RE:WORKING EISENMAN

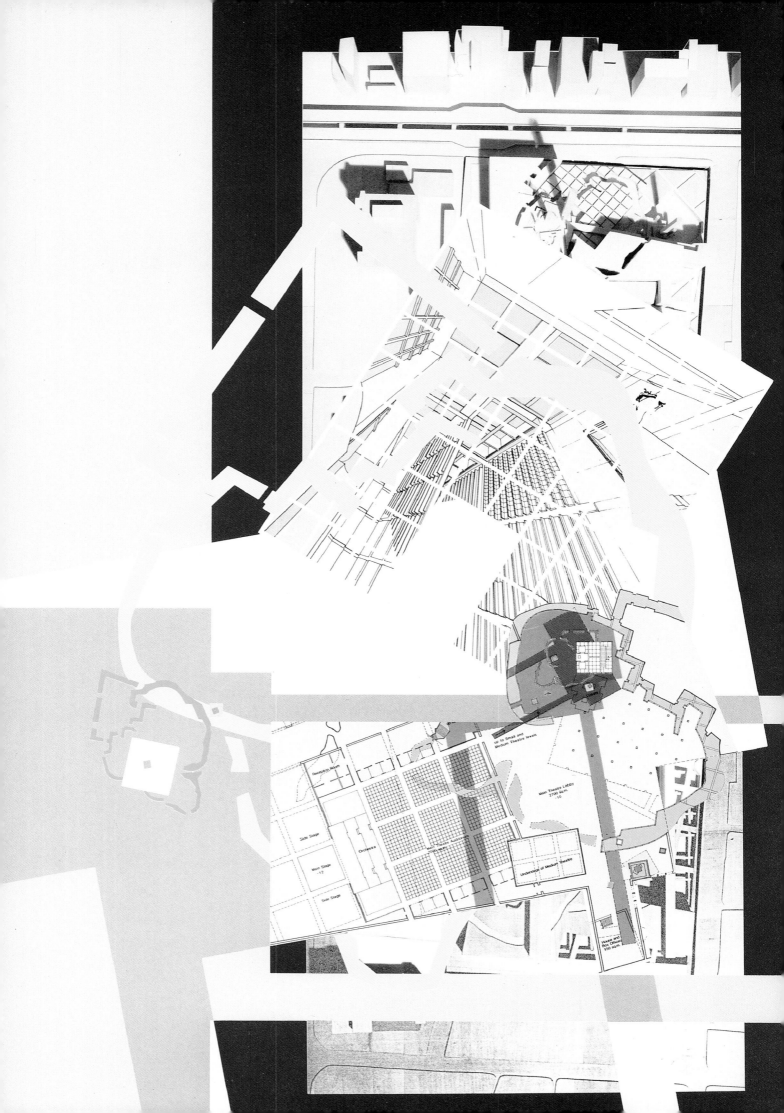

RE:WORKING EISENMAN

A.D. ACADEMY EDITIONS • **E&S** ERNST & SOHN

ACKNOWLEDGEMENTS

Editorial Offices
42 Leinster Gardens London W2 3AN

Editorial and Design Team: Andrea Bettella (Senior Designer);
Maggie Toy (House Editor)
Annamarie Uhr, Meret Gabra-Liddell, (Design)
Nicola Hodges, John Honderich, Sophie Ovenden (Editorial)

Cover: Columbus Convention Center
Page 2: Tokyo Opera House (*A+U* Special Issue, Aug 1988.
Artists: Hiroshi Maruyama/Judy Geib)
Page 6: Berlin IBA Housing (*A+U* Special Issue, Aug 1988.
Artists: Hiroshi Maruyama/Judy Geib)
Pages 10,18: Moving Arrows, Eros and Other Errors (*A+U* Special
Issue, Aug 1988. Artists: Hiroshi Maruyama/Judy Geib)
Pages 40,44: Cannaregio (*A+U* Special Issue, Aug 1988.
Artists: Hiroshi Maruyama/Judy Geib)
Pages 50,58,72: Wexner Center for the Arts
(Collage: Hiroshi Maruyama, 1989)
Pages 78,98,106,114: La Villette (*EISENMANAMNESIE*, *A+U*
Special Issue, Aug 1988. Artists: Hiroshi Maruyama/Judy Geib)
Pages 124,132: University Art Museum, Long Beach
(*EISENMANAMNESIE*, *A+U* Special Issue, Aug 1988.
 Artists: Hiroshi Maruyama/Judy Geib)

First published in Great Britain in 1993 by
ACADEMY EDITIONS
An imprint of the Academy Group Ltd

ACADEMY GROUP LTD
42 Leinster Gardens London W2 3AN
ERNST & SOHN
Hohenzollerndamm 170, 1000 Berlin 31
Members of VCH Publishing Group

ISBN 1 85490 112 5 (HB)

Distributed to the trade in the United States of America by
ST MARTIN'S PRESS

CONTENTS

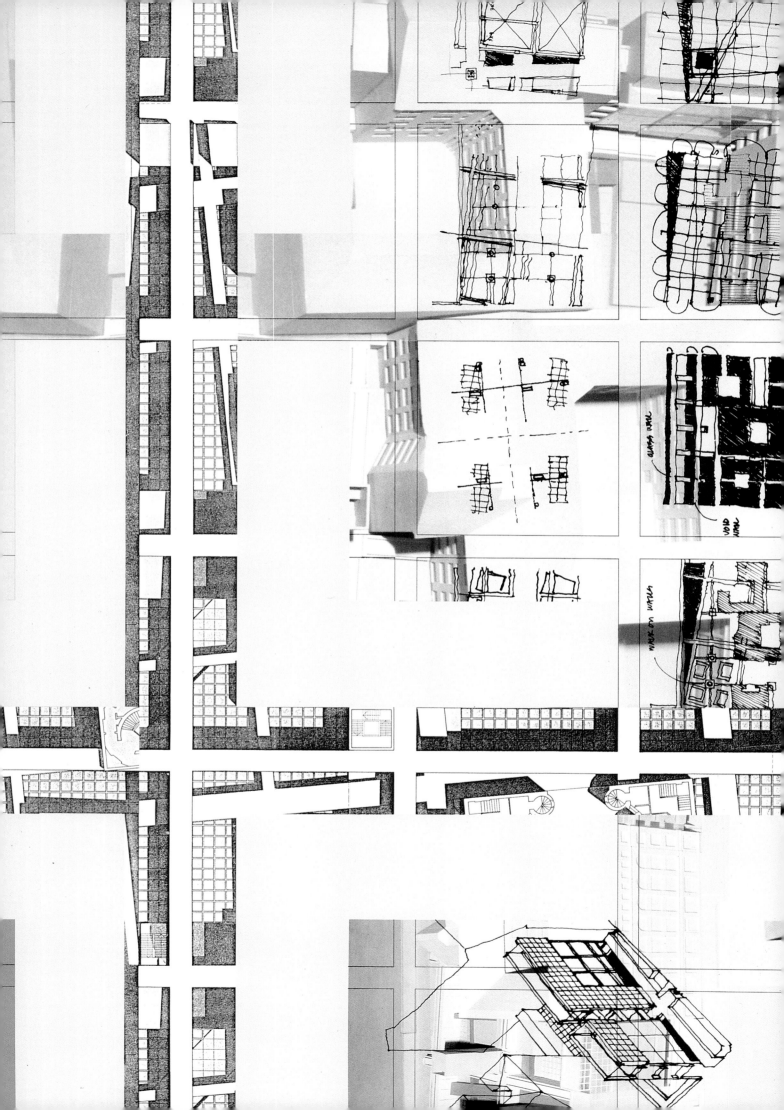

RE:WORKING EISENMAN: WORK AND NAME
ANDREW BENJAMIN

Emphasising work — presented as the disruptive continuity of reworking — is linked to use rather than being a mere display of work. Here the work in question is intended to be one of use (and at use). The array of different texts, images, contrasting orientations, etc, are intended to reinforce the claim that there is no one way that this architectural practice, its representation, is ever able to sanction only one approach, one piece of work, etc. What this means here is that there is a type of mirroring between architect and manual. Moreover, it entails that despite the need for a way in, no introduction, no matter what its guise, even apparent simplicity, can pretend to operate within a strict form of completion and therefore of totality. And yet the continuity of opening and the abeyance of totality are not intended to affirm the ineliminable presence of either the idiosyncratic, or the radically subjective or unrestricted dissemination. Rather it involves, as a beginning, a stance made in relation to the possibility of being complete. In the absence of a singular object to be known there is the inescapable need for the criteria of judgement. Judgement, in eschewing and thus distancing the interplay of totality and knowledge, will affirm the inevitability of positionality. The positioning however will be in relation to work rather than the dominance of the proper name.

What is involved here, therefore, is primarily work. Despite this affirmed primacy, caution must still be exercised, since work is often identified — though in the end misidentified — by (and with) a proper name. Conventionally, a proper name will be used to group, classify and sort work. Work, in that instance, is possessed. Within such an ambit, work attains the passivity of the already completed. Furthermore, with work's reduction to the proper name, such that it becomes the name's work, and with the posited, though still errone-ous, conflation of work and name, the primacy of work is eventually effaced. In this instance however and in contra-distinction to such an effacing, the primacy of work will be maintained. Nonetheless, its being maintained will not entail, as a direct result, the automatic elision of the name. (More is at stake here than that which could ever be established by the exclusive presence of an either/or.) Work's centrality involves the removal of the name. Here, complexity emerges, for in being re-moved, it is being retained. It is, of course, a retaining that no longer retains the proper name's pre-given dominance. And yet as the power of the proper name cannot be lightly dismissed, this complexity of retaining is marked by an almost inescapable fragility. While the complexity of retaining and the move from name to work provide a way of accounting for the nature of this work, they mirror, at the same time, that architecture usually identified with (and by) the proper name Eisenman.

The formulations of these opening deliberations are of course deliberate. They intend to stage — even though it is staging that will be continued in this introduction — the philosophical, theoretical and interpretive problems raised by the proper name. The proper name when proposed in this particular way works to differentiate itself from the person and thus from any forced and thus enforced humanism. The opening also works to indicate — again an indication that will be developed — that despite his (Eisenman's) own personal generosity, what is actually at play here is a body of work. It is the centrality of the work as has been suggested that makes both the initial presence and then any latter reintroduction of the proper name problematic. With the enforced presence of work — with, that is, an insistence on work's centrality — what must be taken up is the question of what — apart from the proper name and with its propriety, the interweaving either of architect and hero, or architect and God — will give the work its unity? More emphatically, what can give it any unity?

Answering these questions will necessitate developing a more sustained conception of the work than that of simple and undifferentiated activity. With such a development it may be that unity emerges with the removal of the certainty provided by that conception of the architectural in which it is posi-tioned, given, by the unquestioned reiteration of architecture's own *telos*. In other words unity may inhere in the openings provided by the abeyance of this dominance. As such it will allow for an account of why this work — the work presented here — is continually presented with or within, or in conjunction with a specific theoretical or philosophical position. These posi-tions may have been employed as tools rather than as the attempt to establish a named affinity in which the philosophy or theory in question gives its name to the architecture and is therefore taken to have legitimated it.

In more general terms what this means is that the application of philosophical names to the architectural, as though the specificity of the architecture in question is identified thereby and in being given an identity legitimised, is to confuse work and name and therefore is not simply banal, it homogenises the differing ways the philosophy/architecture relation can be taken.

Work is an activity; and yet action alone is not sufficient, for here what is activated will have to resist any automatic incorporation into the teleological space of origination and completion. There will be another work which incorporates the two-fold stance, a stance incorporating its own points of overlap. The first part of the stance refers to the site of interpretation; both the site's construal and the conception of interpretation demanded by the site. The second refers to the specific articulation of that site within a movement of reiteration and distancing. It is this latter point that is succinctly captured by Eisenman in his exchange with Derrida. While it is not articulated as such within the letter, it will still be suggested that Eisenman's recognition is linked to the affirmed presence of a specific logic of the gift.

> . . . architecture . . . in its displacement of the traditional role of function . . . does not deny that architecture must function, but rather suggests that architecture may also function without necessarily symbolising that function .[1]

Taking up the point made in the letter means that introduced into the architectural work is the effect of chance. Chance will emerge however not as the opposite to reason — that would be to do no more than retain the dominance of the exclusive opposition by an act of simple counter positing — but as the response to prediction and therefore the given. Chance will not be unreasonable. Chance is not the incursion of the irrational. As will be suggested, chance occurs in the distancing. For architecture, chance may take the form of philosophy.

Reiteration and distancing would seem, in the simultaneity of their presence, to suggest a paradox. How could it be that both are present at the same time? Answering this question will involve indicating that it is precisely their co-presence that marks the inherent radicality of part of the work identified by the proper name —the name Eisenman — while at the same time establishing the limits, if not the conceptual difficulties of other projects identified by the 'same' proper name.[2] What this entails is that what is marked out by the proper name will have become the site of judgement. Differing and conflicting judgements that take work as the point of orientation therefore will rob the proper name of any pre-given essentiality or singularity. The proper name is incorporated into projects; its projection accompanies work. Its own presence is henceforth effective as it will have formed part of its own reworking. The name will have been put to work.

How is the interplay of reiteration and distancing to be understood? The force of this question is that any answer will be implicated in an active process whose presence is inescapable because it is a present as a gift. (It goes without saying that this is to deploy a terminology which while situating what follows may differ significantly from the terminology used in actual texts.) The gift in question is the work of tradition, present as that which has always already been given. Here the gift is present as a constraint. The presence of this constraint is signalled by the use of the term 'must'. The unequivocal insistence on Eisenman's part that, 'architecture must function' will become, perhaps with a certain irony, the affirmation of the architectural. The question that must be asked here concerns how the constraint is to be understood. The initial answer is that the constraint marks out the presence of reiteration.

Architecture's necessity to function as architecture — and thus to hold itself apart from sculpture, engineering, etc — and to work within a repetition or reiteration of architecture's *telos*, is itself architecture's possibility. It is this possibility that indicates that the co-presence of reiteration and distancing have to be thought within the frame of repetition. (Repetition holds the site that is to be determined.) And yet repetition provides no essential unity within which it is to be understood. Repetition opens up at least two possibilities. The first is that repetition is to be explicated as taking place within the domain of the same; ie the repetition of the self-same. The other would be another possibility for repetition, perhaps one in which it — repetition — had been subjected to the process that it named. Here it would be that form of repetition in which what takes place again, takes place for the first time. It is in terms of this distinction — a distinction which overlaps and interweaves — that reiteration and distancing are to be situated. One becomes a location for the other. The distancing intervenes at this precise moment.

Distancing is not indifference. Distancing is not destruction. It is rather that distancing is that other possibility given by the logic of the gift. If the gift, that which is always already given, is architecture's possibility, then retaining architecture necessitates working with the gift. The gift's presence is the constraint. However what follows from the acceptance of the gift — the gift's force reinforced by the possibility that it will always allow itself to be reworked in terms of the conditions of possibility for architecture — need not be given. At the precise point there is an opening in which another chance for architecture will intrude. It will be essential to return to this intrusion. What is held open is precisely that possibility that is signalled in the letter and in relation to which the disruptive force of Eisenman's work can be identified.

There will be a corollary here. It will involve the logic of the gift. This time, however, the gift's presence is in terms of that which is given to be understood or more straightforwardly given to be experienced. (Neither understanding nor experience are simply cognitive; they also work with that which is set out in advance in order that they are possible.) With this other gift there will be a constraint in the sense that if what is given to be experienced as architecture is to be experienced as such, then there must be — as a minimal condition — the actual possibility of its being experienced (understood) as being architecture. Here, of course, a similar division occurs. If the way this takes place — the way that the experience/ understanding happens — is itself explicable in terms of that which is given to be experienced, then what is occurring can be accounted for in terms of the repetition of the self-same. If, however, in contradistinction to the dominance of the same, that which is given is recognised as architecture but with the questions of how and in what way it functions (works) as architecture left open, then there is an abeyance, a distancing from the all-pervasive, and thus all-inclusive dominance of function. Approached in this way, function, rather than being trapped in its simple opposition to form becomes a term that figures within repetition.

Here the actual formulation in the letter needs to be followed carefully. What is suggested is that, '. . . architecture may also function without necessarily symbolising that function, that the presentness of architecture is irreducible to the presence of its function or its signs.' What is being set out here is central. Function is retained. Directly after the announcement of its retention, the necessary link between form and function is sundered. Caution is still necessary however; for, in suggesting that the building need not symbolise function, what is not being suggested is that the building's appearance will have become the site of an orchestrated ornamentation that disguised, or displaced, or dispersed the presence of function. Such a move would be the lot of Post-Modernism. The break in necessity that is being signalled will mean that the actual distinction between form and function will have become recast.

It is clear from many of the projects included in this work that the retention of function is not uncritical. In other words, while functionality is retained — with its retention the constraint is acknowledged and thus the gift accepted — the buildings, their work, enact the continuous reworking of what is entailed by a building having that particular function. (A complex set-up that involves, as has been suggested, a repetition in which something takes place again for the first time.) This questioning (and here it must be added immediately that it is a questioning that does contain or house the answer, indeed another architecture of questioning is in play) is not an accidental part of the project. On the contrary, it is part of the building's work. It is part

therefore of what makes the project what it is.

Of the many consequences of this state of affairs, one important one is that the building's potential, its possibility, can never be reduced to its materiality or assumed functionality. It is as though it contains other yet to be realised possibilities. This disruptive possibility is once again the building's work. The work of the buildings will never be exhausted by any one instance of the buildings being at work. This is to rethink building in terms of a specific and thus regional dynamic. It may involve a different geometry — a geometry that accepted and incorporated the imposition of distortions.

Finally, the continual relationship between Eisenman and philosophical names: for example, Chomsky, Thom, Derrida, Deleuze. Clearly, the relationship cannot be thought through in terms of names. The temptation, while great, will have results which will be facile. There are two points that have to be made. The first is obvious: these names have to be approached in terms of work. The second is related to the first even though it is more difficult. Distancing involves an opening in which that other possibility figures, and in figuring provides for a dramatic recasting of the given. This is the place of philosophy. This is the use, for example, of the fold in the project in Rebstockpark. Folding works in the opening, providing the means of maintaining distancing as effective; for it is folded, quite literally, back into the project's inherent functionality. In being folded back the function is maintained but recast at the same time. The recasting, the reworking, has a complex temporality in that what the project is — its being as project — is not reducible to its being so at one point in time. What this means is that the reworking sunders the ontology of stasis in terms of the ontology proper to complex repetition; ie, a giving which in happening again is an-original happening. It is thus that what the name identifies is the complex site worked by the two-fold presence of reiteration and distancing. The attempt to articulate the specificity of this site will allow it to be judged. Construed this way, judgement will pertain to the named presence of the work's work. An instance, perhaps even an example of this naming, will be Eisenman. Opening up this name, tracing its work, noting its own coming to presence may necessitate the name's reworking.

NOTES
1   *Re:working Eisenman*, p79.
2   I have tried to develop this point in 'Architecture et Contraint', *Chimeres* No 17, 1992.

miMISes READING: does not mean A THING
PETER EISENMAN

Architecture has traditionally been thought of as producing an object with meaning. Recently this meaning has been confused with a different idea, that of an architectural text. The presumption is that simply because something has meaning, the now fashionable term 'text' can be applied to it. A text, however, may be distinguished from an object. While an object (whether concrete or written) may also be a text, a text differs from an object in that it is a reading or an analysis of another object. Hence, while all texts can be objects, not all objects are necessarily texts. Texts always contain something else. That something else is the approximation or simulation of another object. A text does not represent or symbolise this other object, it attempts to reveal or simulate its structure.

Traditional architecture looks for formal order, such as sequences, closures, or proportions: the interval between columns, the relationship of wall lengths, the ratios of solids to voids or parts to the whole. It is concerned with the aesthetic aspect of architectural metaphysics. Architecture is traditionally concerned also with meaning, and this meaning unfolds in the analysis of metaphor, of something which is described in terms of something else; the facade as a face, the chimney as a backbone etc. The 'meaning' of a text is, however, a structural meaning, not a metaphoric one. A structural meaning is one in which there is a differentiation and not a representation. Symbols are metaphoric; they are objects that represent other objects. Signs, however, are textual in that they differentiate one element from another in a set of structural, rather than formal or metaphoric, relationships. Signs are notational devices that will not yield to formal and symbolic analysis, and, therefore, are self-referential: that is, they do not participate in a formal or symbolic whole. For example, the slot in the facade of Mies van der Rohe's Concrete Country House is a sign (not a symbol) of the absence of the floor plane. The slot signals the difference between presence and absence, and it is, therefore, neither a formal nor a symbolic element, but a textual one. A sign of difference and a trace of presence are textual notations. It is the operation of these kinds of notations which is usually ignored by the traditional analysis of meaning; the textual level is left unconsidered. Because of a fixation on symbol-as-metaphor, sign-as-difference is suppressed. Thus, the idea of text must be 'teased out' from the systems of conflicting notation — formal, symbolic, and textual — that may be present in any object.[1]

Traditionally in literature — in which the simulating or analytic text is always outside of or parallel to the object — it is thought that object and text are different. This notion has been challenged by the deconstructionist critique, which suggests that there is no difference between an analytic text and an object, that they are mutually embedded.[2] Similarly, while architecture has always enjoyed a tradition of the external text in the form of architectural criticism, there has always been another text embedded within its object. As opposed to language, where signs represent 'absent' objects, in architecture the sign and the object are both present. It suggests that while in language there is a need for a congruence between sign and object, in architecture the reverse may be true. Since the sign and the object in architecture exist in reality together, there may be a need to uncouple them if a sign is to be disengaged from a symbol. This textuality is found in architecture when symbol and form can be extracted from the object. This extraction discovers two things: one, the object stripped of its former symbolic content; two, a structure that simulates (since it cannot be the object without its former context) this condition. This structure can be considered a text.

The work of Mies van der Rohe has never been examined in the light of this possible textuality. Even Manfredo Tafuri and Francesco Dal Co, who in their provocative writings propose a non-traditional interpretation of Mies, do not view the work as text.[3] Nonetheless, it is possible to see in Mies' work a strong textuality, especially in his preoccupation with precise dissonances that cannot be ignored. Although these may seem to have no symbolic or formal significance, it is precisely because of this lack, it will be argued, that they are the essence of what is textual.

Text emerges in Mies' architecture when the symbolic connection between man and the object (and hence symbol and object) loses its relevance and thus can be taken apart. Instead of simulating the vertebrate structure of man, Mies' architecture simulates a textual structure. The separation of an architecture from the mimesis of man is the production of a simulation: this is the nature of a text. The 'text' in this context can be seen in the attempt to break away from the symbolism, hierarchy, and mimesis that linked the symmetrical axis of objects to the vertebrate axis of the human body. When this break occurred, Mies' objects became unstable, non-hierarchical. Their asymmetry signalled that the elements had broken apart from their vertebrate or organic structure. With Mies' break from mimesis there was also a break from traditional representation. This break for Mies is manifested in an unusual juxtaposition, the contamination of the Modern by the classical.[4]

The key here is the reintroduction of classical elements (axiality, symmetry etc) in a non-classical manner. This contamination is not so much a dialectical insertion of the classical into the Modern (the object into the text) as it is a damming up or a transgression of the classical. It is presented in the context of a rupture with traditional representation. Consequently, Mies' work should be read as an argument that proposes something apart, a suspension as the unresolved condition of being. It is important to see the work in this non-synthetic light.

Mies van der Rohe's projects from 1923 to 1935 fall into three phases that form an internal, almost self-referential narrative: the early work (namely, the Brick and Concrete Country Houses); the middle work (the Barcelona Pavilion and the Tugendhat House) and the late work of this period (summarised in the Hubbe House and, to a lesser extent, in the Ulrich Lange House). The narrative has two aspects. First, one detects a movement from a formalist (classical aesthetic concern) through a Modernist (break-up of the subject and object) to a textual architecture, where embedded in the formal (useful, meaningful, and sheltering) object is a parallel discourse — a text (or a series of textual notations). Second, this narrative is not a sequence of signs that refer to other objects, but a narrative that indicates the difference between objects — presence, absence, process, etc — which can be considered textual. It is important to understand that text does not deny the presence of a meaningful, aesthetic, useful shelter. It suggests rather that the representation or symbolisation of these issues is no longer its primary concern. Mies van der Rohe was not conscious of this idea of text; he did not intend 'textuality' in his work. Yet the evidence of a growing and evolving textuality is powerful; it is only necessary to find the way to it. In order to do this, Mies must be misread, that is, read from inside, as if from his own unconscious.

The first indication in Mies' work of textual notation is found in the Brick Country House.[5] This project begins to explore the limits of the independence of the object from the subject and how these limits can be articulated. It is concerned with a first order of textuality, the reduction of symbolic objects to mere objects, ie, objects without the traditional narrative of man. With the Brick Country House, Mies begins to deploy the elements of architecture as textual counters. The first of these is the wall. Here the walls speak to the fact that there is no space in the house. The walls do not define space: rather, they define their own condition of being — that is, their capacity to support and their capacity to divide.

Traditionally, walls are read as the perimeter of space: they contain, enclose, or exclude space. But the walls in the Brick Country House are merely object presences, divisions where there is no space to divide or where the space has been removed and only surfaces exist. Van Doesburg's 1918 painting *Rhythm of a Russian Dance*, which is often cited as the original model for the Brick Country House, in fact does not reflect such an attitude toward space. It utilises no such absence of space; in it space is active as a ground. For Mies, the absence of space eliminates a major classical element — the ground — leaving the walls as suspended figures. It is merely a case of Mies recognising in Van Doesburg a vehicle from which to elaborate these ideas.

Likewise, the glass planes in the Brick Country House do not contain: again, they are merely a void presence. It, too, signals a breakdown of the idea of the house as a metaphysical enclosure and abandons the traditional distinction between inside and out. The house encloses and shelters, but it does not represent or symbolise shelter and enclosure. Above all, the house remains an object in the metaphysical sense, although there is a displacement from classical mimesis.

This displacement of mimesis is only a part of the entire thesis of the Concrete Country House, for here there is a second development. Whereas in the Brick Country House there is the absence of space, here that absence is marked by a sign. This is the first indication of a text. It is neither a representational nor an aesthetic gesture. It is now the object-as-sign, a sign of the object's own condition. This marks the pivotal shift from the object as a representation of the condition of man to the idea of a text within the object.

Mies begins this shift with a negation of man's plane. Even though there is a classical podium, it is used to signal that the symbolic plane of man, the ground plane, is stripped as such from the object. In the elevation drawing, the plane of the floor is read as a slot. There is an actual floor plane inside, but it is not marked on the facade. This cut in the vertical surface also denies an expected relationship to the windows above. While there are many different window solutions that would have related to the rest of the fenestration, Mies chose, instead, to mark the floor plane with a cut that both marks the absence of man's plane and suggests that the metaphor of support in the concrete wall is being eroded. It is as if Mies purposely undercut the wall's 'meaning' as clear and logical support.

The Brick and Concrete Country Houses were followed by the Barcelona Pavilion and Tugendhat House, which exemplify the next period of Mies' work. In the Barcelona Pavilion, particularly, one can discern an important stage in Mies' on-going confrontation with the classical notion of enclosure and the enclosing wall. Here Mies converts two additional architectural elements into textual counters: the column and the roof. Though the theme is the court house type, Mies, instead of enclosing a court, breaks it open to reveal the column and the roof. The two elements previously employed textually, the wall and the podium, operate in the same way. Again, the wall is not the wall of finitude — the wall that makes space and symbolises the classical relationship between man and object. These walls cleave space; they begin and end in response to no greater order; rather, they obey only their own mute existence.[6]

The podium in the Barcelona Pavilion, as in both of the earlier houses, is not entered axially. (As will be seen, axial entry will become a textual counter when classical elements become embedded in Mies' work.) In fact, the early schemes in many of Mies' projects have a formalist bias. These are then worked through until they ultimately become textual. In the early studies of the Barcelona Pavilion there are further tentative gestures toward what might be termed a 'latent classicality', for example, the alignment of the pool with the main podium. This alignment would have caused the direction of the main entry to be reinforced by the line of the podium and the pool, thus erecting a virtual barrier between the outside and the inside. In the realised project, the pool is pushed out into the landscape, up against the corner of the wall. It is no longer framed by a terrace, but now penetrates the wall, seeming to intrude from the outside. In the early schemes the entire podium except for the small utility pavilion was enclosed by an uninterrupted perimeter rectangle. In the realised scheme, this perimeter is fractured at every corner, almost imperceptibly but enough to engender instability. The principal motive for the fracturing is to disengage the roof plane formally from the floor plane, and then to engage it as a signifier, ie, as another textual counter.

The condition of the roof plane in the Barcelona Pavilion is in opposition to Le Corbusier's Maison Domino, where the stature and status of man is symbolised by the roof plane/podium as coupled horizontal datums. With the Barcelona Pavilion, the hovering roof, formerly a symbol of shelter and enclosure, is stripped of this meaning. It hovers, but symbolically shelters and encloses nothing — it is extracted from its former symbolic presence and recast as a sign. Indeed, there is no interior space in the pavilion; its symbolic presence is one of spacial continuity and the denial of usable interior space.

The Barcelona Pavilion is the first use of the column in Mies' work; it, too, becomes a notational device. For Le Corbusier, the column was the quintessential symbol of the new architecture. His columns were typically round and set back from the facade, creating the canonical 'free plan' and 'free facade' that were to become trademarks of Modernist architecture. For Mies, the column is employed as a sign, not a symbol. In the Barcelona Pavilion, the columns, though detached from the walls, are set forward rather than back; because of their cruciform shape they seem intended to define the corners of an *en suite* sequence of square bays. But, in fact, they signify the absence of corners. This is emphasised by Mies' use of reflective stainless steel, which causes the columns to mirror and double their own infinitude — their absent presences.[7] When the corners disappear, the negative space is read as presence (even though void). The glass planes further mirror and enforce these voids as presences (echoing the roof's function — to shelter nothing), thus becoming the signs of absent enclosure. (In fact, the glass doors were intended to be taken down every day and only put up for security at night.) The stainless steel mullions that divide and frame the glass also provide yet another level of optical self-reference and the signification of absence — they seem as absences in a present glass screen.

In the Tugendhat House, Mies introduces another aspect of text: the reduction of shape and texture to a system of signs. In it are found two curved forms: one is the entry staircase and the other separates the main living area from the dining area. The curve of the staircase is in opaque glass; that of the living room is in wood. Typically, a curve-ended staircase is used somewhat arbitrarily to create a formal tension and interest in an otherwise uninflected orthogonal scheme, or to accentuate function. In the Tugendhat House, Mies inflates this form into a larger text. It is no accident that Mies intersects the wooden curve with the opaque glass plane. If any of the white walls is taken as a neutral datum, it is seen as solid in contrast to the opaque, glazed curve of the entry staircase. Yet remarkably, when the same opaque glazing — now as a 'flat plane' — is seen against the wooden curve of the living room, the opacity dematerialises by the force of the abrupt contrast. The two similar curves articulated in dissimilar materials textually engage the physicality of the opaque, planar walls in a dialogue of difference. The same opaque glass material becomes, in each case, a different sign — in both cases negative: in the former case it is a positive shape; in the latter, a 'negative' or neutral shape.

In the Tugendhat House there is also a use of furniture as text. In most of Mies' projects there are two Barcelona chairs side by side and another placed away from the pair. Landscape architects group trees in this way to create the appearance of a natural ensemble and to allow a flowing continuity through space. In the Tugendhat House there is an even number of chairs (three Barcelona, three Tugendhat), which are grouped such that a symmetry is established and then abruptly denied by a destabilising third. Significantly, this strategy contravenes normal function (disrupting the groups of two or three), thereby suggesting that there is another intention to the grouping.

The final period of concern here, the years 1933-35, is distinguished by the return of openly classical elements embedded in a Modernist setting, as exemplified by two houses with similar plans: the Ulrich Lange House and the Hubbe House.[8] This embedding raises an interesting problem. On the one hand, classical elements are being embedded in a Modernist setting, while on the other hand, this strategy is being used to separate the traditional symbolism of man from architecture. The Hubbe House is a Modernist house which contains its opposite — a classical insertion. But this embedding of the classical is not a 'negative object' (since architecture is always a constructive project).[9] Nor is it a void, the traditional idea of the negative in architecture.[10] Instead, it is absence as a constructive presence. It is a Modernist object hosting an alien simulation; the text of a classical object embedded within it. It is an object of superposition. Superposition differs from super*im*position of figure on ground: the courtyard house as Modernist ground and the row of columns as classical ordination superimposed on it. This kind of layering and transparency can be found in Cubist collage and in Le Corbusier's plans: the overlay of two systems that resolve themselves as figure and ground. But the Hubbe House is not the same. It becomes a textual object in which a simulation of a classical object is superposed with a Modernist object. There is no ground but, instead, a relationship of figure to figure. Figure to figure suggests a possible condition of textuality; an architecture without origin in shelter, use, form, or symbol; rather, a free-floating set of interchangeable integers. The erosion of the traditional iconic structure of architecture is achieved by this superposition, the simultaneous presence of two systems (classical/Modern, symmetry/asymmetry, absence/presence).

The textual mark or trace as the presence of absence is further signalled in the Hubbe House by the unresolved nature of the figures. Like the Barcelona Pavilion and the Ulrich Lange House, the Hubbe House is a courtyard house that has been broken apart, irreparably split into two figures. The first fracturing is generated by a double row of symmetrically placed cruciform columns which split the house in two. Unlike the columns of the Barcelona Pavilion which run with the grain, these run counter to it. At Barcelona they signal a Modernist ground; at Hubbe, a classical intrusion. They signify both the introduction and denial of a classical ordination. It is this state of being and non-being, of embedding and contamination, which becomes the textuality of the house. These columns first introduce and define an axis of symmetry that becomes an eroding device. This is then itself systematically eroded. The columns are asymmetrically placed within both the long (front to back) side of the house, and the short, closed sides of the house, initiating a textual reading. The first pair of columns is symmetrical within the terrace that is pushed forward of the house, but asymmetrical in terms of the exterior wall. The second pair of columns is symmetrical in terms of their flanking walls, but the furniture in the entrance bay is arranged asymmetrically to them. In fact, each bay contains a sequence of quite precise and detailed countermanding symmetries and asymmetries. In the second bay, for example, the wall, which seems to have broken off from the exterior closure, is both too long to fit into its 'former' position, and is shifted away from it. In the third bay, the fireplace wall is asymmetrical about the vertical axis of the bay but symmetrical about the horizontal axis. The fireplace wall becomes a conceptual screen, a cleavage for two symmetries on either side, neither of which, however, operates symmetrically with the other. Within the wall, the fireplace itself is placed symmetrically with its edge aligned with the absent axis of the table on the other side. The seating, placed symmetrically about the fireplace opening, further accentuates the shift. On the other side of the wall the dining room table is symmetrically placed with respect to the wall. Hence, the wall becomes a textual fulcrum for the countermanding symmetries with their opposite asymmetries indicated as absences by edges rather than centres. These always occur about a wall-as-fulcrum, ie, as text. The sequence of free-floating wall elements, seemingly fragments of a former symbolic cruciform, is the final stage of Mies' reconsideration of the wall from structure to text, from symbol to sign.[11]

A focal point of this notation of absence, the transition from symbol to sign, can be located in the single odd column that can be found in the Hubbe House. How is it to be explained? Possibly as a sign that there are other missing columns, which would be present either as a spine along the length of the middle of the building or as an entire field of columns. In any case, the isolated presence of this single column can only imply absences, including its own. This column is textual, a sign, because it is neither supporting, aesthetic, nor indicative of the history of the column. It is detached from the history of the symbolism of 'the column'.

Furthermore, in the architecture of Mies, there is a level of detailing as an indication of significant gesture that has resisted interpretation. It is necessary to penetrate this resistance — the inclination to ignore what are significant details — in order to effect a textual analysis. For example, if the notations of the relationship of tile gridding to monolithic floor materials are taken as significant, then a series of fractured cruciforms for which there is no resolution can be seen. The first of the cruciforms has three whole arms and one fractured one. The horizontal arms are formed by the living quarters, the lower vertical arm is the living/dining area, and the upper vertical arm is erased by the superposition of the tile pattern of the forecourt. Not only is this cruciform fractured, but its arms are also in a state of imbalance: the left arm is widened and the right arm is elongated. Two smaller cruciforms to the right and left of the larger one are similarly fractured and imbalanced, echoing the larger cruciform. Together these fractured cruciforms are signs of the destabilisation of the whole.

Finally, the Hubbe House raises another textual issue of the court house. The court house as a type is an attempt to enclose space; yet it also encloses nature. In the Hubbe House, Mies explores textually the inversion of man and nature. Tafuri and Dal Co in their view of Mies van der Rohe propose the idea that the courts of Mies' court house were not so much contained within the walls looking out on nature, but in fact were the framing of nature behind glass; ie, nature was reduced to an unnatural object, a sign of nature.[12] There is thus another absence, real nature, made present as absence by the use of unnatural, man-made nature as a sign.

Mies' court house simulates nature by the virtual enclosure of it. With the rupture of the type in the Hubbe House, unnatural nature is ironically contaminated by exposing it to real nature. The glass that separated man from nature is now a glass that separates man from the simulation of nature; unnatural nature becomes framed behind glass. Glass, rather than being seen as the outside of the inside, is now the inner-outside of the outside. This glass frames neither man nor space, but frames nature in an unresolved duality.[13] The type is now not merely a simulation of nature, but rather becomes nature as text. In the Hubbe House, Mies objectifies the denial of nature into a sign, with all its meaning and symbolism.

The design of negatives, that is, both presence and absence, and the reversal of symmetries and asymmetries, are Mies' signature. The absence of space becomes the sign of a sign, the sign of a text and the denial of symbolised, functional, aesthetic, meaningful shelter. The sign of a sign is a redundancy produced by opposites. Mies' signification as achieved through the very fact of the opposition, through the seeming irresolution of the system. The expectancy of the system as a whole is betrayed by an order which itself is broken apart, and neither of which is dominant. These signs or texts do not symbolise nor represent. They function but do not make function their theme. Rather, they split symbolic and objective reality, which have become, since the Renaissance, powerfully unified in the linking of man's vertebrate axis with the pitched roof, symmetrical hearth — symbolic of the axis of the world.

Texts that split symbol from object in order to form signs dislocate architecture. But architecture is sustained by this dislocating energy, which is creative and critical rather than stabilising and institutionalising. Mies' separation of symbol and reality creates the dislocation of the metaphysic of architecture necessary for its maintenance. The history of architecture is a constant struggle enacted between the limits of maintenance and dislocation.[14] Mies van der Rohe's texts probe those limits.

NOTES

1 See Barbara Johnson, 'The Critical Difference', *Diacritics* 8, 2, 1978, p3.
2 See J Hillis Miller, 'The Critic as Host', in *Deconstruction and Criticism*, New York, 1979, pp217-53.
3 See Manfredo Tafuri and Francesco Dal Co, *Modern Architecture*, New York, 1982, pp153-7.
4 This idea has been suggested by Tafuri and Dal Co (Note 3), but not for the reasons of text.
5 Although the Concrete Country House is chronologically prior to the Brick Country House, it is not the first in the textual sequence. The ideas in the Concrete Country House can only be understood after the statement of the Brick Country House.
6 This is as opposed to the organisation of walls in any of Le Corbusier's projects which obey a proportional order that is ultimately linked to his modular proportional system. While based on the Fibonacci series, the dimensions of the modular are linked to an ultimate anthropomorphism in the figure of modular man.
7 Colin Rowe has, from a different point of view, maintained that an analysis of the changing column section in Mies van der Rohe would make a useful thesis, as well as a way to understand the formal development of Mies' work.
8 Although the Ulrich Lange House was done after the Hubbe House, it is in some ways its precursor. Compared to the Hubbe House, however, it is unresolved and lacks the separation of sign and symbol. The Ulrich Lange House is not a criticism, an elaboration, or a transformation of the Hubbe House. It 'sounds' and looks like the Hubbe House, but it does not have quite the same meaning.
9 See Jacques Derrida, *The Maintenance of Architecture*, Trento, Italy, 1986, for a discussion of the idea of architecture as a constructive project.
10 See Tafuri and Dal Co (Note 3), p157.
11 This is different from the Tafuri and Dal Co proposition of the impossibility of significances in the work of Mies. For them, the signs in Mies are 'no longer organic components of a language. Where the avant-garde was projecting continuity, Mies designed separations. His architecture isolates itself: meditation on the impossibility of dialogue, it reduces itself to a montage of signs that have mislaid, with never a trace of nostalgic regret, the universe of significance.' Tafuri and Dal Co (Note 3), p153.
12 Ibid, p155: 'Nature was made part of the furnishings, a spectacle to be enjoyed only on condition that it be kept impalpably remote.'
13 Ibid, p157: 'The natural relationship with the surroundings is a mystification to be replaced by an artificial construction.' It is my contention that this artificial construction is a text.
14 See Derrida (Note 9) for a more complete discussion of this idea.

ARCHITECTURE AS A SECOND LANGUAGE: THE TEXTS OF BETWEEN
PETER EISENMAN

To be able to read off a text as a text without interposing an interpretation is the last form of inner experience . . .
Nietzsche, *Will to Power.*

With the influx of non-native English speaking students to American colleges and universities, it is now possible to see college course offerings entitled 'English as a Second Language'. The idea behind the title is that these courses will be offered to students whose first language is not English. The word 'second' in this context does not mean merely to come after in a temporal sense because the idea of a first language or mother tongue implies an originary and even moral value. Thus the idea of a second language suggests the absence of these values as a negative condition.

The idea of temporality and original value becomes key if this notion of 'second language' is transferred to the idea of architecture. In one sense, 'second language' would suggest that architecture is always a second language even to those who speak and read it. In another sense, the term could suggest that architecture is grounded in other disciplines, that it is secondary to philosophy, science, literature, art and technology. But finally, there is a third possibility for the idea of a second language in architecture; that is, architecture as text.

While the term 'text' is at present quite fashionable, its value as an idea is almost obscured by its intellectual currency as a catch-all for anything related to meaning. The concept of a text has a very precise and necessary condition as a strategy for dislocation in architecture, and more precisely for dislocating what is thought to be the natural or 'first language' of architecture itself.

For the purpose of this discussion a more specific use of the term 'text,' which incorporates two recent developments, will be used. As a result of these two developments, text is no longer a vague and generic term for meaning, but is in fact a term which always dislocates the traditional relationship between a form and its meaning.

In the first of these developments, text is not so much the representation of a narrative but rather the representation of the structure of the form of the narrative. In the second, text 'is no longer something complete, enclosed in a book or its margins, it is a differential network. A fabric of traces referring endlessly to something other than itself'. In this latter sense, text displaces the 'conventional' or the 'natural' idea of the literary work. Whereas the concept of text as the structure of the work referred inwardly to the work itself, text in this sense is a fundamental condition of displacement; it depends on no terms of internal reference such as structure. It is neither a complete work nor a meta-language. It is not a 'stable object' but a process, a 'transgressive activity which disperses the author as the centre, limit and guarantor of truth . . .'

What do these developments of the idea of text mean for architecture? What is an architectural text and how can it inform a strategy for dislocation? First it must be understood that the extended idea of a text, whether in architecture or not, is the idea of essential multivalence. It does not cancel or deny prior notions of narrative or structure nor does it necessarily contain them, but exists simultaneously with them. Text never allows a single signified. Everything is shown to mean more than one thing.

Architecture, because of its presence, its here and now, its time and space specificity, was traditionally seen as necessarily univocal. Thus, it would be resistant to the dislocating multivalency of text. The implications for an architecture of texts would be the same as that of the second language, in other words, non-originary and unnatural. Thus in architecture it is possible to say that text is what always exceeds the immediate response to a visual or sensory image, ie that which we see on the surface as the story, or that which we see as the beautiful. This is the heart of the matter.

Since the terms of the natural in architecture have always been thought to be the specificity of time and place, it might be useful to examine this textuality, the dislocation of time and place, in another medium. Film is a discourse that is constantly impacted by a 'second language.' Film is the *sine qua non* of a dislocated place and time because it always has at least two times and two places: the actual time and place of watching, and the narrative time and place. In its early history the fact that film moved in linear time was thought to mean that the narrative moved in chronological time. However, when sound was introduced into film in the 1930s, this coincidence of linear time and chronological time was brought into question; textual time, that is the multivalence of time, developed out of chronological time.

For example, in David Lynch's film *Blue Velvet*, the story, but not the text, is about an average young American couple in a small town in North Carolina in the 50s and their adventures related to a bizarre murder in the town. But *Blue Velvet* is not only about this. It is not about the 50s as a temporal narrative but, among other things, it is about time as text. In fact it is about the dislocation or the dissolution of narrative time in film seen as a natural or first language. All of the icons which are used in this film in a seemingly innocuous and straightforward way set up a condition whereby the space of narrative time in the film is dissolved. This is accomplished particularly, though not exclusively, through the soundtrack. For example, the lead song 'Blue Velvet' is from 1951 when it was sung by Tony Bennett. It was restylised by a group called The Statues in 1960, and that version was covered by Bobby Vinton in 1963 (which is the version used in the film). So there is already a first temporal dislocation in the soundtrack itself. In the film the star, Isabella Rossellini, sings the same song in a nightclub over a microphone which is certainly of a 1940s vintage, if not earlier. Another major song in the film, 'In Dreams' by Roy Orbison, also dates from 1963. Further, the convertible car that Jeffrey drives is a 1968 Oldsmobile, and when he first visits the Lincoln apartments, a single 1958 Fleetwood Cadillac is conspicuously framed in the film. Equally, to drink a Heineken beer in a local Southern bar before the late 50s is clearly anachronistic in the film, as is the earring in one of the male characters' ears.

Blue Velvet is textual in that one of its intrinsic 'image' components, sound, is not about the film's narrative structure of a time and place in the 50s. The complex and intentional tissue of superpositions of future and past create a temporal dislocation. While those images and sounds are present so are their displacements. In other words, the text of the film is about something else. And yet, the film is crafted so as to render the gap between these disjunctions as virtually natural. This is an example of a text of 'between' — between, but not a structure of between — where time is out of focus and interstitial. Textual dislocation comes about from the juxtaposition of two structures of sound and image, a narrative one and a chronological one, neither seen nor heard as dominant or original. One does not know what the 'truth' of these sounds and images is. They do not appear to be related to the narrative but to something other than narrative, some other structure of relationships outside the film's structure. This 'something other' than the narrative is the text between. The dislocating play of sound and images is uniquely possible in the temporal play of the film medium.

Such an idea of a text in relationship to a narrative or representational form such as a plot becomes a condition of a second or non-natural language. The dislocation of narrative time in *Blue Velvet* is exemplary for the case of text in architecture for two reasons. First, because it illustrates another text in an aesthetic medium, but more importantly because of its dislocation of the concept of an internal time or time of narrative. Film, the media *par excellence* for displaying internal time, is used in *Blue Velvet* to dislocate the very phenomenon of narrative time supposedly natural to it.

Architecture, unlike literature or film, has never had the capacity to contain or display a linear or internal time. This has problematised the concept of an architectural text. Despite the critique made by Colin Rowe and Bob Slutzky, much is still made of Sigfried Giedion's notion of space, time and architecture, that is, the potential of new materials and new spatial organisations — in particular, glass and the free plan — to collapse time in such a way that the user could experience different aspects of a plan or its facades from a single vantage point, this is still time as an aspect of the experience of the subject and not internal.

The question of how time could be introduced into architecture itself, rather than merely as the experience of our response to architecture, remained unanswered. Architecture, because it was thought to have the single temporal dimension of the now, and because the static object of architecture was incapable of displaying a multivalent time, was thought not to be textual. However, architecture as text does not reside in the aesthetic or functional presence of the object, but rather as a state of between. Therefore, textual time can be introduced into architecture to produce an architecture which dislocates not only the memory of internal time but all the aspects of presence, origin, place, scale, and so forth. The potential for this textual time was always there and it was always hidden by matching narrative time with chronological time as in early films.

A dislocating architecture confronts originary or authorial value; it does not represent an original source of imagery or figuration; nor does it represent the uses of an object or even an outside discourse. Dislocating architecture displays its multiple meanings by representing the various relationships between other texts, between an architectural text and other texts. The nature of these other texts is the subject of the remainder of this paper.

A dislocating text is always a second language. In retrospect, the potential for a dislocating text in architecture can be found at least since the Renaissance. Alberti took the form of the traditional Greek temple front, which by the 15th century had become almost a banal vernacular form with an internalised iconography, and synthesised it with the triumphal arch of Septimius Severus in Rome to form the facade of Sant'Andrea in Mantua. This synthesis conflated the symbol of the sacred (the Greek temple front) with the symbol of man's power (the triumphal arch). Although this architecture did not dislocate the 'isms' of occupation — the rituals of the church remained intact — one can find in it the operation of a text between; it displayed a between of the theocentric world and the anthropocentric world and its references were spatially between Greece and Rome and temporally between the present and the past. But the actual superimposition of two formal systems or types, one of which remained dominant (that is, symbolising the church), produced an incipient betweenness, but no dislocation.

Any interpretation of a text which is thought to be natural to the discourse of architecture can be called a text of authority, that is, given correctness and value by architecture itself. Architecture is constantly writing texts of authority without realising that it is engaging in this activity. For example, representation is a text of authority. Representation is a false authority that suggests some sort of correct truthful relationship between the object of architecture and what it is signifying. The apparent truth of architecture is in its claims for the univocality of the representation of the architectural object, that is, that object which has an immediate aesthetic and a function that it represents in its presence. The idea of presence and the representations of presence represses all other interpretations, represses textuality. The idea that the classical orders or a functional type is natural to architecture is an example of the representation of presence.

The dislocating text attacks the terms by which presence is represented, that is that origin, beauty, function, truth are 'natural' (ie, authentic) and not conventional to architecture. The dislocating text does not deny function or beauty but denies their authority and thus shifts the perception of them.

A dislocating text in architecture confronts this idea of originary (or what is thought to be the originary) or authorial value; ie, that there is a correct way to read the object. Text, therefore, is not an originary source of imagery or figuration; it is not the representation of use or the aesthetic of an object. These are texts but are not dislocating. A dislocating text is or represents the various relationships between these other texts. In this sense, text is always a strategy which seems to be dislocating and thus a second language.

In a dislocating text the object is seen and read as different, as between its abstract and necessary object being and some known iconic form, which in its iconicity contains the traditional architectural text. Dislocating texts refuse any single authoritative reading. They do not appeal to the logic of grammar or the reason of truth. Their 'truth' is constantly in flux. Although they are directed they are authorless. They are directed in the sense that they suggest a way of reading which seems to be internal to the object. But, at the same time, they deflect any single reading.

Text is then perhaps a term that can be used for any and all strategies and conditions which dislocate architecture from its authorial or natural condition of being; that is, the detaching of what architecture looks like from the need to represent function, shelter, meaning and so forth. It is not so much that the look of architecture will change (architecture will always look like architecture) but rather the style and significance of its look will be different. The idea of text is not in opposition to the reality of architecture, just as the imaginary is not the opposite of the real; it is an other discourse. Text surrounds reality at the same time that it is internal to reality.

The Romeo and Juliet project for the castles of the same name outside of Vicenza in Montecchio for the Venice Biennale of 1986, because of its already having in place an other text, that is the play by the same name, presented an ideal opportunity to present an architectural text that was no longer guaranteed by the tradition of architecture. Here, for the first time, there was a text of between; a fabric of images referring to something other than itself in order to create a dislocation in time and space. Traditional textuality (which includes the Modernist idea of dispersal, incongruity and fragment) is ultimately projected to return the system to closure. The textuality of the Romeo and Juliet project is as a set of fragments which are internally incomplete. They signal the impossibility of a return to more traditional forms of text in architecture such as the relationship of form to type or form to man. The object is no longer identical to a substance.

In the Romeo and Juliet project, the texts are made to close on themselves by insisting on a condition of self-similarity which countered any single authoritative scale and detached this analogous process from the pursuit of a geometric ideal. It is this closure potential afforded by superposition which opens the possibility for a text between. Within the project, a process which moved towards closure, rather than end, guaranteed that there was something yet to be written before the reality of the castle sites in Montecchio and after the narratives of the Verona of Romeo and Juliet. This 'yet to be written' is a temporal dimension outside of the present tradition of architecture, yet exists within the specific project. The design process is no longer governed by a teleology which moves it from an origin to a final goal of truth, but rather is an open-ended series of superpositions.

The Romeo and Juliet project also necessarily confronts the traditional authority of architectural representation. Traditionally, architecture is represented in a set of drawings and models subservient to and depicted by a single object. Thus, this representation in its singularity mediates and separates text from object. In Romeo and Juliet, on the other hand, each manifestation differed from the other creating the between, the figuration united with discourse to create text.

Romeo and Juliet is an example of what Jeff Kipnis calls an immanent text. An immanent text is one that is not authorised by architecture. It is a text which is authorised by the programme and by the site not in architecture but rather in using this idea of text to denote a strategy for the dislocation of traditional ideas of time and place in architecture.

Using this idea of the superposition of two texts to generate a strategy for the dislocation of time and place in architecture also can be seen in our project for the Via Flaminia in Rome. In this project, the first text was the actual site in Rome, and the second text was the dislocation of the sites along the Via Flaminia in time, place and scale. Traditionally an axis such as the Via Flaminia represented a linear progression in time, a continuous and indifferent movement between two or more points, which in themselves have a meaning and a relationship because of the axis. Again through a process of superposition of elements of a different scale and place, similar to the one used in Romeo and Juliet, the elements of such an axial progression are continuously dislocated, appearing to be simultaneously in a different place.

This was achieved by superposing the end points of any three different length segments (in this case the segment of the Via Flaminia from the Ponte Milvio to Sant'Andrea, and from Sant'Andrea to Piazza del Popolo, and the entire segment from Ponte Milvio to Piazza del Popolo) and thus making them the same length. In this way their analogous relationship, as end points of different segments of an axis, is revealed. While these segments become the same length, they obviously become different scales. This in turn dislocates the traditional notion of a dominant scale typically generated by the human body or the aesthetic preferences of the eye. Each of these segments now loses its real dimension, location, place and time; ultimately the whole notion of the axis as a form bound to linear time with its implicit hierarchy and continuity is subverted. More importantly, because elements along each of the axes are relocated, they also begin to superpose other elements to reveal unexpected correspondences, the architectural analogue to the rhetorical figure catachresis, which in their former state would have remained unexpressed. What is revealed from the initial superpositions cannot be predicted.

These superpositions result in a dislocation of origin and destination, of time and space. By incorporating in an end point of the Via Flaminia, such as the Piazza del Popolo or the Ponte Milvio, an assemblage from disparate but analogous elements of other sites on the axis, such as Vignola's Church of Sant'Andrea, the two figures occupy origin and destination contemporaneously. At the same time, movement along the axis of the Via Flaminia toward a destination (supposedly the Piazza del Popolo) seems to result in a return to origin, the beginning of the axis at the Ponte Milvio.

In this way, the idea of a place along the axis of the Via Flaminia is both reinforced and denied. While new places are created, the traditional notion of place is undercut because each place is actually many places at once. The result is a text which displaces the traditional notion of time and space. It does not deny traditional and privileged ideas of context and aesthetic presence as Modernism attempted to do, but subverts them.

While the elements of the site seem to be in their original position, that is they seem to be located according to their previous condition of formal structure (events at the beginning, middle and end of such axes), they in fact are not. Origin and destination are perceived contemporaneously while movement toward the destination results in a return to origin. The perception at one point of all the elements of the progression, rearranged in scale and distance, dislocates the relationship between time and space. In the same way, one might proceed along the axis encountering the same elements several times. Time and space, figure and form, are thus collapsed as interdependent entities. This allows these elements — time, space, place, form, figure — to be deployed in a system which contains its own contradictions, the meaning of space and time is freed from a linear symbolic representation. The definition of time as linear or circular, and of space as dynamic or static, now has no meaning in the traditional sense.

Most importantly, the received system of meaning, ie, the cultural significance of a form, is denied without denying the form: but now the forms in themselves have neither transcendental nor *a priori* meanings. They are cut off from the authority of their former singular significance. The architecture is between the signs.

The two conditions of text thus far described maintain the idea of text and reading within the tradition of architecture. However, there is yet another condition of text, of a text between, which in its displacement does not return to the authority of traditional architecture. The idea of a text between requires an initial condition of two texts. The texts themselves are not dislocating. The dislocation or condition of between is the result of the texts being seen, initially, as two weak images; that is, not having a strong aesthetic, iconic or functionally recognisable image. This weak image in itself leads to an idea of reading as dominant.

In the Frankfurt Biocentrum project, two texts, one not from architecture and one not from biology, but rather between both, were used; neither was strictly authorised by the project. Here the form of the biology building was the result of the superposition of two texts, one displaced from biology and the other displaced from architecture. In the former, three aspects of the DNA's protein production were articulated as the processes of replication, transcription and translation. These three processes were seen to have analogous processes in three dimensions in something called fractal geometry which is also outside of architecture's Euclidean or topological geometries and is, interestingly enough, a 'between' geometry — that is, its forms are between whole number dimensions.

At first, the question to be asked was why should a biology building look like or be the result of the processes of biology. But in fact neither the processes of DNA nor of fractal geometry are themselves the issue nor produce the form; they are merely the second text, from which the text of architecture generates the text between.

Questions concerning the idea of text in general, and more specifically, a dislocating text, have been resisted or repressed in architecture. Perhaps because this idea of text removes the restraint of morality, that is the responsibility of form to the traditions of architecture. What text demonstrates is that a building may function, shelter, be constrained by site, have an aesthetic and be meaningful without necessarily symbolising in its forms these conditions. It can in fact do all of these things and still speak of something else. In a sense it radicalises such formal concerns which in the past had been constrained by a morality without even realising it, because formalisms assume such a morality to be natural and thus neither constrained nor morally impacted. When these constraints are removed then form can be read as a text, a text between, as both outside the author's intentions and outside the authoriality of architecture.

Therefore, the idea of a text between is necessarily dislocating. It does violence to the former celebrations of architecture as an object of desire (of an aesthetic pleasure); as a reification of man (anthropomorphism and human scale); as an object of value (truth, origin and metaphoric meaning). Such a between text is not place-specific, time-specific, or scale-specific. It does not symbolise use, shelter or structure. Its aesthetic and history are other. Its dislocation takes place between the conventional and natural. Thus, what is being violated is the maintenance of the system as a whole.

THE END OF THE CLASSICAL: THE END OF THE BEGINNING, THE END OF THE END
PETER EISENMAN

Architecture from the 15th century to the present has been under the influence of three 'fictions'. Notwithstanding the apparent succession of architectural styles, each with its own label — Classicism, Neo-Classicism, Romanticism, Modernism, Post-Modernism, and so on into the future — these three fictions have persisted in one form or another for 500 years. They are *representation, reason,* and *history.*[1] Each of the fictions had an underlying purpose: representation was to embody the idea of meaning; reason was to codify the idea of truth; history was to recover the idea of the timeless from the idea of change. Because of the persistence of these categories, it will be necessary to consider this period as manifesting a continuity in architectural thought. This continuous mode of thought can be referred to as the *classical.*[2]

It was not until the late 20th century that the classical could be appreciated as an abstract system of relations. Such recognition occurred because the architecture of the early part of the 20th century itself came to be considered part of history. Thus it is now possible to see that, although stylistically different from previous architectures, Modern architecture exhibits a system of relations similar to that of the classical.[3] Prior to this time, the 'classical' was taken to be either synonymous with architecture conceived of as a continuous tradition from antiquity, or, by the mid-19th century, an historicised style. Today the period of time dominated by the classical can be seen as an 'episteme', to employ Foucault's term — a continuous period of knowledge that includes the early 20th century.[4] Despite the proclaimed rupture in both ideology and style associated with the Modern Movement, the three fictions have never been questioned and so remain intact. This is to say that architecture since the mid-15th century has aspired to be a paradigm of the *classic*, of that which is *timeless*, *meaningful*, and *true*. In the sense that architecture attempts to recover that which is classic, it can be called 'classical'.[5]

The 'Fiction' of Representation:
The Simulation of Meaning

The first 'fiction' is *representation*. Before the Renaissance there was a congruence of language and representation. The meaning of language was in a face value conveyed within representation; in other words, the way language produced meaning could be *represented within* language. Things *were*; truth and meaning were self-evident. The meaning of a Romanesque or Gothic cathedral was in itself; it was *de facto*. Renaissance buildings, on the other hand — and all buildings after them that pretended to be 'architecture' — received their value by representing an already valued architecture, by being simulacra (representations of representations) of antique buildings; they were *de jure*.[6] The *message* of the past was used to verify the *meaning* of the present. Precisely because of this need to verify, Renaissance architecture was the first simulation, an unwitting fiction of the object.

By the late 18th century, historical relativity came to supersede the face value of language as representation, and this view of history prompted a search for certainty, for origins both historical and logical, for truth and proof, and for goals. Truth was no longer thought to reside in representation but was believed to exist outside it, in the processes of history. This shift can be seen in the changing status of the orders: until the 17th century they were thought to be paradigmatic and timeless; afterwards the possibility of their timelessness depended on a necessary historicity. This shift, as has just been suggested, occurred because language had ceased to intersect with representation — that is, because it was not *meaning* but a *message* that was displayed in the object.

Modern architecture claimed to rectify and liberate itself from the Renaissance fiction of representation by asserting that it was not necessary for architecture to represent another architecture; architecture was solely to embody its own *function*. With the deductive conclusion that form follows function, Modern architecture introduced the idea that a building should express — that is, look like — its function, or an *idea* of its function (that it should manifest the rationality of its processes of production and composition).[7] Thus, in its effort to distance itself from the earlier representational tradition, Modern architecture attempted to strip itself of the outward trappings of classical style. This process of reduction was called *abstraction*. A column without a base and capital was thought to be an abstraction. Thus reduced, form was believed to embody function more 'honestly'. Such a column looked more like a *real* column, the simplest possible load-carrying element, than one provided with a base and capital bearing arboreal or anthropomorphic motifs.

. This reduction to pure functionality was, in fact, not abstraction; it was an attempt to represent reality itself. In this sense functional goals merely replaced the orders of classical composition as the starting point for architectural design. The Moderns' attempt to represent 'realism' with an undecorated, functional object was a fiction equivalent to the simulacrum of the classical in Renaissance representation. For what made function any more 'real' a source of imagery than elements chosen from antiquity? The idea of function, in this case the message of utility as opposed to the message of antiquity, was raised to an originary proposition — a self-evident starting point for design analogous to typology or historical quotation. The Moderns' attempt to represent realism is, then, a manifestation of the same fiction wherein meaning and value reside outside the world of an architecture 'as is', in which representation is about its own *meaning* rather than being a *message* of another previous meaning.

Functionalism turned out to be yet another stylistic conclusion, this one based on a scientific and technical positivism, a simulation of efficiency. From this perspective the Modern Movement can be seen to be continuous with the architecture that preceded it. Modern architecture therefore failed to embody a new value in itself.

For in trying to *reduce* architectural form to its essence, to a pure reality, the Moderns assumed they were transforming the field of referential figuration to that of non-referential objectivity. In reality, however, their 'objective' forms never left the classical tradition. They were simply stripped-down classical forms, or forms referring to a new set of givens (function, technology). Thus, Le Corbusier's houses that look like modern steamships or biplanes exhibit the same referential attitude toward representation as a Renaissance or classical building. The points of reference are different, but the implications for the object are the same.

The commitment to return Modernist abstraction to history seems to sum up, for our time, the problem of representation. It was given its Post-Modern inversion in Robert Venturi's distinction between the 'duck' and the 'decorated shed'.[8] A duck is a building that looks like its function, or allows its internal order to be displayed on its exterior; a decorated shed is a building that functions as a billboard, where any kind of imagery (except its internal function) — letters, patterns, even architectural elements — conveys a *message* accessible to all. In this sense the stripped-down abstractions of Modernism are still referential objects: technological rather than typological ducks.

But the Post-Modernists fail to make another distinction which is exemplified in Venturi's comparison of the Doges' Palace in Venice, which he calls a decorated shed, and Sansovino's library across the Piazza San Marco, which he says is a duck.[9] This obscures the more significant distinction between architecture 'as is' and architecture as message. The Doges' Palace is not a decorated shed because it was not representational of another architecture; its significance came directly from the meaning embodied in the figures themselves; it was an architecture 'as is'. Sansovino's library may seem to be a duck, but only because it falls into the history of library types. The use of the orders on Sansovino's library speaks not to the function or type of the library, but rather to the representation of a previous architecture. The facades of Sansovino's library contain a message, not an inherent meaning; they are signboards. Venturi's misreading of these buildings seems motivated by a preference for the decorated shed. While the replication of the orders had significance in Sansovino's time (in that they defined the classical) the replication of the same orders today has no significance because the value system represented is no longer valued. A sign begins to replicate or, in Jean Baudrillard's term, 'simulate' once the reality it represents is dead.[10] When there is no longer a distinction between representation and reality, when reality is only simulation, then representation loses its *a priori* source of significance, and it, too, becomes a simulation.

The 'Fiction' of Reason: The Simulation of Truth

The second 'fiction' of post-Medieval architecture is *reason*. If representation was a simulation of the meaning of the present through the message of antiquity, then reason was a simulation of the meaning of the truth through the message of science. This fiction is strongly manifest in 20th-century architecture, as it is in that of the four preceding centuries; its apogee was in the Enlightenment. The quest for origin in architecture is the initial manifestation of the aspiration toward a rational source for design. Before the Renaissance the idea of origin was seen as self-evident; its meaning and importance went without saying; it belonged to an *a priori* universe of values. In the Renaissance, with the loss of a self-evident universe of values, origins were sought in natural or divine sources or in a cosmological or anthropomorphic geometry. The reproduction of the image of the Vitruvian man is the most renowned example. Not surprisingly, since the origin was thought to contain the seeds of the object's purpose and thus its destination, this belief in the existence of an ideal origin led directly to a belief in the existence of an ideal end. Such a genetic idea of beginning/end depended on a belief in a universal plan in nature and the cosmos which, through the application of classical rules of composition concerning hierarchy, order, and closure, would confer

25

a harmony of the whole upon the parts. The perspective of the end thus directed the strategy for beginning. Therefore, as Alberti first defined it in *Della Pittura,* composition was not an open-ended or neutral process of transformation, but rather a strategy for arriving at a predetermined goal; it was the mechanism by which the idea of order, represented in the orders, was translated into a specific form.[11]

Reacting against the cosmological goals of Renaissance composition, Enlightenment architecture aspired to a rational process of design whose ends were a product of pure, secular reason rather than of divine order. The Renaissance vision of harmony (faith in the divine) led naturally to the scheme of order that was to replace it (faith in reason), which was the logical determination of form from *a priori* types.

Durand embodies this moment of the supreme authority of reason. In his treatises formal orders become type forms; and natural and divine origins are replaced by rational solutions to the problems of accommodation and construction. The goal is a socially relevant architecture; it is attained through the rational transformation of type forms. Later, in the late 19th and early 20th centuries, function and technique replaced the catalogue of type forms as origins. But the point is that from Durand on, it was believed that deductive reason — the same process used in science, mathematics, and technology — was capable of producing a truthful (that is, meaningful) architectural object. And with the success of rationalism as a scientific method (one could almost call it a 'style' of thought) in the 18th and early 19th centuries, architecture adopted the self-evident values conferred by rational origins. If an architecture *looked* rational — that is, *represented* rationality — it was believed to *represent* truth. As in logic, at the point where all deductions developed from an initial premise corroborate that premise, there is logical closure and, it was believed, certain truth. Moreover, in this procedure the primacy of the origin remains intact. The rational became the moral and aesthetic basis of Modern architecture. And the representational task of architecture in an age of reason was to portray its own modes of knowing.

At this point in the evolution of consciousness something occurred: reason turned its focus onto itself and thus began the process of its own undoing. Questioning its own status and mode of knowing, reason exposed itself to be a fiction.[12] The process for knowing — measurement, logical proof, causality — turned out to be a network of value-laden arguments, no more than effective modes of persuasion. Values were dependent on another teleology, another end fiction, that of rationality.

Essentially, then, nothing had really changed from the Renaissance idea of origin. Whether the appeal was to a divine or natural order, as in the 15th century, or to a rational technique and typological function, as in the post-Enlighten-

ment period, it ultimately amounted to the same thing — to the idea that architecture's value derived from a source outside itself. Function and type were only value-laden origins equivalent to divine or natural ones.

In this second 'fiction' the crisis of belief in reason eventually undermined the power of self-evidence. As reason began to turn on itself, to question its own status, its authority to convey truth, its power to prove, began to evaporate. The analysis of analysis revealed that logic could not do what reason had claimed for it — reveal the self-evident truth of its origins. What both the Renaissance and the Modern relied on as the basis of truth was found to require, in essence, faith. Analysis was a form of simulation; knowledge was a new religion. Similarly, it can be seen that architecture never embodied reason; it could only state the desire to do so; there is no architectural image of reason. Architecture presented an aesthetic of the experience of (the persuasiveness of and desire for) reason. Analysis, and the illusion of proof, in a continuous process that recalls Nietzsche's characterisation of 'truth', is a never-ending series of figures, metaphors, and metonymies:

> In a cognitive environment in which reason has been revealed to depend on a belief in knowledge, therefore to be irreducibly metaphoric, a classical architecture — that is an architecture whose processes of transformation are value-laden strategies grounded on self-evident or a priori origins — will always be an architecture of restatement and not of representation, no matter how ingeniously the origins are selected for this transformation, nor how inventive the transformation is.

Architectural restatement, replication, is a nostalgia for the security of knowing, a belief in the continuity of Western thought. Once analysis and reason replaced self-evidence as the means by which truth was revealed, the classic or timeless quality of truth ended and the need for verification began.

The 'Fiction' of History:
The Simulation of the Timeless

The third 'fiction' of classical Western architecture is that of *history*. Prior to the mid-15th century, time was conceived non-dialectically; from antiquity to the Middle Ages there was no concept of the forward movement of time. Art did not seek its justification in terms of the past or future; it was ineffable and timeless. In ancient Greece the temple and the god were one and the same; architecture was divine and natural. For this reason it appeared 'classic' to the 'classical' epoch that followed. The classic could not be represented or simulated, it could only *be*. In its straightforward assertion of itself it was non-dialectical and timeless.

In the mid-15th century the idea of a temporal origin

emerged, and with it the idea of the past. This interrupted the eternal cycle of time by positing a fixed point of beginning. Hence the loss of the timeless, for the existence of origin required a temporal reality. The attempt of the classical to recover the timeless turned, paradoxically, to a time-bound concept of history as a source of the timeless. Moreover, the consciousness of time's forward movement came to explain a process of historical change. By the 19th century this process was seen as dialectical. With dialectical time came the idea of the *Zeitgeist*, with cause and effect rooted in presentness — that is, with an aspired-to timelessness of the present. In addition to its aspiration to timelessness, the spirit of the age held that an *a priori* relationship existed between history and all its manifestations at any given moment. It was necessary only to identify the governing spirit to know what style of architecture was properly expressive of, and relevant to, the time. Implicit was the notion that man should always be in harmony — or at least in a non-disjunctive relation — with his time.

In its polemical rejection of the history that preceded it, the Modern Movement attempted to appeal to values for this (harmonic) relationship other than those that embodied the eternal or universal. In seeing itself as superseding the values of the preceding architecture, the Modern Movement substituted a universal idea of relevance for a universal idea of history, analysis of programme for analysis of history. It presumed itself to be a value-free and collective form of intervention, as opposed to the virtuoso individualism and informed connoisseurship personified by the post-Renaissance architect. Relevance in Modern architecture came to lie in embodying a value other than the natural or divine; the *Zeitgeist* was seen to be contingent and of the present, rather than as absolute and eternal. But the difference in value between presentness and the universal — between the contingent value of the *Zeitgeist* and the eternal value of the classical — only resulted in yet another set (in fact, simply the opposite set) of aesthetic preferences. The presumedly neutral spirit of the 'epochal will' supported asymmetry over symmetry, dynamism over stability, absence of hierarchy over hierarchy.

The imperatives of the historical moment are always evident in the connection between the representation of the function of architecture and its form. Ironically, Modern architecture, by invoking the *Zeitgeist* rather than doing away with history, only continued to act as the midwife to historically significant form. In this sense Modern architecture was not a rupture with history, but simply a moment in the same continuum, a new episode in the evolution of the *Zeitgeist*. And architecture's representation of its particular *Zeitgeist* turned out to be less 'modern' than originally thought.

One of the questions that may be asked is why the Moderns did not see themselves in this continuity. One answer is that the ideology of the *Zeitgeist* bound them to their present history with the promise to release them from their past history; *they were ideologically trapped in the illusion of the eternity of their own time*.

The late 20th century, with its retrospective knowledge that Modernism has become history, has inherited nothing less than the recognition of the end of the ability of a classical or referential architecture to express its own time as timeless. The illusory timelessness of the present brings with it an awareness of the *timeful* nature of past time. It is for this reason that the representation of a *Zeitgeist* always implies a simulation; it is seen in the classical use of the replication of a past time to invoke the timeless as the expression of a present time. Thus, in the *Zeitgeist* argument, there will always be this unacknowledged paradox: a simulation of the *Zeitgeist* history, too, is subject to a questioning of its own authority. How can it be possible, from within history, to determine a timeless truth of its 'spirit'? Thus history ceases to be an objective source of truth; origins and ends once again lose their universality (that is, their self-evident value) and, like history, become fictions. If it is no longer possible to pose the problem of architecture in terms of a *Zeitgeist* — that is, if architecture can no longer assert its relevance through a consonance with its *Zeitgeist* — then it must turn to some other structure. To escape such a dependence on the *Zeitgeist* — that is, the idea that the *purpose* of an architectural style is to embody the spirit of its age — it is necessary to propose an alternative idea of architecture, one whereby it is no longer the purpose of architecture, but its inevitability, to express its own time.

Once the traditional values of classical architecture are understood as not meaningful, true, and timeless, it must be concluded that these classical values were *always* simulations (and are not merely seen to be so in light of a present rupture of history or the present disillusionment with the *Zeitgeist*). It therefore becomes clear that the classical itself was a simulation that architecture sustained for 500 years. Because the classical did not recognise itself as a simulation, it sought to represent extrinsic values (which it could not do) in the guise of its own reality.

The result, then, of seeing classicism and Modernism as part of a single historical continuity is the understanding that there are no longer any self-evident values in representation, reason, or history to confer legitimacy on the object. This loss of self-evident value allows the timeless to be cut free from the meaningful and the truthful. It permits the view that there is no one truth (a timeless truth), or one meaning (a timeless meaning), but merely the timeless. *When the possibility is raised that the timeless can be cut adrift from the timeful (history), so too can the timeless be cut away from universal-*

ity to produce a timelessness which is not universal. This separation makes it unimportant whether origins are natural or divine or functional; thus, it is no longer necessary to produce a classic — that is, a timeless — architecture by recourse to the classical values inherent in *representation, reason,* and *history*.

The Not-Classical: Architecture as Fiction

The necessity of the quotation marks around the term 'fiction' is now obvious. The three 'fictions' just discussed can be seen not as fictions but rather as simulations. As has been said, fiction becomes simulation when it does not recognise its condition as fiction, when it tries to simulate a condition of reality, truth, or non-fiction. The simulation of representation in architecture has led, first of all, to an excessive concentration of inventive energies in the representational object. When columns are seen as surrogates of trees, and windows resemble the portholes of ships, architectural elements become representational figures carrying an inordinate burden of meaning. In other disciplines representation is not the only purpose of figuration. In literature, for example, metaphors and similes have a wider range of application — poetic, ironic, and the like — and are not limited to allegorical or referential functions. Conversely, in architecture only one aspect of the figure is traditionally at work: object representation. The architectural figure always alludes to — aims at the representation of — some *other* object, whether architectural, anthropomorphic, natural, or technological.

Second, the simulation of reason in architecture has been based on a classical value given to the idea of truth. But Heidegger has noted that error has a trajectory parallel to truth, that error can be the unfolding of truth.[13] Thus to proceed from error or fiction is to counter consciously the tradition of 'mis-reading' on which the classical unwittingly depended — not a presumedly logical transformation of something *a priori*, but a deliberate 'error' stated as such, one which presupposes only its own internal truth. Error in this case does not assume the same value as truth; it is *not* simply its dialectical opposite. It is more like a *dissimulation*, a 'not-containing' of the value of truth.

Finally, the simulated fiction of Modern Movement history, unwittingly inherited from the classical, was that any present-day architecture must be a reflection of its *Zeitgeist*; that is, architecture can simultaneously be about presentness and universality. But if architecture is inevitably about the invention of fictions, it should also be possible to propose an architecture that embodies an *other* fiction, one that is not sustained by the values of presentness or universality and, more importantly, that does not consider its purpose to be the reflection of these values. This *other* fiction/object, then, clearly should eschew the fictions of the classical (represen-

tation, reason, and history), which are attempts to 'solve' the problem of architecture rationally; for strategies and solutions are vestiges of a goal-oriented view of the world. If this is the case, the question becomes: What can be the model for architecture when the essence of what was effective in the classical model — the presumed rational value of structures, representations, methodologies of origins and ends, and deductive processes — has been shown to be a simulation?

It is not possible to answer such a question with an alternative model. But a series of characteristics can be proposed that typify this aporia, this loss in our capacity to conceptualise a new model for architecture. These characteristics, outlined below, arise from that which can *not* be; they form a structure of *absences*.[14] The purpose in proposing them is not to reconstitute what has just been dismissed, a model for a theory of architecture — for all such models are ultimately futile. Rather what is being proposed is an expansion beyond the limitations presented by the classical model to the realisation of *architecture as an independent discourse*, free of external values — classical or any other; that is, the intersection of the *meaning-free*, the *arbitrary* and the *timeless* in the artificial.

The meaning-free, arbitrary, and timeless creation of artificiality in this sense must be distinguished from what Baudrillard has called 'simulation':[15] it is not an attempt to erase the classical distinction between reality and representation — thus again making architecture a set of conventions simulating the real; it is, rather, more like a *dissimulation*.[16] Whereas simulation attempts to obliterate the difference between real and imaginary, dissimulation leaves untouched the difference between reality and illusion. The relationship between dissimulation and reality is similar to the signification embodied in the mask: the sign of pretending to be *not* what one is — that is, a sign which seems not to signify anything besides itself (the sign of a sign, or the negation of what is behind it). Such a dissimulation in architecture can be given the provisional title of the *not-classical*. As dissimulation is not the inverse, negative or opposite of simulation, a not-classical architecture is not the inverse, negative, or opposite of classical architecture; it is merely different from or other than. A not-classical architecture is no longer a certification of experience or a simulation of history, reason, or reality in the present. Instead, it may more appropriately be described as an *other* manifestation, an architecture *as is*, now as a fiction. It is a representation of itself, of its own values and internal experience.

The claim that a not-classical architecture is necessary, that it is proposed by the new epoch or the rupture in the continuity of history, would be another *Zeitgeist* argument. The not-classical merely proposes an end to the dominance of classical values in order to reveal other values. It proposes, not a new value or a new *Zeitgeist*, but merely another condition — one of reading architecture as a text. There is nevertheless no question that this idea of the reading of architecture is initiated by a *Zeitgeist* argument: that today the classical signs are no longer significant and have become no more than replications. A not-classical architecture is, therefore, not unresponsive to the realisation of the closure inherent in the world; rather, it is unresponsive to representing it.

The End of the Beginning

An origin of value implies a state or a condition of origin before value has been given to it. A beginning is such a condition prior to a valued origin. In order to reconstruct the timeless, the state of *as is*, of face value, one must begin: begin by eliminating the time-bound concepts of the classical, which are primarily origin and end. The end of the beginning is also the end of the beginning of value. But it is not possible to go back to the earlier, prehistoric state of grace, the Eden of timelessness before origins and ends were valued. We must begin in the present — without necessarily giving a value to presentness. The attempt to reconstruct the timeless today must be a fiction which recognises the fictionality of its own task — that is, it should not attempt to simulate a timeless reality.

As has been suggested above, latent in the classical appeal to origins is the more general problem of cause and effect. This formula, part of the fictions of reason and history, reduces architecture to an added-to or inessential object by making it simply an effect of certain causes understood as origins. This problem is inherent in all of classical architecture, including its Modernist aspect. The idea of architecture as something added-to rather than something with its own being — as adjectival rather than nominal or ontological — leads to the perception of architecture as a practical device. As long as architecture is primarily a device designated for use and for shelter — that is, as long as it has origins in programmatic functions — it will always constitute an effect.

But once this self-evident characteristic of architecture is dismissed and architecture is seen as having no *a priori* origins — whether functional, divine, or natural — alternative fictions for the origin can be proposed: for example, one that is *arbitrary,* one that has no external value derived from meaning, truth, or timelessness. It is possible to imagine a beginning internally consistent but not conditioned by or contingent on historic origins with supposedly self-evident values.[17] Thus, while classical origins were thought to have their source in a divine or natural order, and Modern origins were held to derive their value from deductive reason, not-classical origins can be strictly arbitrary, simply starting points, without value. They can be artificial and relative, as

opposed to natural, divine, or universal.[18] Such artificially determined beginnings can be free of universal values because they are merely arbitrary points in time, when the architectural process commences. One example of an artificial origin is a *graft,* as in the genetic insertion of an alien body into a host to provide a new result.[19] As opposed to a collage or a montage, which lives within a context and alludes to an origin, a graft is an invented site, which does not so much have object characteristics as those of process. A graft is not in itself genetically arbitrary. Its arbitrariness is in its freedom from a value system of non-arbitrariness (that is, the classical). It is arbitrary in its provision of a choice of reading which brings no external value to the process. But further, in its artificial and relative nature a graft is not in itself necessarily an achievable result, but merely a site that contains *motivation* for action — that is the beginning of a process.[20]

Motivation takes something arbitrary — that is, something in its artificial state which is not obedient to an external structure of values — and implies an action and a movement concerning an internal structure which has an inherent order and an internal logic. This raises the question of the motivation or purpose from an arbitrary origin. How can something be arbitrary and non-goal oriented but still be internally motivated? Every state, it can be argued, has a motivation toward its own being — a motion rather than a direction. Just because architecture cannot portray or enact *reason* as a value does not mean that it cannot argue systematically or reasonably. In all processes there must necessarily be some beginning point; but the value in an arbitrary or intentionally fictive architecture is found in the *intrinsic* nature of its action rather than in the direction of its course. Since any process must necessarily have a beginning and a movement, however, the fictional origin must be considered as having at least a methodological value — a value concerned with generating the internal relations of the process itself. But if the beginning is in fact arbitrary, there can be no direction toward closure or end, because the motivation for change of state (that is, the inherent instability of the beginning) can never lead to a state of no change (that is, an end). Thus, in their freedom from the universal values of both historic origin and directional process, motivations can lead to *ends* different from those of the previous value-laden *end.*

The End of the End

Along with the end of the origin, the second basic characteristic of a not-classical architecture, therefore, is its freedom from *a priori* goals or ends — the end of the end. The end of the classical also means the end of the myth of the end as a value-laden effect of the progress or direction of history. By logically leading to a potential closure of thought, the fictions of the classical awakened a desire to confront, display, and even transcend the end of history. This desire was manifest in the Modern idea of utopia, a time beyond history. It was thought that objects imbued with value because of their relationship to a self-evidently meaningful origin could somehow transcend the present in moving toward a timeless future, a utopia. This idea of progress gave false value to the present; utopia, a form of fantasising about an open and limitless end, forestalled the notion of closure. Thus the Modern crisis of closure marked the end of the process of moving toward the end. Such crises (or ruptures) in our perception of the continuity of history arise not so much out of a change in our idea of origins or ends than out of the failure of the present (and its objects) to sustain our expectations of the future. And once the continuity of history is broken in our perception, any representation of the classical, any 'classicism', can be seen only as a belief. At this point, where our received values are in crisis, the end of the end raises the possibility of the invention and realisation of a blatantly fictional future (which is therefore non-threatening in its truth value) as opposed to a simulated or idealised one.

With the end of the end, what was formerly the process of composition or transformation ceases to be a causal strategy, a process of addition or subtraction from an origin. Instead, the process becomes one of *modification* — the invention of a non-dialectical, non-directional, non-goal oriented process.[21] The invented origins from which this process receives its motivation differ from the accepted, mythic origins of the classicists by being *arbitrary*, reinvented for each circumstance, adopted for the moment and not forever. The process of modification can be seen as an open-ended tactic rather than a goal-oriented strategy. A strategy is a process that is determined and value-laden before it begins; it is *directed*. Since the arbitrary origin cannot be known in advance (in a cognitive sense), it does not depend on knowledge derived from the classical tradition and thus engender a strategy.

In this context, architectural form is revealed as a 'place of invention' rather than as a subservient representation of another architecture or as a strictly practical device. To invent an architecture is to allow architecture to be a cause; in order to be a cause, it must arise from something outside a directed strategy of composition.

The end of the end also concerns the end of object representation as the only metaphoric subject in architecture. In the past, the metaphor in architecture was used to convey such forces as tension, compression, extension, and elongation; these were qualities that could be seen, if not literally in the objects themselves, then in the relationship between objects. The idea of the metaphor here has nothing to do with the qualities generated between buildings or between buildings and spaces; rather, it has to do with the idea that the internal process itself can generate a kind of non-representational figuration in the object. This is an appeal, not to the classical aesthetic of the object, but to the potential *poetic* of an architectural text. The problem, then, is to distinguish texts from representations, to convey the idea that what one is seeing, the material object, is a text rather than a series of image references to other objects or values.

This suggests the idea of architecture as 'writing' as opposed to architecture as image. What is being written, is not the object itself — its mass and volume — but the *act* of massing. This idea gives a metaphoric body to the act of architecture. It then signals its reading through an other system of signs, called *traces*.[22] Traces are not to be read literally, since they have no other value than to signal the idea that there is a reading event and that reading should take place; trace signals the idea to read.[23] Thus a trace is a partial or fragmentary sign; it has no objecthood. It signifies an action that is in process. In this sense a trace is not a simulation of reality; it is a dissimulation because it reveals itself as distinct from its former reality. It does not simulate the real, but represents and records the action inherent in a former or future reality, which has a value no more or less real than the trace itself. That is, trace is unconcerned with forming an image which is the representation of a previous architecture or of social customs and usages; rather, it is concerned with the marking — literally the figuration — of its own internal processes. Thus the trace is the record of motivation, the record of an action, not an image of another object-origin.

In this case a not-classical architecture begins actively to involve an idea of a reader conscious of his own identity as a reader rather than as a user or observer. It proposes a new reader distanced from any external value system (particularly an architectural-historical system). Such a reader brings no *a priori* competence to the act of reading other than an identity as a reader. That is, such a reader has no preconceived knowledge of what architecture should be (in terms of its proportions, textures, scale, and the like); nor does a not-classical architecture aspire to make itself understandable through these preconceptions.[24]

The competence of the reader (of architecture) may be defined as the capacity to distinguish a sense of *knowing* from a sense of *believing*. At any given time the conditions for knowledge are deeper than philosophic conditions; in fact, they provide the possibility of distinguishing philosophy from literature, science from magic, and religion from myth. The new competence comes from the capacity to read *per se*, to know how to read and more importantly, to know how to read (but not necessarily decode) architecture as a text. Thus the new 'object' must have the capacity to reveal itself first of all as a text, as a reading event. The architectural fiction proposed here differs from the classical fiction in its primary condition as a text and in the way it is read: the new reader is no longer presumed to know the nature of truth in the object, either as a representation of a rational origin or as a manifestation of a universal set of rules governing proportion, harmony, and ordering. But further, knowing how to decode is no longer important; simply, language in this context is no longer a code to assign meanings (that *this* means *that)*. The activity of reading is first and foremost in the recognition of something as a language (that *it is*). Reading, in this sense, makes available a level of *indication* rather than a level of meaning or expression.

Therefore, to propose the end of the beginning and the end of the end[25] is to propose the end of beginnings and ends of value — to propose an *other,* 'timeless' space of invention. It is a timeless space in the present without a determining relation to an ideal future or to an idealised past. Architecture in the present is seen as a process of inventing an artificial past and a futureless present. It remembers a no-longer future.

This paper is based on three non-verifiable assumptions or values: timeless (originless, endless) architecture; non-representational (objectless) architecture; and artificial (arbitrary, reasonless) architecture.

The author wishes to thank the following people who have helped in the preparation of this article: Carol Burns, Giorgio Ciucci, Kurt Forster, Judy Geih, Nina Hofer, Jeff Kipnis, Joan Ockman and Anthony Vidler.

NOTES

1 Jean Baudrillard, 'The Order of Simulacra', *Simulations,* Semiotext(e), New York City, 1983, p83. Jean Baudrillard portrays the period beginning in the 15th century by three different simulacra: counterfeit, production, and simulation. He says that the first is based on the natural law of value, the second on the commercial law of value, and the third on the structural law of value.

2 The term 'classical' is often confused with the idea of the 'classic' and with the stylistic method of 'classicism'. That which is classic, according to Joseph Rykwert, invokes the idea of 'ancient and exemplary' and suggests 'authority and distinction': it is a model of what is excellent or of the first rank. More importantly, it implies its own timelessness, the idea that it is first rank at any time. Classicism, as opposed to the classical, will be defined here as a method of attempting to produce a 'classic' result by appealing to a 'classical' past. This accords with the definition given by Sir John Summerson, for whom classicism is not so much a set of ideas and values as it is a *style.* He maintains that while much of Gothic architecture was based on the same proportional relationships as the 'classical' architecture of the Renaissance, no one could confuse a Gothic cathedral with a Renaissance palazzo; it simply did not have the look of classicism. In contrast, Demetri Porphyrios argues that classicism is not a style, but instead has to do with rationalism: 'as much as architecture is a tectonic discourse, it is by definition transparent to rationality . . . the lessons to be learned today from classicism, therefore, are not to be found in classicism's stylistic wrinkles but in classicism's rationality.' Porphyrios here confuses classicism with the classical and the classic, that is, with a set of values privileging the 'truth' (that is, rationality) of tectonics over 'expression' and error. The fallacy of this approach is that classicism relies on an idea of historical continuity inherent in the classical: therefore it does not produce the timelessness characteristic of the classic. The classical, by implication, has a more relative status than the classic: it evokes a timeless *past,* a 'golden age' superior to the modern time or the present.

3 Michel Foucault, *The Order of Things,* Random House, New York City, 1973. It is precisely Michel Foucault's distinction between the classical and modern that has never been adequately articulated in relationship to architecture. In contrast to Foucault's epistemological differentiation, architecture has remained an uninterrupted mode of representation from the 15th century to the present. In fact, it will be seen that what is assumed in architecture to be classical is, in Foucault's terms, modern, and what is assumed in architecture to be modern is in reality Foucault's classical. Foucault's distinction is not what is at issue here, but rather the continuity that has persisted in architecture from the classical to the present day.

4 Foucault, pxxii. While the term 'episteme' as used here is similar to Foucault's use of the term in defining a continuous period of knowledge, it is necessary to point out that the time period here defined as the classical episteme differs from Foucault's definition. Foucault locates two discontinuities in the development of Western culture: the classical and the modern. He identifies the classical, beginning in the mid-17th century, with the primacy of the intersection of language and representation: the value of language, its '*meaning*', was seen to be self-evident and to receive its justification within language: the way language provided meaning could be represented within language. On the other hand, Foucault identifies the modern, originating in the early 19th century, with the ascendance of historical continuity and self-generated analytic processes over language and representation.

5 'The End of the Classical' is not about the end of the classic. It merely questions a contingent value structure which, when attached to the idea of the classic, yields an erroneous sense of the *classical.* It is not that the desire for a classic is at an end, but that the dominant conditions of the classical (origin, end, and the process of composition) are under reconsideration. Thus it might be more accurate to title this essay, 'The End of the Classical as Classic'.

6 Franco Borsi, *Leon Battista Alberti,* Harper and Row, New York City, 1977. The facade of the church of Sant' Andrea in Mantua by Alberti is one of the first uses of the transposition of ancient building types to achieve both verification and authority. It marks, as Borsi says, 'a decisive turning away from the vernacular to the Latin' (p272). It is acceptable in the 'vernacular' to revive the classical temple front because the function of the temple in antiquity and the church in the 15th century were similar. However, it is quite another matter to overlay the temple front with the triumphal arch. (See R Wittkower, *Architectural Principles in the*

Age of Humanism, WW Norton, New York City, 1971, and also DS Chambers, *Patrons and Artists in the Renaissance*, Macmillan & Co, London, 1970.) It is as if Alberti were saying that with the authority of God in question, man must resort to the symbols of his own power to verify the church. Thus the use of the triumphal arch becomes a message on the facade of Sant' Andrea rather than an embodiment of its inherent meaning.

7 Jeff Kipnis, from a seminar at the Graduate School of Design, Harvard University, 28 February 1984. 'Form cannot follow function until function (including but not limited to use) has first emerged as a possibility of form.'

8 Robert Venturi, Denise Scott Brown, Steven Izenour, *Learning From Las Vegas: The Forgotten Symbolism of Architectural Form*, revised edition, MIT Press, Cambridge, Massachusetts, 1977, p87.

9 See the film *Beyond Utopia: Changing Attitudes in American Architecture*, Michael Blackwood Productions, New York City, 1983.

10 Baudrillard, pp8-9. In referring to the death of the reality of God, Baudrillard says 'metaphysical despair came from the idea that images concealed nothing at all, and that in fact they were not images . . . but actually perfect simulacra . . .'

11 Leone Battista Alberti, *On Painting*, Yale University Press, New Haven, 1966, pp68-74.

12 Morris Kline, *Mathematics. The Loss of Certainty*, Oxford University Press, New York City, 1980, p5.

13 Martin Heidegger, 'On the Essence of Truth', from *Basic Writings*, Harper & Row Publishers, 1977. 'Errancy is the essential counter-essence to the primordial essence of the truth. Errancy opens itself up as the open region for every opposite essential truth . . . Errancy and the concealing of what is concealed belong to the primordial essence of truth.'

14 Gilles Deleuze, 'Plato and the Simulacrum', *October*, no 27, MIT Press, Cambridge, 1983, pp52-52. Deleuze uses a slightly different terminology to address a very similar set of issues: he discusses the Platonic distinction between model, copy and 'simulacrum' as a means of assigning value and hierarchical position to objects and ideas. He explains the overthrow of Platonism as the suspension of the *a priori* value-laden status of the Platonic *copy* in order to: 'raise up simulacra, to assert their rights over icons or copies. The problem no longer concerns the distinction Essence/Appearance or Model/Copy. This whole distinction operates in the world of representation . . . The simulacrum is not degraded copy, rather it contains a positive power which negates both original and copy, both model and reproduction. Of the at least two divergent series interiorised in the simulacrum neither can be assigned as original or copy. It doesn't even work to invoke the model of the Other, because no model resists the vertigo of the simulacrum' (pp52-3). Simulation is used here in a sense which closely approximates Deleuze's use of copy or icon, while dissimulation is conceptually very close to his description of the pre-Socratic simulacra.

15 Baudrillard, p2. In the essay 'The Precession of Simulacra' Baudrillard discusses the nature of simulation and the implication of present-day simulacra on our perception of the nature of reality and representation: 'Something has disappeared: the sovereign difference between them (the real and . . . simulation models) that was the abstraction's charm.'

16 Baudrillard, p5. Distinguishing between simulation and what he calls 'dissimulation', Baudrillard says that 'to dissimulate is to feign to have what one hasn't . . . "Someone who feigns an illness can simply go to bed and make believe that he is ill. Someone who simulates an illness produces in himself some of the symptoms." (Littre.) Thus feigning . . . is only masked: whereas simulation

threatens the difference between "true" and "false", between "real" and "imaginary". Since the simulator produces "true" symptoms, is he ill or not?' According to Baudrillard, simulation is the generation by models of a reality without origin: it no longer has to be rational, since it is no longer measured against some ideal or negative instance. While this sounds very much like my proposal of the not-classical, the not-classical is fundamentally different in that it is a dissimulation and not a simulation. Baudrillard discusses the danger in the realisation of the simulacra — for when it enters the real world it is its nature to take on the 'real' attributes of that which it is simulating. Dissimulation here is defined differently: it makes apparent the simulation with all of its implications on the values of 'reality', without distorting the simulacra or allowing it to lose its precarious position, poised between the real and the unreal, the model and the other.

17 What is at issue in an artificial origin is not motivation (as opposed to an essential or originary cause, as in an origin of the classical) but rather the idea of self-evidence. In deductive logic reading backward inevitably produces self-evidence. Hence the analytic process of the classical would always produce a self-evident origin. Yet there are no *a priori* self-evident procedures which could give one origin any value over any other. It can be proposed in a not-classical architecture that any initial condition can produce self-evident procedures that have an internal motivation.

18 The idea of arbitrary or artificial in this sense must be distinguished from the classical idea of architecture as artificial nature, and from the idea of the arbitrariness of the sign in language. Arbitrary in this context means having no natural connection. The insight that origins are a contingency of language is based on an appeal to reading: the origin can be arbitrary because it is contingent on a reading that brings its own strategy with it.

19 Jonathan Culler, *On Deconstruction: Theory and Criticism after Structuralism*, Cornell University Press, Ithaca, 1982. This is basically similar to Jacques Derrida's use of 'graft' in literary deconstruction. He discusses graft as an element which can be discovered in a text through a deconstructive reading: 'deconstruction is, among other things, an attempt to identify grafts in the text it analyses: what are the points of juncture and stress where one scion or line or argument has been spliced with another? . . . Focusing on these moments, deconstruction elucidates the heterogeneity of the text.' (p150). The three defining qualities of graft as it is used in this paper are: (1) graft begins with the arbitrary and artificial conjunction of (2) two distinct characteristics which are in their initial form unstable. It is this instability which provides the motivation (the attempt to return to stability) and also allows modification to take place. (3) In the incision there must be something which allows for an energy to be cut off by the coming together of the two characteristics. Culler's discussion of deconstructive strategy contains all of the elements of graft: it begins by analysis of text to reveal opposition. These are juxtaposed in such a way as to create movement, and the deconstruction (graft) is identifiable in terms of that motivation. This paper, which concentrates on transposing these ideas from a pure analytic framework to a programme for work, is more concerned with what happens in the process of consciously making grafts than finding those that may have been placed unconsciously in a text. Since a graft by definition is a process of modification, it is unlikely that one could find a static or undeveloped moment of graft in an architectural text: one would be more likely to read only its results. Graft is used here in a way that closely resembles Culler's analysis of Derrida's method for deconstruction of opposition: To deconstruct an opposition . . . is not to destroy it . . . 'To deconstruct an opposition is to undo and displace it, to situate it differently.' (p150).

'This concentration on the apparently marginal puts the logic of supplementarity to work as an interpretive strategy: what has been relegated to the margins or set aside by previous interpreters may be important precisely for those reasons that led it to be set aside.' (p140). Derrida emphasises graft as a non-dialectic condition of opposition: this paper stresses the processual aspects which emerge from the moment of graft. The major differences are of terminology and emphasis.

20 Culler, p99. 'The arbitrary nature of the sign and the system with no positive terms gives us the paradoxical notion of an "instituted trace", a structure of infinite referral in which there are only traces — traces prior to any entity of which they might be the trace.'
This description of 'instituted trace' relates closely to the idea of *motivation* as put forth in this paper. Like Derrida's 'instituted trace', motivation describes a system which is internally consistent, but arbitrary in that it has no beginning or end and no necessary or valued direction. It remains a system of differences, comprehensible only in terms of the spaces between elements or moments of the process. Thus, motivation here is similar to Derrida's description of *différance* — it is the force within the object that causes it to be the dynamic at every point of a continuous transformation.

21 Jeff Kipnis, 'Architecture Unbound', unpublished paper, 1984. Modification is one aspect of extension which is defined by Kipnis as a component of decomposition. While extension is any movement from an origin (or an initial condition), modification is a specific form of extension concerned with preserving the evidence of initial conditions (for example, through no addition or subtraction of materiality). On the other hand, synthesis is an example of extension which does not attempt to maintain evidence of initial conditions but rather attempts to create a new whole.

22 The concept of trace in architecture as put forward here is similar to Derrida's idea in that it suggests that there can be neither a representational object nor representable 'reality'. Architecture becomes text rather than object when it is conceived and presented as a system of differences rather than as an image or an isolated presence. Trace is the visual manifestation of this system of differences, a record of movement (without direction) causing us to read the *present* object as a system of relationships to other prior and subsequent movements. Trace is to be distinguished from Jacques Derrida's use of the term, for Derrida directly relates the idea of *différance* to the fact that it is impossible to isolate 'presence' as an entity. 'The presence of motion is conceivable only insofar as every instant is already marked with the traces of the past and future . . . the present instant is not the past and future . . . the present instant is not something given but a product of the relations between past and future. If motion is to be present, presence must already be marked by difference and deferral.' (Culler p97). The idea that presence is never a simple absolute runs counter to all of our intuitive convictions. If there can be no

inherently meaningful presence which is not itself a system of differences, then there can be no value-laden or *a priori* origin.

23 We have always read architecture. Traditionally it did not induce reading but responded to it. The use of arbitrariness here is an idea to stimulate or induce the reading of traces without references to meaning but rather to other conditions of process — that is, to stimulate pure reading without value or prejudice, as opposed to interpretation.

24 Previously, there was assumed to be an *a priori* language of value, a poetry, existing within architecture. Now we are saying that architecture is merely language. We read whether we know what language we are reading or not. We can read French without understanding French. We can know someone is speaking nonsense or noise. Before we are competent to read and understand poetry we can know something to be language.

25 Compare Franco Rella, 'Tempo della fine e tempo dell'inizio' (The Age of the End and the Age of the Beginning), *Casabella* 489/499, Jan/Feb 1984, pp106-8. The similarity to the title of Franco Rella's article in coincidental, for we use the terms 'beginning' and 'end' for entirely different purposes. Rella identifies the present as the age of the end, stating that the paradoxical result of progress has been to create a culture that simultaneously desires progress and is burdened with a sense of passing and the chronic sense of irredeemable loss. The result is a culture which 'does not love what has been but the end of what has been. It hates the present, the existing, and the changing. It therefore loves nothing.' Rella's article poses the question of whether it is possible to build today, to design in a way that is with rather than against time. He desires the return to a sense of time-boundedness and the possibility of living in one's own age without attempting to return to the past. The mechanism by which he proposes to re-create this possibility is myth. He differentiates myth from fiction, and it is this difference which illuminates the opposition between his proposal and the propositions of this paper. Myth is defined as a traditional story of ostensibly historical events that serves to unfold part of the worldview of a people in the traditional value-laden sense, giving history and thus value to timeless or inexplicable events. Rella dismisses fiction as verisimilitude, merely creating the appearance of truth. Instead of attempting to return to the past, myth attempts to create a new beginning, merely situating us at an earlier, and less acute, state of anxiety. But a myth cannot alleviate the paradox of progress. Against both of these, 'The End of the Beginning and the End of the End' proposes dissimulation, which is neither the simulation of reality as we know it, nor the proposal of an alternate truth, which appeals to the identical terrifying structures of belief — that is, origins, transformation, and ends. 'The End of the Classical ' insists on maintaining a state of anxiety, proposing fiction in a self-reflexive sense, a process without origins or ends which maintains its own fictionality rather than proposing a simulation of truth.

REPRESENTATIONS OF THE LIMIT: WRITING A 'NOT-ARCHITECTURE'

PETER EISENMAN

Throughout the history of architecture there has been a concern for the question of its limits, a concern that is manifest in any discipline. Traditionally, in architecture, this has been studied from within the discourse itself — for this is the way in which the limits have been classically conceived. Consequently, any discussion of limits has always begun from the centre and worked outwards. For example, the drawings of Piranesi were understood in the 18th century to define a certain set of limits. They were seen to be not buildable (or not-building) precisely because a traditional convention of architectural representation, perspective, was intentionally contravened. Again, in the 20th century the constructions of Lissitsky and Schwitters were limit-provoking in that they transgressed, metaphorically, the laws of gravity — a convention of construction. Limits arrived at through transgression or contravention of convention are limits reached from within.

But it is possible that the discovery of the limits of a discipline can also be approached from without, that is by discovering what it is not. Rosalind Krauss, for example, in a recent essay attempts such a task for the new 'sculpture' by invoking two bracketing notions to landscape and architecture: 'not-landscape' and 'not-architecture', which she uses to delimit a sculptural analytic matrix. Borrowing from her matrix, it might inform a search for the limits of architecture to deploy an architectural analytic matrix delimited by (sculpture: building: not-sculpture: not-building).

Alternatively, and more directly, it might be possible to locate the limits of architecture by simply examining its complement, 'not-architecture'. Unlike a just 'not architecture', which is a state of having nothing to do with the subject, a not-architecture would be intimate with architecture, would know it, would contain it, as architecture would know and contain a not-architecture; it would constitute a relationship to being by not being. It is, of course, this intimacy, this 'insideness', that raises the possibility of limit discovery, although the model already suggests that a well-disciplined boundary is a delusory goal, that the limits will be found to be mutable, amorphous — an episode of transition in perpetual flux. It is within the domain of the transitory that the drawings of Daniel Libeskind must be situated. But further, and perhaps more interestingly, they must be *read,* and read as not-architecture.

First, what is it to read a drawing? Traditionally, we read writing and see drawing. But if we transgress that custom, then we accrue to drawing the privilege of the autonomy of the reader. If we limited ourselves to seeing drawings as drawings then there would be no possibility of 'unhooking' signs from objects (and thus not-architecture from architecture), a privilege of reading. In architectural drawing, there is no metaphysics of 'hooking' — the image is not conceived of as 'hooked' to the object in the way that a sign is to a signified in writing. Traditionally, in a text, there is no necessary image relationship between the sign and its object or meaning; this is not the case in drawing since the image is a replication, representation or abstraction of an object — but it is not significant of it. The notion of unhooking is crucial to discovering the not-architecture in Libeskind's work, for it is in its free play of signing, its signing of signing, that we read these drawings as writings, and thus as a not-architecture.

To insist that these are drawings, that they are working documents for real physical form (whether as a three-dimensional model or a constructed building, ie, the traditional role of architectural drawing) would disappoint us. The three-dimensional artefact that would result could at best echo but could not contain, represent, or signify the content of these drawings, for the drawings exceed the existing cause and effect of drawing/building or drawing/model by a destruction of it. That exceeding sets them loose, unhooks them as an architectural writing from the traditional architectural drawing.

The prerogative of reading Libeskind's drawings as writing leads to the issue of the reader's privilege of naming. Why, for example, are these works architectural and not sculptural or simply concrete poetry? This is similar to the question: At what point is a shelter a 'house', or when is a structure 'architecture' and not merely building? Or, in what context is a line drawn on the ground or lines on a piece of paper architectural, rather than graphic or sculptural? Do they relate to architecture by a function: defining outside from inside, sacred from profane, shelter from not shelter? To invoke 'architectural' by a function is again to seek limits from inside, a return to form in a causal relationship to function. *Libeskind's drawings are intimate with architecture by the act, the will, and only the will of a reader to name them so.* Further, the act of reading these works, naming them writings, reinforces their status as architecture, for reading insists on their having a significance that as graphics they could not have. As graphics they could only represent architecture. The act of reading these drawings as writings, however, is insufficient to locate these particular works as not-architecture, a stronger condition than architectural, one beyond the naming authority of the reader. What is it about these works that is outside yet intimate? Why do we read Libeskind's works as not-architecture?

To begin this not-architecture reading, Libeskind's drawings must be situated within the present context of architectural drawing. Drawing in this sense is a narrative and often literal representation of a building or its parts. It achieves its status as architectural through the use of a conventional, well-defined vocabulary: windows, doors, walls, etc. But Libeskind's drawings are a critique of this tradition of drawing in architecture. Within the realm of orthodox architectural drawing perhaps only Aldo Rossi has achieved such a critique of drawing in drawing today — an inversion of the mode of representation wherein a realised building becomes a representation of a drawing. Libeskind, however, is not interested in inversions nor in mere representation. He is interested in de-assembly. De-assembly is for drawing what deconstruction is for writing; it is a knowing use, an emphasis of the fact that drawing is always in part writing.

Libeskind began the investigations that led to the works at Cooper Union, where he initially developed a set of serial and gridded collages as fragments of both paintings and architecture, and of his own projects. This fragmentation was the beginning of an attempt to set elements free from their function in both their tectonic and formal sense — from the causality of function and form. In his next phase there were the Constructivist-like works, his first de-assemblies. Similar, superficially, to the investigations of the Constructivists, Suprematists, and Elementarists, the intent was different. While the former were interested in disassembly as a process of revealing the manifest essentiality of the isolated element, Libeskind's de-assembly demonstrated the inessentialness of transitory components; they were a denial of elementality. Next in the Micromegas works, any idea of causality or essentiality was superseded by raw process, a kind of 'writing'. These projects were studies in process-as-element, the essential of kinetic or dynamic, stop action flicker-films where there is no element or series of elements but only a directional serial energy. Finally in his latest drawings, he further eliminates the essentiality of the vector in favour of an 'other' seriality. Their various positions defy constancy, either in element or in direction. They examine a contained transitoriness. The Micromegas were carefully projected within the bounds of zero and infinity. Now in these drawings even the non-limits of Libeskind's beginning and end have been erased, leaving only traces of the journey of his process.

These traces as writing are no longer within the canons of an architecture as defined by the classical tradition of drawings. As such these 'writings' or 'scores' require Foucault's new reader subject — an 'agnostic' aesthete — and a new object which is outside of the discipline of known origins and finite ends. This new object is no longer an object but a process — a trace of objects, outside the universe of tonal or a-tonal relationships. This new process/trace cannot be understood within a traditional formal analysis of the drawings because these 'writings' do not believe in the compositional requirements for harmony; for hierarchy, ordination, or closure. Nor is it fruitful to make an aesthetic judgement — that one looks better than another or that one seems right. These judgements assume an *a priori* notion of the value of images again according to a classical set of values of objects, that again, writing denies. Then what gives them any value at all? What distinguishes them from any set of lines?

It is precisely because they are not any random set of lines yet at the same time are not a precise set of lines conforming to a representation of an image. They are neither, they are *other*, and it is because of their otherness that they begin to define from outside the limits of architecture — that is, they become a not-architecture in the traditional sense of naming or writing. They are unhooked signifiers which begin to encircle their former signified. As such, they are an unsentimental trace of their own history. How far they can go before their progressive opacity (a quality of distance between signifier and signified) reveals its own transparency is the question of limit — their question of being.

ARCHITECTURE AND THE CRISIS OF REALITY
PETER EISENMAN

Last autumn I attended a conference in the small German town of Brakel. There, six so-called leading international architects were gathered to present their new designs for a series of doorknobs. The conference's location, subject and audience all raise fundamental questions about architecture. Its location raises the question of authenticity, its audience the question of reality, and its subject the crisis of design today in relation to authenticity and reality.

The town of Brakel is about as far as it is possible to be from 'anywhere', before you begin to go back to 'somewhere'. Like many other small, isolated German towns, it has been passed over by present-day reality (including the ravages of World War II). It looks like something out of the 19th century. It has no electric neon signs, no Post-Modern simulations of old buildings. It seems to be an 'authentic' environment, in that it has no other spatial and temporal referents than its own. Traditionally, authenticity was seen as the result of such a specificity of time and place. It was conferred onto a product through its relation to an origin. This notion of origin as referent, whether that origin identifies location, time, or, most importantly, an author, has generally gone unquestioned.

The town of Brakel, while it remains time and place-specific, has lost authorial presence in its architecture precisely through its span of time. So while on first glance Brakel appears to be an authentic environment, it may upon reflection be only a form of reality. Brakel may not be so much an issue of authenticity as it is a lesson in presence.

Reality is a condition of the here and now. While the real is often confused with the authentic, its difference lies in its reliance on presence. This raises the second question posed by the conference at Brakel, that of a crisis of reality. The audience at this conference was real in the sense of being present, but they were not authentic in a traditional sense of spatial and temporal specificity. Sixty representatives from the news media, television, newspapers and magazines from all over Germany and Western Europe attended the conference. But what sort of conference did that make? Was it that what was advertised as a design conference was in reality a news conference? For if it was seen as a design conference, and its audience was authentic, the purpose of the conference could be seen as simulated. In a sense, the whole event could be seen as

'inauthentic', unless design is seen as a practice largely defined by media.

The simulation of reality challenges the essence of presence. Although it often is, presence in architecture should not be confused with authenticity. For architecture will always register some form of presence without necessarily being authentic. In fact, architecture throughout history has been *sine qua non* the repository of presence. It can, in fact, be defined as the reification of presence — that is, the objectification of the metaphysics of presence. This is because architecture primarily deals with notions of shelter, enclosure and structure. Architecture could be said to reside in the public consciousness as a metaphor of reality. It has assumed this position precisely because its bricks and mortar are the locus of what is thought to be real. It is not merely accidental that architecture's recent popularity coincides with a deep-seated public need for a return to those things which are thought to be real.

In an era of mass production and industrialisation, these traditional ideas of authenticity and reality have become difficult to sustain; in particular, the idea that authoriality is part of both origin and the authentic. For example, there is no question that a mass-produced piece of Thonet bentwood furniture is authentic, but now the name of the author has been replaced by that of the manufacturer. As Walter Benjamin points out, the photograph loses its aura of authenticity, that is, its relationship to an original (no matter who the author is), because of its inherent potential for reproduction. In mechanical reproduction the immediacy of time and place specificity is also relinquished.

This leads to an idea which is neither authentic nor real, neither inauthentic nor unreal. This is the *banal*; it is between the authentic and the real. Banality is not time-specific. Instead, banal qualities are acquired over time. But, more importantly, what differentiates banality from the authentic or the real is that banality cannot be authored. To be authored means to bear the mark of the designer who imposes a will from the outside. But banal qualities are always internal to the object. Therefore, banality concerns presence, that is the real, as much as it does the unreal. The specific quality of unauthored design, or what is seemingly unauthored, can be seen in many examples of authored design. What in its time was very precisely designed looks undesigned today. For example, silver from a distance of 200 years lacks the presence of individual authority; it takes on a 'dumbness' over time. Thus, while in its time Georgian silver could be called authentic, today it seems banal. It has no sense of time or any nostalgia for the past. But further, it appeals to an internal type or norm for its authority, rather than to any external design decisions.

This brings us to the third issue raised by the Brakel conference: the crisis of design or, more appropriately, the aestheticisation of the banal. The doorknob presents a problem of banality. It conforms very strictly to a functional type, to some set of internal or functional, normative requirements: it must fit the hand, be located at an appropriate height, be able to assist in opening a door. In fact, architects are always looking for a 'dumb' or banal doorknob — one that seems undesigned. That is, one that conforms as much as possible to the functional type, but more importantly one that lacks authorial presence and time specificity. There exists in manufacturers' catalogues and common production a multitude of such 'dumb' doorknobs. But for some reason the German hardware manufacturers (who already produce some of the best Bauhaus-designed artefacts, including doorknobs) who hosted the conference decided to introduce architect-designed (interestingly enough, not industrial designer-designed) door handles. Why the need today to author banal objects?

Why is it not possible to buy in an ordinary hardware store a 'dumb' spoon or fork, that is, one whose authorship is not evident? Why is it only possible to find aestheticised imitations or 'designer' forks and spoons, cheaply made and mass-produced, poorly proportioned and with meaningless decoration? Why is it that only in a 'designer' hardware store, in an antique flea-market, or in a London cutler's could something that looks undesigned or dumb be purchased? This is because in this particular consumption-crazed period there is a nostalgia for the aura of the authenticised object.

This nostalgia involves, among other things, a desire for truth. In the transition from the authentic authored object to the banal mass-produced one there is thought to be a loss of truth. This truth is thought to reside in an unauthored aesthetic. By aestheticising the banal, a supposedly new authenticity is sanctioned, a new form of truth. Authenticity traditionally involved an idea of truth, but because authored design has become cosmetic and aestheticised it has lost the possibility for truth to reside in its facture. The designed product has become so pervasive in contemporary culture that it is impossible to find any banality. Today's hyper-designed environments, from the 'good taste' Scandinavian modern to the exotic 'Italian avant-garde', run in the face of banality.

Today the crisis of reality can be seen in the proliferation of this nostalgia for truth. This is seen in the many attempts to recreate the commonplace. While recreations can be authentic, such as in the example of the Georgian silver, they also are most often inauthentic. Shopping malls are quintessentially representative of these attempts at recreation. They recreate by simulating the iron, steel and glass-enclosed arcades of the 19th century, or the typical American 'main street'. An authentic environment cannot be recreated; instead, recreations of the commonplace are kitsch. An aporia is cast on both the no-place, kitsch design of the shopping mall and the profusely designed placelessness of the home. It seems to be a case of too much design and too little authenticity. This is because design has been reduced to the aestheticisation and cosmeticisation of the banal. The traditionally authored object becomes an aestheticised simulation, an atopos of time and place — but an atopos which nevertheless maintains the classical dialectic of formal categories. Thus, between the aestheticisation of the banal, which can be seen as the nostalgia for authenticity, and the simulation of reality, is there a choice?

Because the banal cannot be directly authored, it may be a desired result but it can never be progress. While it may be possible to achieve a banal result, it is not an operative process in design; rather, it is more critical. It is in this sense of the critical that this text colludes with the aforementioned nostalgia for authenticity. Instead of respecting the categories of 'authenticity', 'truth' and 'reality', I might instead have attempted to dislocate them. And in this dislocation I might perhaps find an authenticity in difference.

Authenticity in the traditional sense was seen as inherent in a correct or truthful artefact, that is, one that was truthful to a norm, a type, a category or a process. In other words, the process of authentic design was an attempt to 'get it right'. For example in photography an authorial act was thought to be to print or to take a 'good' photograph. But in an age of mechanical reproduction, perhaps an authorial act could be to 'get it wrong'. To *purposely* print a photograph badly (as opposed to merely printing it badly) is to violate the conventions concerned with printing it right, and thus to imbue the object with a different authorial intent. This is an authoriality between the authentic and the banal. It is an authoriality revealed in the violation of these same categories, a violation that reveals good and bad as a repression. What would be an equivalent violation of such repressive categories in architecture?

Traditionally, in architecture, to propose a design that followed a rational, factual programme was thought to be an authentic act. Such a response would produce a functional building. It would shelter, structure and enclose an intended use. It would not only be meaningful, it would also have an aesthetic value. Any dislocation would concern the violation first and foremost of the idea of architecture as a natural, as opposed to a conventional act. What would be violated is the idea of reading the object in a truthful way, that is, as fulfilling a functional or meaningful programme. A new reading, of the kind proposed here, would do violence to the former categories of architecture as an object of desire (of an aesthetic pleasure), as a reification of man (anthropomorphism and human scale), and as an object of value (truth, origin and metamorphic meaning). Such a dislocation is not necessarily place-specific, time-specific or scale-specific. It does not symbolise use, shelter or structure. The dislocation takes place, then, between the conventional and the natural.

What is being violated is the maintenance of the dialectical categories of the system as a whole. Difference is now internal rather than external. This is the other topos of authenticity.

Both Ohio State and Long Beach bear traces of this process of violence. In the Ohio State project, the violence is also literal, as in the cutting of the existing buildings or in the fragmenting of the armoury. At OSU the fragments of the armoury have figure but no figural value; they remain within the architectural metaphysic of shelter, enclosure and habitation without using these for their symbolic value. In the Long Beach project there is also a literal violation of the land and also the found objects of the oil derricks and the Rainbow Pier. However, they are not merely literal objects any more than they are represented meanings. The old distinction between an object which has aesthetic value (the signified) and the text (the signifier) is erased; objects mean and texts sensate.

The authenticity of difference recognises the repressed topos internal to the atopia of reality. This atopia of the present must be recognised as such before a new (other) topos can be found. The new topos lies repressed in atopia. It no longer sees this as a crisis but as an opportunity, a condition of its own internal being. This is its authenticity and its difference.

TEXT AS ZERO: OR: THE DESTRUCTION OF NARRATIVE
PETER EISENMAN

Today, simulation, the simulacrum of what was formerly 'real', has erased the opposition between reality and fiction. Whereas before, fiction (representation) simulated the real, and thus followed from it, now it is the real which simulates and follows from fiction. To understand this phenomenon one has only to watch a presidential news conference to see a president being 'presidential', that is, acting as he is told he is supposed to be, rather than being as he is. Or, similarly, to watch the performance of the 'winning coach' affecting the reality of a winner in a post-game interview. Or consider the 'reality' of a live horse race at a racetrack where much of the race is obscured by a giant television screen showing a simulcast of what it is obscuring. In each situation 'reality' becomes a simulation or a *framing* of a simulation.

In his film *Zelig*, Woody Allen uses the inevitable exhaustion which occurs when a simulation can (because of sheer technical capacity) be made to be indistinguishable from reality as a frame for criticism. The film simulates a 'real' biography of a man called Zelig, and it is through the use of its framing mechanism — that is, by putting quotation marks around this seeming reality — that Allen is able to return the film to a fiction, one which at that point becomes critical of its own simulation, that is, it becomes a framing within a framing.

In architecture, Post-Modernism, rather than confronting this crisis of reality, becomes a participant in it by a framing of its own. But unlike the self-criticism of Woody Allen's film, Post-Modernism exhibits a failure to be critical. It posits the frame as a mask, as a dissimulation, which says 'this is not reality'. What Post-Modernism does not add, which is its implicit message and which would be its critical gesture, is that this 'not-reality' is all that is left of the reality of architecture.

The Post-Modernists put their dissimulations forward as an authentic architecture, but they can be seen as another kind of framing: a fiction which is not critical of architecture, which does not acknowledge its own unreality. It is not that their architecture becomes unreal, for it does not surrender its own metaphysic; rather architecture becomes meta-theatre, the art of the giant stage set. When, for example, a Michael Graves uses 'papier-mâché' keystones such as the one for the Portland Building, or a Robert Venturi paints the words 'William and Mary' on a cartooned version of the original piece of furniture, these cry out, 'This is not-reality.' They are in fact the residue of a former and now empty reality. They speak of the impossibility of reuniting Foucault's figuration and discourse (facture and meaning) in a relativistic world where reality no longer exists as such but only as a parody of its former self.

As dissimulation is the last tactic of relativism, it also is the initial strategy of the absolutist. It is in this context that the stage-set houses of Lars Lerup sound a similar chorus. To begin, for Lerup, is to frame existence. Saying, 'This is not reality; this is a dream, or a shadow', is to begin with an abdication placed in a stage-set storefront to nothingness. By violently framing or de-framing (even de-faming) the traditional metaphysics of an anthropocentric architecture — the mimetic conventions of narrative, of use, of site, of vertebrate structure — Lerup attempts to recapture a 'former' architecture that, because it never was, can never be.

Here he consciously traps us in the futility of a paradox. He asks the question: In the world as simulation, where there is and can be no 'reality', how can there be a 'representation of reality', that is, what was formerly known as architecture? Thus his narrative emerges as a text on the emptiness of the classical architectural text: his architecture stands perpetually deferred from and expectant of its own mute dreams — an architecture degree zero, but not a *tabula rasa*: a de(sign). A sign of its own silence and displacement, it becomes a site for potential meaning.

Unlike Graves or Venturi's historicising figures, which attempt to gain value from a dissimulation of history, Lerup's dissimulations have figure but no figural value: they remain within the architectural metaphysic of shelter, definition and habitation, without deploying these for their symbolic value. They are text as zero. But they are no longer literal objects any more than they are represented meanings. The old distinction between aesthetic object (the signified), and text (the signifier) is erased; objects and texts are now equivalent: objects mean and texts sensate. These are Lerup's 'new sentences'.

In an age of simulation perhaps the one remaining example of a vanishing authenticity is violence, the destruction of the 'frame', the deframing of reference. For Lerup the text now becomes the assault, an authentically violent assault on the paradigm of 'frame' itself, the stability of the metaphysic of 'house'. But it is no longer 'house' as merely an object which is the locus of this violence, but rather 'house' as text. While architects such as Frank Gehry or Site Inc *represent* destruction, their houses remain aesthetic objects rather than sites for reading. For Lerup, on the other hand, the process of the narrative becomes the axis of destruction.

In a way, Lerup's text houses remind one of John Hejduk's poetic and mystic notations. Hejduk's is a textuality which also attempts to break down anthropocentrism. His 'houses' begin to look like prehistoric animals, his sites like the savannah of a mystical planet. While Hejduk's anamorphic creatures possess a primitive and furry warmth, Lerup's seemingly familiar objects become distant dream machines and cool dissimulations.

But for all this, Lerup's texts remain encumbered with a certain logocentrism in the form of a justification for this absent architecture. His texts continue to appeal to 'the' correct reading, that is, to the intention of an author who himself can only be furthest away from knowing such a correctness.

It is this desire for correctness that reveals in Lerup a nostalgia for the 'aura' of the absolute, for that which is real. Lerup becomes symptomatic of the current state of modernity: an absolutist knowing himself to be inescapably caught within and at the same time compelled to escape from anthropocentric paradigms (particularly from the classical paradigm of the absolute). Lerup, who believes in the avant-garde, can thus only dissimulate as a displacement of Platonic idealism. It is only in the desire for the authority of the authentic that the drive of man to transcend man, to distinguish music from noise, poetry from reportage, and meaning from gibberish, can produce an *other* text, a text which attempts to elude the closure of anthropocentrism, without being thematic of another centrism.

For example, Lerup's text makes an initial attempt to leave anthropocentrism in the tripartite symmetry of Love/House. In its triadic structure Lerup intends to echo the psychological structure: unconscious, preconscious, conscious. However, the unconscious and the conscious are not opposites which can be reflected in a tripartite symmetry of presence. The unconscious is essential absence, which can only be 'traced' in presence. Presence therefore is no longer whole; it can no longer account for all that is real.

Equally, Lerup's modern androgynous 'person' is no longer whole. While sexuality can be simulated and conflated, the psyche and the ego cannot. Today's 'people' may be physically the same size as our former male husbands and female wives, but the comfortable illusion of these figures as mentally the same has been blown apart. The architectural needs of today's 'people' are fundamentally in question. No longer is the mimesis of their vertebrate structure in the image of the central hearth sufficient to sustain the concept of 'house'. No longer is the representation of their union sustained under one gabled roof. The grand abstraction of man as the measure of all things can no longer be maintained. Before Freud, man knew himself inasmuch as he was present to himself, inasmuch as he felt himself to be. After Freud's exposition of the unconscious, this naïve anthropocentrism was rendered untenable. Hence the shadow houses of Lerup's work; they attempt to remake the unconscious. They represent as much a despair for reality as a concern for the unconscious.

Unlike Roland Barthes, who has written that 'the text needs its shadow', Lerup makes the text a shadow, both as the unconscious and as a mask, a dissimulation that says, 'I am not conscious, I am not real'. The remaking of the unconscious in Lerup's Love/House is one example of a dissimulation that contains the masking of conscious reality. This masking is a walk through Lerup's own life, and it is here that the genuine desire for an authentic architecture is wedded to a nostalgia for a real Lerup. His nostalgia for the sensuality and comfort of symmetry is seen in his drawings, which reveal, like the sexual organs of an androgynous plastic human torso, a Dionysian who subsumes the classical aesthetic value of that same symmetry — not as an aesthetic object but in the violent deconstruction of the rationality of process. In Lerup's writings there is a nostalgia for a lost Eden in such phrases as 'logical integral clarity' or 'text as zero', the 'zero degree' plan as the 'new wilderness'. *Alienation* is formed in the 'axis of equipment', and *redemption* is desired in the 'new significance'. However, in the return to the aura of the authentic, in the replacement by one narrative of another, Lerup slips back into his own tendentious autobiography.

Because he is not able to distance himself totally from his classical background, Lerup's architectural graphs remain anthropocentric: chimneys as vertebrate symmetries, floor plans as horizontal ground datums, all measures of anthropocentrism. The metaphysics of plan conventions that he abandons in the Nofamily House and Love/House are also abandoned in the section of Texas Zero, but there the abandonment is violated by a new anthropomorphism. It is Lerup's aesthetic predilection for tripartite (closed, hierarchical, static) classicism which intrudes on his argument.

While Lerup desires to replace the narrative of man with the narrative of architecture, ultimately his architectural replacement remains, in its anthropocentrism, tied to man. However, it is in The Final Transformation that Lerup's assault finally emerges most vigorously in his architecture. The fragments are at last cut loose from their anthropocentric spine, from their own aesthetic and figural objecthood. They are now but graphic counters, the traces of a process, and as such violent to the idea of centre, of spine, and of wholeness and enclosure.

In a world of simulation, it is the authentic violence of process which supplants the futile nostalgia for the aura of the authentic object. This is the last critique by architecture of its own discourse. This, then, is the only authentic reality; the insatiable desire for the absolute. As such, it cannot be known, cannot be achieved; it can only be dreamed for. For Lerup it is not enough to be critical; one senses that it is now time for him to propose. Lerup's houses dream this.

THE REPRESENTATIONS OF DOUBT: AT THE SIGN OF THE SIGN
PETER EISENMAN

The sign must remain a sign, must speak only of its renunciation of having value and only by means of this renunciation will it be able to recognise its true functions and its own destiny: only a language illuminated by its own limits will be able to operate.
Massimo Cacciari, *Eupalinos on Architecture.*

The invention of perspective as a system of representation in the 15th century may have been ultimately a more decisive issue in architecture than it was in painting. Perspective necessarily replaces a naïve, narrative representation of reality — three-dimensional objects disposed in space — by an internally coherent set of graphic conventions which require a strictly controlled order. Indeed, architecture was an essential instrument for this kind of representation. In fact, most significant paintings of the new perspectival type in the early 15th century employed architecture as their convenient setting.

For, while this convention allowed painting to represent depth in space more naturally, it allowed architecture to represent deep space on a facade surface and thus to become more like painting. In painting it provided the illusion of reality; in architecture it reduced real space to the illusion of flat space on the painted surface. Thus perspective introduced into the built object both a connection to and a distinction between architecture and the image of architecture. The possibility now existed of the representation of space in architecture, that is, a representation of architecture by architecture; now, rather than imitating 'nature' in the way that a Corinthian capital represents nature, architecture might itself be its own representation.

With the introduction of perspective, architecture was no longer merely a form of reality itself, but also *imitated* reality. The vertical plane as a surface for the representation of deep space necessarily forced architecture to become both reality *and* representation. Perspective also forced an explicit change in the relationship of the viewer to the object, by reducing the temporal dimension of narrative of the subject's experience of the object, from sequential, linear, time to time understood as a particular place. This representation for the architects of the Renaissance was always related to 'natural' space. For them perspective was considered a law of nature, not a representation of it. Perspective was the mediation between man and nature, between what man sees and how he sees. For Palladio perspective was artificial and not natural; it could be used to break apart the relationship between man and nature. For Palladio, man becomes the new nature and perspective becomes transformed from a state of nature to a tool of representation — a technique in relationship to man.

According to Giulio Argan, Palladio's architecture does not set out to represent space, that is, to represent natural law, but rather to represent a system of logical manufacture of absolute value apart from all meaning.[1] This absolute value was architecture itself. In Palladio, architecture thus rejects perspective and its representation. It is in Argan's terms 'non-perspectival'. For Palladio, the image becomes a sign and the sign is not so much a representation of something else, as it is a code for its own internal system. This introduced a second angle in the relationship between subject and project. Now the object has become the house of man, not the house of nature. And when the object becomes dwelling it begins to erode the traditional subject/object relationship. Thus Palladio was concerned not so much with the representation of 'natural' conditions of building, but more with this altered condition of the object produced by the concept of perspective.

Palladio deliberately disconnects and disintegrates the relationship to previous architecture. The destruction of these prior relationships produces the quality of unrelatedness or absoluteness in the individual forms. This destruction produces a third change between subject and object. Now, the flatness of a Palladian facade is counter to the perspectival flatness of a canvas. This produces an uncertainty as to the exact nature of the object. Where previous architecture attempted to mirror the certainty of nature, Palladio's architecture mirrored this doubt over the status of the object.

The idea of Modernism in architecture was apparently preoccupied with a similar move away from the representation of the 'natural' order of things towards the so-called order of the 'object itself'. This was supposedly accomplished through a process of abstraction. A blank facade or a column without capital or base were thus thought to be abstractions of 'facade' or 'column'. But, unless one assumes that a column with a Doric, Ionic or Corinthian base and capital is the *natural* state of 'column' and that a facade with string courses, mouldings, friezes and pediment represents a *generic* state of plane, this proposition does not hold. In fact, of course, a blank facade and an unadorned column are not abstractions of architecture, but simply the elemental conditions of architecture. The classical orders and Renaissance facades were themselves only elaborations of such elemental conditions; in this sense the supposed 'abstractions' of Modern architecture operate in a traditional way as representations of architectural elements. The conventional signs of classicism, embodied in the orders and their proportions, referred to and represented a condition of nature: to nature's harmonies, to the forms of natural objects, to the human body. This mode of representation linked subject and object together in an assumed relationship of signification. The subject read the object which, as a sign of something else, offered up its meaning.

Modern architecture, despite its apparent abstraction and seeming self-reflexivity, merely reproduced such a relationship. The 'abstract' column referred, albeit negatively, to the tradition of columns; similarly the 'abstract' plane referred to a tradition of facades, and so on. In most Modern architecture, therefore, the relationship of the subject to the object remains largely unchanged with respect to the Renaissance tradition. The 'abstract' column is still a sign of something else to be decoded by an observing subject.

But Modernism, as developed in the other arts, in philosophy, literature, music and painting, broke decisively with this subject/object relationship. In Modernism the dominant mode of reading was an attempt to have the object refer not to a reading subject, but to its own condition of being. It proposed a neutral, self-reflexive object and a detached, self-reflexive subject. Architecture, however, unlike its sister arts, remained narrative and representational. Modernism as embodied in this changed condition of subject and object, except in rare cases, was not achieved in Modern architecture. This was also the case with its form of representations.

When Modern architecture substituted the axonometric for perspective, the dominant form of representation since the Renaissance, this supposed a change in the relation of object to object. Even though the 'analytic' quality of the axonometric intended the object to be viewed clinically from above in all of its true dimensions, the subject still remained an observer and a reader of signification. However, the axonometric did change the traditional relationship between subject and object in subtle ways: the dimensions of the object, undistorted by the mechanisms of the human eye, could hardly be mistaken for a representation of 'natural' reality. But the object still contained the locus of a meaning which referred outside of itself.

What then might be seen as a Modernist condition of the architectural object, or for that matter any architectural object? For this, a form of representation that no longer, like perspective or axonometric, sees the object as a representation for a subject, has yet to be proposed. Throughout all of this the status of the model remained unexamined from the Renaissance through to the architecture of the Modern period.[2] A model is usually thought to be merely a replica of a building, albeit a reduced and in some cases impoverished representation of that reality. Because of this, the model was seen to be the least self-reflexive condition of a sign and thus it was rarely considered as a vehicle of Modernist intention. But the model, beyond being merely a means of representation, can also question the relationship between viewer and object. Through its three axes, scale, time and representation, it raises issues of the nature of reality, the objecthood of the actual building, and also becomes a critique of drawing as representation.

This question of what was the nature of reality and thus the nature of representation — what was an architectural sign? — concerns the limits of architecture itself. This concern became focused in the sequence of Eisenman's houses from House I to House El Even Odd. And by the last house it had completely dominated the work, but had also introduced a second question — that is, the condition of the reading subject.

House I was built like a model. Its connections between beam and columns could only have been fabricated as one builds a model aeroplane; they were sanded and glued by hand. But further, what appeared to be the columns and beams which were exposed in the space did not function as structure, but rather as signs of structure. And if the idea of this reduction was lost on anyone, there was even the outline of a missing column on the floor of the house.[3]

In House I the code was, if anything, metaphoric. On the other hand, House II was deliberately coded to remove it from reality. It was built to look like a model. In fact, in many published photos of the actual building the caption reads 'model photo of House II'. House II looks like a model because all of the traditional means of identifying built reality — coping lines, flashing lines, frames, sills and mouldings — were purposely absent. The building was fabricated out of steel and wood and then wrapped in a silicone material which obliterated all of those identifying traces. The difference between House I and House II already suggested some movement away from the traditional idea of the nature of the reality of the built object. Whereas House I was built like a 'life-size' model, House II was a representation of such a model. In both cases, what was the reality and what was the sign of that reality were thrown into question.

House VI also looks like a model. It is also a model in that it 'represents' a series of transformational diagrams, the process of the house which is its reality. Instead of the house being the result of a process of transformation as in House II and IV, the house now *is* the process of transformation.

In House X, for the first time in Eisenman's work, the actual building was no longer a metaphorical model. But conversely, the building was no longer the final reality, the model was. But the model was also now moving toward the intersection of two modes of representation, drawing and model.[4] It was an axonometric model. Usually a scale model is a three-dimensional representation of a three-dimensional reality. An axonometric drawing is a two-dimensional representation of a three-dimensional reality. An axonometric model differs from an axonometric drawing in that while it is a representation, it is not representing an actual object, but a transformation of an object. It is both process and reality. As such it begins to represent drawing rather than building.[5] It is both a statement of the potential object-autonomy of a model and at the same time a representation of the approximate nature of the sign in the process of the realisation of the house. Thus, it is both object and representation.

Usually a model is stationary and the viewer moves around, above and even below it to understand it. While both a model and a drawing depend on a reading subject, the information conveyed from a drawing does not change from different viewpoints. There is no fixed or frontal viewing as in an axonometric drawing. The axonometric model, in contrast, changes depending on the position of viewing. From the sides and from eye level it is seen as a distortion of reality — its vertical planes raking in different directions. Then from a slightly raised angle on the oblique, it appears to be a conventional orthogonal model. Finally, when viewed frontally at a 45-degree angle to its orthogonal co-ordinates, with one eye closed, it appears to flatten out and assumes the precise aspect of an axonometric drawing. The viewer, forced into a frontal and monocular view, sees the building as if through a camera.

Usually a photograph of a building is a narrative record of a fact — a representation of reality. A photograph unlike a painting presumes an actual object. A painting may not be representational but a photograph in some way always is. This is particularly true of architectural photography, which in most cases tells us more about the object than our actual experience of the object. It is a medium and traditionally the medium is representational. When the medium or the process can become the object as in House VI, then the nature of the object is thrown into question. For House X, the medium — the photograph — is the reality of the model because it is the view which reveals its *conceptual essence* as an axonometric drawing. The black and white photographs of the axonometric drawing (collage) and of the axonometric model are one and the same.

The project for House 11a represented the intersection of model and building. If House I and House 11 questioned the nature of the sign, and if House VI and House X explored the axis of time, then House 11a can be seen to explore the axis of scale.

In figurative sculpture the scale of the maquette or model is usually known, since the model is referring to some known object, ie a rider and a horse in the case of an equestrian statue. When Modern sculpture shifted away from representation to abstraction it moved from what could be called scale-specific to scale non-specific. How large is a Brancusi or a Sol LeWitt, and what makes something a model of a Donald Judd or a Joel Shapiro? When sculpture ceased to be anthropomorphic, then its scale ceased to be a dimension of representation. Architecture has always been scale-specific. That is because it always had doors and windows which gave it scale in relationship to man. Thus scale has always been the crucial axis which has linked the object of architecture to its subject. Could there be an architecture which was scale non-specific and if so, what would be the nature of its model?

The project for Cannaregio took House 11a and built it as three differently scaled objects. One of the objects is about four feet high; when it is in the urban space of Cannaregio, because of its size, it is seen as the model of a house. If the same object is taken and put in a second House 11a, built, this time, at normal human house scale, the act of putting the model or smaller object inside the larger object changes the function of the larger object. It is no longer a house, but a kind of mausoleum. Once the larger object memorialises the smaller one, it is no longer the model of an object; it has been transformed from a four-foot high object which was a model of something else, into a real thing — an object in itself.

When a third object is placed in the same context which is larger than the other two, that is, larger than 'reality', larger than an anthropomorphic necessity, it completes a self-reflexive cycle. And if the largest one now contains both the middle-sized one and the little one, it becomes, as it were, a museum of the memorial of the model. Because of the change in scale, all three objects take on different meaning, not in relationship to the individual but to their own change in scale — they become self-reflexive.

Because of the changes in scale, these objects suggest a set of ideas which have nothing to do with the size of man in relationship to the size of the object (whether it is larger, smaller, or the appropriate size for man's use).

The idea for House El Even Odd took up where House X left off. It started from the notion that the house itself could begin with 45-degree sloped/vertical planes so that an actual representational model of it would look like an axonometric model. This was its so-called neutral or 'even' condition. From this two axonometric projections could be made: one backwards towards the vertical and one forwards towards the horizontal.

These transformations produce two other objects. The first produces an object that is a flattened surface. (Since an axonometric projection is taken at a 45-degree angle to the vertical and horizontal, when an already 45-degree condition is projected another 45 degrees, all lines fall into the horizontal plane.) The second transformation reverses the seemingly axonometric projection of the original state. The new object becomes a regular rectilinear el-shaped volume. So that two opposing axonometric projections of an axonometric model produce what in reality are a normal model and a plan. All three states projected simultaneously become El Even Odd. Thus, the model of this house appears to be simultaneously a three-dimensional object, an axonometric projection, and a plan.

This simultaneity of readings takes on a real ambiguity when the object is placed in a site model that is constructed axonometrically. When the site is read, because of its 45-degree angle, as being axonometric, then the building object is read as an axonometric transformation. Since parts of the object are in axonometric projection, the site model causes the viewer to think that the real house (as opposed to the model) is a retransformation of the parts into some other rectilinear object. However, if the object is taken as a real representation of the actual house-object, then the sloping sides of the axonometric site can be read as sloping in reality rather than in axonometric projection. This fluctuation of readings is the first dislocation experienced by the viewer.

There is a second dislocation which occurs when the object is turned upside-down and placed below ground. Now the flat element that was seen to be a plan is located at ground level and is actually a roof. A person literally walks on this plan. Now a fluctuation occurs between what looks to be a plan but is, in fact, a second transformation of an axonometric, and what looks to be an axonometric but is, in fact, a plan. Thus the model of House El Even Odd is not an axonometric model. It is the representation of a house which in itself is the simultaneous representation of three states in a process of transformation. Each stage of the process does not deny or erase the prior one. The process is not linear; all stages exist simultaneously in the model. It is an architecture which 'generates its own house. It is a process that represents itself in order to become its own representation.'[6]

House El Even Odd moved this process one step further toward its limits. As a programme it is intransigent, so self-reflexive that it exists not as an object but merely as its own representation. There is no object now, merely the representation of one. This becomes a 'truth' of architecture. The drawings, plans, projections, models, the traditional processes are perhaps radical architecturally, and, almost by afterthought, socially. They dislocate the conventional house and the social relations encoded therein. The relationship between subject and object in architecture, from the Renaissance to the Modern period, is exemplified and confirmed in

the concept of *dwelling*. Indeed we might see that the primary shift in this relationship, from an architecture that imitates nature to one that represents the object, was forced by the act of making a dwelling for man.

For Argan the shift represented by Palladio's architecture, from an architecture that sets out to 'represent' or construct the space of nature to an architecture of 'mere manufacture', is precipitated by the demand on Palladio to construct dwellings. A dwelling 'as object produced by man for man'[7] cannot be merely an imitation of nature but is forced simply to replicate the act of its own construction. For Palladio, the making of a dwelling was primary, and perspective was merely a means of articulating the elevation of dwelling to the status of architecture. But, for Palladio and succeeding architects, the shift from nature/object to object/man implied in the building of dwelling, still resided in the traditional subject/object relationship. This was undisturbed in the entire production of Modern architecture.

But the object of Modernism would preclude any such mirroring of the subject in dwelling: in effect, a truly Modernist object could not be at the same time a 'dwelling' and self-reflexive. Modernism and the idea of a dwelling are in this sense mutually exclusive. The permutations of the mode, as a model of representation that allows for the composition of a self-reflexive object, begins a progressive dissolution of the concept of dwelling.

The models in Eisenman's work take up this theme. They deliberately manifest the present impossibility of the making of dwelling. In this void is substituted the possibility of the making of architecture. Where, for Palladio, the perspectival image became a *sign* of dwelling, the model in Eisenman's work allows the possibility of an architecture that is not a system of representation — an image of something else — but rather a system that can exist also as the sign of itself — that is, of its own architectural condition.

The house traditionally is the locus of memory. It is the constant sign of the nostalgia for dwelling. In House El Even Odd there is an indifference to dwelling which is expressed in neutral signs. The formal structuring corresponds to a maximum absence of images. The language of absence is a testimony to the absence of dwelling.

The dislocation has become enormous. From the idea of a house as a sign of dwelling, to the idea of a house as a representation of a model in Houses I and II, through a model of House X which is not a representation of a house, but rather an object in itself, to a model of House El Even Odd which is not an object, but a sign — a representation of itself. The dislocation involves not only the model/building relationship, but also the subject itself. It is a shift from a programme for a known subject to a disclosure that the subject is in doubt. 'The model now like that of Cézanne and Johns *is* doubt.'[8]

The idea for the first part of the title 'Representations of Doubt' comes from Maurice Merleau-Ponty's essay 'Cézanne's Doubt', published in English in Art and Literature 4, *Spring 1965, Lausanne, Switzerland, pp106-25. The idea for the second part of the title 'At the Sign of the Sign', was first suggested to Eisenman in an interview with David Shapiro and Lindsay Stamm. See 'A Poetics of the Model: Eisenman's*

Doubt', Idea as Model, IAUS Catalogue 3, *Rizzoli International, New York, 1981, pp121-5.*

The extract from Massimo Cacciari is taken from 'Eupalinos on Architecture', Oppositions 21, *Summer, 1981, published for IAUS by MIT Press, Cambridge, Massachusetts, p115. He is referring to Manfredo Tafuri and Francesco Dal Co's* Architettura Contemporanea, *pp342-5.*

NOTES

1 Giulio Carlo Argan, 'The Importance of Sanmicheli in the Formation of Palladio', *Renaissance Art*, ed C Gilbert, p173.

2 While Alberti had already suggested the importance of models, in Book II, chapter 1, he makes the following observation: 'I would add another consideration which appears to me most pertinent: The architect who exhibits coloured models, made more attractive by pictorial adornment, reveals he does not simply wish to present his project, but is misled by his ambition to attract attention with superfluities, distracting the mind from a measured examination of the model, and all its parts which can be admired. Hence, it is better not to make impeccable finished and adorned models, elegant and glittering, but stripped and simple ones, so as to emphasise the strength of the concept, and not the accuracy of execution in the model.' (Leon Battista Alberti, *L'Architettura*, translated by Giovanni Orlandi, Milan, 1966, p88.) Kurt Forster contends that Alberti's insistence on completely bare, conceptualised models in unpainted wood — usually dark, dense wood such as chestnut — is similar, in intention, to my own desire to make actual houses look like unadorned, unpainted white models.

3 As to the early contribution of perspective to the 'representations of doubt', one only has to look at the Brunelleschi interior of San Lorenzo with its even columnar intervals and their projection onto the floor by means of bands in the pavement. In Schinkel's atrium at Slöss Tegel, the plan betrays the idea of the four-columned atrium (tetrastyle), but only two columns are in place. The twin piers in the back are left over from the existing wall of the old Schlösschen in Tegel. Hence the 'perspective' of the history of architectural members: from the massive pier, to the column, to the absence of the column. This observation was pointed out to me by Kurt Forster in private communication.

4 The model was made, if not conceived, after working drawings were completed, and after it was decided not to build the house. It can thus be seen as the ultimate reality of the work.

5 The idea of transferring the qualities of an axonometric drawing to a model was first attempted in the exhibition 'Idea as Model'. There the idea was to reduce a model to the properties of a drawing. Using the House II diagrams, an attempt was made to overlay the diagrams onto a Plexiglas model. The result, however, was a conventional model of the axonometric diagrams, rather than an axonometric model.

6 Hal Foster, 'Pastiche/Prototype/Purity', in *Artforum*, March 1981, New York, pp77-9.

7 Op cit Argan, p74.

8 Johns is quoted by David Shapiro in 'Imago Mundi', *Art News* vol 70, no 6, October 1971, pp40-1 and 66-8. 'I prefer disastrous relationships. I like to cast doubt on everything', after speaking of Buckminster Fuller's positive attitude which consisted in 'distributing clear information'. For Shapiro, Johns changed the discursive colour code of Fuller's world map (say, blue for cold regions, green for forests) into a random colour code emphasising the disjunction between models and any referentiality. Names for islands, countries and continents were displaced and floated far from their usual positions. Shapiro points out the obvious other examples of the doubt which are the ontological questions of the status of map-as-painting, target and numeral as privileged places where 'aboutness' is questioned. According to Shapiro: 'Eisenman's problematic concerning the poignancy of perspective systems is a sensuous analogue to Johns's question concerning the reality of the "seeming" given in alphabet, target, flag. Both prefer to represent representations, to be nakedly about "aboutness" and little else, but making that little the largest subject. Both have been criticised as "linguistic" artists. Both may be regarded, like Blooms's Wallace Stevens, as meditating on Wittgenstein's dark aphorism: "What the solipsist *means* is correct." ' (David Shapiro, from a forthcoming essay, 'Johns and Eisenman'.)

STRONG FORM, WEAK FORM
PETER EISENMAN

Architecture has traditionally been a strong form discipline. This is usually taken to mean that there is a one-to-one correlation between meaning and function, meaning and structure, meaning and form. As a strong form discipline, architecture is also a very problematic discipline, because it has a weak condition of sign: in other words, it does not have a system of explicit signs. It is difficult to express happiness, sadness, goodness, badness — any emotional or philosophic concept. What language can deal with, architecture cannot. Language is also a strong form system. There is a very direct correlation between the word 'wolf' and a person named Wolf. But we realise in language that 'wolf' means not only that person, but many other people and many other nuances in language other than an animal. For example it is a person who chases women. They sometimes meet and overlap, these 'wolfs'. Language also has a symbolic connotation, where there is not a one-to-one correspondence between word and sign. Literature and poetry try to make opaque the transparent relationship between sign and signified. On the other hand, in journalism, when we read the newspaper we read for clarity. It is edited for clarity, for a strong relationship between sign and signified. When we read literature, like Shakespeare, we are not reading for clarity but rather for the possible opacity in the language. Because when we read Shakespeare, we already know the story, we know the history of Henry V, we know the history of Romeo and Juliet, we have read the story in some other form before. So we are not reading to understand. Language has a very clear way of representing opacity, in literature and in poetry. But in architecture, sign and signified have always been together; function, symbolism, aesthetic form have always been merged, not separated, whereas in traditional views of language they have been separated.

In traditional structuralist thought the signified and the signifier are seen as separate entities. Post-structuralism says, however, that these two have always been together. Now this is just like the situation in architecture, because in architecture they have always been together. Thus in architecture, in order to find a transparency in this given opacity, in order to have a possibility of meanings, one has to pull the sign and signifier apart. One has to pull apart the one-to-one relationship between structure, form, meaning, content, symbolism etc, so that it is possible to make many meanings.

This pulling apart is what I call a displacement. Vienna is the city where displacement and ideas of displacement obviously were born, through Sigmund Freud; so the concept of displacement is not a new one.

The question is, why do we want to displace architecture today? Why is it necessary to separate function and structure from symbolism, meaning, and form? Because in the past architecture always symbolised reality. In other words, while language was one kind of reality, poetry another, music another, architecture was perhaps the ultimate condition of reality, because it dealt with physical facts, with bricks and mortar, house and home. It was physical place, the fundamental condition of reality.

The cosmology in which we exist has changed. In the 14th century there was a change from what can be called a theocentric cosmology to an anthropocentric one. It changed in the 19th century from an anthropocentric one to a technocentric one, to a mechanical view of the world — that is a scientific, mathematical, rational view of the world. This lasted through the Second World War. After the Second World War the cosmology again changed: the mechanistic, technocentric world became an informational world, a world ordered by electronics; it is now a world of media.

Let me give you a few examples of this changed view of reality. In the televising of sports there is something which is called 'instant replay'. This means that a good play is played over again, a goal is shown in four different ways. Children grow up as 'instant replay junkies'. Because of this they have lost the faculty of watching a real game. They are more interested in the commercials (and in a mediated world, maybe the commercials are better). Thus reality changed, reality became the instant replay and the commercials. The eating habits of children also changed. They would say we need to eat at McDonald's, then they would change to Wendy's. Basically, they were eating commercials. In other words, it did not matter whether the meat was good or bad, they were not eating the meat, actually, but the commercials. When there is no instant replay at the game, they do not know how to watch that reality. But this has been corrected now, in the United States. First they had huge television screens in the stadium, on which you could watch instant replays. And then they realised there was something better than instant replay — you could actually have a big television screen, but huge, the size of a wall, and you could actually watch the game on television at the game, complete with instant replay.

My son is a disc-jockey in very exotic nightclubs in New York City: Mars, Morrisey, etc. And what he does is he scratches records. What is scratching? To take the structures of rock or pop music, and take their strong forms away — that is, the rhythm, the harmonics, the melody, the narrative sound — and produce in essence weak music. In other words, something with no bass, no melody, no harmony. And hundreds of people move to this music which he creates. It is of a particular moment in time. It has lost its condition of narrative time, which is something repeatable or static in time. It is now no longer repeatable. It is now about music as performance, as event. And what we realise is that time of narrative, that is moving from here to there as a rational discourse, in music, in the latest music that people are listening to, has been replaced by another structure. This guy my son has a collection of records, each week he's got to buy a hundred new records, because the people don't want to hear the same scratched stuff the next week. So he has to 'remix' every week, because they do not tape it and save it. It is all prima. That is the essence of going to a discotheque to have something of the original. But this is a different kind of original from what Walter Benjamin meant when he spoke of 'the aura of the original of the work of art'; it's now the original of mechanical reproduction, it is the original of media. It is mediated originality without. And no longer is the time of reality the time of stasis, the time of history, the time of this room. It is a different kind of time, the time of the event.

For example, in the past a news conference was something where somebody was to say something important. And people came to hear something that was real. Now a news conference is set up for the ten o'clock news. The ten o'clock news has got certain time slots called 'soundbites' — 15 seconds, 20 seconds, 30 seconds. So the President, before he speaks, is mediated by his consultants to say something in a certain 15-second period that the television people will put on the nightly news. The rest does not matter, because all people hear is what is on TV. They do not read any more. In fact now we have newspapers that are formatted like television.

All of this makes one understand that reality has become mediated. Now people can no longer even watch minute-long commercials. Now they are 15 seconds. Now in one minute you are getting four different commercials. The condensation, another Freudian term, is so strong that it only takes 15 seconds to deploy it. And when one is hit with information at 15-second intervals, that is real condensation.

Architecture's reality needs to be reconsidered to stand in a mediated world. To do that means to displace the conditions of architecture as they used to be. In other words, the conditions that saw architecture as reasonable, as understandable, as clearly functioning. Now this displacement

does not mean that architecture should not function. Rather, the displacement concerns the conditions of architecture as defined by Vitruvius. Vitruvius said that a building had to have *utilitas, firmitas, venustas*. Which literally means utility, firmness, pleasingness. But he did not mean it should function well, because all buildings function well, or that it should be structured well, or that it should contain well, or that it should be aesthetically well. What he meant was, it should 'look like' it functions well, it should look like it is built well, etc. Thus, he permanently elided actual function and symbolic function in what I call a strong form relationship. When Le Corbusier said, 'A house is a machine to live in', he did not mean it should really be a machine, because basically he was building bourgeois houses with 19th-century functions. He meant that the house should look like a machine. And so they built an ordinary house with all the ordinary functions and made it look like a machine.

What I am suggesting is that, yes, a building has to function, but it does not have to look like it functions. Yes, a building has to stand up, but it does not have to look like it stands up. And when it does not look like it stands up, or it does not look like it functions, then it functions and stands differently. Now when I did a museum for the Wexner Center in Columbus, Ohio, I said, 'We have to exhibit art, but do we have to exhibit art the way art has been traditionally exhibited, that is, against a neutral background? Because,' I said, 'you know, art has always been critical of life, that is what gave art its potency, its poetry. And architecture should serve art, in other words, be a background for art? Absolutely not,' I said. 'Architecture should challenge art and this notion that it should be a background.' And the proof of this for me, is that in Cincinnati, where I am doing what I think is an important building, they just had a recent show of Robert Mapplethorpe's photographs, and they are about to lock up the director — they are having a trial, a pornography trial in Cincinnati, trying to prove, which they will prove, that the director is a pornographer. I have been desperately wishing someone would put me on trial as a pornographer, me the architect, right? And maybe try and put me into jail. Because we accommodate, we allow, we never critique society, or art, or life, we accommodate life, we accommodate art, we roll over. You have never heard of one architect being threatened because his or her work was politically active, that is, it threatened anybody. Most people do not care. Yet poets get locked up, artists get locked up. You know, William Butler Yeats helped bring about the Irish Rebellion. Corbu? They did not care. They used him. He even went and begged Mussolini to give him work. He would have begged anybody so as to build.

What I am saying is that we need to displace this concept of architecture as a service, as an accommodating profession, as one that people inhabit. Just the notion of inhabit means 'to grow used to'. And the habitual is what people want from an architect; in other words, architecture is OK as long as it indulges the habits of people. But once you question the habit, that is, the way museum curators show works, the way art critics write about works in a museum, you upset the balance, you cause a stir. The art critics hate my Wexner Center building. The curators hate it. Why? Because it provokes them to have to think again about the relationship between painting and the space of painting. Because they cannot hang easel paintings on the walls of my building. And yet, what is interesting is that artists are talking about recontextualising art. If you remember, Michelangelo's work was in a context, it was not to be put in a museum. They did not scrape Michelangelo, Giulio Romano, the Carraccis off the walls and hang them in museums, they painted *in situ*. Art was *in situ*. Artists are now saying they want art to be *in situ*. That is, they want to take painting off the easel and sculpture off the pedestal and make it site-specific. Except when it comes to galleries and museums. Then the most radical artist wants architecture to roll over and be a pedestal and an easel. And architects are all too willing to provide pedestals and easels for artists. We need to rethink this idea of architecture.

Now, what to do about it? In school — let me tell you how corrupt the relationship between student and teacher is: basically it is 'don't bother me if I don't bother you.' The teacher comes in on the first day of the design studio and says, 'We are going to design a library.' And not one student says, 'Why? Why not a school, or a jail, or a zoo?' There's no questioning. Maybe a smattering of grumbling. They are not going to be library specialists. Students never ask why they study structures, by the way, or why they study mechanical engineering in an architectural curriculum. I have never designed a structure — I do not need to know anything about it. I failed structures, as you could probably tell from my buildings, but it does not matter, because I am not allowed to design a structure in the United States or I would be sued, right? I have to hire a structural engineer, a mechanical engineer.

So, then the teacher says, 'We are going to do research. Go and research libraries.' As if you needed to research libraries to do a library. But it has been decided that the history of libraries influences what we should do today. In other words, that the way to learn about libraries is to research not just the architecture of libraries, but how books are made, how they are checked out, how they are processed, stored, etc. I do not know how a library works. If I were going to do a library I would go hire somebody who knew what libraries were about — as I did when we did the convention centre. Who knows what happens in a convention centre? Basically, the study of programme is useless. In any case, let us assume now that the student brings the project in, and the teacher first of all says, 'Why did you do this?' And the student will start to answer why he or she did this, 'Well, because I needed to have a clear entry. I needed to have a clear circulation system, I needed to show what the building symbolically meant in the street, I needed to respond.' Right? And if the student gets all of the responses right, that is clear and reasonable, the teacher will say, 'That's good.' Even though it may be horrible-looking. As long as all the answers are 'motherhood' answers, it is OK. *You* try as a student to answer a teacher when he says, 'Why did you do that?' with 'I don't know.' Or, 'It doesn't matter why I did it.' Or, 'What does it mean? I have no idea. You make it up.' These kinds of responses would mean expulsion from any school, anywhere.

Architecture has a serious problem. Advances in science have always been made because someone did not believe what the teacher was telling them. They did not believe, in fact, in the principle of the non-loss of materiality, they did not believe in the notion of narrative time. They did not believe in the philosophical terms of teleology or ontology, or even typology. The only way to advance in a discipline is to displace knowledge. And the only discourses that remain healthy are those that are displacing discourses. The ones that cling to their theory and their tradition and their rationality, die. Now architecture may already be dead, I do not know, I do not think anybody cares. As long as people make money in building what sells, they will be published anyway, because public relations people will make sure they get published, because journalists have to have something to write about. Media in the end is debilitating. Because what we all want, media, is the killer of creativity in any time.

The press keeps saying, 'We want something new, do you have anything new for us?' And they keep getting more work only to stay — to stay real. Because they assume that 'the image' in the media is their reality. And if they lose that, it is like losing their shadow. They are so desperate, we are so desperate, that we cannot work any more. Society often has no satisfaction from the actual product of our labour, people are only interested in the mediated result.

Weak form derives from several ideas: that there is no single truth; that there is no decidability (things have to be undecidable, arbitrary); that things are no longer essential (there is no essence to architecture, there is no essence to anything); that it is all in the excess. If you look at David Lynch it is about excess. If you look at anything in contemporary discourse, it is about the condition of excess, that is, nothing relying on essence. Weak form is arbitrary, undecidable, excessive, and has no ontology or teleology of value, that is, no strong relationship to narrative space or time.

ARCHITECTURE AND THE PROBLEM OF THE RHETORICAL FIGURE

PETER EISENMAN

Now let us, by a flight of imagination, suppose that Rome is not a human habitation, but a psychical entity with a similarly long and copious past — an entity, that is to say, in which nothing that has once come into existence will have passed away and all the earlier phases of development continue to exist alongside the latest one.
Sigmund Freud, *Civilisation and its Discontents.*

Sigmund Freud, in an unintended cultural repression, assumes later in the same text that 'if we want to represent historical sequence in spatial terms we can only do it by juxtaposition in space . . . The same space,' he says, 'cannot have two different contents.' But this is only true if we assume that architecture is place, time, and scale-specific. What if this is not the case? What if this assumption merely represents 500 years of a cultural repression known as Classical Architecture? What if it is possible to reinvent a Rome, a Rome free of these repressions, a Rome which is no longer place, time, and scale-specific? But first, what is the nature of these repressions?

They assume the metaphysics of architecture (that is, shelter, aesthetics, structure, and meaning), and the vocabulary (elements such as columns, capitals etc) to have the status of natural law. The assumed factual nature of this assumption stems from the fact that it is the nature of architecture, unlike any other discipline, to establish centre, to manifest presence, to be the agent of reality — bricks and mortar, shelter and function, house and home. Architecture, because it *is* bricks and mortar, holds out the promise of reality, authenticity and genuine truth in a surreal world where truth is a managed item developed by committees, produced by writers and sold by media spokesmen. Our only source of value today is a memory of value, a nostalgia; we live in a relativist world, yet desire absolute substance, something that is incontrovertibly real. Through its being, architecture has become, in the unconscious of society, the promise of this something real. But it is also true that architecture, more than any other discipline, must confront and dislocate this deeply rooted perception in order to be. This is because, contrary to popular opinion, the status quo of dwelling does not define architecture. What defines architecture is the continuous dislocation of dwelling, to dislocate, in other words, what it in fact locates.

To dislocate dwelling, architecture must continually reinvent itself. Architecture accomplishes this out of itself, out of the stuff that holds it together. Palladio did not know what a country villa was. He invented it out of architecture. One could almost say that architecture is the continuing invention of dwelling. It is the need to dislodge dwelling that has maintained architecture throughout history. It is the power of architecture's nature to centre that renders its task to decentre and thus recentre so difficult.

Architecture creates institutions. It is a constructive activity. Architecture, by its very creation, is institutionalising. So for architecture to be, it must resist what it must in fact do. In order to be, it must always resist being. It must dislocate without destroying its own being, that is, it must maintain its own metaphysic. This is the paradox of architecture. Thus in order to reinvent a site, whether it be a city or a house, the idea of site must be freed from its traditional places, histories, and systems of meanings. This involves the dislocation of the traditional interpretation of its elements so that its figures can be read rhetorically as opposed to aesthetically or metaphorically. What does it mean to read rhetorically? What is a rhetorical figure?

Traditionally in language there is a relationship between a sign and what it stands for. For example, a cat, c-a-t, has a fixed relationship to an animal which walks around on four legs and meows. It is not a question of how the letters look. If you change the letters around from c-a-t to a-c-t, they are the same letters, but now it does not mean a four-legged animal. It means something else. So there is a fixed relationship within the structure of the letters and a fixed relationship between that particular fixed structure and an object. Now it has been suggested that it is possible to cut the fixed and supposedly immutable relationship between sign and signified. That is, the relationship which always has been, which is thought to be as much a natural law as architectural elements are to architecture. Cutting this relationship would produce what might be called free-floating signs without necessary meanings or the necessary relationship to their object — cut from cultural, historical, accumulated meaning. Now the difference between literature and architecture is enormous. Linguistic signs are traditionally transparent. That means that with 'cat' we do not look at the letters c-a-t and examine the relationship between the c and the a; we go right away to the four-legged animal. What literature tries to do is to dam up this transparency of signs. So that what the art of writing — poetry — attempts to do is make less transparent the relationship between the sign and the signified. Language can do this because it has a very elaborate syntax, that is, it can dam up the transparency and make the words opaque, giving them substance in themselves. Now (paradoxically) that substance is like a cutting. When you start to make words opaque, you start cutting the relationship between the sign and the signified. You cut or obscure or deny the easy flow from the word to its meaning. Jacques Derrida has suggested that traditionally, language suppresses the aesthetic in favour of the rhetorical. Now in architecture, it is almost the reverse. The presence in the object is dominated by the aesthetic; the absence, or the rhetorical quality is repressed. Thus we do not have either an agreed-upon sign system or an elaborated grammar. In fact, architecture is perhaps the least representative of all the arts. In architecture, when you build a wall, not only is it really opaque, but its relationship to a signified plane is very difficult to articulate. A wall is a wall, it is not a word, it *is*, it is never *about*. It is the thing that the word 'wall' refers to, it is the opposite condition of a word: words are transparent whereas walls are opaque. In this opacity, walls also have traditional meanings as elements of a thought-to-be immutable vocabulary of architecture. When Michael Graves says that what Peter Eisenman is doing is not architecture, he means that it is outside what he assumes to be the natural vocabulary of architecture. Outside the traditional associative feelings about the content of a wall. If we want to make a wall more of a sign — that is, more rhetorical — we have to reduce its traditional opacity, that is its traditional elemental, structural, and aesthetic content. This requires the introduction of an absence in the *is* of architecture, an absence in its presence. Absence has been traditionally repressed by presence. This requires a strategy.

Let us go back to our words 'cat' and 'act' and suggest another relationship. If we add a third term, the verb 'is', we have the forms 'cat is' and 'act is'. Now, if we superpose them and produce a third form, 'cactis', it is a sign which does not mean anything in itself. While it is similar to 'cactus', it does not in itself represent or suggest the plant or the desert. This process first fragments and recombines the fragments like a new word. There is both loss and gain in each transaction. The new form contains the loss of the prior forms as well as the loss of its own meaning. Therefore there is an absence. This is what I am calling provisionally a rhetorical figure. This is in order to distinguish the metaphorical figure which is both rhetorical but also representational, from what I define as a rhetorical figure. This is in reality a *catachresis* which is

thus not representational, as will be explained later. Now how does this operate in architecture? The representational figure stands for something outside. So there is also an absence. But this absence is about, it is outside, it is not contained within the *is*. The rhetorical figure, like the cactis, stands for its own absence — it does not refer outside — its own absence *is*. Architecture has always assumed that like language and like art, it has signs, ie, that its figuration is representational. But this idea of rhetorical figuration in architecture is not representational. A representational figure represents a thing in its absence. A rhetorical figure contains its absence, that is, it contains its open-endedness.

The classical history of architecture is not without rhetorical figures, but this implicit rhetoric was always univocal, spoken in the classical language of architecture, understanding that rhetoric in itself is not culturally free. The attempt here is to loosen the culture of architecture from the monotony of classical architectural rhetoric, that is, to use the freedoms that architecture potentially makes available. In his use of the 'duck' and the 'decorated shed', Robert Venturi actually made this attempt to distinguish between representational and rhetorical, although he did not explicitly define it as such. A duck is a representational figure; the decorated shed a rhetorical figure. Venturi actually initiated Post-Modern historicising in architecture by condemning representational ducks. This is because the rhetorical decorated shed uses (or represents) the traditional vocabulary of architecture.

In Graves, there is a rhetorical and a representational aspect of his figures. Graves' rhetorical figures differ from mine in that he assumes that the vocabulary of architecture is the vocabulary of architecture. His work is similar to the traditional literary aspects of rhetoric (that is, it is rhetorical in a traditional representational mode). Traditional architecture has by its very nature been writing one text of authority — that is, its reality was seen as history or aesthetic in an attempt to reduce anxiety. Graves' figures are texts of authority. What Graves does not acknowledge is that columns or capitals did not always exist in the conventional vocabulary of architecture. They were invented out of the rhetorical potential of architecture.

Now today, Graves' work presents a very interesting case because while it is artfully presented to look like invention in the assumption of the givenness of the column and the capital, that is in the givenness of the vocabulary of architecture, he in fact works to end the possibility of invention. This is because the representational figure, like its predecessor the abstract figure, works to narrow the suggestive (or rhetorical) nature of the sign.

What one is arguing thus far: (1) That the Post-Modernist impulse in architecture quite rightly restored figuration. (2)

That in doing so, it copied the idea of figuration as a linguistic invocation; that figuration was aesthetically, rather than rhetorically, based. (3) That when its figural sign was rhetorically based, as in the case of Graves, it was done within and accepting the traditional and elemental vocabulary of architecture (ie columns, beams, walls, doors). It assumes this to be natural. (4) Thus what we know as Post-Modern architecture is not Post-Modernist in any conventional linguistic or literary (or even philosophical) sense. It is merely another kind of classical or traditional figuration. Thus one must now search for a Post-Modernist rhetorical figure in architecture which is not marginalised or repressed.

The idea of the rhetorical figure which is being proposed here is rhetorical in two senses. First, because it writes texts other than the approved texts of architecture. Second, because it writes texts other than texts of presence. That is, other than texts of elemental scale, original value, and aesthetic or metaphorical meaning.

In my proposal for rhetorical figures, architecture is no longer elements but an *other* grammatical counter, proposing an alternate reading of the idea of site and object. In this sense, a rhetorical figure will be seen to be inherently contextual in that the site is treated as a deeply scored palimpsest. But traditional Contextualism is representational and analytic, treating place as a physical presence known as a culturally determined idea containing powerful symbolic and evocative meanings. The analogic or rhetorical rather than analytic character of this process dislocates site implications from their culturally predetermined meanings by superposing two old contents to create a new content. In the resulting rhetorically (as opposed to aesthetically, structurally, or historically) determined figuration, there is the revelation in the site of a repressed text. This text suggests that there are other meanings which are site-specific by virtue of their pre-existence, however latent, within the context.

For example, traditionally an axis represents a linear progression in time, a continuous and indifferent movement between two (or more) points which in themselves contain meaning and relate to each other in a hierarchical way. Through the process of superposition, elements of such an axial progression are dislocated continuously, appearing at once at a different scale and in a different place. By superposing the endpoints of any three different length segments, and thus making them the same length, we reveal their analogous relationships as endpoints of different segments of an axis. When these segments become the same length, they obviously become different scales. This in turn dislocates the traditional notion of scale as given by the human body or the human eye. Each of these segments now loses its real dimension, location, place, and time; ultimately,

the whole notion of the axis as a form bound to linear time, hierarchy and continuity is subverted. More importantly, because elements along each of these axes are relocated, they begin also to superpose on other elements to reveal unexpected correspondences which in their former reality would have remained unintelligible. What is revealed from the initial superpositions cannot be predicted. These are the so-called 'repressed texts' that are found by reading these new rhetorical figures. Superpositions result in a dislocation of origin and destination, of time and space. By incorporating in any site the assemblage from disparate but analogous elements of other sites, the two figures occupy origin and destination contemporaneously. At the same time, movement along an axis toward a destination results in a return to origin. The misreading suggested by these figures hints at other misreadings of place. In this way, the idea of place is both reinforced and denied. While new places are created, the traditional notion of place is undercut because each place is actually many places at once. The result is a text which displaces the traditional notion of time and space. It denies traditional and privileged ideas of context and aesthetic presence. It recognises that absence is an essential condition of a rhetorical figure, but not absence as the opposite of presence, rather absence *in* presence. (The only constant truth now about the idea of a thing is that it is not the thing itself, and therefore, contains the presence of the absence of the thing.) Any site contains not only presences, the memory of previous presences and the immanences of possible presence. The physical difference between a moving thing (dynamism) and a still one (stasis) is that the moving one contains the trace of where it has been and where it is going. The introduction of this trace, or condition of absence, acknowledges the dynamic reality of the living city.

This process assembles this repressed text as a fiction. These rhetorical figures are fictional because while the elements of the site seem to be in their original position, that is they seem to be located according to their previous condition of formal structure (axes and events at the beginning, middle, and ends of such axes), they in fact are not. Origin and destination are perceived contemporaneously while movement toward the destination results in a return to origin. The perception at one point of all the elements of the progression, rearranged in scale and distance, dislocates the relationship between time and space. In the same way, one might proceed along the axis encountering the same elements several times. Time and space, form and figure are thus collapsed as interdependent entities, space becomes independent of time (actual and historical) and space (more precisely, place and locus) becomes independent of form. This allows the conception of these elements, time, space, place, form, figure, in a system which contains the possibility of its own contradiction. The meaning of space of time is freed from a symbolised representation: the definitions of time as linear or circular, and of space as dynamic or static, now have no meaning in the traditional sense. The system of meaning (cultural structure) of a form is denied without denying the form: but now the forms in themselves have no transcendental or *a priori* meaning. They are cut off from their former givenness. The meaning is in the relationship; the architecture is between the signs. These seeming conditions of presence make these analogies co-existent with their precedents and yet suspend them in a condition of absence. It dislocates the conceptual essence of their previous typical structures (hierarchy, time, space, place, etc). The elements are now devoid of their 'original' meaning, they are not embedded in culture, history, place, scale, or time. They are both the 'new' and the 'old', now timeless, placeless, and spaceless in terms of scale, distance, and direction. This means that their form and figure do not relate directly to an inevitable structure of time and place.

This repressed text is a fiction which recognises its own fictive condition. In its way, it begins to acknowledge the fictional quality of reality and the real quality of fiction. Culture, history, and ultimately architecture are not fixed or merely additive, but are a continual process of reiteration and simultaneous dislocation which at every moment modifies the previous instant of meaning and structure.

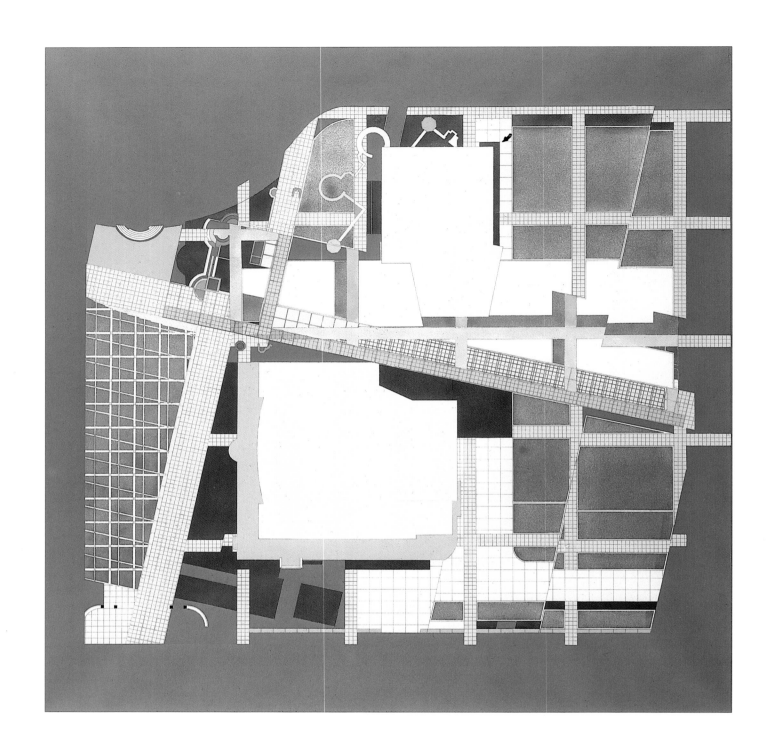

UNFOLDING EVENTS: FRANKFURT REBSTOCK AND THE POSSIBILITY OF A NEW URBANISM
PETER EISENMAN

The entry of Germany on the scene of philosophy implicates the entire German spirit which, according to Nietzsche, presents little that is deep but is full of foldings and unfoldings.
Gilles Deleuze, *Le Pli.*

The German soul is above all manifold [vielfältig] . . . its disorder possesses much of the fascination of the mysterious; the German is acquainted with the hidden path of chaos . . . the German himself is not, he is becoming, he is developing.
Friedrich Nietzsche, *Beyond Good and Evil.*

Throughout the design arts, we are experiencing a paradigm shift from the mechanical to the electronic; from an age of interpretation to an age of mediation. Mechanical reproduction, the photograph, is not the same as electronic reproduction, the facsimile. The former is the essence of reproduction because change can occur from the original; the latter, because there is no change from the original, that is, no interpretation, has no essence at all. While in both cases the value of an original is thrown into question, mediated reproduction proposes a different value system precisely because there is no interpretation. Contemporary media undermine the essence and aura of the original, indeed the very nature of reality. Media environments, such as advertising, or synthetic realities such as Disney World, have now become so potent that they form a new reality. Whereas architecture formerly served as a baseline for reality — bricks and mortar, house and home, structure and foundation were the metaphors that anchored our reality — what constitutes this reality today is not clear.

Traditionally, architecture was place-bound, linked to a condition of experience. Today, mediated environments challenge the givens of classical time, the time of experience. For example, on a Sunday afternoon anywhere in the world, whether it be at the Prado in Madrid or the Metropolitan in New York, there are literally hordes of people passing in front of art works, hardly stopping to see, at best perhaps merely photographing their experience. Not only do they have no time for the original, they have even less for the experience of the original. Because of media the time of experience has changed; the soundbite — infinitesimal, discontinuous, autonomous — has conditioned our new time.

Architecture can no longer be bound by the static conditions of space and place, here and there. In a mediated world, there are no longer places in the sense that we used to know them. Architecture must now deal with the problem of the event. Today, rock concerts might be considered the only form of architectural event. People go to them not to listen, because you cannot hear the music, but to become part of the environment. A new type of environment is being projected, comprised of light, sound, movement. But this kind of event structure is not architecture standing against media, but architecture being consumed by it. Media deals neither with physical facts nor with interpretation but with the autonomous condition of electronic reproduction. The rock concert with amplified sound and strobe lighting attempts to deny physical presence. This architecture cannot do. However, architecture can propose an alternative, some other kind of event, one in which a displacement of the static environment is not merely an electronic one-liner but rather one in which interpretation of the environment is problematised, where the event comes between sign and object.

Traditional architecture theory largely ignores the idea of the event. Rather, it assumes that there are two static conditions of object: figure and ground. These in turn give rise to two dialectical modes of building. One mode concerns figure/ground contextualism, which assumes a reversible and interactive relationship between the solid building blocks and the voids between them. A typical example of contextualism would say that there exist in any historical context the latent structures capable of forming a present-day urbanism. The other mode concerns the point block or linear slab isolated on a *tabula rasa* ground. Here there is no relationship between old and new or between figure and ground. Rather the ground is seen as a clear neutral datum, projecting its autonomy into the future. In each case, the two terms figure/object and ground are both determinant and all-encompassing; they are thought to explain the totality of urbanism. But as in most disciplines such all-encompassing totalities have come into question; they are no longer thought to explain the true complexity of phenomena. This is certainly true of urbanism.

Germany and specifically Frankfurt seem always clearly to trace changes in western urbanism. In the late 18th and early 19th centuries the typical perimeter housing and commercial block of German cities defined both the street space and the interior court space as positive. These spaces seemed literally to have been carved out of a solid block of the urban condition. In the mid-19th century, with the development of the grand boulevards and *Allees*, a new kind of spatial structure appeared in German cities. The streets were still positive spaces but were lined with ribbon buildings, so that the rear yards became left-over space. This idea led to the development of the German *Siedlung* where, since there were no streets adjacent to the buildings, the backs and fronts were now the same. Now all of the open space was in a sense left over; the 'ground' became a wasteland. The object buildings seemed detached, floating on a ground that was no longer active.

Nowhere was this *Siedlung* urbanism more prevalent than in the developing ring around the urban centre of Frankfurt. While Ernst May's pre-war housing was revolutionary, its corrosive effect on the urban fabric is now everywhere to be seen. In the postwar era, with the expansion of the *Autobahn* and air travel, a new, more complex task faced urban development. No longer was the simple *Siedlung* nor the figure/ground perimeter block adequate to contain the new complex urban realities; the city no longer totally defined the possible context of an urbanism. Yet the form of the perimeter block of the historic urban centres became the basic unit of an urban theory known as Contextualism, the vogue of Post-Modern urbanism. But its nostalgia and kitsch sentimentalism never took into account the *manifold* realities of contemporary life.

What is needed is the possibility of reading object-figure/ground from another frame of reference. This new reading might reveal other conditions which may have always been immanent or repressed in the urban fabric. This reframing would perhaps allow for the possibility of new urban structures and for existing structures to be seen in such a way that they too become redefined. In such a displacement, the new, rather than being understood as fundamentally different to the old, is seen instead as being merely slightly out of focus in relation to what exists. This out-of-focus condition then, has the possibility of blurring or displacing the whole, that is both old and new. One such displacement possibility can be found in the form of the fold.

It was Leibniz who first conceived of matter as explosive. He turned his back on Cartesian rationalism, and argued that in the labyrinth of the continuous, the smallest element is not the point but the fold. From Leibniz, one can turn to the ideas of two contemporary thinkers concerning the fold; one is Gilles Deleuze, and the other is René Thom. In the idea of the fold, form is seen as continuous but also as articulating a possible new relationship between vertical and horizontal, figure and ground, breaking up the existing Cartesian order of space.

Deleuze says the first condition for Leibniz's event is the idea of extension. Extension is the philosophical movement outward along a plane rather than downward in depth. Deleuze argues that in mathematical studies of variation, the notion of the object is changed; no longer is it defined by an essential form. He calls this idea of the new object an object/event, an 'objectile' — a modern conception of a technological object. This new object for Deleuze is no longer concerned with the framing of space, but rather a temporal modulation that implies a continual variation of matter. The continual variation is characterised through the agency of the fold. For Deleuze, the idea of the fold was first defined culturally in the Baroque. He differentiates between the Gothic, which privileges the elements of construction, frame, and enclosure, and the Baroque, which emphasises matter, where the mass overflows its boundaries because it cannot be contained by the frame which eventually disappears. Deleuze states that the fold/unfold are the constants today in the idea of an object/event.

The linking of fold and event also influences work in other disciplines, specifically in mathematics with René Thom. In his catastrophe theory Thom says that there are seven elementary events or transformations. These transformations do not allow any classical symmetry and thus the possibility of a static object, because there is no privileged plan of projection. Instead of such a plan there is a neutral surface formed from a variable curvature or a fold. This variable curvature is the inflection of a pure event. For Thom, the structure of the event of change is already in the object but cannot be seen, only modelled (by the neutral surface of the catastrophe fold). Thus, while a tiny grain of sand can trigger a landslide, the conditions leading up to the moment of movement are already seen to be in place in the structure. Thom's seven catastrophes were proposed to explain precisely this phenomenon.

In one sense catastrophe theory can also explain abrupt changes in the state or form of such control as figure to ground, urban to rural, commercial to housing, by means of a complex fold that remains unseen. This type of folding is more complex than origami, which is linear and sequential and thus ultimately involves a frame. This quality of the unseen in the folding structures on our site deals with the fact that 'the folded object' neither stands out from the old nor looks like the old, but is somewhere in between the old and something new. Such an in-between or third figure may be likened to the *passe-partout* which is the matter between the frame and the figure in a painting. However, the idea of a *passe-partout* is always another framing, a reframing in a certain way. It can never be neutral; it always will be more or less than what is there. The fold in this sense is neither figure nor ground but contains aspects of both. Architecture could then interpret the fold which is essentially planar in three-dimensional volumes. These folds would not be merely an extrusion from a plan as in traditional architecture, but rather something which affects both plan and section. The neutral surface of the catastrophe fold is already between figure and ground, between plan and section, yet it is homogeneous; it is not merely the appearance of a third; it is a third in its own being.

By introducing the concept of the fold as a non-dialectic third condition, one which is between figure and ground, yet reconstitutes the nature of both, it is possible to refocus or reframe what already exists in any site, and specifically other possible immanent conditions latent in Frankfurt. This reframing changes what exists from that which was repressed by former systems of authority (such as figure and ground) to a potential for a new interpretation of existing organisations. Through the concept of the fold, it is possible to refocus what already exists in Frankfurt.

The fold then becomes the site of all the repressed immanent conditions of existing urbanism which, at a certain point, like the drop of sand which causes a landslide, have the potential to reframe existing urbanism, not to destroy it but to set it off in a new direction. The idea of the fold gives the traditional idea of edge a dimension. Rather than being seen as an abrupt line, it now has a volumetric dimension which provides both mediation and a reframing of conditions such as old and new, transport and arrival, commerce and housing. The fold then can be used not merely as a formal device, but rather as a way of projecting new social organisations into an existing urban environment.

Thus as we near the end of one era and are about to enter a new one, there is an opportunity to reassess the entire idea of a static urbanism, one which deals only with objects rather than events. In a media age static objects are no longer as meaningful as timeful events, where the temporal dimension of the present becomes an important aspect of the past and the future.

A LETTER TO PETER EISENMAN
JACQUES DERRIDA

MY DEAR PETER,

I am simultaneously sending this letter, with the cassette that accompanies it, to Hillis, who must talk with us over the course of the anticipated meeting. As he must also moderate and enliven it, but for other reasons as well, Hillis is therefore, along with you, the first addressee of these questions. He understands better that any other the labyrinth, as we all know. And what I am going to say to you will probably reverberate in a sort of labyrinth. I am entrusting to the recording of the voice or the letter that which is not yet visible to me and cannot guide my steps towards an end/exit, that can barely guide them towards an 'issue'. I am not even sure myself whether what I am sending you holds up. But that is perhaps by design, and it is of this I plan to speak to you. In any case, I very much regret the necessity of depriving myself of this meeting with you, the two of you, all of you.. But now, do not worry, I am not going to argue with you. And I am not going to abuse my absence, not even to tell you that you perhaps believe in it, absence, too much. This reference to absence is perhaps one of the things (because there are others) that has most troubled me in your discourse on architecture, and if that were my first question you could perhaps profit from my absence to speak about it a little, about absence in general, about the role that this word 'absence' will have been able to play at least in what you believed you could *say* if not *do* with your architecture. One could multiply examples, but I am limiting myself to what you say about the presence of an absence in *Moving Arrows, Eros, and Other Errors*, which concerns Romeo's chateau, 'a palimpsest and a quarry', etc. This discourse on absence or the presence of an absence perplexes me not only because it bypasses so many tricks, complications, traps that the philosopher, especially if he is a bit of a dialectician, knows only too well and fears to find you caught up in again, but also because it has authorised many religious interpretations, not to mention vaguely Judeo-transcendental ideologisations, of your work. I suspect a little that you liked and encouraged these interpretations even as you discreetly denied it with a smile, which would make a misunderstanding a little more or a little less than a misunderstanding. My question has to do not only with absence, but with God. *Voilà*, if I did not come it is not just because I am tired and overworked, held up in Paris, but precisely to have the opportunity to ask you directly a question about God that I would never have dared to do in Irvine if I had been present in person; instead, I am glad that this question comes to you by way of this voice, that is to say, on tape. The same question brings up others, a whole group of closely related questions. For example, at the risk of shocking you: Whether it has to do with houses, museums, or the laboratories of research universities, what distinguishes your architectural space from that of the temple, indeed of the synagogue (by this word I mean a Greek word used for a Jewish concept)? Where will the break, the rupture have been in this respect, if there is one, if there was one, for you and for other architects of this period with whom you feel yourself associated? I remain very perplexed about this subject and if I had been there I would have been a difficult interlocutor. If you were to construct a place of worship, Buddhist, for example, or a cathedral, a mosque, a synagogue (hypotheses that you are not obliged to accept), what would be your primary concern today? I will make allusion shortly to Libeskind's project in Berlin for a Jewish Museum. We spoke about this the other morning in New York, but let us leave that behind for the moment.

Naturally, this question concerns also your interpretation of *chora* in 'our' 'work', if one can say in quotations our work 'in common'. I am not sure that you have detheologised and deontologised *chora* in as radical a way as I would have wished (*chora* is not the void, as you suggest sometimes, nor absence, nor invisibility, nor certainly the contrary from which there are, and this is what interests me, a large number of consequences). It is true that for me it was easier, in a certain way. I did not have anything to 'do' with it and would not have been able to do anything with it, that is, for the city of Paris, for La Villette, the little city; you see what I mean (and the whole difference is perhaps between us). But I would like you to say something to our friends in Irvine, while speaking to them of the difference between our respective relations to discourse, on the one hand, and to the operation of architecture, to its putting into action, on the other hand. Profit from my absence in order to speak freely. But don't just say whatever, because as everything is being recorded today, and memory, always the same, not being at all the same, I will know all that you will have said publicly. I had the feeling, and I believe that you said it somewhere, that you have judged me to be too reserved, in our 'choral work', a little bit absent, entrenched in discourse, without obliging you to change, to change place, without disturbing you enough. It is doubtless true that there would be a great deal to say about this subject, which is complicated because it is that of the place (*chora*) and of displacement itself. If I had come, I would have spoken perhaps of my own displacement in the course of 'choral work' but here it is you who must speak. Therefore tell me whether *after Choral Work* (as you yourself said in Irvine in the spring) your work took, in effect, a new direction and engaged itself in other paths. What has happened? What for you is this period? This history? How does one determine the boundaries of it or put rhythm into it? When did we begin to work together, had we never done so, on this *Choral Work* that is not yet constructed but that one sees and reads everywhere? When will we stop?

This all brings me directly to the next question. It also concerns a certain absence. Not my absence today in Irvine where I would have so much liked to see you again along with other friends, even more so since I was one of those who had wished for and prepared this meeting (and I must ask you to forgive me and to make others forgive me); but absence like the shadowed sound of the voice — you see what I mean by this. What relations (new or archi-ancient, in any case different) does architecture, particularly yours, carry on, must it carry on, with the voice, the capacity of voice, but also therefore with telephonic machines of all sorts that structure and transform our experience of space every day? The question of the nearly immediate telephonic address, certainly *nearly* immediate, and I underline, but also the question of telephonic archivation, as is the case right here, with the spacing of time that telephonic archivation at once supposes and structures. If one can imagine a whole labyrinthlike history of architecture, guided by the entwined thread of this question, where would one be today and tomorrow, and you?

This question of history, as the history of spacing, like the spacing of time and voice, does not separate itself from the history of visibility (immediately mediate), that is to say, from all history of architecture; it is so great that I will not even dare to touch upon it, but will 'address' this question, as you say in English, through economy and through metonymy, under the form of a single word, glass (*glas, glass*).

What is there of glass in your work? What do you say about it? What do you do with it? How does one talk about it? In optical terms or in tactile terms? Regarding tactility, it would be good if, continuing what we were saying the other morning in New York, you would speak to our friends of the erotic tricks, of the calls of desire, do I dare say, of the sex appeal of the architectural forms about which you think, with which you work, to which you give yourself up. Whether its directions are new or not, does this seduction come as supplement, into the bargain, as precisely the 'subsidy/bonus of seduction' or 'subsidy/bonus of pleasure'? Or is it essential? Isn't the subsidy/bonus essential, at least? But, then, what would the subsidy/bonus *itself* be? Subsidy/Bonus? For the author of *Moving Arrows, Eros, and Other Errors*, what is the relation between subsidy/bonus and the rest in the calculations and the negotiations of the architect? As my American students sometimes disarmingly ask me, Could you elaborate on that? I return now to my question, after this long parenthesis on your desire, my question about glass that is not perhaps so far off. What terms do we use to speak about glass? Technical and material terms? Economic terms? The terms of urbanism? The terms of social relations? The terms of transparency and immediacy, of love or of police, of the border that is perhaps erased between the public and the private, etc? 'Glass' is an old word, and am I wrong if I believe that you are interested in glass, that you perhaps even like it? Does it only have to do with new materials that resemble glass but are no longer it, and so on? Before letting you speak about glass, I bring up a text by Benjamin, *Erfahrung und Armut*, which I'm sure you know (it also concerns architecture and was published in 1933, which is not just any date, in Germany or elsewhere). From it I extract at the outset only the following, on which our friends will certainly like to hear you comment.

> But Scheerbart — to return to him — most values that his people, and according to their model, his fellow citizens, live in apartments that correspond to their rank: in houses of moving and slippery glass, such as those that Loos and Le Corbusier have since erected. It is not for nothing that glass is such a hard and smooth material upon which nothing attaches itself. Also a cold and concise material. Things made of glass have no 'aura' [Die Dinge aus Glas haben keine 'Aura']. In general, glass is the enemy of secrecy. It is also the enemy of possession. The great poet André Gide once said, 'Each thing that I wish to possess becomes opaque for me.'

(Here we return to the question of desire and glass, of the desire of glass: I have elsewhere tried to follow this experience of desire as the experience of glass in Blanchot, especially in *La Folie du jour* and in *L'Arrêt de mort*.)

> Do people such as Scheerbart dream of glass masonry [Glasbauten] in order to have recognised a new poverty [Bekenner einer neuen Armut]? But perhaps a comparison here will reveal more than the theory. Upon entering a room of the 80s, and despite the 'comfortable intimacy' ['Gemütlichkeit'] that perhaps reigns there, the strongest impression will be, 'You have nothing to look for here.' You have nothing to look for here because there is no ground here upon which the inhabitant would not have already left his trace: by knick-knacks on shelves, by doilies on the armchair, by the sheer curtains at the windows, or by the fire screen in front of the fireplace. A beautiful word from Brecht here helps us go far, farther: 'Erase your traces!' [Verwisch die Spuren!], so says the refrain of the first poem in Anthologie pour les habitants des villes . . . Scheerbart and his glass and the Bauhaus and its steel have opened the way: they have created spaces in which it is difficult to leave traces. 'After all that has been said,' declares Scheerbart 20 years later, 'we can easily speak of a "culture of glass" ["Glaskultur"]. The new environment of glass will completely change man. And the only thing left to hope for now is that the new glass culture will not encounter too many opponents.'

What do you think, Peter, of these propositions? Would you be an 'opponent', a supporter? Or, as I suppose, but perhaps wrongly, neither one nor the other? In any case, could you say something about it and why?

Benjamin's text speaks, as you have seen, of a 'new poverty' (homonym if not synonym for a new expression, a new French concept, to designate a wandering group of poor people, indeed, of the 'homeless', which is irreducible to categorisations, classifications, and former localisations of marginality or of the social ladder: the low income, the proletariat as a class, the unemployed, etc). And the new poverty, the one about which Benjamin speaks, and none other, should be 'our' future, already our present. From this fascinating text that is politically ambiguous and that must not be too fragmented, I extract the following:

> Scheerbart is interested in the question of knowing what our telescopes, our airplanes, and our rockets do to men of the past in transforming them into completely new creatures, worthy of notice and affection. Furthermore, these

creatures already speak in an entirely new language. And what is Decisive [das Entscheidende] in this language is the tendency towards the Arbitrary Construct [zum willkürlichen Konstruktiven], a tendency that particularly resists the organic. It is through this tendency that the language of these men, or rather of Scheerbart's people, cannot be confused with any other; because these people object to this principle of humanism that calls for the correspondence with humans. Even up to their proper names . . . Poverty of experience [Erfahrungsarmut]: one must not understand by this that these men desire a 'New Experience'. No, they want to liberate themselves from experience, they want a world in which they can make their poverty be recognised — the exterior and eventually also the interior — in such a pure and distinct way that something decent comes of it. And they are not always ignorant and inexperienced. One can say the opposite: they have consumed [gefressen] all of that, 'culture' and 'man' until they are satiated and tired . . . We have become impoverished. We have abandoned one piece after another of the heritage of humanity and often we should have wagered it to Mont-de-Piété [the Mount of Piety] for a hundredth of its value, in order to receive as an advance the few coins of the 'Present' [des 'Aktuellen']. In the door stands economic crisis, behind her a shadow, the war to come. Today, to attach oneself to something has become the business of the small number of the powerful, and God knows whether they are not more human than the majority; for the most part more barbarous, but not in the good sense [nicht auf die gute Art]. The others, however, must settle in once again and with Little. They relate it to the men who created the Fundamentally New [das von Grund auf Neue zu ihrer Sache gemacht], and who founded it upon understanding and self-denial. In its buildings [Bauten], its paintings, and its histories, humanity prepares itself to outlive [überleben], if necessary, culture. And most important, humanity does this while laughing. Perhaps this laughter here and there sounds barbarous. Good [Gut]. Therefore let he who is an individual [der Einzelne] occasionally give a little humanity to the mass, which one day will return it to him with interest. [trans P Beck and Stiegler]

What do you think of this text, Peter, in particular of a poverty that *should* not cause another one to be forgotten? What do you think of these two barbarities that must not be confused and as much as possible — is it possible? — must not be allowed to contaminate each other? What do you think of what Benjamin called the 'present' and of his 'few coins'? What, for you, would be 'good' barbarity in architecture and elsewhere? And the 'present'? I know that there is a present that you do not want, but what best breaks (today? tomorrow?) with this present? And you who want to abstract architecture in proportion to man, in proportion even to his scale, how do you understand this 'destructive', in Benjamin's sense, discourse in the mouth of 'these people [who] object to this principle of humanism that calls for [architecture's] correspondence with humans. Even up to their proper names'?

Therefore, Peter, I would like, and your listeners in Irvine, I imagine, will perhaps like, to hear you speak about the relations between architecture today and poverty. All poverties, the one about which Benjamin speaks and the other; between architecture and capital (the equivalent today of the 'economic crisis' occurring in 1930 *'in der Tur'*, in the 'opening of the door'); between architecture and war (the equivalent today of the 'shadow' and of what 'comes' with it); the scandals surrounding social housing, 'housing' in general (not without recalling what we have both said, which is a little too complicated for a letter, of the habitable and inhabitable in architecture), and the 'homeless', 'homelessness' today in the United States and elsewhere.

This letter is already too long. I shall speed up a little to link schematically other questions or requests to the preceding ones. I cited this text by Benjamin, among other reasons, to lead you to ruin and to destruction. As you know, what he says about 'aura' destroyed by glass (and by technology in general) is articulated in a difficult discourse on 'destruction'. In the

Trauerspiel (and certainly elsewhere but I don't remember where anymore), Benjamin talks about the ruin, especially about the 'baroque cult of the ruin', 'the most noble matter of baroque creation'. In the photocopied pages I am sending you, Benjamin declares that for the baroque 'the ancient inheritance is comparable, in each one of its components, to the elements from which is concocted the new totality. No, they build it. Because the achieved vision of this new thing is that: the ruin . . . The work [of art] confirms itself as ruin. In the allegoric edifice of the *Trauerspiel*, these ruined forms of the salvaged work of art clearly have always already come unfastened.' I will say nothing about Benjamin's concept of the ruin, which is also the concept of a certain mourning in affirmation, indeed the salvation of the work of art; I will, however, use this as a pretext to ask you the following.

First, is there a relationship between your writing of the palimpsest, your architectural experience of memory (in *Choral Work*, for example, but also everywhere else), and 'something' like the ruin that is no longer a thing? In what way would you say, and would you say it, is your calculation, reckoning, of memory not baroque in this Benjaminian sense, despite some appearances? Second, if all architecture is finished, if therefore it carries within itself the traces of its future destruction, the already past future, future perfect, of its ruin, according to methods that are each time original, if it is haunted, indeed signed, by the spectral silhouette of this ruin, at work even in the pedestal of its stone, in its metal or its glass, what would again bring the architecture of 'the period' (just yesterday, today, tomorrow; use whatever words you want, Modern, Post-Modern, Post-Post-Modern, or Amodern, etc) back to the ruin, to the experience of 'its own' ruin? In the past, great architectural inventions constituted their essential destructability, even their fragility, as a resistance to destruction or as a monumentalisation of the ruin itself (the baroque according to Benjamin, right?). Is a new image of the ruin to come already sketching itself in the design of the architecture that we would like to recognise as the architecture of our present, of our future, if one can still say that, in the design of your architecture, in the past future, the future perfect, of its memory, so that it already draws and calculates itself, so that it already leaves its future trace in your projects? Taking into account what we were saying previously about Man (and God), will we again be able to speak of 'the memory of man', as we say in French, for this architecture? In relation to the ruin, to fragility, to destructability, in other words, to the future, could you return to what we were talking about the other morning in New York, about excess and 'weakness'? Every time that excess presents itself (it never presents itself except above and beyond ontological oppositions), for my part, I hesitate to use words of force or of weakness. But it is certainly inevitable as soon as there is announcement. This is nothing more than a pretext so that *you* talk about it, Hillis and you.

Finally, from fragility I turn to ashes, for me the other name or the surname for the essence (not the essential) of the step, of the trace, of writing, the place without place of deconstruction. There where deconstruction inscribes itself. (In 'Feu la cendre' — excuse my reference to something that dates from nearly 20 years ago — this conception of ashes, as the trace itself, was principally reserved for, or rather entrusted to, the 'burn everything' and to the 'holocaust'.) To return to our problem and to hear again the fragile words of 'fragility', of 'ashes', of 'absence', or 'invisibility', of 'Jewish' or not 'Jewish' architectural space, what do you think of the Berlin Museum Competition, about which we also spoke the other morning in New York? In particular, what do you think of the words of Libeskind, the 'winner' of the 'competition', as printed in a recently published interview in the newsletter of the architecture school at Columbia? Here I must content myself with quoting:

> *And in turn the void materialises itself in the space outside as something that has been ruined, or rather as the solid remainder of an independent structure, which is a voided void. Then there is a fragmentation and a splintering, marking the lack of coherence of the museum as a whole, showing that it has come undone in order to become accessible, functionally and intellectually . . . It's conceived as a museum for all Berliners, for all citizens. Not only those of the present, but those of the future and the past who must find their heritage and hope in this particular*

form, which is to transcend passive involvement and become participation. With its special emphasis on housing the Jewish Museum, it is an attempt to give a voice to a common fate — to the contradictions of the ordered and disordered, the chosen and the not chosen, the vocal and the silent. In that sense, the particular urban condition of Lindenstrasse, of this area of the city, becomes the spiritual site, the nexus, where Berlin's precarious destiny is mirrored. It is fractured and displaced, but also transformed and transgressed. The past fatality of the German Jewish cultural relation to Berlin is enacted now in the realm of the invisible. It is this invisibility which I have tried to bring to visibility. So the new extension is conceived as an emblem, where the invisible, the void, makes itself apparent as such . . . It's not a collage or a collision or a dialectic simply, but a new type of organisation which is really organised around a void, around what is not visible. And what is not visible is the collection of this Jewish Museum, which is reducible to archival material, since the physicality of it has disappeared. The problem of the Jewish Museum is taken as the problem of Jewish culture itself — let's put it this way, as the problem of an avant-garde of humanity, an avant-garde that has been incinerated in its own history, in the Holocaust. In this sense, I believe this scheme joins architecture to questions that are now relevant to all humanity. What I've tried to say is that the Jewish history of Berlin is not separable from the history of modernity, from the destiny of this incineration of history; they are bound together. But bound not through any obvious forms, but rather through a negativity; through an absence of meaning and an absence of artefacts. Absence, therefore, serves as a way of binding in depth, and in a totally different manner, the shared hopes of people. It is a conception that is absolutely opposed to reducing the museum to a detached memorial.

Once again void, absence, negativity, in Libeskind as in you. I leave you alone to deal with these words, dear Peter, dear Hillis; I will tell you what I think some other time, but I suggested what I think at the beginning. Once again I have spoken too much and naturally I abuse my absence. I admit it as a sign of love. Forgive me, Hillis and you, and ask our friends, your listeners, to forgive me for not being there to speak with them and to listen to you.

Affectionately,

Jacques

PS (1) This tape was recorded and this transcription finished when I read, at the end of an interview (in the special edition of the Spanish magazine *Arquitectura* devoted to 'Deconstruction' [270] — it's the title of the introduction), the following lines from you that were already anticipating my questions: 'I never talk about deconstruction. Other people use that word because they are not architects. It is very difficult to talk about architecture in terms of deconstruction, because we are not talking about ruins or fragments. The term is too metaphorical and too literal for architecture. Deconstruction is dealing with architecture as a metaphor, and we are dealing with architecture as a reality . . . I believe post-structuralism is basically what I mean by Post-Modernism. In other words, Post-Modernism is post-structuralism in the widest sense of the word.' I certainly believe that I would not subscribe to *any* one of these statements, to *any* one of these seven sentences, not to one nor to two not to three nor to four nor to five nor to six nor to seven. But I cannot explain it here and I, truly, never talk much *about* deconstruction. Not spontaneously. If you wish, you could display one, two, three, four, five, six, seven before the listeners and try to convince them by refuting the contrary propositions or you could let this postscript fall to the side.

PS (2) I was forgetting the fundamental question — the question of foundation, of what you do at the foundation of the foundation or at the foundation of the foundation in your architectural design. Let's talk about Earth itself. I have questioned you in a noncircuitous way about God and Man. I was thinking about the Sky and the Earth. What does architecture, and primarily yours, have to see and do with *experience*, ie with the voyage that makes its way outside of Earth? Then, if we don't give up architecture, and I believe that we are not giving it up, what are the effects on 'design' itself, of terrestrial architecture, of this possibility? Of this definite possibility from now on of leaving the terrestrial soil? Will we say that the architecture of a rocket and of astronomy in general (already announced by literature, at least, and long before becoming 'effective'), that they dispense with foundations and thus of 'standing up', of *the* 'standing up', of the *vertical* stance of man, of the building in general? Or do these architectures (of rockets and astronomy in general) recalculate foundations and does the calculation remain a terrestrial difference, something which I somewhat doubt? What would be an architecture that, without holding, without standing upright, vertically, would not fall again into ruin? How do all these possibilities and even questions (those of holding up, holding together, standing or not) record themselves, if you think that they do? What traces do they leave in what you could build right now in Spain, in Japan, in Ohio, in Berlin, in Paris, and, tomorrow, I hope, in Irvine?

Post/El Cards: A REPLY TO JACQUES DERRIDA
PETER EISENMAN

DEAR JACQUES,

After many months I find the time and the calm distance to reply to your extraordinary letter. I was pleased that you would take the time to write a letter of such energy and length, but also disturbed by what I perceived as an implied criticism in your words. I was also quite literally left speechless by your questions, questions that I could not answer personally, questions that, indeed, must be directed to architecture for a reply.

Why was I so stunned, so taken aback? Perhaps, on first thought, because I felt in your criticism a rejection of my work. However, after many re-readings, I no longer feel that same rush of defensiveness but rather a certain exhilaration, a certain sense of an *other* freedom. Why? Because in a way you are right. Perhaps what I do in architecture, in its aspirations and in its fabric, is not what could properly be called deconstruction. But things are not quite so simple: if my work is not something, then it raises questions as to what it is not. In attempting to interrogate what it is not, I will not give answer to all of your questions. Indeed, I do not think that the spirit of your letter was one of inquisition. Rather, your questions seem to outline a provocative framework for thinking about architecture. So I will attempt to follow suit, to elaborate through questions yet another framework, or perhaps a post/work, for architecture.

A question, in one sense, is a frame for an answer, a frame for a discourse that may not be the discourse of the reply. Thus I will use your three numbered questions (only two of which are actually numbered, question 3 beginning instead with the word *finally*) as posts to support me (or perhaps as the cards I might play). Indeed, knowing your fondness for precision and numbers, should I inquire further as to what happened to the missing 3, which is, after all, a reflection of the letter *E*?

How, for example, does one respond to such questions as 'Do you believe in God?' or 'What do you think of a culture of glass?' or 'What about the homeless?' without sounding either evasive or irrelevant? How does one assert that certain urgent problems such as homelessness or poverty are no more questions of architecture than they are of poetry or philosophy without sounding callous? These are indeed human problems, but architecture, poetry, and philosophy are not the domains in which they will be solved. In that sense, such issues are no more relevant than my inquiring about your own domestic, suburban home in relationship to your work. Yet, if I fail to answer, others will ask why. No answer will be interpreted as an answer: as a refusal to answer or an inability to answer or a lack of concern to answer, but never the real answer. The real answer: that to answer is impossible either in the medium of letter or of glass.

Your questions probably require a volume, several volumes, inscribed for you. Perhaps with that you, too, would be led to 'ruin and destruction'. But if I do not answer some of your questions, it is not through lack of time, interest or compassion, but rather the questions, perhaps, cannot be answered in architecture.

I publish this letter with yours because I think that every architect should witness philosophy against the wall, should have to answer, for themselves, some of your questions. And possibly some day you, too, will problematise architecture in your discourse and thus be forced to answer these same questions. I wonder in passing if the fact of your questions points to problems that architecture poses for something that is now named deconstruction and for the 'you' that may now have become the aura of Jacques Derrida. Therefore my response may be less to answer to the specific questions, frames, frame-ups that you have proposed than to place my cards on the table, cards that, perhaps, cause you some fraction of dis/ease.

Jacques, you ask me about the *supplement* and the *essential* in my work. You crystallise these questions in the term/word/material *glas/s*. You glaze over the fact that your conceptual play with the multifaceted term *glas* is not simply translatable into architectural glass. One understands that the assumption of the identity of the material glass and your ideas of *glas*, in their superficial resemblance of letters, is precisely the concern of literary deconstruction; but this becomes a problem when one turns to the event of building. This difference is important. For though one can conceptualise in the building material glass, it is not necessarily only as you suggest — as an absence of secrecy, as a clarity. While glass is a literal presence in architecture, it also indexes an absence, a void in a solid wall. Thus glass in architecture is traditionally said to be both absence and presence.

Yes, I am preoccupied by absence, but not in terms of this simple presence/absence dialectic, as you might think. For me as an architect, each concept, as well as each object, has all that it is *not* inscribed within it as traces. I am preoccupied with absence, not voids or glass, because architecture, unlike language, is dominated by presence, by the real existence of the signified. Architecture requires one to detach the signified not only from its signifier but also from its condition as presence. For example, a hole in a plane, or a vertical element, must be detached not only from its signifier — a window or a column — but also from its condition of presence — that is, as a sign of the possibility of light and air or of structure — without, at the same time, causing the room to be dark or the building to fall down. This is not the case in language where you and I can play with *glas* and *post*, *gaze* and *glaze*, precisely because of the traditional dialectic of presence and absence.

It is improbable to effect in architecture what you do in language. Opacity is the possibility of the poetic in language. It screens the distance between sign and signifier. Opacity and density are possible in glass, even in clear glass, which, in your quotation, is 'the enemy of secrecy'. The textuality of glass in architecture is different from the textuality of *glas*, the letters *g*, *l*, *a*, *s*. Modes of translation from one language to another, from one syntax to another, can do things with the word *glass* that architecture cannot. For that matter, the hinge between Derridean thought and architecture is in neither glass nor ash (gash or ass may be better). It would be naïve to think so, particularly in the face of your work. It is no longer possible to simply accept naïveté in your thought about architecture or in thought in general about architecture. One may have started there. Yet that *there*, which is not the there of my architecture, is difficult because it is dominated by what is already there in architecture: another tradition of sign and signified. Your idea of glass is eminently utilitarian and transparent; whereas there is no transparency in your *glas*, perhaps only *verre* and not truth, no (-)*itas*. Wordplay which produces both opacity and transparency in language has no easy equivalent in architecture. The closest, perhaps, is the classical ideal of virtual space, or the Gesalt of figure-ground. Even so , neither of these concepts moves architecture from its belief in the theory of origins to something *other*. Only when the thought-to-be essential relationship of architecture to function is undermined, that is, when the traditional dialectical, hierarchical, and supplemental relationship of form to function is displaced, can the condition of presence, which problematises any possible displacement of architecture, be addressed. It is not that there is no possibility of deconstruction in architecture, but it cannot simply take issue with what you have called the metaphysics of presence. In my view, your deconstruction of the presence/absence dialectic is inadequate for architecture precisely because architecture is not a two-term, but a three-term system. In architecture, there is another condition, which I call *presentness*, that is neither absence nor presence, form nor function, neither the particular use of a sign nor the crude existence of reality, but rather an excessive condition between sign and the Heideggerian notion of being: the formation and ordering of the discursive event that is architecture. As long as there is a strong bond between form and function, sign and being, the excess that contains the possibility of presentness will be repressed. The need to overcome presence, the need to supplement an architecture that will always be and look like architecture, the need to break apart the strong bond between form and function, is what my architecture addresses. In its displacement of the traditional role of function it does not deny that architecture must function, but rather suggests that architecture may also function without necessarily symbolising that function, that the presentness of architecture is irreducible to the presence of its function or its signs.

All of these issues lead into our differences on the question of aura. You want no aura, or the deconstruction of aura, and I want this aura that is the aura of the third — this excess that is presentness. My architecture asks, Can there be an *other* in the condition of aura in architecture, an aura that both is secret and contains its own secret, the mark of its absent openness? This may involve the difference between the thing as word, and the thing as object, between language and architecture. Unlike language, which is understandable through the gaze alone, in architecture there is no such thing as the sign of a column or a window without the actual presence of a column or a window. Both the gaze and the body are implicated by the interiority of architecture. This interiority, this necessity to enclose, is not found in language or even in painting or sculpture. Thus, you may be right that architecture strives for an aura, one having nothing to do with text, or good or bad, or truth or God, but, nevertheless, with something that needs to be explained. Presentness is the possibility of another aura in architecture, one not in the sign or in being, but in a third condition. Neither nostalgic for meaning or presence or dependent on them, this third, non-dialectical condition of space exists only in an excess that is more, or less, than the traditional, hierarchical, Vitruvian preconditions of form: structure, function, and beauty. This excess is not based on the tradition of plenitude. This condition of aura is perhaps something that also remains unproblematised in your work, despite your protestations to the contrary. I believe that by virtue of architecture's unique relationship to presence, to what I call presentness, it will always be a domain of aura. After all, aura is presence of absence, the possibility of a presentness of something else. It is this *else* that my architecture attempts to reveal.

I say this because when I read your work on Valerio Adami, I am fascinated by your discourse, yet when I look at the painting, I find it lacking: it lacks the aura possible in marking a surface with lines, paint, colour, texture, etc. I feel the same way about psychoanalysts who put symbolic and ritualistic drawings and paintings in frames on the walls of their offices and think of them (because they are framed) as art. While these works may have psychological content and intent, they are, for me, illustrated psychology, not art, because they do not establish a critical relationship to traditional art. They are not analytical or critical in the terms of their own medium, either painting or drawing. They do not take into account the history and specificity of painting. No matter how important your thoughts on Adami are, he remains uninteresting to me as an artist because of this very lack of aura. Now you probably believe that this painterly aura I speak of is one of secrecy and distance, a traditional aura of an original work ripe for deconstruction. But I am not talking about this kind of Benjaminian aura — the aura of metaphysical fullness — but rather of an *other* aura evolving from the remainder of the here and now after its deconstruction: presentness, not the presence, of the work. Traditional architecture collapses presentness into presence and has always viewed their separation as dangerous. In my view, the most virulent translation of undecidability in architecture rests on this point.

My architecture holds that architecture could write something else, something other than its own traditional texts of function, structure, meaning, and aesthetics. So, as you have observed, it always has strived, implicitly, for this other aura. Now, it is one thing to speak theoretically about these matters and it is another thing to act on them. You see, Jacques, when you leave your own realm, when you attempt to be consistent, whatever that might mean in architecture, it is precisely then that you do not understand the implications for deconstruction in architecture — when deconstruction leaves your hands. For me to toe the party line is useless; for in the end, Jacques, you would be more unhappy with an architecture that illustrates deconstruction than with my work, wherein the buildings themselves become, in a way, useless — lose their traditional significance of function and appropriate an other aura, one of excess, of presentness, and not presence. No amount of talking about absence, or of word play between *presence* and *present* can create such an aura that distances architecture in building from the past and future of building.

In the end, my architecture cannot be what it should be, but only what it can be. Only when you add one more reading of my work alongside your reading of it in pictures and texts — that is, a reading in the event of a building — only there will you see the play between presence and presentness, only then will you know whether I have been faithful.

Yet, I remain yours faithfully,

Peter Eisenman

ACCIDENTS WILL HAPPEN
ROBERT E SOMOL

To the phantasmagorias of space to which the flanêur abandons himself, correspond the phantasmagorias of time indulged in by the gambler. Gambling converts time into a narcotic.
Walter Benjamin, 'Paris, Capital of the Nineteenth Century', *Reflections*.

In classic Aristotelian philosophy, substance is necessary and the accident is relative and contingent. At the moment, there's an inversion: the accident is becoming necessary and substance relative and contingent . . . At the end of the 19th century, museums exhibited machines; at the end of the 20th century, I think we must grant the formative dimension of the accident its rightful place in a new museum. They ought to exhibit — I don't know how yet — train derailments, pollution, collapsing, buildings, etc.
Paul Virilio, *Pure War*.

Passing time, Jacques Derrida and Peter Eisenman have recently been exchanging personal notes and building up a public debt. Interested in and speculating on the truth in architecture, Derrida's signed IOU closes with a series of inquiries on the credits and liabilities of his account with Eisenman. At the end of his second postscript, Derrida would have Eisenman establish his standing:

> *What would be an architecture that, without holding, without standing upright, vertically, would not fall again into ruin? How do all these possibilities and even questions (those of holding up, holding together, standing or not) record themselves, if you think that they do? What traces do they leave in what you would build right now in Spain, in Japan, in Ohio, in Berlin, in Paris, and, tomorrow, I hope, in Irvine?*[1]

For his part, Eisenman promises to 'attempt to follow suit' and 'place my cards on the table'.[2] But since this exchange the issue of Eisenman's debt to Derrida (and vice versa) has continued without resolution and it remains uncertain as to whether the gambit of laying cards on the table was played in order to take a trick (*faire un pli*) or to fold. Now, however, with the Rebstockpark project for the development of offices and housing in Frankfurt, Eisenman has begun to size up the point of standing, and it is an account that relies exactly on this undecidability of the fold.

In part, the stand-off between the partners Eisenman and Derrida involves the double set of books they are keeping about the work, over the issue of whether the pair 'presence/absence' is being thought dialectically or not, on the position of the homeless and the value of aura, and on who will take responsibility for the losses incurred due to the displacement of the one and the deconstruction of the other. For Eisenman, architecture — unlike writing — must struggle against its literal presence, which has traditionally been reinforced by the icons of 'strong form'. As a non-dialectical condition between presence and absence (and perhaps, too, between the beautiful and the sublime), Eisenman posits the term 'presentness' as one possibility for a 'weak' practice,[3] the hazard of the architectural event. Thus, the play of folds in the Frankfurt scheme has more to do with the untimely than the unhomely, and the project emerges as an urban analogue to the cinematic chronography of Robbe-Grillet's *Last Year at Marienbad*. The between condition of presentness necessitates a consideration of the arbitrary, the accidental.

Traditionally, architecture and urbanism have been generated and evaluated on the basis of a theorisation of the object. For example, in Colin Rowe's post-war discourse on Modernism both the phenomenal transparency of Corbusier's Garches and the literal transparency of the Bauhaus's machine-like repetition of space can only be considered as bounded objects, autonomous products of intentionality that allow for a decidable meaning through interpretation. Similarly, 'complexity and contradiction' are also criteria that assume a metaphysical fullness of presence, that require a clearly framed object in order to initiate readings of depth. The Frankfurt project, however, compels a rethinking of architecture and urbanism from a theory of the accident rather than the object. Complexity and contradiction (and decidable interpretation) characterise the object; chaos and catastrophe (and mediation) elicit aspects of the accident. As an index, the accident occurs between objects, and subjects.[4] In bidding accidents to occur, a weak practice must operate between strong form categories while supplanting intentions with intensities.

A 'weak' or textual or 'between' architecture and urbanism cannot simply displace strong form by rejection since that would result merely in a 'radical', though ultimately containable, expressionism, one that reaffirms established procedures of the discipline. In other words, previous oppositional practices have acted as a series of exceptions to the rule that require and reinforce a decidable frame of reference for the successful transmission of their 'critical' message. Since strong form categories can be neither simply abandoned nor reproduced, the dialectical economy of same and other must be elided, and Eisenman's Frankfurt scheme attempts this through an initial investigation of three traditional integers of strong form design: typology, morphology and archaeology. The project then operates to blur these decision frames — the proper categories that authorise univocal meaning and strong narrative — by subjecting them to chance affiliations in order to expose repressed or secondary readings and to activate the latent conditions within strong codes and contexts. Through a rigorous rereading of the history and morphology of the site, the programme requirements, and a reconsideration of the dominant building forms in and around Frankfurt, Eisenman's design process begins to weaken or loosen the determinacy of a categorical or transcendental typology, the figure-ground gestalt of morphology, and the historical or mythological symbolism of archaeology, while multiplying the reframing possibilities of the outside text(s).

Rebstockpark falls within the third green belt that encircles Frankfurt, halfway between the historic downtown and the international airport, and is itself framed by a branch of the autobahn to the north and railway lines to the south. In addition to providing five million square feet of office and housing space, the Rebstockpark programme indicated that the solution should consider the site as a gateway to Frankfurt, a city whose name (ford or crossing of the Franks) suggests its historically important location as a transportation route along the Main River. Given the proximity of Rebstockpark to the Messe, the location of Frankfurt's annual book fair, as well as the significance of the area to the history of printing and book publishing, the Frankfurt project assumes the site to be 'already written', to exist as the signature of a book. But rather than treat the folding of the signature as a transcendental and neatly repeatable function, Eisenman loosens the direct attachment of the fold to the organised legitimacy of a locally specific referent. In other words, in order to open itself to a textual reading the fold must undergo an 'accident', a mistranslation, and this consists of its fortuitous (and necessary) alignment with the catastrophe theory of René Thom.

While differential calculus can be employed to describe phenomena where change is smooth and continuous, René Thom's mathematical model can account for events that are discontinuous and possess a bimodal distribution of probabilities. For example, when contradictory stimuli or input are present there is a much greater probability for movement between extreme actions or outcomes rather than the establishment of a balanced, 'neutral' position. Thom's

seven archetypal catastrophe models are able to describe these abrupt moments of instantaneous and imperceptible change where extreme conditions suddenly drop off into one another without coming to rest in a neutral middle ground. Each of these seven forms possess an aspect of the 'fold' internal to it where there is a kind of 'jump cut' between extreme positions on a graph, where there is almost a simultaneous inhabitation of alternative possibilities. For Eisenman's entry to the Frankfurt competition the 'butterfly catastrophe' was appropriated as figure and process, a complex five-dimensional catastrophe that can only be appreciated in section. As an initial approximation of the formal character of this butterfly fold one may imagine the double underlooping of the bow tie, which refers coincidentally (or not) to Eisenman's own folded, sartorial signature.

Rather than imposing an abstracted folding process on a *tabula rasa* site, the Eisenman scheme imaginatively re-reads Rebstockpark as the site of a catastrophe, as an already folded moment in the urban fabric. In addition to noticing the repeated morphology of variously scaled 'pleats' that fall within the site itself, this framing of the park exposes one aspect of the involution in the history of the development of Frankfurt. As a result of air attacks during World War II, which left traces on the Rebstock site in the form of bomb craters, the postwar development of the city folded back upon itself, such that the 'oldest' buildings of the central city were in fact the most recently (re)constructed. In addition to thematising circulation and transformation in the city of 'the crossing of the Franks', the folded gateway of Rebstockpark recognises the temporal disjunction of reversal of 'old' and 'new' simulated within Frankfurt's limits.

It is precisely the kind of temporal dislocation exhibited in the Rebstock project that Paul Virilio has suggested demonstrates the obsolescence of a bounded urban space:

> The city was the means of mapping out a political space that existed in a given political duration. Now speed — ubiquity, instantaneousness — dissolves the city, or rather displaces it. And displaces it, I would say, in time . . . When we know that every day there are over 100,000 people in the air, we can consider it a foreshadowing of future society: no longer a society of sedentarisation, but one of passage . . . one concentrated in the vector of transportation . . . Before, you had to leave in order to arrive. Now things arrive before anyone's leaving.[5]

Eisenman's Frankfurt scheme marks this interchangeability of here and there, *da* and *fort*, in the contemporary situation of 'generalised arrivals'. As with Thom's catastrophic types, the plan(e)s of Rebstockpark mark an instantaneous collapse of inside and outside, vertical and horizontal, object and setting. Rather than a narrative (strong time) succession of presents, these event-folds inhabit 'peaks of present' where there is a coexistence of a present of the future, a present of the present, and a present of the past. In describing the time-image found in the work of Robbe-Grillet, Gilles Deleuze writes:

> An accident is about to happen, it happens, it has happened; but equally it is at the same time that it will take place, has already taken place and is in the process of taking place; so that, before taking place, it has not taken place, and, taking place, will not take place . . . etc.[6]

In the undecidability of whether the Rebstock site has contracted to absorb a neutral exterior net or is in the process of expanding to unfold its information across a larger area, the project offers an urban version of peeks at presentness, similar to the literary and cinematic visions of Robbe-Grillet and the mathematical models of Thom. In both large and small scale episodes there is a multiplication of tenses: already folded, folding, not yet folded.

As an urban initiative, the Rebstockpark plan occupies a place between a utopian internationalism and a nostalgic regionalism. As suggested above, it attempts neither to predict the future nor reclaim the past, but evinces a condition of 'presentness', Derrida's *maintenant*, a 'nowness' that Lyotard has associated with the sublime and the endeavour to create events.[7] In part, this condition signals a catastrophe between the vertical and horizontal, figure and ground, in contrast to the approach articulated by Colin Rowe in *Collage City*. For Rowe, urban space requires a texture, a balance between figure and ground, or solid/object and void/space, where both maintain an iconic presence, a meaning. The collage technique Rowe associates with Picasso is intended to enforce a 'balancing act' between scaffold and exhibit, structure and event. In distinction to the structured events of this collage urbanism, the typologies deviated through the folded net of Eisenman's project establish opportunities for mutual exchange between the residential area and the office park. While horizontal bands are each marked by specific intensities depending on where they fall along the fold, the system frustrates any oppositional reading of presence; landscape, inter- and intra-building relations, and intervals become one, an irresolution in which neither figure nor ground can maintain plenitude or integrity. Due to the vagaries of folding, some forms are joined fortuitously to create new, monstrous formal and programmatic types while others occupy multiple sites or moments, as when ground plane infects elevation like muddy turf caught in the face mask of a football helmet. In this multidimensional urbanism, plan is no longer an adequate tool for either the production (extrusion) or reception

(gestalt) of solids and voids, and there is no stable iconic referent for understanding the whole or its parts. Any two-dimensional mediation of the scheme ultimately serves to sign its own inadequacy; plan, elevation and section all act as bluffs to raise the ante of architecture. It is when the project outbids itself, when there is a move beyond the limits of any single interpretive system, technique, or decision frame, that there is a chance for textuality to replace texture.

The urbanism of Rebstockpark attempts to change the dialectical condition — the necessity of the pair — on which classical-humanist difference has been founded and from which it has always been reduced to sameness. Wagering on the arbitrary and accidental, the topological folds and faults of this weak urbanism open the possibility for a 'third', an imperceptible and non-dialectical term that may be more than two but which may also be something less than one, a multiplicity without number or unity: a pure function of multiplication (the *x*-fold). Whereas the structure of the pair attaches things to function, utility and propriety, the Frankfurt project proposes the double without a pair, the activation of the supplements that operate between dialectical opposites. Located on the outskirts of Frankfurt, between the interior and exterior of the city, the Rebstockpark project makes excessive its status as an urban *passe-partout*.[8] In the discourse of framing, the *passe-partout* is the mat that serves to separate the interior edge of the figure with the exterior edge of the frame. Often made of cardboard, the *passe-partout* is traditionally an invisible supplement that, with respect to either object-figure or context-background, disappears into the other.

Eisenman's proposal activates its secondary status by both pulling in context beyond the perimeter of the site (eg the autobahn and swimming pool) and extending its reconfigured morphology beyond its limits (eg the S-Bahn stop). Through involutions of the *passe-partout*, periphery can no longer be thought of as edge and centre cannot be equated with figure. Like the paragon, the *passe-partout* of this project 'perverts all the links between part and whole', and opens 'the play of dis/appearing to the possibility of dis-pairing.'[9]

Experimenting with processes of the fold entails a significant doubling back from a dialectical thinking through the horizontal and vertical cuts of plan and section. Thus, the Frankfurt project follows a path other than the Guardiola House and Koizumi, each of which tended to substitute section for plan, and thus simply exchanged one organising cut for another. Despite the respective successes of both, section came to assume, naturally, some of the transcendental qualities of plan in each. Frankfurt is not a sectional scheme because it does not privilege any cut, but rather thinks plan sectionally, since the fold hinges on the mutual-becoming of both the horizontal and the vertical. The folds of Rebstockpark activate the *passe-partout* twice over, once typologically, between building and ground, and then morphologically, between site and non-site. In each case a traditionally invisible edge or frame is opened up to its own figurative possibilities. Moreover, the fold eliminates the nostalgia for the cut of the historical avant-garde, for the mechanico-physical aspect of early 20th-century collage and montage. Instead, the logic of the fold mimes electronic processes of dubbing and sampling since it generates seamless loops that lapse back on themselves to establish new tracks. It invents and inhabits an *other* plane, one where neither vertical nor horizontal is a dependant variable of the other, where both are copies without origin that possess no legitimate line of evolution or revolution.

The modern age presents itself as an enlightened dialectic between two, strong-form bounded conditions, the autonomy of the object and the determinacy of interpretation, which together constitute an identical economy of inside (subjective interiority) and outside (projective exteriority). As Julia Kristeva suggests, interpretation is allied with semiology in that both attempt to 'relate a sign (or event-sign) to a signified in order to *act* accordingly, consistently, consequently'.[10] This modern sense of interpretation as transformation or cure requires an excavation of the depths (whether Marx's dialectic or Freud's unconscious) to arrive at a truth that lies somewhere beyond or beneath the contingent surface. With the demise of a discourse organised around the subject of man and the integrated (hierarchical) sign, this type of inquiry has been eclipsed. On all levels of discussion, the outraged 'What does it mean?' that attended Modernism has been replaced by the familiar 'What's that from?' This post-interpretive posture represents one aspect of what has come to be called the Post-Modern, an age of citation or mediation.

Throughout various levels of cultural production in the late 19th century — including the European master narratives or deep logics — the 'Classical Age' expressed itself through a compulsive unwillingness to let chance count as chance. With the rise of the social sciences at the time of the White City and Beaux Arts urban planning came a commitment to causation, will, and subjective contract between sovereign individuals. For example, the resistance to the development of tort law in American legal practice required that mass industrial accidents be framed as issues of contract and autonomous choice. A common problematic in historical moments of technological change, the dominant discourse in late 19th-century science, literature, art, philosophy, law and politics seemed to revolve around the question of accident versus will, a difficulty Rowe continues to negotiate in his attempt to balance an urbanism of event and structure.

In large part, the discussion of action and accident around the turn of the century can be attributed to concerns arising with the early history of photography. As Walter Benn Michaels indicates the early discourse of photography revolved around the question of intentionality and will, of whether this new mechanical procedure retained enough aspects of individual choice and autonomy to be counted as an art.[11] Again, this new technology of representation led to a renewed effort to repress chance and the accident. For Michaels, this effort manifests itself in the scientific and literary concern with gambling during the period, and the attempt to describe such acts as the expression of will and intent. Curiously, it is precisely photography and gambling — the primary threats to the 19th-century view of liberal-humanist subjectivity — that often serve as analogies for Eisenman's own projects and situate his relationship to them. Significantly, as John Berger says of photographs, gambling acts are not unintended but are 'weak in intentionality'.[12]

In contrast to the interpretative deep logics and strong forms of the last century, the chance Eisenman takes at Frankfurt is for an urbanism and architecture that exhibit characteristics more like those of gambling and photography, that preserve the accident, that display a 'weak intentionality', and allow a weakening of architecture's meaning system. The indexical signature here becomes the face of an event, like gaming or taking a picture. As the ruins (and windfalls) of catastrophe theory, the structural faults of Rebstockpark preserve the possibility of the accident, the undecideable, through a spatial and temporal dilation, the moment of being here and there, now and then. Thus, Eisenman's urbanism, too, learns from Las Vegas, but unlike that of Robert Venturi the experience it takes from the untimely and unhomely desert of Nevada is indexical not iconic.

As Jacques Derrida has written, 'unexpectability conditions the very structure of an event',[13] and it is, finally, the hazard of the event that is at stake in a 'weak' practice. In his tentative defence of Robert Venturi as an architect of the event, Geoff Bennington takes up the argument that Modernism failed to address adequately the separation between inside and outside, suggesting that perhaps architecture, unlike Derridean discourse, is constitutionally unable to do so: 'A radical "flowing space" would not simply reduce the wall to a sheet of glass, but would show that the inside is merely a fold or invagination in a more generalised "outside".[14] It is precisely this challenge of the fold that the Rebstockpark scheme pursues, a coincidence that should not pass without a certain humour as Bennington's article eventually develops a critique of Eisenman's work against that of Venturi and Tschumi.

In distinguishing 'the event' from a narrative sequence organised by plot, John Rajchman maintains that it is 'a moment of erosion, collapse, questioning, or problematisation of the very assumptions of the setting within which a drama may take place, occasioning the chance or possibility of another, different setting'.[15] Events are not in themselves accidental so much as the fact that their occurrence engenders the realisation that what has been taken to be the necessary and natural is accidental. The Rebstock project directs an architectural 'event', a manifestation of 'weak time', to the extent that it elicits an active reframing of typology, context, function and archaeology. Neither historicist nor progressive — and therefore other than the category of the *possible*— this kind of time can be thought of as *virtual*: 'a reality of which we do not yet possess the concept.'[16] The virtual is merely an historical impossibility, not a logical or necessary one. As an investigation of the virtual, the Rebstock proposal performs an experimentation rather than an interpretation. And it is through this experimental quality — presentness as the untimely — that the scheme projects a 'virtual reality'. In this way the two avant-gardes may begin to be distinguished, in the interval that separates the new from the now, the up-to-date iconicity of the machine from the indexicality of disappearance. It is on the becoming-imper-

ceptible of the between that weak practice wagers its ability to notice the difference.

After the advent of the fold the question remains open as to whether the virtual event forms of the Frankfurt competition will stand: a chance: to collapse the discourse of Modern urbanism or to serve as adequate collateral to the enquiries of Derrida. In the trajectory from object to accident one recalls, vaguely, a past discourse within Modernism against theatre and the event, a religion of the original that enforced its other, the codification of rules for its exact reproduction, and the legislation against the daily hazard of experimentation. But, in ANY event, we are all mediators and mistranslators most or all of our lives. Presentness is trace [sic].

Quotations are taken from: Walter Benjamin, 'Paris, capital of the Nineteenth Century', in Reflections, *edited by Peter Demetz, Schocken Books, New York, 1986, p159; and Paul Virilio and Sylvere Lontringer,* Pure War, *translated by Mark Polizzotti, Semiotext(e), New York, 1983, pp32-3.*

NOTES

1 Jacques Derrida, 'A Letter to Peter Eisenman', *Assemblage* 12, August, 1990, p13.

2 Peter Eisenman, 'Post/EL Cards: A reply to Jacques Derrida', *Assemblage* 12, August, 1990, pp14-15.

3 This idea of presentness is in contrast to Michael Fried's usage of the concept in his defence of high Modernism. For Fried, presentness implies a bounded object of depth and plenitude, the quality of which is instantaneously self-evident such that it induces immediate faith and conviction. In some ways, Eisenman's usage has more in common with the perpetual reframing and temporal limitlessness of minimalist work that Fried was arguing against. See Michael Fried, 'Art and Objecthood', *Artforum*, June 1967.

4 As early as the Guardiola House, Eisenman had invoked the notion of the 'controlled accident'. This begins to suggest a connection to gaming since Roland Barthes describes the initial delivery of the panchinko player in the same terms. Moreover, it begins to situate 'weak urbanism' in terms of the tradition of the Picturesque, as Uvedale Price's attempts at 'directing accidents' attests. See, eg, Sidney Robinson, *Inquiry into the Picturesque,* University of Chicago Press, Chicago, 1991. A full discussion of the parallels and differences between these two attitudes is beyond the scope of the present paper.

5 Ibid, pp60, 64 and 68.

6 Gilles Deleuze, *Cinema 2: The Time-Image,* University of Minnesota Press, Minneapolis, 1989, p100.

7 See Jacques Derrida, 'Point de folie — Maintenant l'architecture', *AA Files*, 1986, pp65-75, and Jean-Francois Lyotard, 'The Sublime and the Avant-Garde', *Artforum*, April, 1984, pp36-43.

8 For a discussion of this concept, see Jacques Derrida, *The Truth in Painting*, translated by Geoff Bennington and Ian McLeod, University of Chicago Press, Chicago, 1987.

9 Ibid, pp343, 376.

10 Julia Kristeva, 'Psychoanalysis and the Polis', *Critical Inquiry*, September 1982, p79.

11 See, eg, Walter Benn Michaels, *The Gold Standard and the Logic of Naturalism*, University of California Press, Berkeley, CA, 1987.

12 John Berger and Jean Mohr, *Another Way of Looking*, New York, 1982, p90.

13 Jacques Derrida, 'My Chances/*Mes Chances*', in *Taking Chances*, edited by Joseph H Smith and William Kerrigan, Johns Hopkins University Press, Baltimore, 1988, p6.

14 Geoff Bennington, 'Complexity Without Contradiction in Architecture', *AA Files* 15, Summer 1987, p16.

15 John Rajchman, *Philosophical Events: Essays of the '80s*, Columbia University Press, New York, 1991, pviii.

16 Ibid, p160.

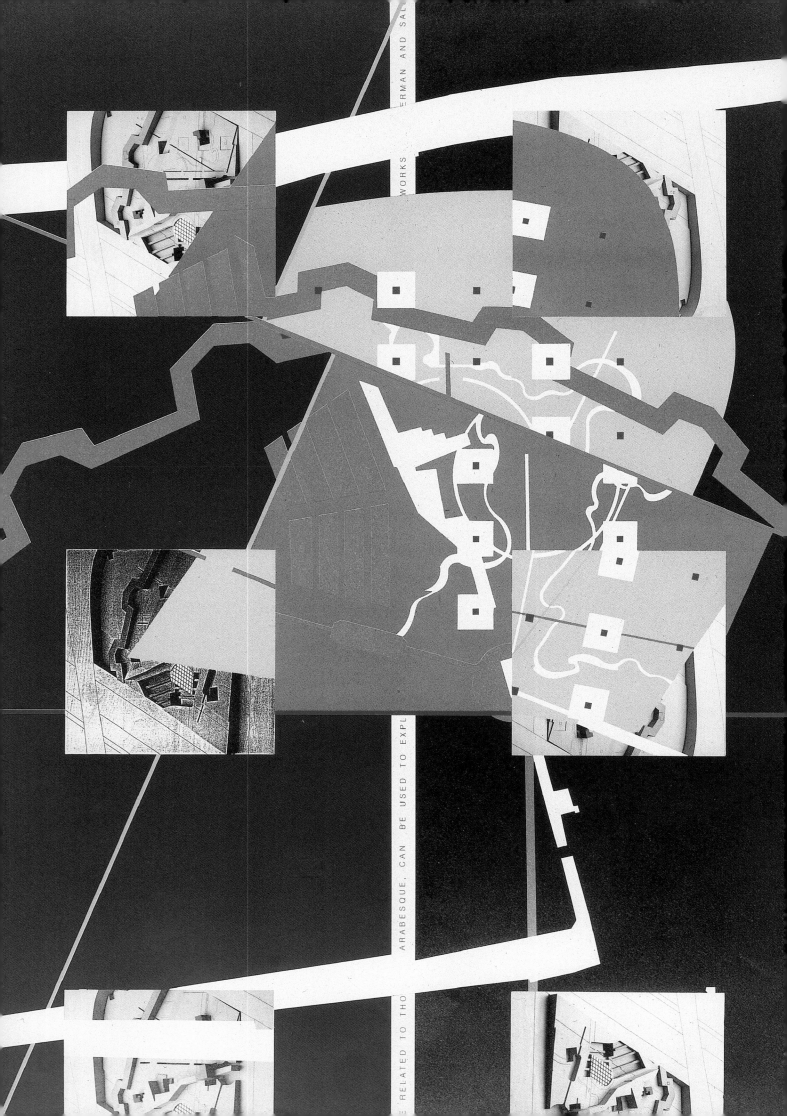

ARABESQUE, CAN BE USED TO EXPL… WORKS …ERMAN AND SAL… …E RELATED TO THO…

REFUSING ARCHITECTURE
MARK C TAYLOR

The absence of unity and coherence in life as well as in art does not remove the desire to create continuity where there is none. In June of 1988, Philip Johnson attempted to bring a semblance of order to the disorder of contemporary architecture by mounting an exhibition at the Museum of Modern Art entitled 'Deconstructivist Architecture'. The show included exemplary work by seven architects. In his introductory essay for the catalogue, Johnson is tempted to draw a parallel between the Deconstructivist show and the exhibition devoted to 'International Style Architecture' which he and Henry-Russell Hitchcock had sponsored in the same museum 60 years earlier. But Johnson wisely resists the temptation, for he realises that 'Deconstructivist architecture represents no movement; it is not a creed. It has no "three rules" of compliance. It is not even "seven architects".'[1]

In their exploration of what Johnson labels 'violated perfection', the architects Johnson assembles reject the pure formalism of Modernism as well as the frivolous figuration of Post-Modernism. Each in their way seeks a third course that is neither Modern nor Post-Modern. But beyond this common quest, they share little. They are not even all interested in the philosophical style of critical analysis that lends the show its name: Derridean deconstruction. Of the architects included in the MOMA show, only two demonstrate serious and sustained interest in deconstruction: Tschumi and Eisenman. But even here, differences outweigh similarities. While Tschumi reads deconstruction through Bataille, Eisenman approaches deconstruction with Derrida. These alternative deconstructions lead to different architectures. Though Tschumi and Eisenman both seek a third way *between* Modernism and Post-Modernism, Eisenman's refusal is more disruptive than Tschumi's re-fusal.

Heralded and attacked as 'the first deconstructive structure ever built', Le Parc de La Villette is, in the words of its architect, 'the largest discontinuous building in the world'. The Park, Tschumi explains, 'can be seen to encourage conflict over synthesis, fragmentation over unity, madness and play over careful management' (CF, vii).[2] Tschumi's architecture is guided by the notions of discontinuity, distortion, fragmentation, repetition, transference, rupture, interruption, and dislocation. By disfiguring Modern forms and Post-Modern figures, Tschumi probes the uncanny 'place' where 'space mingles with the unconscious'. If Bataille's

texts perform writing-as-experience-of-limits, and Masson's art embodies painting/drawing-as-experience-of-limits, then Tschumi's deconstructions stage architecture-as-experience-of-limits. The site of this liminal architecture is the border that is approached in 'borderline states'.

The Park is located at the edge of an edge, margin of a margin, and border of a border of Paris. 'La Villette', Tschumi points out, 'is right on the edge of one of the walls, with the suburbs just beyond' (CV, 26). But the Park is not only *on* a border; it *is* a border that joins and disjoins two cities within the city. Le Parc de La Villette is suspended between La Cité de la Musique and La Cité des Sciences et de L'Industrie.

Begun in 1983 as one of the *Grands Projets d'urbanisme parisien*, Le Parc de La Villette is located on a 125-acre site in the northeast corner of Paris. Responding to the programme's charge to create an 'urban park for the 21st century', La Villette contains cultural and entertainment facilities ranging from art galleries, music halls and open-air theatres, to restaurants, computer displays and playgrounds. The City of Music, designed by Christian de Portzamparc, is located at the southern entrance to the Park. In the midst of the City of Music stands the Grande Halle that provides space for temporary exhibitions and performances. The literature distributed by the Park's information centre unwittingly describes the hall in Bataillian terms: 'Constructed in 1867 by Jules de Mérindol, student of Louis Janvier, the Grand Hall was, from 1869-1974, the "Temple" of the sale of beef in the area of the cattle market de la Villette.'

The northern entrance to the Park is dominated by the imposing City of Sciences and Industry. Adrien Fainsilber's construction clearly expresses the principles of modern science and technology it is designed to exhibit. Combining references to classical Greece with the most advanced technology and industrial materials, Fainsilber creates a structure that is not merely Modern but Futuristic. The multiform and interactive interior offers a variety of settings for an extraordinary array of exhibitions devoted to the natural and physical sciences. When one passes through the gates of this City, one enters a world that approaches the realm of science fiction.

Between the City of Music and the City of Sciences and Industry, Tschumi locates his Park. The dominant feature of the Park is a series of 10-metre red cubes, which are symmetrically placed on plots of 120 square metres. These are La Villette's famed Follies. Each Folly is a distinctive variation on the common cubic structure. The Follies that have been completed provide space for the information centre, a postal station, a café, video studios, and playrooms for children. Between the Follies are open lawns, occasional gardens and waterways. Numerous walkways transect the Park on different levels. Complex and apparently unstable support systems complement an undulating 15-foot-wide cantilevered canopy to transform parts of the Park into a labyrinthian maze.

At the border of the Park, along the margin where reason meets folly and civilisation encounters madness, there looms *Le Géode*, a giant sphere 36 metres in diameter that encloses *la salle de spectacle*. This massive reflective sphere recalls a similar structure that is the logo for Disney's Magic Kingdom of the society of spectacle — EPCOT Center. The pristine surface of the sphere, which gathers earth and sky by mirroring each in the other, is comprised of 6,433 triangular plaques. Neither precisely solar nor lunar, the Géode appears to be a brilliant silver sun whose superficial triangles recall the pyramidal monuments of the Egyptian god Ra. Such pyramids are built to cover the abyss over which (the) all is suspended. The crystalline geometry of abstract constructions represents the desire to find an exit from the labyrinth of death and decay by stopping time.

In an important essay entitled 'Questions of Space: The Pyramid and the Labyrinth (or the Architectural Paradox)', Tschumi contrasts Modern architecture with his version of deconstructive architecture through the images of the pyramid and the labyrinth.[3] While the pyramid represents reason and civilisation, the labyrinth is the sign of folly and madness. For Modernists, Tschumi argues, architecture is the creation of the rational mind in which every trace of irrationality and sensuality is refused. In designing their 'dematerialised' buildings, proponents of Modernism endlessly manipulate linguistic models in an effort to discover ideal forms and essential structures that resist the corrosive effects of time and history. Tschumi insists that Modernism's 'white crusade' involves a hygienic search for 'absolute truth' in which the material and sensual aspects of life are purged. In their flight from death, however, Modernists rush into its arms. Whether explicitly or implicitly, structures that repress Eros are devoted to Thanatos.

In contrast to the death-defying pyramid, the labyrinth entangles us in time ever more deeply. For Tschumi, the labyrinth figures the empirical dimension of space that affects the senses before reason. The opposition between the pyramid and the labyrinth repeats Nietzsche's distinction between Apollonian and Dionysian forms of art. This opposition is, according to Tschumi, insurmountable and hence architecture is irreducibly paradoxical. He does not try to resolve or dissolve this paradox by collapsing one side into the other but contends that 'the definition of architecture may lie at the intersection of logic and pain, rationality and anguish, concept and pleasure' (MT, 9). To redress the imbalance created by Modernism's repressive Apollonian approach, Tschumi develops a Dionysian architecture that is guided by the pleasure principle.

In what appears to be a claim designed to provoke, Tschumi insists that 'architecture is the ultimate erotic "object".'[4] Following Bataille, Tschumi argues that '*eroticism is not the excess of pleasure, but the pleasure of excess.*'[5] The excess that gives pleasure is the remainder or refuse refused by systems and structures constructed to dominate and control everything that is unruly. By soliciting the repressed, Tschumi attempts to subvert Modernism's purist aesthetic and puritan ethic. When understood in this way, the practice of architecture is inseparable from transgression. Tschumi's 1976 manifesto underscores the interplay of Eros and transgression in architecture: 'If you want to follow architecture's first rule, break it. Transgression. An exquisitely perverse act that never lasts. And like a caress is almost impossible to resist. TRANSGRESSION'[6] (AM, 3). By stressing its transgressive nature, Tschumi insists that the pleasure of architecture does not result from the absence of rules but from their infraction. Rules, which are represented in forms and structures, are not simply destroyed but are preserved *as faulty*. Instead of covering faults and mending tears, the architect, who seeks perverse pleasure, opens wounds that never heal by deconstructing structures that once seemed whole. The pleasure of Tschumi's Folly *is not* the salvific pleasure that comes from a return to the Garden or the realisation of the Kingdom, but is rending Dionysian pleasure that arrives with the confession that there is no escape from what Bataille describes as 'the deleterious absurdity of time'.

In Le Parc de La Villette, Tschumi attempts to construct his deconstruction of Modern architecture by means of a method he labels 'superimposition'. Superimposition is a 'strategy of differences' that counters Modernism's totalising syntheses with the dissociation and dis-integration of de-structured structures. In the Park, Tschumi superimposes three different systems — points, lines, and surfaces — without making any effort to unify or integrate them. In superimposition, Tschumi explains,

> the principle of heterogeneity — of multiple, dissociated and inherently confrontational elements — is aimed at disrupting the smooth coherence and reassuring stability of composition, promoting instability and programmatic madness ("a Folie"). Other existing constructions add further to the calculated discontinuity.

Though Tschumi maintains that his design is rigorously non-hierarchical, the point grid actually dominates the other two systems. The grid both imitates the abstract plan of Paris and plots the pattern of the Park. Tschumi's appropriation of the grid, which plays such an important role in Modern art and architecture, is subversive. By turning the grid against itself, he uses it to open rather than close structure. 'Just as [the grid] resisted the humanist claim to authorship,' he argues,

> so it opposed the closure of ideal compositions and geometric dispositions. Through its regular and repetitive markings, the grid defined a potentially infinite field of points of intensity: an incomplete, infinite extension, lacking centre or hierarchy (CF, vi).

While the grid traditionally has been used to centre and ground structures by providing a secure foundation, Tschumi employs the grid to create a decentred structure that is 'utterly discontinuous and often unpredictable'. Indirectly invoking Foucault, whose work informs so much of the Park, Tschumi notes that the grid 'suggests the bars of the asylum or prison, introducing a diagram of order in the disorder of reality'.[7] But the repressed returns to disrupt and disorder systems and structures of control. The point of (no) return is (the) folly.

There is, of course, a long tradition of follies in architecture. The word 'folly' implies the eroticism that Tschumi associates with deconstructive architectural practice. 'Folly' derives from the stem '*beu*' (swelling, flowing, flowering), which it shares with the Greek '*phallos; phallus, ithyphallic* (*ithy*: erect: carried at festivals of Bacchus [*who is also known as Dionysus*])'.[8] Follies historically have been associated with parks and gardens that serve as Arcadian retreats. By providing an escape from the regulations that police routine behaviour, follies become associated with sites of pleasure, excess, and transgression. In the recessive grottoes of these gardens of delight, the refused resurfaces. But, as we have seen, Eros cannot be separated from Thanatos. Follies often include ruins that mark the site where Dionysus meets Cronus. Gardens, Jean Starobinski maintains,

> teach us that we are ephemeral, that we pass on as generations before us have passed on, that wisdom lies in the acceptance of passing seasons and the vicissitudes of life . . . Nature . . . leads us in ecstasy to the idea of ruin and the decay of matter. Our final delight is in abandoning ourselves to death, an exaltation that anticipates the darkness into which we will vanish.[9]

It was not, however, until the Age of Reason that the folly became 'the figure of unreason'. As Tony Vidler points out, 'epitomising a gamut of negative qualities, the folly took on the essential nature of the opposite pole, of extreme undesir-ability, of absolute contradiction. As the emblem of foolish luxury, it offered a warning to spendthrifts and unproductive investors; as totally without function, it provided a spectre of emptiness and uselessness without which function itself was meaningless; close to madness.'

Tschumi's Follies reflect and extend the encounter between madness and civilisation that begins in the Enlightenment. Folly inhabits rational structures as the refuse through whose refusal reason constitutes itself. While the Park's Follies recall works of the Russian Constructivists, their function in Tschumi's overall scheme is deconstructive. Neither inside nor outside the grid, the Follies dislocate the structure within which they are inscribed. In contrast to Modernist Post-Modern architects, who disfigure by adding ornaments and figures to abstract forms, Tschumi's disfiguration deconstructs formal structures by dislocating them from within. Each Folly begins as a cube that is then transformed through a process Tschumi names 'deviation'. 'Deviation is both the excess of rationality and irrationality. As a norm, it contains the components of its own explosion. As a deviation, it frees them. Normality tends towards unity, deviation towards heterogeneity and dissociation' (CF, 27). The Folly is the site of dissociation, which, in Derrida's terms, 'gathers together what it has just dispersed; it reassembles it *as* dispersion'. Never integrated totalities but always divisible in themselves, the Follies are points of 'rupture, discontinuity, disjunction' (CV, 15). As the juncture of disjunction, the Follies explode structure. The deconstructed cubes are 'points of intensity' where forces that come together fly apart and forces that fly apart come together.[10]

In a certain sense, the Follies are useless; they are pointless points. The 'explosion' of structure releases a latter-day potlatch in which expenditure without return becomes consumption that knows no end. In a 1974 manifesto entitled *Fireworks*, Tschumi declares: 'Good architecture must be conceived, erected and burned in vain. The greatest architecture of all is the fireworkers': it perfectly shows the gratuitous consumption of pleasure' (AM, 1). The pleasure of architecture cannot be reappropriated in any productive system, for it remains utterly useless. Rather than a weakness, this uselessness is a strength in a society governed by the principle of profit. Tschumi's architecture works by not working. In other words, when it works, it fails.

The pointlessness of Tschumi's architecture not only points to its uselessness but to its meaninglessness. Though the Follies are sensual, they are not sensible; their sense is nonsense. Modern architects, Tschumi insists, are obsessed with the idea of *presence* in the form of the presence of the idea. For the Modernist, the architect is the master of meaning who constructs significant forms. Since knowledge is power, to master meaning is to gain control. One of the most important aspects of Tschumi's deconstruction of Modernism and Modernist Post-Modernism is his critique of knowledge and meaning. In one of his descriptions of the Park, Tschumi offers his most concise summary of his differences with Modern and Post-Modern architecture:

> The project takes issue with a particular premise of architecture, namely, its obsession with presence, with the idea of a meaning immanent in architectural structures and forms which directs its signifying capacity. The latest resurgence of this myth has been the recuperation, by architects, of meaning, symbol, coding and 'double coding' in an eclectic movement reminiscent of the long tradition of 'revivalisms' and 'symbolisms' appearing throughout history. This architectural Post-Modernism contravenes the reading evident in other domains, where Post-Modernism involves an assault on meaning or, more precisely, a rejection of a well-defined signified that guarantees the authenticity of the work of art. The La Villette project, in contrast, attempts to dislocate and de-regulate meaning, rejecting the 'symbolic' repertory of architecture as a refuge of humanist thought . . . La Villette is a term in constant production, in continuous change; its meaning is never fixed but is always deferred, differed, rendered irresolute by the multiplicity of meanings it inscribes.[CF, vi-vii.]

To stimulate rather than repress multiple meanings, Tschumi attempts to erase the preprogrammed programme by shifting the locus of the production of meaning from the masterful architect to a plurality of readers. This gesture enacts what Roland Barthes describes as 'the death of the author'.

Barthes' essay 'The Third Meaning: Research Notes on Some Eisenstein Stills' indirectly illuminates the nonsense of Tschumi's Follies. In contrast to the more or less transparent informational and symbolic levels, Barthes' third meaning is not obvious but is 'obtuse'. 'Obtuse meaning,' Barthes explains,

> is not directed towards meaning . . . does not even indicate an elsewhere of meaning . . . it outplays meaning — subverts the whole practice of meaning . . . Obtuse meaning appears necessarily as a luxury, an expenditure with no exchange.

In light of the importance of Bataille for Tschumi's architectural theory, it is noteworthy that Barthes explicitly draws on Bataille's interpretation of the carnival to develop his notion of obtuse meaning. The exteriority of Barthes' non-synthetic third is a strange exteriority. Obtuse meaning 'is outside (articulated) language while nevertheless within interlocution.' Barthes designates this outside that is inside 'the

filmic'. 'The filmic', he explains, 'is that in the film which cannot be described, the representation which cannot be represented. The filmic begins only where language and metalanguage end.'[11] As if to screen Barthes' filmic, Tschumi constructs a 'cinematic promenade' that snakes through the Park. This serpentine path extends the practice of superimposition by appropriating Eisenstein's method of montage for architectural purposes. Since the master architect does not impose meaning on form, each element in the Park is an 'empty slot' — 'la case vide' — where meaning must be produced instead of discovered.[12] At each point along the way, the meaning of the fragments shifts and slides until it becomes completely undecidable. Tschumi's cinematic techniques are not only polymorphous; they are perverse. Their aim is not meaning but its lack. In what is, perhaps, his most revealing comment on the Park, Tschumi confesses: 'La Villette, then, aims at an architecture that means *nothing*, an architecture of the signifier rather than the signified — one that is pure trace or play of language' (CV, vii). The point — the point that means nothing — is not Tschumi's but Bataille's point, or Tschumi's refiguration of Bataille's point. The point of La Parc de La Villette is to reissue Bataille's call to summon all of man's tendencies into a point:

> To summon all of man's tendencies into a point, all of the 'possibles' that he is, to draw from them at the same time the harmonies and the violent oppositions, no longer to leave outside the laughter tearing apart the fabric of which man is made . . . in this respect, my efforts recommence and undo Hegel's Phenomenology. *Hegel's construction is a philosophy of work, of 'project'. The Hegelian man — Being and God — is accomplished, is completed in the adequation of the project. The only obstacle in this way of seeing . . . is what, in man, is irreducible to project: nondiscursive existence, laughter, ecstasy, which link man — in the end — to the negation of the project that he nevertheless is — man ultimately ruins himself* [s'abîme] *in a total effacement — of what he is, of all human affirmation. Such would be the* easy *passage from the philosophy of work — Hegelian and profane — to sacred philosophy, which the 'torment' expresses.*[13]

This is the passage Tschumi plots in the Park, that he superimposes on the site of the slaughterhouses of Paris. The red of La Villette is the trace of the blood of sacrifice. The Follies are what Didi-Huberman describes in another context as 'the torn-rent image' of 'an Acéphelic god', who is the tragic god of ecstasy. Dionysian ecstasy is madness, which is both overwhelmingly terrifying and irresistibly attractive. Eurydice is another guise of madness, Orpheus another mask of the architect whose quest leads him to the underworld. In his folly, Tschumi, like Orpheus, transgresses the prohibition against 'looking at the point where life touches death'. In 'Architecture and Transgression' he wilfully embraces an important passage from the opening pages of Breton's *Second Manifesto of Surrealism*:

> Everything tends to make us believe that there exists a certain point of the mind at which life and death, the real and the imagined, past and future, the communicable and the incommunicable, high and low cease to be perceived as contradictions.[14]

This is the point toward which Tschumi's architecture is directed. His refusal of Modern architecture expresses the *desire* for a re-fusal with what is, in effect, the sacred. The point of the Follies repeats Schelling's *Indifferentzpunkt*. Though Tschumi insists that re-fusal is infinitely deferred, he continues to long for the oneness that Modernism promises but cannot deliver.

There is, however, another way to read the nonsense of the point. A few pages after dismissing Schelling's *Indifferentzpunkt* as 'the night in which all cows are black', Hegel begins his analysis of the experience of consciousness by examining what seems to be a sensible point — the *hic et nunc* of sense-certainty. As the point of departure, this point is the limit of the Hegelian System. But no sooner has Hegel begun than he loses his point. From the beginning, indeed before the beginning, the systematic exposition of consciousness seems pointless. The presence of the *hic et nunc* disappears; the point of departure turns out to be the departure of the point. Preoccupied with the certainty of sense, Hegel finds the nonsense of the point unbearable. With a flick of his dialectical wand, he tries to translate the nonsensical absence of the point into the sensible presence. But his effort fails and thus his labour remains pointless. The evasion of the point both allows presence to appear and inscribes an inevitable disappearance in the very midst of presentation. This withdrawal points towards a different refusal.

The *absence* of the point is present in the midst of Tschumi's Park. Something is missing from his project. It is planned but has not been constructed. Along the cinematic promenade, one of the gardens that remains absent is Choral Work, whose architects are Peter Eisenman and Jacques Derrida. By deconstructing Modernism and Modernist Post-Modernism differently, Choral Work disrupts La Parc de La Villette as if from within. Perhaps it is no accident that Choral Work has not been constructed; perhaps it cannot be constructed; perhaps La Villette cannot contain it; perhaps Tschumi cannot bear it. Perhaps. But such speculation is pointless.

To begin again, we must return to the non-sense of the point — not Tschumi's but Hegel's point. Hegel's systematic

effort to recover presence (here) in the present (now) of the point is bound to fail. The presentation of spatial and temporal presence presupposes something that is never present and yet is not absent. Neither present nor absent, this strange third allows appearance to appear by disappearing. The presence of the present and the present of presence are always dislocated as if from within by something that eludes the economy of presence and thus remains irreducibly unrepresentable. This dislocation disrupts presence by spacing the present and interrupts the present by timing presence. Derrida names this becoming-space of time and becoming-time of space *différance*. Never present without being absent, the site of *différance* is a certain non-site. The impossible task of Eisenman's deconstructive architecture is not simply to build differently but to construct *différance*.

This venture cannot be approached alone; it must be a joint undertaking. To build deconstructively is, in effect, to construct a joint whose origin is not (the) one. Choral Work is such a joint project. Duplicity begins with the title. Choral Work is both a text with a strange architecture and an architectural project that is textual. The origin of Choral Work is at least double — Derrida and Eisenman. Though they cooperate, these two never become one. In a certain sense, the title *is* the work. As Derrida has long insisted, the strange logic of the supplement can be captured by neither the either/or of Aristotelian logic nor the both/and of Hegelian logic. The supplement implies (but does not represent) 'something else' — something so different that it is 'unnameable.' Thus unnameable is figured in the disfiguring of Choral Work.

Whose title is Choral Work: Derrida's or Eisenman's? The answer, it seems, is neither one nor the other. At the time of their first encounter, Derrida was writing a text on Plato's *Timaeus* entitled 'Chora'. In the course of the dialogue between Derrida and Eisenman, the suggestion emerges — it is not clear from whom — to form a title for their joint work by introducing yet another supplement: the addition of an 'L' to 'Chora' to form Choral Work. This supplement is far from innocent. As we shall see, it both haunts the margins of Derrida's most sustained interrogation of art, *The Truth in Painting,* and is Eisenman's signature. The title 'Choral Work' embodies a madness different from Tschumi's madness. The madness embodied in the Follies reflects polysemy run wild. In such plurivocality, the double coding characteristic of Post-Modernism is multiplied but not interrupted. The undecidable title 'Choral Work' *disseminates* meaning. 'The difference between discursive polysemy and textual dissemination is precisely *difference* itself, "an implacable difference".'[15] This 'implacable difference' can be heard *between* the lines of Derrida and Eisenman's conversation. They repeatedly misunderstand each other. The effect is often comic, sometimes *almost* tragic. Even when they seem to concur, agreement is provisional and not final. Blanchot's account of *le pas au-delà* effectively describes the exchange or nonexchange between Derrida and Eisenman.

> *Behind discourse speaks the refusal to discourse, as behind philosophy would speak the refusal to philosophise: the non-speaking speech, violent, concealing, saying nothing and suddenly crying.*[16]

This cry of refusal is the echo of chora. In his analysis of the place or, more precisely, the non-place of chora in Plato's *Timaeus,* Derrida refigures his 'non-concept' *différance.* Chora, Derrida argues, 'is the spacing that is the condition for everything to take place, for everything to be inscribed' (CW, 3). In other words, chora is the margin of the between that articulates the differences constitutive of identity. 'This third kind, or genus,' Derrida argues, 'is neither the eternal eidos nor its sensible copy, but the place in which all those types are inscribed — *chora.*' [CW, 3] This third is not dialectical or synthetic. Neither sensible nor intelligible, it eludes the strictures of classical Western ontology. And yet, it is inextricably entangled in structures that cannot include it. Inasmuch as it is 'the spacing that is the condition for everything to take place', chora is, in a certain sense, antecedent to all that exists. However, as the condition of the possibility of existence, chora itself does not exist. Nor is it nothing. Chora is 'more ancient' than being or nonbeing. The past of this 'ancient of ancients' has never been present; it is an absolute past whose perpetual withdrawing opens the space for all presence to appear and creates the time for every present to transpire. Emmanuel Levinas labels this radical past '*anarchie*'. The arche of an-archie *is not* the traditional arche of archi-tecture but is the arche of the archi-trace. This trace produces a certain anarchy by faulting the foundation of classical and modern architecture: form, structure, presence, meaning, origin, synthesis, unity etc.

According to Eisenman, the history of architecture from classicism through Modernism is governed by what he, following Heidegger and Derrida, describes as 'the metaphysics of presence'. Eisenman divides this history into four chapters that are organised around the shifting relations among what Kant identifies as the three regulative ideas that guide all reflection: God, self, and world. Eisenman's story of Western architecture is not continuous but is punctuated by at least three ruptures. Prior to the 15th century, God mediated between man and world, thereby establishing order and ensuring meaning. Human thought and action sought to re-present the truth established by the divine architect of creation. With the Renaissance, anthropocentrism replaces theocentrism. The third chapter in Eisenman's story begins in the 19th and ends in the 20th century. In the face of

the recognition of this fundamental human estrangement, man's sense of himself came into 'crisis.' Modern architecture arises in response to this crisis.[17] Technology, the Modernist believed, would make it possible to realise the Utopian future that neither God nor man had delivered. But the dream of Modernity was short-lived; it ended in the nightmare of the Second World War. Eisenman's architecture is calculated to deepen the 'existential anxiety' he believes is endemic to the Post-Modern world.

Like other members of the New York Five, Eisenman's early work is deeply influenced by Modernism. In a series of houses, most of which were never built, Eisenman extends Modern formalism by adapting Noam Chomsky's transformational grammar to architectural practice. The procedure Eisenman follows in these houses is not unlike Tschumi's treatment of the Follies. Eisenman begins with a cube and programmes variations on this basic structure. The goal of Eisenman's 'syntactic' investigations is to identify the 'structural essence' of architecture. It should be clear that this search for an architectural eidos is thoroughly logocentric. But even in these early works, it is possible to discern anticipations of Eisenman's eventual break with Modernism. The houses are not integral structures but are interrupted by disturbing elements that serve no function.

After reading Derrida, Eisenman gives up his dream of presence. A passage in the draft of 'Misreading Peter Eisenman', which is conspicuously missing from the published version of the essay, suggests Eisenman's shift away from architectural principles that presuppose a metaphysics of presence: 'Figure in the current work is none other than the manifestation of absence through presence, the presence of absence, the very strategy of dislocation.' To realise his strategy of dislocation in which formal presence is disrupted by a recessive absence, Eisenman develops a *textual* architecture. His notion of the text is thoroughly Derridean. The text, Eisenman explains, 'is no longer something complete, enclosed in a book or its margins, it is a differential network. A fabric of traces referring endlessly to something other than itself.' It is not a 'stable object' but a process, a 'transgressive activity' that disperses the author as the centre, limit and guarantor of truth.'[18] Within this differential network, meaning is a function of the relationship between and among signs. Since everything is always already coded and signs always refer to other signs, there is no thing in itself. In contrast to speculative or imaginal idealism, however, this network is not self-contained but is put in play by 'something other than itself' that can never be represented. This other is the ever-withdrawing point of non-identity that renders every integrative synthesis impossible. In the absence of wholeness and integrity, the text becomes a 'tissue of superpositions' in which differing strands intersect to dislocate space and time.

In his important article 'Architecture as a Second Language: The Texts of Between' Eisenman illustrates his understanding of textuality with David Lynch's film *Blue Velvet*. What fascinates Eisenman about the film is Lynch's use of detail to create a sense of temporal dislocation. The most notable instance of Lynch's technique is the lack of temporal coincidence between the narrative and the soundtrack. While the film is set in a small North Carolina town in the l950s, the version of the song 'Blue Velvet' that plays in the background did not appear until a decade later. 'Blue Velvet' was first sung by Tony Bennett in 1951, covered by The Statues in 1960, and finally recorded by Bobby Vinton in 1963. Lynch uses Vinton's rendition to create a disruptive space between the time of narrative and the time of the music.

> *While those images and sounds are present so are their displacements. In other words, the text of the film is about something else. And yet, the film is crafted so as to render the gap between these disjunctions as virtually natural. This is an example of a text of 'between' . . . One does not know what the 'truth' of these sounds and images is. They do not appear to be related to the narrative but to something other than narrative, some other structure of relationships outside the film's structure. This 'something other' than the narrative is the text between.*[19]

Eisenman's analysis of Lynch's film is particularly helpful, for it indirectly provides his clearest explanation of his complex strategy of 'scaling'. Scaling is the means by which Eisenman attempts to introduce time into the space of architecture. The time that preoccupies Eisenman is no ordinary time but is a time which, though it allows presentation to occur, is itself never present and thus disrupts every form of presence. What Eisenman is attempting to trace by scaling is the anachronistic time of *différance*. In his Romeo and Juliet project, developed for the 1986 Venice Biennale, Eisenman uses the process of scaling to create a complex architectural scheme. The text that presents this project, which is entitled *Moving Arrows, Eros, and Other Errors*, consists of 30 superimposed plastic transparencies that bear a narrative explanation and drawings done to different scales. Eisenman generates his architectural text and textual architecture from yet another text that is not one but multiple. The 'origin', in other words, is already divided and dispersed. There are at least three versions of *Romeo and Juliet*, one by Da Porto, one by Bandello, and one by Shakespeare. Weaving different strands of these texts together, Eisenman creates a site that is 'a palimpsest and a quarry'. But the narratives not only constitute the site, the site also shapes the narratives. 'Each narrative', Eisenman points out,

> *is characterised by three structural relationships, each having its own physical analogue: division (the separation of the lovers symbolised in physical form by the balcony of Juliet's house); union (the marriage of the lovers symbolised by the church); and their dialectical relationship (the togetherness and apartness of the lovers as symbolised in Juliet's tomb). The three structural relationships that pervade the narrative also can be found to exist at a physical level in the plan of the city of Verona: the cardo and decumans divide the city; the old Roman grid unites; and the Adige River creates a dialectical condition of union and division between the two halves.*[20]

By juxtaposing different narratives and superimposing contrasting scalings, Eisenman produces a labyrinth from which there is no exit. For example, in one scaling, he relocates Verona within the castle of Romeo to represent Romeo's effort to unite the city, which had been divided by the feud between the Capuletti and Montecchi families. The failure to achieve union is depicted by another scaling in which the tomb of Juliet is enlarged and superimposed on the cemetery of Verona in such a way that the entire city becomes the grave of the young lover. Multiple texts and sites are put into play in such a way that synthesis — dialectical or otherwise — becomes impossible. The death of Juliet marked by the tomb/city figures the impossibility of union.

The strategy of scaling is developed further in Choral Work. In their contribution to Tschumi's Park, Eisenman and Derrida 'attempt to bring into figuration an idea of chora'. This undertaking, however, is impossible, for as Derrida insists, 'chora cannot be represented' (CW, 8). The architectural task, then, becomes to represent the impossibility of representation. Toward this end, Eisenman and Derrida develop a way of disfiguring that is neither Modern nor Post-Modern.

In Choral Work, three texts again generate the project. In this case, the textual web is even more tangled, since, as Eisenman notes, each text is on another text: 'Bernard's [text] can be seen as a text on mine for Venice; mine will be a text on Jacques Derrida's; his a text on Plato's *Timaeus*' (CW, 8). As Choral Work develops, its intertextuality becomes even more complex. Derrida and Eisenman superimpose their work on Tschumi's La Villette plan. But Tschumi's work is superimposed on Derrida's theory and, it appears, on Eisenman's strategy of scaling, which, in turn, is also superimposed on Derrida's notion of deconstruction. Eisenman suspects that Tschumi stole his notion of scaling and transformed it into his own method of superimposition. Eisenman's appropriation of Derrida's reading of textuality is calculated to compound the problem of authorship and origin. He superimposes two additional texts on Tschumi's point grid: the Romeo and Juliet project with its intricate layering of texts and signs, and his plan for a housing project on Cannaregio, a small island near Venice. In developing his Cannaregio design, Eisenman appropriates the point grid scheme Le Corbusier had used in his plan for a hospital that was to have been built on the site of the island's abattoirs. Apparently dismissing any concern about Tschumi's unacknowledged appropriation of the strategy of scaling, Eisenman stresses the intricacy of the site he devises in La Villette.

But Eisenman protests too much. It is precisely the question of authorship that he is raising. This extraordinarily complex question is, in the final analysis, inseparable from a theological problematic. Since the author-architect is made in the image of God, the death of God implies the disappearance of the author-architect, and vice versa. It is possible, however, that the death of God does not result in the mere absence of presence but implies an alterity that cannot be figured in terms of being and nonbeing. This third alternative is suggested by a detail relevant to the Cannaregio project about which Eisenman remains silent. Cannaregio was not only the site of slaughterhouses but was also the island where the Jewish population of Venice lived. In Choral Work, Eisenman and Derrida, who are both Jewish, call into question the incarnational theology that implicitly informs the work of Tschumi and his Surrealist precursors. I shall return to this theological issue in what follows.

As I have noted, Choral Work has not been built. Promises continue but fulfilment is deferred. To find a deconstructive construction, we must look elsewhere. In the course of his dialogue with Derrida, Eisenman remarks: 'What is interesting for me as I read the "chora" text is that I feel that I was actually making "chora" before I knew about it' (CW, 8). Nowhere is Eisenman's deconstruction *avant la lettre* more evident than in his most acclaimed building: Wexner Center for the Visual Arts, located on the campus of Ohio State University. Wexner Center is neither Modern nor Post-Modern but something else, something other. The displacements effected by Wexner are multiple: it is a Center without a centre; a museum that calls into question the metaphysics and ideology of the museum; a structure that is poststructural; a construction that is deconstructive. Oscillating between abstraction and figuration, Wexner Center disfigures otherwise than either Modernism or Post-Modernism. Here, as elsewhere, everything begins along the margin, border, edge . . . with the tear, wound, cut.

Eisenman begins by disfiguring. Before the beginning, there seemed to be one — one building. But this 'original' one was actually two: Mershon Auditorium and Weigel Hall. Eisenman cuts the link, severs the cord joining them and thereby opens the time-space of the between in which his building is suspended. Wexner Center is a (w)edge driven

between two other buildings. Actually, it is not really one but many wedges; wedges within and without create an irreducibly open structure that 'is' nothing but edge. When read in this way, Wexner Center prefigures Choral Work.

Along the edge of the between, in what Venturi describes as 'residual space', Eisenman inserts a series of galleries, various performance spaces, studios, a fine arts library, and administrative offices. This structure is difficult but not whole. Its spaces are demanding and frustrating for artists, curators, and visitors. Wexner Center does not conform to expectations of what a museum should be. The galleries are interrupted by pillars and posts, some of which are themselves interrupted. Eisenman exploits this marginal site in a way that critically engages both Modernism and Post-Modernism. He does not attack the formalism of Modernism or the ornamentalism of Post-Modernism from without but uses structure and figure against themselves to dislocate Modern and Post-Modern architecture as if from within.

Eisenman's deconstruction of Modernism is most obvious in his use of the grid in Wexner Center. In addition to serving as Eisenman's logo in his early work, the grid is an essential structure for Modern artists and architects. In her classic essay 'Grids', Rosalind Krauss argues that 'one of the most Modernist things about [the grid] is its capacity to serve as a paradigm or model for the antidevelopmental, antinarrative, and antihistorical.'[21] In its Modern variations, the grid is the figure of essential form and eidetic structure that remains when figures and ornaments are erased. Eisenman subverts the Modern notion of the grid and the metaphysics of presence that it presupposes by using grids ornamentally to reintroduce time into space. The grids that structure and ornament Wexner Center assume multiple forms. Doubling and redoubling, they repeatedly shift, oscillate and alternate until it becomes impossible to locate stable axes that provide orientation. Layered grids function like moiré patterns that tremble ever so slightly. The superimposition and intersection of the grids opens the 'Center' by allowing the outside in and turning the inside out until the gridwork points beyond (the) structure both spatially and temporally. Through a careful orchestration of grids, Eisenman links Wexner Center with the rest of the campus, the University's gridiron, the city of Columbus, the state of Ohio, and even the rest of the world by way of the Columbus airport. The result is not simply one more Post-Modern effort to recontextualise buildings but something far more complex. In this structure, time invades the space of the grid to open a gap that never closes. In situating Wexner Center spatially, Eisenman invokes traces of the past. Through his method of scaling, he superimposes the Jefferson and Olmsted grids on the Wexner site to create the trace of another trace — the Greenville Trace. The territory of Ohio was initially plotted by two teams of surveyors: one working from north to south, the other working from south to north. One of the aims of the surveyors was to integrate the traditional Jefferson grid with smaller, more localised grids. The grids were supposed to meet on an axis that passes through Columbus. But the surveyors failed; they missed the mark and thus the grid was disrupted by a gap. This gap is named the Greenville Trace. Eisenman figures this trace in the labyrinthian maze of gardens that falls between Wexner's ornamental grid and the streets of Columbus. In one of the walls of this underground that is above ground, there is a fissure that disfigures what is supposed to be an all-inclusive grid. This figureless figure is a trace of the spacing of time that can never be re-covered.

The unrecoverable past also returns in Wexner Center's explicit deployment of figure. In contrast to typical Post-Modern uses of ornamentation, Eisenman refigures the past in such a way that the very possibility of re-presentation is called into question. The figures that supplement Eisenman's dis-integrated structures are taken from the armoury that was on the site until 1958. But just as Eisenman turns structures against Modernism, so he turns figures against Post-Modernism. The trace of the past is 'present' as 'absent' in Wexner Center. As is so often the case, an accident proves productive. In the plan for the site, Eisenman preserved what remained of the original foundation of the armoury. By mistake, however, workers removed the remains of the foundation. Committed to inscribing the trace of the past in the present, Eisenman reconstructs the outline of the armoury's foundation. Like the fragile lines of a text, this faint outline traces the site of the withdrawal of the original foundation. What appears to commemorate the presence of a solid foundation turns out to mark the absence of a grounding structure. Though apparently a representation by which the past enriches the present, Eisenman's 'textual' supplement is a depresentation through which the inaccessibility of the past hollows out the present. By following Eisenman's non-foundational outline, it becomes possible to read Modernism's desire for clarity and transparency, as well as Post-Modernism's ironic play with the past, as two versions of nostalgic longing for an impossible presence.

The remote proximity of the inaccessible past is figured in the disfigured tower. 'The separation effected by temporalisation' generates a 'spacing' that splits stable structures. As structures crack, the tower, which is supposed to be the site of (panoptical) surveillance, becomes a blind spot that is the locus of a lapse. The lapse of time exposes the opening of space that never was, is, or will be closed. Intended to be a symbol of security, the faulty tower can now be read as a sign of inescapable insecurity. From a certain perspective, the tower appears to be whole. But as one shifts one's angle of vision, things fall apart. More

precisely, one discovers that the whole was never whole but was 'originally' a fragment. That which is (always already) rent cannot be whole. The pieces simply do not fit together. Lines that appear to converge do not meet; walls that seem complete break off; the grid etched in brick abruptly ends; perpendiculars become diagonals; rectangles and squares are cut to form wedges. As one walks around the tower, the circle disappears in a ceaseless play of edges that figure and refigure Eisenman's coup. Something is forever missing from Derrida's texts and Eisenman's architecture. They are always writing and building something else — something that cannot be written or built but can only be traced by a certain disfiguring. To figure the trace that figures the unfigurable, we must retrace our thoughts by returning to the supplement that transforms 'chora' into 'Choral Work': 'L.' Not one L but two — one is the L of Derrida, one the L of Eisenman. Edmond Jabès indirectly poses the question poetically:

EL
LE
L

Stages of the experience from fore-book to absent book.[22]
How is L . . . ELLE . . . to be read? What is L? Who is L? Where is L?

Derrida's L is at least double. L is ELLE, or so it appears. Throughout his 'Chora' essay Derrida repeatedly notes that Plato figures chora as feminine — 'the mother, the matrix, or the nurse'. And yet these 'names' are improper, for chora is neither masculine nor feminine but a third genre that approximates the neuter. 'So chora is not mother, not the nurse who nurtures infants' (CW, 3). The supplemental L of Choral Work is but is not not ELLE, and thus is something el-se.

L appears el-sewhere in the Derridean corpus. *The Truth in Painting* is not a seamless book but a torn text. The first section of this work, which is entitled 'Parergon', is repeatedly interrupted by the figure of a disfigured L: this faulty L is something like a frame within a text that is devoted to the question of the frame. In 'Parergon', Derrida reframes Kant's Third Critique by reading the *Critique of Judgment* as a frame. As the margin of difference between the First and the Second Critiques, the *Critique of Judgment* is a non-synthetic third that cannot be figured within the economy of ontotheology. Contrary to expectation, this different difference creates the opening for another Post-Modernism in which the religious can be thought otherwise. 'If Modernism distinguishes itself by striving for absolute domination,' Derrida argues,

> then Post-Modernism might be the realisation or experience of its end, the end of the plan of domination. This Post-Modernism could develop a new relationship with the divine that would no longer be manifest in the traditional shapes of the

*Greek, Christian, or other deities, but would still
set the conditions for architectural thinking.*[23]

The 'historical figure' of this other religion, Derrida suggests, is 'a certain Judaism'.[24]

Eisenman refigures the L that marks the margin of Derrida's text in a seemingly insignificant supplement to his textual architecture — a detail that is suspended above a threshold that is supposed to open doors. It is a doorhandle in the shape of an L, or, more precisely, in the shape of three Ls that intersect in a point. The L is repeated many times on the plate supporting the handle. Once recognised, the L appears everywhere in Eisenman's work — early as well as late, in drawings as well as buildings. Every house which is not a home is, in effect, 'House El'. And yet Eisenman never talks or writes about the significance or insignificance of L. It is as if the letter (if it is a letter) were unpronounceable, unspeakable. Why?

El, the head of the Canaanite pantheon, was the creator and father of the other gods. It appears that El was something of an architect, for one of his most common epithets in Ugaritic literature is 'Builder of Things Built'. El, architect of the universe, had a Dionysian streak that sometimes led to grotesque excess. In one ancient text he 'is portrayed as drinking himself into a stupor and wallowing in his own excrement and urine'.[25] Philo of Byblos, a Greek historian, identifies El with Cronos — the same Cronus with whom Derrida associates Dionysus.[26] In this guise, El appears to be the god whose Bacchanalian revel is celebrated in Bataille's writings and Tschumi's architecture. But elsewhere El appears otherwise. El is also the 'name' of YHWH. Though

usually hostile to Canaanite gods and goddesses, Israel identified YHWH with El. Thus 'El' is a substitute for 'YHWH.' But 'YHWH' is itself a substitute for the ineffable name of God. As a substitute for a substitute, El 'names' that which is absolutely unnameable. During their first meeting, Eisenman confesses to Derrida:

*Through your work directly, and indirectly through
such writers as Susan Handelman and Mark
Taylor, I have recently begun to consider Hebraic
thought and its implications for architecture. There
were no graven images in the temple, and, as I
understand it, the Hebrew language contains no
present tense of the verb 'to be' — only 'was' and
'will be.' Thus Hebraic thought deals more with
absence than presence. [CW, I]*

. . . No present tense . . . only 'was' and 'will be' . . . For Eisenman, presence is never present and thus the Utopia never arrives. To believe in (its) presence is madness — sheer folly. In the absence of presence, all re-fusals — be they archeological or teleological, gardens or kingdoms — must be refused. Every habitation is uninhabitable; every *Heim, unheimlich*. Always displaced by an other that cannot be domesticated, architecture unsettles rather than settles; dislocates rather than locates. In the wake — the interminable wake — of Modernism and Modernist Post-Modernism, only exile remains. Exile with no hope of return. The nonplace of exile is the desert — the desert where a certain disaster lurks. This is Eisenman's point, and it marks a point of no return. It is towards this point that we are inexorably drawn today — here and now — *ici et maintenant*.

NOTES

1 Philip Johnson, Preface, *Deconstructivist Architecture*, ed Philip Johnson and Mark Wigley, Museum of Modern Art, New York, 1988, p7.

2 For the sake of convenience, I have cited the following works in the body of the text: Bernard Tschumi, *Architectural Manifestoes,* Architectural Associates, London [AM]; Bernard Tschumi, *Cinégramme Folie, La Parc de La Villette*, Princeton Architectural Press [CF]; Bernard Tschumi, *La Case Vide*, Architectural Association, Landeer, 1985 [CV]; Jeffrey Kipnis, ed, *Choral Work*, Rizzoli International, New York, 1992 [CW]; and Bernard Tschumi, *The Manhattan Transcripts*, Architectural Design, London, 1991 [MT].

3 Bernard Tschumi, 'Questions of Space: The Pyramid and the Labyrinth (or the Architectural Paradox)', *Studio International*, September/October 1975, pp136-42. In developing the reading of Bataille that informs his architectural theory, Tschumi was deeply influenced by Dennis Hollier's *La Prise de la Concorde*. In the English translation of this book Hollier underscores the importance of the slaughterhouses of La Villette for Bataille and, by extension, for Tschumi. See: 'Bloody Sundays', *Against Architecture: The Writings of Georges Bataille*, translated by Betsy Wing, MIT Press,

Cambridge, 1988, ppix-xxiii.

4 Bernard Tschumi, 'Architecture and Transgression', *Oppositions,* vol 7, winter, 1976, p59.

5 Tschumi, 'The Pleasure of Architecture', *Architectural Design*, no 3, 1977, p217.

6 Tschumi freely admits that transgression involves violence. In an essay entitled 'Violence of Architecture' he argues: 'The integration of the concept of violence into the architectural mechanism — the purpose of my argument — is ultimately aimed at a new pleasure of architecture. Like any form of violence, the violence of architecture also contains the possibility of change, of renewal. Like any violence, the violence of architecture is deeply Dionysian.' *Artforum*, vol 20, no 1, September 1981, p44.

7 Tschumi, 'Madness and the Combinative', *Precis*, Fall 1984, p150.

8 Joseph Shipley, *The Origins of English Words*, John Hopkins University Press, Baltimore, 1984, p24.

9 Quoted in Michel Saudan and Sylvia Saudan-Skira, *From Folly to Follies: Discovering the World of Gardens*, Abbeville Press, New York, 1987, p195.

10 Though Tschumi does not cite Lyotard, Deleuze, or Guattari, he

clearly borrows his notion of 'points of intensity' from their work. See: Jean-François Lyotard, *Des dispositifs pulsionnels*, Christian Bourgois, Paris, 1980; *Économie libidinale*, Les Éditions de Minuit, Paris, 1974; and Gilles Deleuze and Félix Guattari, *Anti-Oedipus: A Thousand Plateaus*.

11 Roland Barthes, 'The Third Meaning: Research Notes on Some Eisenstein Stills', *Image — Music — Text,* translated by Stephen Heath, Hill and Wang, New York, 1977, pp62, 55, 61, 64. As we shall see in what follows, Eisenstein is also very important for Tschumi.

12 'La case vide' designates the empty box in a chart or an unoccupied square on a chessboard. As such, it marks the site of the indeterminate and unexpected.

13 Georges Bataille, *Inner Experience*, translated by Leslie Boldt, State University of New York Press, Albany, 1988, pp80-1.

14 André Breton, *Manifestoes of Surrealism*, translated by Richard Seaver and Helen Lane, University of Michigan Press, Ann Arbor, 1969, p123.

15 Jacques Derrida, *Dissemination,* translated by Barbara Johnson, University of Chicago Press, 1981, p351.

16 Maurice Blanchot, *Le Pas au-delà*, Gallimard, Paris, 1973, p158.

17 Peter Eisenman, *House of Cards*, Oxford University Press, New York, 1987, p170.

18 Peter Eisenman, 'Architecture as a Second Language: The Texts of Between', *Restructuring Architectural Theory, Threshold,* vol IV, Spring, 1988, p71.

19 Ibid, p72.

20 Peter Eisenman, *Moving Arrows, Eros, and Other Errors*, Architectural Association, London, 1986, pp6-7.

21 Rosalind E Krauss, 'Grids', *The Originality of the Avant-Garde and Other Myths*, MIT Press, Cambridge, 1986, p22.

22 Edmond Jabès, *The Book of Questions: EL, or the Last Book,* translated by Rosmarie Waldrop, Wesleyan University Press, Middletown, CT, 1984, p71.

23 Jacques Derrida, 'Architetture ove il desiderio può abotare', *Domus,* no 20, 1986.

24 Jacques Derrida, *Truth in Painting,* translated by Geoffrey Bennington and Ian McLeod, University of Chicago Press, 1987, p134.

25 *Harper's Bible Dictionary,* ed Paul Achtemeier, Harper and Row, New York, 1985, p252.

26 See Jacques Derrida, *Glas*, translated by John Leavy and Richard Rand, University of Nebraska Press, Lincoln, NB, 1986, pp231-2.

FIG 1

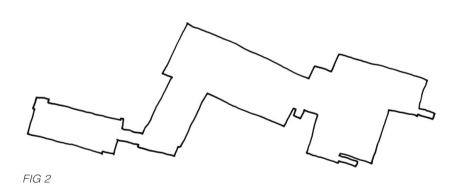

FIG 2

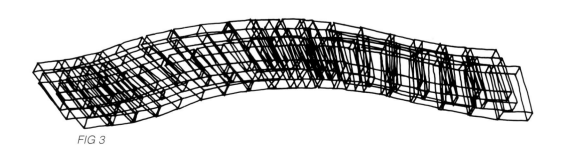

FIG 3

THE GENIUS OF MATTER: EISENMAN'S CINCINNATI PROJECT
SANFORD KWINTER

Peter Eisenman's design for the Department of Architecture, Art, and Planning at the University of Cincinnati celebrates with vigour and wit the withering of a type of space of which Eisenman himself was the prime inventor. For Eisenman, the qualities of a space were, in fact, never merely sought or discovered in relationships — scale, proportion, symmetry — *inherent* to rational, homogeneous space; they were, rather, something that had always to be *invented* by means of operations committed upon it. While discovery presupposes entities already formed and given in advance, ones that need only be uncovered or brought to the threshold of representation, invention implies difference and transformation, or creation *in time*. It is Eisenman's hallmark never to have questioned the fundamental tenets of traditional Western geometry, but rather to have forced them to submit to this destabilising pressure of time. For even the most regular, immutable, structurally stable form — say, a square or cube — if allowed to move *against itself* in time, that is, not only in relation to the regular grid from which it was born (through excision or extrusion) but in relation to any earlier position, *any segment of its own duration* — will begin to emit qualities entirely irreducible to static geometry. All of Eisenman's early or 'classical' work consisted of variations on this single operation: the mobilisation of the static points of traditional geometry and their transformation into *oscillators*. This meant that every form came accompanied by an 'associated space', one that was never fully the isotropic space of the rational grid, but 'singular', particular only to itself, one that described the double beat of a specific, two-step oscillation. The famous Eisenman 'L' describes the steady state, or interval, of one such oscillation: shift any point on a square to a different point on both the x and y axes — and if the shift is less than the metric of the original square — two Ls will always be produced in inverted, reciprocal, and oscillatory relation to one another (Fig 1).

By maintaining diagrammatically active the two extreme points (this *and* that) as well as the geometric passage between them, Eisenman endowed the all-too-structuralist space of the 1960s and 70s with a modest dynamical window and in so doing, rendered it fundamentally productive — one might provisionally even say 'alive' in the sense that life is sometimes attributed to crystals. But more important, this non-hierarchical suspension of a complex temporal aggregate or structure — even if mostly imprisoned in truncated binary operations — preserved for a later date the deeper questions of development and emergence, as well as the whole set of global structures and phenomena that arise when local movements are correlated through free interaction. More than anything else, the Cincinnati project represents the first signs of emancipation from the limitations of the earlier model.

The Cincinnati project may be said to consist of two formal series in dynamic interrelation: one angular, contrapuntal, 'digital', a disposition of rigid elements in deliberate, regular variation (a linear definition of the existing structures) (Fig 2); and a second, almost randomly undulant, anexact (vague but rigorous), continuous, multiple, and 'soft' (Fig 3). At first view, the project asserts itself as globally structuralist: it seems to proceed by collision and abrasion of forms, opposition of representations, and reversal of effects. The earlier oscillation dynamic — here transposed to a macroscopic scale — clearly remains a powerful motor in the work, though it is no longer determinant, for in migrating upward across thresholds of scale the oscillatory mechanism appears to have taken on a life of its own. No longer content merely to transmit pre-set movements

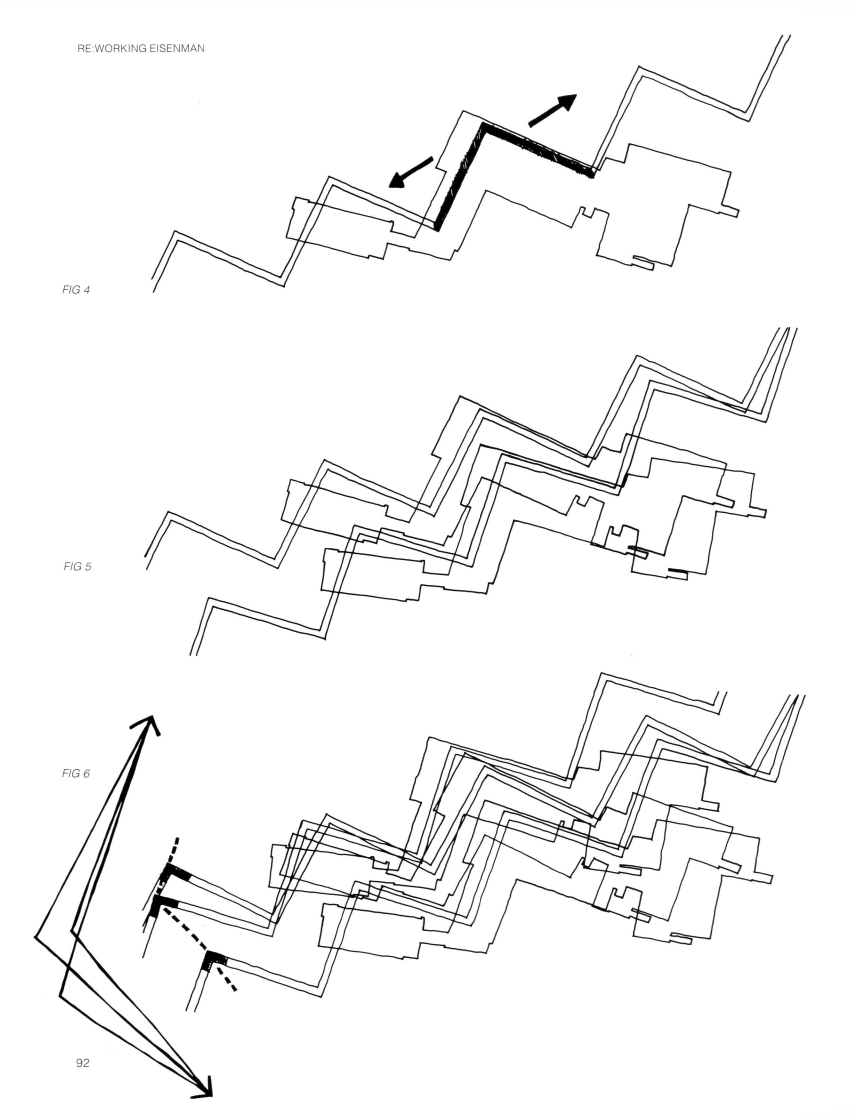

FIG 4

FIG 5

FIG 6

programmed in advance, it generates its programme on the fly, linking and crosslinking movements — flows of information and matter — from all depths and reaches within the system. Indeed it is perhaps only now that one may properly apply this latter term to Eisenman's work. For 'system' implies a shifting network of mobile parts continually self-updating (in relation to one another, and in *real time*), and continually tapping in to flows that originate in other parts of the network. What we are given is a field of individual local interactions capable of triggering or manifesting effects of structure at any (even the global) level.

How and why has this sudden 'phase transition' occurred in Eisenman's work? The answer may be this simple: it has to do with the adoption of a material model — in the case at hand, the geological paradigm of plate tectonics, sedimentation, soft structuration, rigid binding — in order to weaken the earlier semiotic one. Semiotic structures are binary, hierarchical, closed, and proceed by opposition or counterpoint. Simple, uncorrelated oscillation is by far the most complex activity that they are able to generate (alterity, deconstruction). The *material* model however proceeds by diffusion and integration; matter is at once a vehicle for difference-producing processes (eg heat propagation, or any flow along a gradient) and a medium of infinite elasticity and limitless capacity to resolve external forces acting upon it (heat or pressure will change the structural identity of a given matter in both predictable and unpredictable ways). Matter is literally riddled with properties, dissymmetries, thresholds, inhomogeneities, singularities that emerge and vanish depending only on with which other forces they are brought into relation. Matter, in short, is active, dynamic, and creative.

The Cincinnati project approaches and exploits precisely these characteristics. The first thing one notices when examining the work is that none of its structural elements is fixed or oriented, and each seeks to propagate according to its own nature. Each form is associated with a 'tremor field', a parameter space of limited but acceptable movement in which the form may drift at will. This is no longer a simple oscillation space where only the extreme positions may be inhabited and where the dynamical passage space remains highly unstable, but a complex one, a *statistical* space within which the object may take up any position at any time. But there is axial or vectorial movement as well. The disposition of the existing buildings is at the outset emphasised by embedding on-axis a T-square armature into the aggressively protruding angle of the central DAAP building. This simple anchoring structure — a chevron — then emits a pulse from each of its extremities, reproducing itself serially as a regular, periodic, stepped, or partly folded line (Fig 4). The tension between the relentless orthogonality of this regulating pulse, and the desultory, off-axis drifting of the actual buildings is not resolved but rather exacerbated: the entire aggregate structure is seesawed, once forward and once back, bringing it alternately into phase with each of the flanking buildings (Wolfson and Alms) (Figs 5 and 6). The fanning process of dragging the footprints through this complex alternation lays out the first tremor field while imparting a certain viscosity to the medium in which the buildings are suspended. The result of these preliminary site-priming operations is to have rendered the aggregate of initial structures no longer rigid, but *colloidal*.

Following from this, the third type of movement generated concerns the external milieu into which these movements are inserted. The rocking, drifting, pulsing movements are three distinct periodicities which combine as in a chemical reaction network to form a single travelling wave front — like a soliton or bore inexplicably forming on ocean or river systems — that self-assembles at the periphery of the tremor field (Fig 7). This second system (the major addition) represents, in topological jargon, a hyperbolic 'smoothing' of the irregular and elliptical shapes emitted from the first. In this sense one would say that the second system presents a higher — and more complex — level of coherence and integration. Indeed what has transpired between the two 'stages' is a phase transition: the mutual entrainment of the original disparate periodic movements has pushed the existing angular system far enough away from its equilibrium or attractor to cause it to flip into a new, more stable state, only now in relation to a new attractor higher up in the system. What this softly undulating figure lacks in apparent macroscopic, geometric features or asperities, it makes up for in granular structure: that is, in flexibility, complexity, and *activity*. On one level, one might say, what was a rigid, or colloidal *polyphony* in the 'originating' system became a type of soft *harmony* in the second. Yet to stop here would be to ignore the full implications of the multiple, differential and fibrous nature of the sine wave. For the Cincinnati project remains wholly within the basic geologic framework: we continue to deal with the same raw materials and forces, only now in different combinations, their different morphologies reflecting different processes of formation.

One view of the wave clearly encourages a sedimentary reading (microstructural formation by strata), to be apposed to the more igneous morphology of the existing buildings (macrostructural formation from cooling liquid). The horizontal partitioning of the wave into stacked plates nervously fluctuating off of a mean clearly manifests this particular singularity, ie, anexact deposits of silt or flysch, plus soft structuration over time (Fig 8). Yet what is richest about this movement is its relation to its own perturbation or tremor field, that is, to its *basin of attraction*.

The wave is, in fact, made up of multiple simultaneous articulations: first, its loose, flexible, earthworm-like segmentarity; then a series of algorithmic impulses driven lengthwise through the system, beginning with a compression/dilation wave that presses certain segments together and draws others apart (Fig 9). This is followed by a horizontal axis-displacing wave, generated by a 'tilt-equation' that programmes the behaviour (shift) of any individual segment in relation only to the one immediately preceding it, as in a Markov chain (Fig 10). The process is then reiterated, in section so to speak, emitting a dip and dive perturbation wave along the z axis (Fig 11); to this is added a corkscrew deformation pulse (torque wave) (Fig 12), followed by a final kick that knocks the whole system into a state of fibrillation (ie, dangerously out of phase) (Fig 13). The complex overlay of all these conflicting movements and the final kick into fibrillation is what is most interesting, first because each of these individual perturbations is independently actualised (architecturalised) in the resulting fibre bundle, and second, because the fibrillation process causes the fibres to deviate maximally in their trajectories so as to explore the farthest reaches of their tremor field or attractor basin (Fig 14). Whereas in the first (colloidal) system the position of elements is determined probabilistically, here the trajectories seem to vaporise through space wilfully to fill the attractor basin in its entirety. The floating wave structure of the Cincinnati project is determined then by a double articulation: in one direction (looking toward molar forms) it stabilises or smooths the discontinuities generated by the rigidly bound masses of the existing building system, and in the other direction (looking towards molecular, uncoded matter deposits and free action) it sifts and recombines its own internally generated differences, driving itself farther and farther away from equilibrium and toward creative instability.

Both the existing building system and the fibre-wave addition are complex homeostatic systems which manage to express stability from one perspective and instability from another. All form, however, is directly the result of instabilities — those moments when a system is weakened by excitatory disturbances that distance it from its organising attractor — but this is generally masked by static geometric representation. (When a system's dynamic is repressed, so is its morphogenesis.) The Cincinnati schema, in fact, represents a very complex, integrated, self-organising, oscillatory system, with a simple, very clear dynamic. As the wave system stretches to the western part of the site for example, it becomes shallower, less compact, more disordered; unable to maintain its internal tension levels, it begins, like breakers at the seashore, to curl, then disintegrate into new forms, as it makes its way now to a lower attractor in the system. As the wave breaks up it will form discrete pools to be crystallised and bound into cooler, more rigid forms. Stability and instability are simultaneously sustained within both structures, and each feeds, both off of and into, the opposite term in the

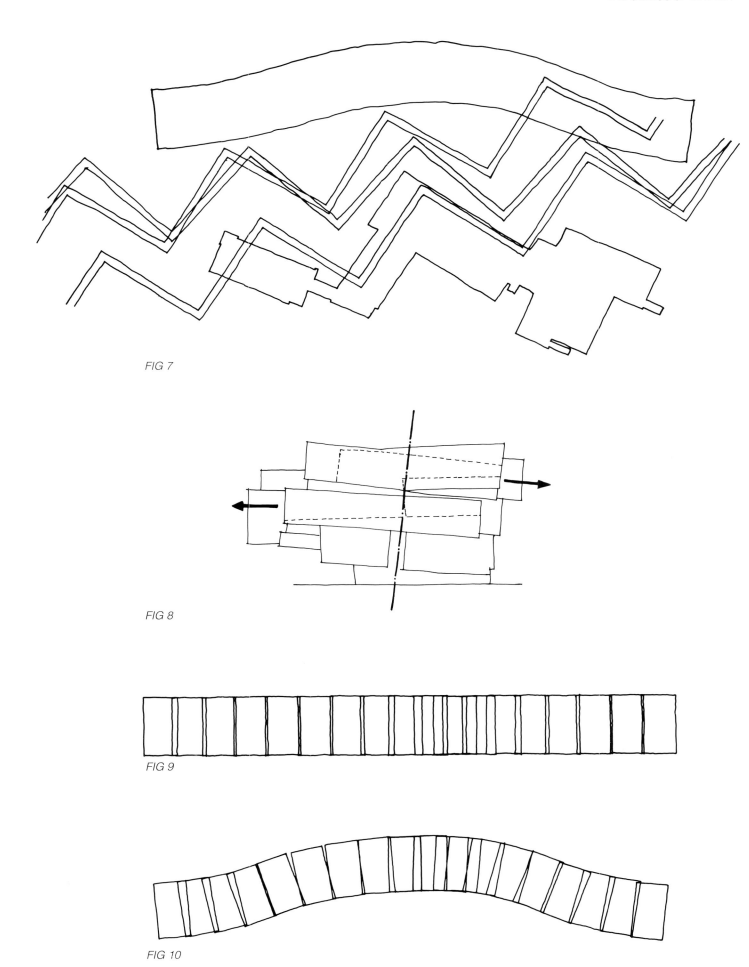

FIG 7

FIG 8

FIG 9

FIG 10

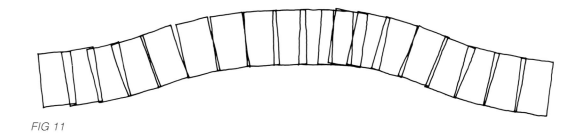

FIG 11

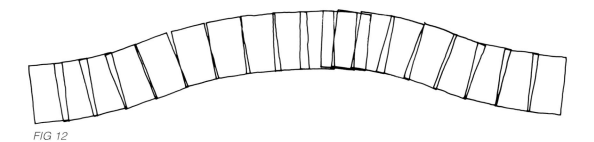

FIG 12

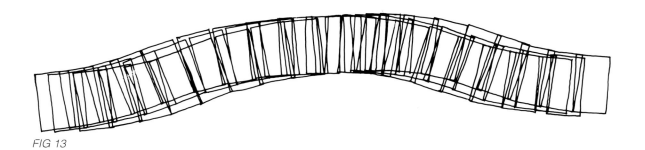

FIG 13

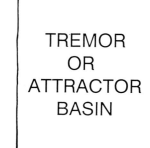

TREMOR
OR
ATTRACTOR
BASIN

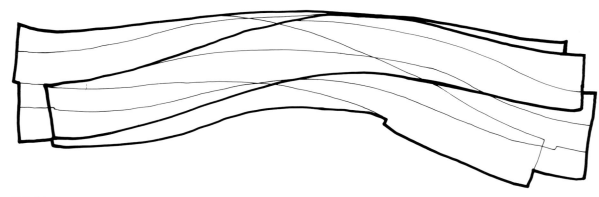

FIG 14

complementary structure. A simple diagram of this relationship would look like Fig 15.

What is most important here is the *cyclic flow* of structure through the entire system. Like the famous Zhabotinsky-Belousov reaction, or chemical clock, the Cincinnati oscillation induces a general, global correlation cutting across all scales within the system, continually ordering and reordering its elements (the solution in the chemical clock correlates every molecule to change from blue to red and back again at precise intervals).

The Cincinnati project is an architecture literally fraught with movement, waves, *flow*, and this guarantees the continual infolding of external influences, the continual recycling and rendering productive of chance perturbations collected in real time at the site. Its movements are finally no longer those of classical translation or displacement through continuous, homogeneous space, but intensive, quality-generating movements that ceaselessly differ, individuate, unfold. There is a new theory of nature emerging today — one based on dynamics, complexity, discontinuities, and events — and a new (though still inchoate) architecture that embraces these same fundamental rhythms of free *becoming*. The 'structures' that interest the late 20th century are no longer those of isolated Forms in disposition, or even in motion, but embedded *matter in the throes of creation*, that is, in free and continuous variation and combination with external forces, perpetually inventing and releasing new capacities, attributes, mixtures, states. Oscillation will be no longer the static operation of sublating two terms across a patch of space, but, as we see it here in the Cincinnati project in nascent form, a veritable engine driving a morphogenetic machine into a new non-linear world in which nothing is predictable save *transformation* itself.

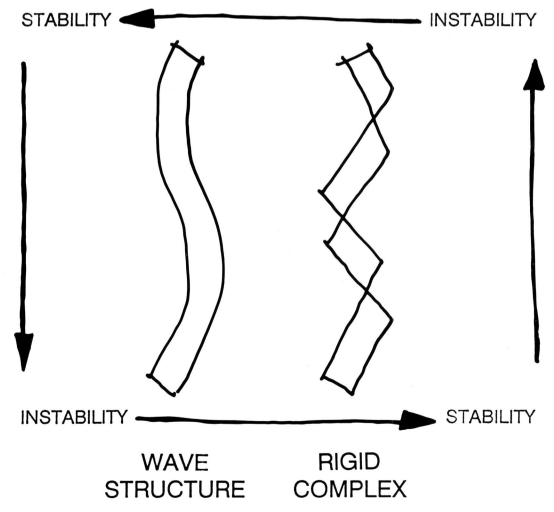

STABILITY ← → INSTABILITY

INSTABILITY → STABILITY

WAVE
STRUCTURE

RIGID
COMPLEX

FIG 15

INeffective DESCRIPTions: SUPPLEmental LINES
GREG LYNN

If there exists a primitive 'geometry' (a protogeometry), it is an operative geometry in which figures are never separable from the affectations befalling them, the lines of their becoming, the segments of their segmentation: there is 'roundness', but no circle, 'alignments', but no straight line, etc. On the contrary, State geometry, or rather the bond between the State and geometry, manifests itself in the primacy of the theorem-element, which substitutes fixed or ideal essences for supple morphological formations, properties for effects, predetermined segments for segmentations in progress.[1]

The recent work of Peter Eisenman has abandoned the dissolution of the cube and the grid for the construction of a less rigid network of lines. The projects have become 'supple' as the coordinates of the grid have disappeared and the proliferation of lines and surfaces which are not straight supply forms which are indescript. Here, the stipulation that geometry necessarily be 'rigid' is abandoned[2] for the provision that geometry can be reconsidered in a more 'supple' manner.[3] The term 'abandon' is used here to describe a movement from a geometric model based on rigidity to a secondary model founded on suppleness. This supple model inscribes the failure of rigidity as the resulting necessity for its discourse, rather than erasing the previous rigid condition and replacing it with itself. To the primacy of 'rigid' geometry, 'supple' geometry is secondary, as it lacks the firmness of ideal structure by which it could be seen as original. 'Supple' geometry's relationship to form is supplemental, as its complaisance makes it contingent on form. The ability for geometry to describe wholistic structure is abandoned for a pliant system of isolated relationships and microstructures which are globally disparate. The qualification of 'supple' geometry as pliant rather than unyielding introduces the 'pli',[4] as the operation of bending and folding.

In Eisenman's latest project for the Frankfurt Rebstock, the 'pli' is the process by which the existing conditions are arbitrarily and unpredictably reframed.[5] This recent work, which is characterised by pliancy, attempts to separate form from its linkage to 'rigid' *formal* description, producing a suppleness which supplies a meaning — neither present nor absent but nevertheless less than ideal. The possibility for a reading of pliancy in Eisenman's recent work indicates a difference from his early projects, which are characterised by complexity and contradiction rather than complaisance and compliancy.

The theory of architecture produced by Eisenman to frame his early work liberates architectural textuality from the discourse of utility. The displacement of architectural meaning occurs through the analytic depletion of the economies of presence. These early processes are characterised by transformation; where latent textuality is formalised through multiple readings and misreadings.

The question to which Eisenman returns, Why does architecture look the way it does?, is thematic in the exhaustion of both functionalism and structuralism through these textual reading strategies. The displacement of architecture's utilitarian discourse occurs with the reinscription of the 'commodious' and the 'firm' within a rhetorical rather than essential discourse of representation. This introductory displacement uncouples architecture's dominant necessity, the utility of function and structure, from its secondary representations, the signification of appearing functional and structural.

The need to overcome presence, the need to supplement an architecture that will always be and look like architecture, the need to break apart the strong bond between form and function, is what my architecture addresses. In its displacement of the traditional role of function it does not deny that architecture must function, but rather suggests that architecture may also function without necessarily symbolising that function, that the presentness of architecture is irreducible to the presence of its functions or its signs.[6]

The opening of the strong bond between the being of architecture, a thing in itself, and the textuality of architecture, a pure sign of itself, has redirected Eisenman's gaze away from the multiplicity of reading strategies and back to the object. This depleted object to which Eisenman *presently* returns has been displaced from the discourse of utility through the erosion of functionalism and structuralism.

Unlike language, where an excess of presence can displace meaning by referring the signifier outside itself to materiality, architecture is already overflowing its meaning by its necessary material presence. It is the simultaneous presence of the object itself with its representation that is specific to architecture's mimetic exchange.

Unlike language, which is understandable through the gaze alone, in architecture there is no such thing as the sign of a column or window without the actual presence of a column or window. Both the gaze and the body are implicated by the interiority of architecture. This interiority, this necessity to enclose, is not found in language or even in painting or sculpture.[7]

Architectural representation is described as already interior to the architectural object, which not only provides for representation's inhabitation of form, but also inscribes inhabitation as architecture's primary discourse. Eisenman's statement that 'reading does not mean a thing'[8] proposes that interpretation alone will not produce an object in presence, therefore identifying the need for an architectural textuality which resides in an *informed* reading. For Eisenman, certain objects are more or less open to the deconstruction of presence, while others offer a greater or lesser resistance, indicating the persistence of essential qualities within the objects themselves. According to Eisenman, the aura of 'presentness' is a residual condition in presence, which remains after architecture's deconstruction. The subject of Eisenman's theoretical work has been the articulation of an architectural textuality which is neither a purely linguistic phenomenon nor essential to the thing itself. His resistance to the complete deconstruction of the object has spurred a new dialogue with philosophy, which is troubled by *any* investment of aura or essence in form, regardless of its strength. For Eisenman, it is this resistance to post-structuralism that distinguishes architecture's difference as a predominantly immanent discourse, where the signifier and signified are simultaneously present. The recent renegotiation of the transaction with philosophy differs from earlier open invitations as architecture is defined by its resistance to deconstruction. This resistance to the dissolution of the object into pure reading defines a residue which resides in neither being nor language but in what Georges Bataille has described as '*informe*'.[9] The condition of textuality in form implies a materiality which is nonetheless formless, as in the 'informe' of Bataille. As the architectural sign necessarily resides in form, any description of it as 'informe' or formless would occur between a failed architectural representation and the thing itself. Unlike 'rigid' geometry, whose ideal structure is primary as it comes before the object itself as original, 'supple' geometry acknowledges the possibility that form may not resemble *anything*. Its pliant structure is complaisant,[10] as it is secondary to *any form*.

From the initial house projects to the Wexner Center for the Visual Arts, the condition of weakness between architectural form and its representation has been signified as an absence within the architectural discourse of presence. This absence is duplicitous, as the initial separation of essential function and structure from the representation of appearing functional and structural, and secondarily, in the early work which relies on contradiction, this separation becomes iconic as the representation of appearing non-structural and non-functional. This dialectic contradiction of utility is iconic in the pairing of utilitarian and anti-utilitarian elements in House VI and the Wexner Center. For example, the green functional stair is contradicted by the inverted red non-functional stair, the columns separating both the double bed in the bedroom and the seats of the dining room table contradict the functional placement of other columns, and the exterior hanging column above the lawn contradicts the firmness of the structure. These operations are reproduced in the Wexner Center, as the brick arch of the armoury is cantilevered along with the beams and suspended columns of the grid at the entry stair. It is not the introduction of absence between the sign and the signifier, but rather its signification, which most troubles Derrida in his 'Postel' correspondence with Eisenman.

A more pliant discourse would offer a resistance to utility through neither resemblance nor contradiction, to which Eisenman's early work appeals, but rather through the acknowledgement that architectural discourse may not resemble anything. Eisenman's qualification of 'presentness' implies not only a potential weak bond between the architectural sign and the necessary utility which it signifies, but also the recent articulation of a graft between conditions which are arbitrary and immanent to architectural discourse. In previous projects the absence of architectural meaning has been effectively signified through the use of latent but immanent texts to erode strong geometric form. It is the ability of these early projects to signify effectively that indicates the prolonged strength of formalism, yet to be dismantled in Eisenman's architecture. Since the erection of the Wexner Center Eisenman's recent work recognises that the displacement of signification implies the ineffectiveness of *any* meaning, including the signification of absence. The attempted separation of the elision between the necessary utility of architecture and its utilitarian signification relies on the conventions of geometry and formalism for its meaning, in the early work. In these projects, the pure form of the grid and cube is eroded by a corrosive process which deposits residual traces. These traces effectively represent the erosion of functionalism and structuralism through formal signification, in the projects leading to and including the Wexner Center. Still, the pure form of rigid geometry is the ground for architectural mimesis, which remains privileged as a residual presence in the early projects; as the EL figure is iconic of the eroded cube. The dominance of the global base figure of the grid, despite its disintegration by textual processes, remains as a ground for orthogonal planimetric meaning. Although gravity indicates the necessity for forms which are horizontal and perpendicular to the ground plane, as the grid is an iconic rather than an actual structure.

Where previously the presence of the 'rigid' structure of the grid was contradicted by the signification of structural and functional absence, in the more recent projects structures are introduced which neither signify nor contradict Vitruvian firmness. Rather, these projects register a deficiency in the ideal qualities necessary for a description of this same rigidity, which is abandoned. The weakness of these 'supple' lines is not iconic, in that it does not reside in the forms themselves, but rather in their resistance to formal description. This separation of forms from their formal description is reciprocal to Eisenman's earlier erosion of the strong bond between utility and its signification as functional and structural.

Any architecture is necessarily geometric, in that its discourse is concerned with the description of *form* as *formal*. As geometry is immanent to any architectural interpretation, even a displaced relationship between form and formalism must pass through a geometric description. This process of translation remains privileged in Eisenman's early projects as a neutral abstraction, as geometry is unaffected by its translation of form into its own discourse. In the most recent projects, the mediation of form by geometry introduces a reciprocal mediation of geometry as it becomes 'supple' and pliant in order adequately to describe form while resisting idealisation and abstraction. The rejection of the Modernist sensibility of abstraction, as the moment where architecture idealises a structure so that it can be effectively described, marks the possibility for geometry's failure as an architectural structure. The addition to the College of Design, Architecture, Art and Planning begins to resist the parallel idealisation of 'rigid' geometry with forms that present themselves obliquely to orthogonal view. In the DAAP project, formal idealisation by geometry is repressed as the curved lines lack the coordinates necessary for the location of a radius or a straight line. The resistance of its 'supple' structure, which is arbitrary to architectural discourse, to a reduction by 'rigid' geometry, which is immanent to architectural discourse, is founded on the project's lack of ideal coordinates, lines, or planes from which its forms could begin to be fixed.

Although the 'supple' lines of the DAAP project are arbitrary to 'rigid' geometric description, they are similar to the landscape forms which are immanent to the curve of the sloped site. The latent curved and sloped conditions of the context suggested the need for a similar building form, which lacked a 'rigid' geometric description. The 'supple' geometric processes were used to generate a curvilinear form which twisted and curved with the site. In this sense, the project suggests a graft between conditions which are immanent, where the project defines itself through the operation of dominant and latent texts which are internal to the programme, site, or existing building, and arbitrary, where non-essential texts are introduced which are external to the programme, site, and existing building. The deflections of the curved lines respond to the recessive forms of the contours which are latent in the site, making a graft possible between the arbitrary forms of the addition and the immanent forms of the site.

> . . . in a sense the work was to find the building in the site. Its vocabulary came from the curves of the land forms and the chevron forms of the existing building setting up a dynamic relationship to organise the space between the two.[11]

The iteration of the existing building by a series of traces, which are deployed across the site based on their latent geometries, relies on the introduction of contradiction into the immanent structure of the existing context, in a similar fashion to the earlier projects. The chevron is derived as a latent structure within the existing DAAP building which extends the logic of the building across the site as an ornamental band of circulation. The chevron relies on the abstraction of the existing building as an ideal geometry to generate the new alignments of the 'Alms', 'DAA' and 'Wolfson' traces. As the orientation of the DAA building is dominant, the traces are aligned to the latent structures of the Wolfson and Alms buildings. These processes displace the opposition of the original context to the addition yet they reinforce the originality of the base figure itself through contradiction. The operations deployed toward the existing building generate originary traces which multiply the base figures which are immanent to the site. As the curved lines pass across the outer boundaries of the three chevrons they shift their width incrementally to the north and south, as if differentially refracted within each chevron zone. The curved lines return to their original position when within the chevron bands and crack along the line of the chevron to their shifted positions.

Despite the fact that the project begins with the tracing of the immanent figures of the existing building, the curved lines introduce a mapping of supplemental traces, which do not refer to the previously existing structures. The horizontal network of lines across the site are supplemental in that they are generated through the affiliations of their segmentation, rather than through a reduction in scale from an ideal global structure. The local affiliations between segments are produced without reference to the resulting global figure of the curved line, which is less than ideal, as its form cannot be predicted from the beginning of its segmentation. However, the horizontality of this network of lines does not premiate the plan, as their differential torquing in section displaces the tableau of the ground plane as an ideal datum. The building's mass oscillates between subterranean 'burrowing' at the western precinct of the site, to a slithering on the site's surface to the east. As RE Somol 'chances' upon the rhizome[12] as an analogy to describe the mapping of the Wexner Center, the DAAP project engenders the rhizome's 'multiplicity of secondary roots'[13] as its primary structure, without residual reference to the eroded pure form of the grid and the cube. In this sense, the earlier contradiction by which the 'rigid' geometry was eroded by traces, is blurred by Somol's articulation of a secondary structure of affiliations. It is this network of chance affiliations which Somol's rhizomatic reading exploits within the contradiction of the competing global alignments of the Wexner Center's grid geometry. The 'supple' structure of the DAAP project is arbitrary to the 'rigid' structure of the existing building and does not derive its meaning by contradiction, but rather through the chance affiliations that it exploits. These moments occur at the connections to the campus at the pedestrian bridge, Crosley Tower, and the garage. The effects of supple geometry rely on a clear[14] reading of molecular affiliations between arbitrary texts, which register the specific and disparate information which the abstraction of an ideal interpretation would repress. The strategy of mapping, rather than tracing, implicit in the analogy of the rhizome, displaces global structure by exploiting affiliations between unpredicted, multiple, disparate and localised connections. The horizontal stratifications of the curved lines are not organised by *molar* or global structures but rather by the *molecular* structures of localised mappings, overlaps, traces, and interferences between adjacent segments. The differential conditions of torque, tilt, and step, in the X, Y, and Z dimensions, are unpredicted between any two segments, as the variable recombinations are out of phase. The mobility of exponential overlapping, tilting and phase shifting generates multiple time frames along the line, composing open rather than closed intervals.[15] It is the introduction of differential intervals within the line's segmentation that generates the molar figure of the curve. The affiliations between segments are regulated at the molecular scale, but lack a molar order necessary for geometric idealisation. This proliferation of lines has roundness without circularity, as the lines are neither radial nor axially straight. The addition resists ideal description as it cannot be coordinated between points. Unlike the identical *repetition* of a Cartesian line, the 'supple' lines of the new building are an *iteration* of localised interstitial intervals, resulting in a mutant flow.[16]

A straight line, from which the supple line originates, is defined by the parallel and tangential alignments of the segments. Into the fixed phasing of the segmented line a sequence of exponentially increasing and decreasing overlaps is placed between segments. The parallel alignments occurring in plan are replaced with exponentially increasing and decreasing angles between adjacent plates. This variable phasing introduces a mobile rather than fixed time sequence which relays along the line's length as a flow of open intervals. The exponent and phase of the plan tilts does not correspond to the exponent and phase of the overlaps, so that a curve results which multiplies without duplicating itself as it is inherently out of phase.[17] The alignments of spacing and tilting are compounded by sectional torquing and stepping whose oblique sectional effects rotate the ideal cutting planes of the plan and section into a multiplicity of views. The plan's dominance, as the ideal ground for architectural meaning, is founded on the firmness of 'rigid' geometries interpretations. As 'rigid' geometry is the dominant ground for the datum of the architectural plan, the 'suppleness' of the DAAP project begins to displace the singular plane of the plan cut, by which architectural form is co-ordinated to either parallel or perpendicular points. This failure of geometry to orthogonally represent the 'supple' geometry of micro-affiliations necessitates the N-dimensional modelling of computer-aided drawings, with which the project can be conceived from multiple cutting planes. Neither horizontal nor perpendicular to the object at any point, this more pliant geometric description of the architectural form can accommodate oblique relationships as it is secondary and non-original. The mobility of this 'supple' geometry abandons the ideal ground of horizontal and frontal presentation which the abstraction of rigid geometry promises in the singular moment of the plan cut and section. The obliquity of the form to its formal interpretation obscures the possibility for the complete and effective representation of architectural form. It is significant that this obliquity is neither essential to the forms themselves nor is it purely a function of their reading by a more 'supple' geometry, but rather, it occurs between their form and its resistance to an ideal interpretation. Therefore, the crooked figure which results as a consequence of the mappings of its segmentation is neither straight nor straightforward.

The 'supple' geometry of the DAAP project generates a molar figure through the molecular mappings of that figure's segmentation. This process of affiliation differs from Eisenman's earlier processes of contradiction whereby molar figures were rigidly opposed for the generation of secondary traces. For instance, the archeological operations of the Romeo and Juliet project introduced a system of cartographic traces (which although they are derived from maps differ from the recent processes described as mapping) which are not only immanent to geometry, but further the latent figures that themselves are immanent to the existing site. So despite the displacement of the originality of the found site through the use of maps, the 'traces' of latent information operate to reinforce the ground of plan geometry for the signification of the project's absent meaning. In a similar manner the Frankfurt Biocentrum and the Carnegie Mellon Research Institute projects introduce external scientific texts into the architectural process as arbitrary structures, yet despite the processes of multiplicity which they introduce, their base forms reinforce the mimetic dominance of 'rigid' geometry, as the integers of the N-cube and the fractal DNA code are *already* formally descript. Their representation of external processes through an already formal structure allows for a reduction into architecture, whereby neither the architectural nor the scientific texts are displaced, as geometry provides an assumed neutral language as the site for translation. Despite their residual status, the figures generated between these base figures are fundamental, as traces which refer to an original 'molar' structure. The status of the global figure as the origin of the residual trace is a result of a primary structure, which is eroded by contradiction rather than by the *chance* affiliations of a secondary, more 'supple' geometry.

> *The tracing has already translated the map into an image; it has already transformed the rhizome into roots and radicles. It has organised, stabilised, neutralised the multiplicities according to the axes of significance and subjectification belonging to it. It has generated, structuralised the rhizome, and when it thinks it is reproducing something else it is in fact only reproducing itself.*[18]

In Eisenman's early work, abstraction's translation of form neutralises the potential displacement of architectural textuality by the arbitrary texts of cartography, biology, and other latent contextual conditions. What distinguishes the DAAP project from these earlier processes of tracing is that the mapping of local residues and microstructures are given originary value in themselves, as the 'molar lines are already undermined by fissures and cracks'.[19] The DAAP project attempts to frame its global structure as a supplementary mapping which is *already* residual rather than a system of traces which refer to a once complete pure form for their reading as residual. The supplemental traces of 'overlap', 'tilt', 'torque' and 'phase shift' are fundamental to the production of the crooked lines, which are indescript as global figures as they lack ideal structure. This distinguishes the 'supple' line as no longer within the 'rigid' geometric system necessary for the firmness of architectural discourse. The global structure abandons the eroded cube and grid, as it is itself a residual structure, contingent on the affiliations of a

multiplicity of microstructures. This condition of 'supple' clarity results from the failed formal description by rigid geometry of an arbitrary form. The resistance of the DAAP project to formal description resides in the multiplicity of affiliations between the disparate molecular structures of segmentation, where the resulting molar structure is ideally deficient. This resistance to a predictable or effective description can be distinguished from Jeffrey Kipnis' recent concept of undecidability, which has been formulated in response to Eisenman's recent work, including the DAAP project. Kipnis finds an excessive multiplicity of meanings disseminated by Eisenman's 'worms'.[20]

> *Most recently, his efforts in the Columbus Convention Center, the University of Cincinnati DAAP addition and the hotel in Banyoles, Spain, are directed toward a design which no longer seeks to embody any specific meaning, architectural or nonarchitectural, but rather to create a formal and material environment capable of engendering many meanings.*[21]

The resistance to the embodiment of a dominant meaning is located by Kipnis in the proliferation of *many* secondary meanings, which the object engenders as an excess of plentitude. This multiplicity which is more than one is governed by the essence of the object, and the resulting deferral of a singular meaning by the presence of simultaneous meanings relies on a contradiction between representations. The competing meanings are *more than adequate* for Kipnis, as their excess is *both* a consequence *and* a contradiction of essential similarities the forms have with other signifiers. The 'governed multiplicity'[22] of Kipnis disturbs any singular meaning with the contradiction of an excessive plentitude, yet the ability of these projects to signify remains intact, so that *any* meaning is as essentially effective as *any other*.

> *In its very negativity, the notion of the un-decidable — apart from the fact that it only has such a sense by some irreducible reference to the ideal of decidability — also retains a mathematical value derived from some unique source of value vaster than the project of* definiteness *itself. This whole debate is only understandable within something like the geometrical or mathematical science, whose unity is still to come on the basis of what is announced in its origin.*[23]

As the undecidable relies on a plenitude of contradiction by a signifier in multiplicity, the affiliations which generate the residual global figure of the DAAP project are a multiplicity which is incomplete, as the molar figure is formally indescript and unpredictable. This resistance of the DAAP project to Kipnis' reading of its undecidability is not its failure to proliferate *many* meanings, but rather, its inability to engender *any one* meaning. The DAAP's affiliation of micro-structures invites a multiplicity which is less than one rather than more.[24] This introduces a lack in form, as the multiplicity *already* within the lines themselves resists any one interpretation. The qualification of Kipnis' abandonment of *any* singular meaning acknowledges that although the contradiction of *many* meanings renders the truthfulness of any one undecidable, the most recent work of Peter Eisenman

problematises *(m)any* meaning(s) as they resist interpretation. The pliancy of these projects invites *many* readings while obscuring *any one* of these by the obliquity of the forms to formal reading. The 'supple' geometry of Peter Eisenman's recent projects displaces the ideal exteriority of interpretation through an internal resistance *in form* to formal description. The multiplicity inherent to these forms resists *any one reading*, while inviting inadequate readings which are *less than more*.   *(Text written in 1990.)*

NOTES

1 Gilles Deleuze and Félix Guattari, 'Micropolitics and Segmentarity', *A Thousand Plateaus: Capitalism and Schizophrenia*, University of Minnesota Press, Minneapolis,1987, p212.

2 For a further discussion of abandonment, in reference to the categories of painting and sculpture in the work of Marcel Duchamp, see John Rajchman: 'For, as de Duve uses the term, to "abandon" something is not just to discard it. It is to register the moment of its loss or "impossibility" within a work in such a way as to open up, or call for, another history.' John Rajchman, 'Duchamp's Joke', *Philosophical Events: Essays of the 80's*, Columbia University Press, New York.

3 '1 supple [ME *souple*, fr OF, fr L *supplic-*, *supplex* submissive, suppliant, lit, bending under, fr *sub-* + *plic-* (akin to *plicare* to fold)—more at PLY] 1a: compliant often to the point of obsequiousness b: readily adaptable or responsive to new situations 2a: capable of being bent or folded without creases, cracks, or breaks: PLIANT < ~ leather> b: able to perform bending or twisting movements with ease or grace: LIMBER <~ legs of a dancer> c: easy and fluent without stiffness or awkwardness <sang with a lively, ~ voice — Douglas Watt>. *Webster's New Collegiate Dictionary*, G & C Merriam Co, Springfield, Massachusetts, 1977, p1170.

4 Gilles Deleuze, *Le Pli*.

5 'By introducing the concept of the fold as a non-dialectic third condition, one which is between figure and ground, it is possible to index other possible immanent conditions latent in Frankfurt. In other words, through the concept of the fold it is possible to reference or reframe what already exists in Frankfurt, to suggest how what exists could be something other than that which was repressed by former systems of authority such as figure and ground.' Peter Eisenman, 'Viel/Faltig/Field/Feld', project description for the Frankfurt Rebstock competition. What is less important to this discussion of the fold is the reference to the uncovering of repressed immanent conditions latent to the site, and rather the external necessity for the arbitrary fold to this process. For a further discussion of the fold as a '*Passe-Partout*' between internal and external categories, see Jacques Derrida: 'But by the same token *is* not: the fold in a lining by which it is, out of itself, in itself, at once its own outside and its own inside; between the outside and the inside, making the outside enter the inside and turning back the antre or the other upon its surface, the hymen is never pure or proper, has no life of its own, no proper name.' Jacques Derrida, 'The Double Session', *Dissemination*, The University of Chicago Press, Chicago, 1981, p229.

6 Peter Eisenman, 'Post/El Cards: A Reply to Jacques Derrida', in *Re:working Eisenman*.

7 Ibid.

8 Peter Eisenman, 'miMISes READING: does not mean A THING', in *Re:working Eisenman*.

9 'A dictionary begins when it no longer gives the meaning of words, but their tasks. Thus "*formless*" is not only an adjective having a given meaning, but a term that serves to bring things down in the world, generally requiring that each thing have its form. What it designates has no rights in any sense and gets itself squashed everywhere, like a spider or an earthworm. In fact, for academic men to be happy, the universe would have to take shape. All of philosophy has no other goal: it is a matter of giving a frock coat to what is, a mathematical frock coat. On the other hand, affirming that the universe resembles nothing and is only formless amounts to saying that the universe is something like a spider or spit.' Georges Bataille. 'Informe (Formless)', *Visions of Excess: Selected Writings, 1927-1939*. Edited and with an introduction by Allan Stoekl, translated by Allan Stoekl, with Carl R Lovitt and Donald M Leslie Jr, University of Minnesota Press, Minneapolis: 1985, p31.

10 'Complaisant' is used here distinctly from complacent, as the structure described is actively rather than passively supplemental.

11 Peter Eisenman, 'College of Design, Architecture, Art and Planning: University of Cincinnati', *Architecture + Urbanism, 90:01*, A+U Publishing Co, Tokyo, 1990, p162.

12 For a reading of chance affiliation in the operation of rhizomatic structures, and their characteristic unpredictability from the outset of a design process in the Wexner Center for the Visual Arts, see RE Somol: The building acts as a weed that proliferates within the spaces left between cultivated areas, between the institutions of cultural Modernism and structures of architectural Modernity. In that sense, Wexner approaches the status of the rhizome — a horizontal, underground stem able to produce the shoot and root systems of a new plant. Unlike the tree that imposes a hierarchical structure, the rhizome circulates underground making unordered connections and affiliations, sometimes penetrating even the rooted trunks of trees and putting them to new uses.' RE Somol, '0-0', *Progressive Architecture, October 1989* , Penton Publishing, Cleveland, 1989, p88.

13 Deleuze and Guattari, 'Introduction: Rhizome', *Plateaus* p5.

14 'That is precisely what clarity is: the distinctions that appear in what used to seem full, the holes in what used to be compact; and conversely, where just before we saw endpoints of clear-cut segments, now there are indistinct fringes, encroachments, overlappings, migrations, acts of segmentation that no longer coincide with the rigid segmentarity. Everything now appears supple, with holes in fullness, nebulas in forms, and flutter in lines . . . A microphysics of the migrant has replaced the macrogeometry of the sedentary.' Deleuze and Guattari, 'Micropolitics and Segmentarity', *Plateaus*, p228.

15 'The smooth and the striated are distinguished first of all by an inverse relation between the point and the line (in the case of the striated, the line is between two points, while in the smooth, the point is between two lines) and second, by the nature of the line

(smooth-directional, open intervals, dimensional-striated, closed intervals).' Deleuze and Guattari, 'The Smooth and the Striated', *Plateaus*, p480.

16 'This is how you tell the difference between the segmented line and the quantum flow. A mutant flow always implies something tending to elude or escape the codes.' Deleuze and Guattari, 'Micropolitics and Segmentarity', *Plateaus*, p228.

17 The operation of 'phase shift' was introduced to Eisenman's work in the Frankfurt Biocentrum project, where the fractal geometry of the plan borrowed the process of transcription from the nucleotides non-repetitive reading of DNA strands. This analogy operates exclusively in the horizontal plane; the fractal processes are iconic as the plan is premiated as the ground for the project's meaning. The CMRI project also utilised a phase shift between differentially organised N-Cubes to generate the asymptotic curve of its site plan.

18 Deleuze and Guattari, 'Introduction: Rhizome', *Plateaus*, p13.

19 Deleuze and Guattari, 'Micropolitics and Segmentarity', *Plateaus*, p224.

20 Jeffrey Kipnis, 'A Matter of Respect', *Architecture + Urbanism. 90:01*, A+U Publishing Co, Tokyo, 1990, p137.

21 Kipnis, 'A Matter of Respect', p134.

22 'Starting from a system of axioms which "governs" a multiplicity, every proposition is determinable *either* as analytic consequence *or* as analytic contradiction.' Jacques Derrida, *Edmund Husserl's Origin of Geometry: An Introduction.* Translated, with a preface and afterword, by John P Leavey Jr, N Hays, Stony Brook, NY, 1978, p53.

23 Derrida, *Introduction*, p53.

24 For a discussion of Deleuzian multiplicity which is 'less than one' in reference to the urban scale projects of Eisenman, see RE Somol: 'Accidents Will Happen', in *Re:working Eisenman*.

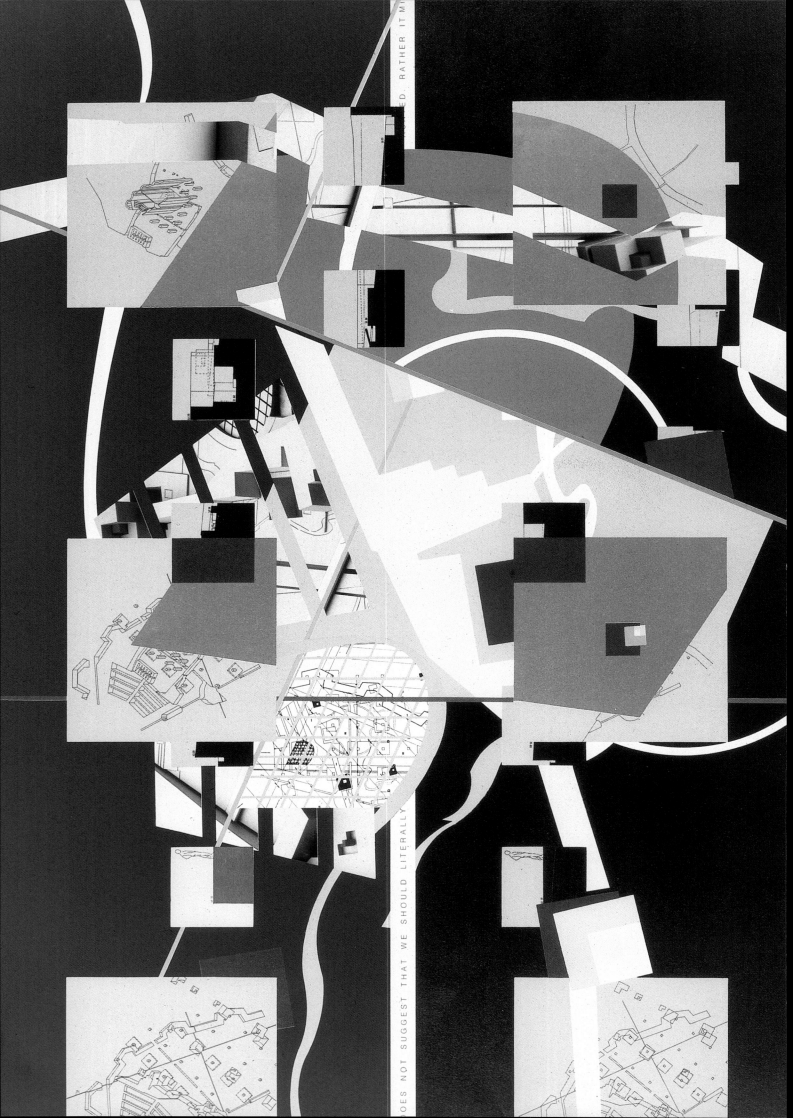

DOES NOT SUGGEST THAT WE SHOULD LITERALLY

FROM TATTOO TO TRINKET
ANTHONY VIDLER

What has become prosaic in itself is not to be reshaped poetically; it can only be dressed up.
Hegel.

The question of ornament appears especially problematic today, when a so-called Post-Modernism, dedicated to the hedonistic proliferation of rediscovered 'architectural motifs', is itself in the process of being countered by a nostalgic revival of Modernism's own motifs. For Modernist motifs, in ideological terms, signal 'no ornament', at the same time as they are, stylistically, no more than ornament. The condition is the same whether we speak of the 'Constructivism' of Tschumi, or the apparently more complicated 'deconstructions' of Coop Himmelblau, Libeskind or Eisenman. Indeed, the very notion of ornament is, in many contemporary projects, thrown into doubt, as the traditional distinction between that which is essential and that which is auxiliary (a distinction that was a necessary condition of 'Post-Modern' irony) is blurred or discarded altogether.

As 'auxiliary light and complement to beauty', in Alberti's terms, ornament presupposed the existence of an original and originating body: hence the organic analogies of classicism, and the sartorial analogies of eclecticism and Modernism. Without such bodies, whether symbolic or structural, the condition for ornament would seem absent. Even in the most 'ornamental' of Post-Modern projects — in the facades of Michael Graves, Charles Moore or Robert Venturi, for example — it is still possible to detect the difference between ornament and what is being ornamented. Indeed, it is such a distinction that makes it possible to identify the 'false' nature of the ornament, or, by contrast, the ornamental nature of the supporting structure. But the facadeless grids and colliding forms of the new deconstructivists seem at once to discard all ornament and assume an entirely ornamental identity.

Here the traditional identification of ornament with its proximity to the architectural 'body' breaks down in front of the apparent paradox of a building comprised of 'total ornament'. Which immediately poses the question: Ornament to what? That is, if the architecture itself has become ornament, with respect to what entity might its ornamental qualities be recognisable? The recently completed Wexner Center for the Visual Arts, Ohio State University, Columbus, by Peter Eisenman, raises this question with regard both to the apparently ornamental grid that fills the passage be-

tween the Center and the adjoining building, and the more properly ornamental grids that pattern the floors and walls of the Center. These constructed and inlaid grids are, in fact, simply extensions and manifestations of grids that compose the whole building, itself formed out of the collisions among at least three grids of different scales, themselves derived from virtual and real grids that map the context. In this situation, how might we distinguish between ornament and non-ornament, or, in other terms, how might we describe a condition of total ornament?

In this context, it might be tempting to refer to Gianni Vattimo's reading of the late Heidegger, and tentatively conclude that Eisenman and his peers are, consciously or unconsciously, trapped in the more general, post-historical, condition of 'weak monumentality', producing an essentially ornamental art that holds a 'background' position. Against the strong metaphysical, monumental tradition of the Hegelian utopia, such monuments would, in Vattimo's terms, provide

> a backdrop to which no attention is paid, and . . . a surplus which has no possible legitimation in an authentic foundation.[1]

For Vattimo,

> what is lost in the foundation and ungrounding which is ornament, is the heuristic and critical function of the distinction between decoration as surplus and what is "proper" to the thing and to the work,[2]

That is, the distinction between essence and auxiliary. This loss, or 'exhaustion' would, in Vattimo's conclusion, be acknowledged in the monument-become-ornament, invaded by the very surplus that was, originally, its reason for being.

And yet, however tempting we might find this notion of the monument as 'residue' of memory, as already ruined trace, as 'pure' decoration, we should perhaps stop at the easy equivalence posed by a 'counter-monument' like the Wexner Center, and the philosophy of a Heidegger recuperated for post-history and counter-nostalgia. For, the evident presence of such a building — a presence equally aspired to by Libeskind's Berlin Wall project and Coop Himmelblau's rooftop schemes in Vienna — clearly indicates a *desire* for an essential monumentality that goes far beyond any ironic backgrounding or fatigued playing. Indeed, behind most deconstructivist projects there hovers the trace, not of an exhausted memory, but of an active and dialectical opposition. Perhaps then, the theoretical conditions for interpreting such 'totalisations' of ornament might be better constructed out of the fault lines of post-Hegelian attempts to *recuperate* monumentality than from any 'post-historical' philosophies of loss or failure.

Along these lines, it might be possible to articulate the conditions for a monumental ornament that has no need of the original monument, ie an ornament that takes its definition from what it implies, rather than from that to which it is added. Hegel, in his paradoxical formulation of the dilemma of architecture, already pointed to this condition. In his discussion of the disappearance of the symbolic form of art, Hegel spoke of the moment when the symbol, dedicated to the perfect unity of inner meaning and external shape, is undermined by the classical will to use and dominate according to a strict separation of means and ends. His example is that of didactic poetry, where the content is entirely developed in its 'prosaic' form to the extent that any artistic shape imposed on this form is external and ornamental: 'What has become prosaic in itself', he concludes,

> is not to be reshaped poetically; it can only be dressed up; just as horticulture, for example, is for the most part just an external arrangement of a site already given by nature and not in itself beautiful, or as architecture by ornament and external decoration makes pleasant the utility of premises devoted to prosaic circumstances and affairs.[3]

In these terms, Hegel maintains, didactic poetry, and by direct implication, architecture, 'cannot be numbered amongst the proper forms of art.' We are thereby confronted with the definition of an art, architecture, the first of all the arts, symbolic in its essence, that refuses artistic status to its subsequent developments. Architecture, Hegel states, of its very nature cannot remain symbolic, having to become prosaic, and therefore, entirely ornamental. In reverse, we are presented with a notion of ornament, that, once distinguished *as* ornament, separately from the essential symbol, undermines the symbolic equation of form and content, fatally marking architecture for an unhappy death long before all the other arts.

Perhaps it is in the light of such a fatality that we might read the post-Hegelian attempts to reconstitute the nature of ornament as an organic extension of bodily display, as so many theoretical expressions of a need to reconstitute monumentality, but now *as* dress. With no pretence to the symbolic, a monument might take on the role of the sign, always assuming that the true nature of this sign — its arbitrariness — might be distinguished at first glance. Ornament thus becomes a proper subject for enquiry on its own terms and is seen, anthropologically and sociologically, as a direct outgrowth of the same instincts for tattooing, ritual

dressing and the wearing of jewellery as constituted society itself. In these terms ornament might even be construed as the very foundation of architectural style.

Thus Gottfried Semper's construction of an architecture that owed its origin to the adornment of the body seems, in retrospect, a means of recuperating architecture once more, this time not as symbol but as ornament — 'adornment is the first important step towards art: in adornment and its laws is contained the complex codex of formal aesthetics.' For Semper all the decorative elements of architecture — those that accentuated the relations of the parts of the structure, those that designated the distinction among the parts, those that pointed to the purpose of the building and finally, those that related the work to the universe as a whole — owed their origin to the adornment of the body and its extensions in the industry of the family. Adornment was what distinguished the human species from all animals, it was what marked the striving for individuality: 'by adorning anything, be it alive or inanimate, I bestow upon it the right of individual life. By making it the centre of relations that pertain to it alone, I elevate it to the rank of a person.'[4] Hence, the principle of 'dressing', or *Bekleidung*, which Semper identifies as the first principle of architecture. Reversing the traditional view of dress as originally invented to cover and decorate the body, later to be adopted, by analogy, in architectural ornament, Semper posits its initial appearance in architecture, only thence to be assumed as a distinguishing mark for the body:

> The art of dressing the body's nakedness (if we do not count the ornamental painting of one's own skin) is probably a later invention than the use of coverings for encampments and spatial enclosures. There are tribes whose savagery appears to be the most primitive, who do not know clothing, yet to whom the use of skins and even a more or less developed industry of spinning, plaiting, and weaving for the furnishing and security of their encampments is not unknown.[5]

In this way, ornament, far from being a mere auxiliary, emerges as the foundation of architecture; dressing and incrustation, traditionally scorned as mere embellishment, become the means by which structure and the division of space are represented, linguistically and socially, as monumental form:

> This tradition of incrustation, in fact, applies to the totality of Hellenic art and prevails, above all, as the true essence of architecture. It limits itself in no way simply to a type of tendentious decorative adornment of surfaces with sculpture and painting, but essentially conditions the art-form in general; in Greek architecture, both the art-form

*and decoration are so intimately bound together
by this influence of the principle of surface dressing that an isolated look at either is impossible.[6]*

Semper thereby counters the Hegelian 'loss' of symbolic form, symptom of division and decline, by an assertion of the very primacy of dressing.

Read in this light, Adolf Loos's apparent 'refusal' of ornament may be seen as the ethical corollary to Semper's materialist justification of dress. Thus the 'principle of cladding' is invoked against the 'Potemkin City' of Vienna, made out of 'canvas and pasteboard' with its historicist facades 'nailed on' to structures whose real and truly Modern identity was thereby hidden. Loos decries this city of frock-coats and fur collars concealing social equals, a bourgeois city pretending to be a city of aristocrats.[7] An 'authentic style', by contrast, would be one that proudly displayed the 'modernity' of techniques and life in the late 19th century, by its open revelation of the distinction between structure and hung enclosure, by its use of materials that reveal their nature: a strict separation maintained between 'the material clad' and 'cladding'.[8]

Such a sartorial ethics, summarised in the formula, 'ornament is something that must be overcome', did not by any means imply the total eradication of ornament; but rather the eradication of ornament of another time, place and role; the destruction of survivals, primitive and otherwise; the breaking down of prejudices, in the same way, for example, that 'the 20th-century woman cyclist' might 'wear pants and clothing that leaves her feet free'.[9] Modern architecture was thereby to be 'dressed down' for action, and ornament, so to speak, became folded into the structure of the object. Hence the notion of the tattoo as a mark of the degenerate and the criminal in the Modern context, where any overtly 'useless' decoration offended propriety and economy. Loos, in this way, shifted the argument from Semper's 'tailorisation' to Modernist Taylorisation.

'The evolution of culture', Loos claims, 'is synonymous with the removal of ornament from utilitarian objects.'[10] Here the evolutionary historicism of the late 19th century is allied to an economics of production:

*The enormous damage and devastation caused
in aesthetic development by the revival of ornament would be easily made light of, for no one, not
even the power of the state, can halt mankind's
evolution . . . But it is a crime against the national
economy that it should result in a waste of human
labour, money and material. Time cannot make
good this damage.[11]*

'Ornament', he concludes, 'inflicts serious injury on health, on the national budget and hence on cultural evolution: . . . ornament is wasted labour power and hence wasted health.'[12]

Thus fashion, that impels continuous changes of ornamental style, supports a consumption economy based on waste and obsolescence, and leads to what Loos describes as 'a premature devaluation of the labour product'. In this cycle of production and consumption, both the worker's time and the material employed are 'capital goods that are wasted'. Loos echoes Frederick W Taylor as he analyses the benefits to worker and society of the repudiation of 'ornament on things that have evolved away from the need to be ornamented'.[13] The wasted labour and ruined material saved by the suppression of ornament may be, so to speak, reinvested in both the worker and society. The worker, working a shorter time, nevertheless produces a more culturally durable, that is non-consumable, product. More durable, thus more valuable to society, this product may then be more expensive to buy. This will then lead to a higher reward for the worker who works for a shorter time not producing ornament, and thence takes home a higher reward. Here Loos has intimated, and it was this aspect of his writing that so appealed to Le Corbusier's economistic approach, a means for architecture aesthetically to respond not only to a generalised 'modernity' but to that specific aspect of the Modern bound to the scientific rationalisation of production.

The ultimate instrument of Taylorised ornament was, of course, the metropolis itself, the preferred environment of Modern man. 'The majority of men would rather live in a metropolis than a small city or in the country', observed Otto Wagner in 1910; 'Making a living, social position, comfort, luxury, the presence of intellectual and physical faculties, entertainment in the good and bad sense, and finally art, motivate this phenomenon.'[14] The architectural expression of this metropolitan sensibility was, following the law of Modernity, a 'uniformity' corresponding to economy and the 'democratic essence' raised by sheer repetition into a principle of monumentality. Here the Taylorised environment would attain its highest expression as the metropolis, so to speak, creates the conditions for its own aesthetic Taylorisation by eliminating ornament. No time would then be lost in contemplating highly decorated monuments, as the ever-rushing inhabitant was urged on by repetition, similarity, and smooth, serially punctured facades.

Already, as Simmel pointed out, the metropolitan inhabitant had been forced to adopt, in self-defence against overstimulation, what he called a blasé attitude. Originally forced on the intellect unable to take in more than a certain quotient of stimulation and sense impression, this blasé attitude had deeper and more functional roots in the money economy:

*The essence of the blasé attitude is an indiffer-
ence toward the distinctions between things. Not*

in the sense that they are not perceived, as in the case of mental dullness, but rather that the meaning and the value of the distinction between things, and therewith the things themselves, are experienced as meaningless. They appear to the blasé person in a homogeneous flat and gray color with no one of them worthy of being preferred to another. This psychic mood is the correct subjective reflection of a complete money economy to the extent that money takes the place of all qualitative distinctions between them in the distinction of 'how much?'[15]

The correct *objective* response of architecture, therefore, would be to produce objects that in no way interfere with this process; objects that demand no waste of time. Hence the uniform facades of Wagner's *Grosstadt* and Loos' own Michaelerplatz building, satirised by nostalgics as looking like a gridded drain cover.

Some years later, Walter Benjamin will speak of the loss of 'aura' surrounding the individual work of art, whose 'presence in time and space, its unique existence at the place where it happens to be' has been destroyed by mechanical reproduction. Concentration, the rapt attention of an individual in front of a work of art, has been replaced by distraction. For Benjamin, the blasé attitude is a distracted one, and, as he notes 'architecture has always represented the prototype of a work of art the reception of which is consummated by a collectivity in a state of distraction.'[16]

In this regard, it is interesting to remember that Simmel, in his own treatment of adornment and ornament, places it in the realm of social distinguishing marks, seeing it as partaking of the same order of distinction, of drawing attention, as the secret: adornment 'although apparently the sociological counter-pole of secrecy', has an analogous structure: even as it forms part of the social structure of secrecy to engender envy and attention, so 'it is the nature of adornment to lead the eyes of others upon the adorned'. Such distinction would be entirely out of place in a Taylorist world without wasted time or ornament: 'this environment looks with much less attention at the unadorned individual, and passes by without including him'.[17] The secret, the adorned, the masked would, in any case, disrupt the total subordination of production and consumption to the managerial economies of time and space.

On one level, of course, this restriction of ornament in building simply shifted the ornamental imperative onto society itself, creating the conditions for the production of what Simmel's student Siegfried Kracauer was to characterise as the 'mass ornament'. For Kracauer, the suppression of ornament had become the watchword of the *neue sacklichkeit*, the new objectivity of architects from Hannes Meyer to Mies van der Rohe. Writing in 1927, Kracauer argued that the increasing lack of ornament in architecture was more and more compensated for by a new phenomena — the ornament of the masses themselves, as exhibited in stadia and street. Thus the masses appear, with their regularity and pattern of bodies as ornament: 'The decisive agent of ornament is the mass.'[18]

Under such conditions, both communities and individuals, 'The community of people and the personality disappear when calculability is demanded; only the human being as a small part of the mass can smoothly climb to the top of the chart and serve machines.'[19] Taylor has, in this sense, destroyed history itself:

Many buildings have been shorn of the ornaments that formed a kind of bridge to yesterday. Now the plundered facades stand uninterrupted in time and are the symbol of the unhistorical change that takes place behind them.[20]

For the masses, Taylorised production develops its own forms of distracted and entirely functional entertainment, itself formed of a reproduction of mass production: 'The capitalistic production process, like the mass ornament', Kracauer wrote, 'is an end in itself.'[21] His favoured example is that of the modern dance troupe — the Tiller girls — whose mechanised motions seem to emulate those of the factory:

The production process runs its course publicly in secret. Everyone goes through the necessary motions at the conveyor belt, performs a partial function without knowing the entirety. Similar to the pattern in the stadium, the organisation hovers above the masses as a monstrous figure whose originator withdraws it from the eyes of its bearers, and who himself hardly reflects upon it. It is conceived according to rational principles which the Taylor system only takes to its final conclusion. The hands in the factory correspond to the legs of the Tiller girls.[22]

In a later essay, 'Girls and Crisis', of 1931, Kracauer developed the analogy:

When they formed an undulating snake, they radiantly illustrated the virtues of the conveyor belt; when they tapped their feet in fast tempo, it sounded like business, business; when they kicked their legs high with mathematical precision, they joyously affirmed the progress of rationalisation; and when they kept repeating the same movements without ever interrupting their routine, one envisaged an uninterrupted chain of motor cars gliding from the factories into the world, and believed that the blessing of prosperity had no end.

With decoration removed from building, and re-inscribed on the body of the mass, the mental revolution called for by Taylor was complete.

On another level, however, as Simmel himself intimated, ornament in architecture was simply displaced to a third and even more triumphant moment. As Simmel remarked,

Everything that 'adorns' man can be ordered along a scale in terms of its closeness to the physical body. The 'closest' adornment is typical of nature peoples: tattooing. The opposite extreme is represented by metal and stone adornments, which are entirely individual and can be put on by everybody. Between these two stands dress, which is not so inexchangeable and personal as tattooing, but neither so un-individual and separable as jewellery, whose very elegance lies in its impersonality. (Emphasis added.) [23]

In one sense, the development of post-Hegelian architectural theory had paralleled this movement: from the monument as binding meaning and form in the symbol, a monument that stood for the analogous human body, to the monument as distinguishing between essence and appearance through the clear play of the sign, and that stood for the 'dressed' body, the possibility was now opened for the monument, (as opposed to the unadorned structure of the prosaic mass-building) to be freed from any but representational use and thus to be seen as total ornament. If Loos was to restrict 'Architecture' to the tomb and the monument, it was for this reason, to return architecture, so to speak, to the 'symbolic' realm, but now in the form of the completely superfluous, the triumphant mask.

As Simmel intimated, ornament was, as the mainspring of social distinction, that distinguishing mark that binds individuality to possession:

As adornment usually is an object of considerable value, it is a synthesis of the individual's having and being; it thus transforms mere possession into the sensuous and emphatic perceivability of the individual himself . . . And this is so, not although adornment is something 'superfluous', but precisely because it is.[24]

For Simmel, adornment, because it was superfluous, expanded far beyond the narrow compass of the necessary and the individual:

the superfluous 'flows over', that is, it flows to points which are far removed from its origin but to which it still remains tied: around the precinct of mere necessity, it lays a vaster precinct which, in principle, is limitless. According to its very idea, the superfluous contains no measure.[25]

Thus, against Mies' 'less', Simmel proposed 'more', a more linked intimately to the processes of the money economy:

In the adorned body, we possess more; if we have the adorned body at our disposal, we are masters over more and nobler things . . . It is, therefore, deeply significant that bodily adornment becomes private property above all: it expands the ego and enlarges the sphere around us which is filled with our personality and which consists in the pleasure and the attention of our environment. This environment looks with much less attention at the unadorned individual, and passes by without including him.[26]

But this criteria, as Theodor Adorno pointed out as early as 1965, can easily be reversed, given the right historical conditions, if, for example, the unornamented, as in the 20s, became a way of drawing attention. Indeed, Adorno was critical of casting the problem of ornament in these terms at all, terms that pose the 'good' return of ornament against its 'bad' exclusion. This was the way of much Post-Modernism, and fell into the same trap as Loos himself, when, following Kant, he rigorously distinguished between the ornamental or purpose-free (*zweckfrei*) and the functional or purposeful (*zweckebunden*). For, as Adorno pointed out, the very definition of what is or is not purposeful changes with time; it is a historically determined category. This is illustrated easily by the perception that often 'what was functional yesterday can . . . become the opposite tomorrow.'[27] Indeed criticism of ornament is often no more than the rejection of something that once had functional and symbolic significance, and has now lost it. Ornament and non-ornament are so historically interconnected, Adorno argues, that their separation becomes a blockage to thinking about design. Even if we rigorously try to avoid, as many functionalist Modernists did, any trace of expression in design, when this work is viewed historically it inevitably is seen as the very expression of its age. Thus Adorno, (in 1965!), concluded against both Modernism and its opposite:

On the one hand, the purely purpose-oriented forms have been revealed as insufficient, monotonous, deficient, and narrowmindedly practical . . . On the other hand, the attempt to bring into the work the external element of imagination as a corrective, to help the matter out with this element which stems from outside it, is equally pointless; it serves only to mistakenly resurrect decoration, which has been justifiably criticised by modern architecture.[28]

The problem lies, Adorno argued, in the way of posing the question in the first place: the posing of handicraft and imagination as two apparently exclusive terms. Even as handicraft, conceived of as anti-art, too easily degenerates into an unimaginative or even antitechnological materialism, so imagination, conceived of as the untrammelled expression of the individual, easily falls into the trap of personal, as opposed to public, wilfulness: 'Where only such expression is striven for', Adorno notes, 'the result is not architecture but filmsets.' [29] Both, when pursued as goals in and of themselves, forgetting they exist also for others, become fetishes. The argument falls into a contradiction that pervades Modernism and its critics:

> On the one hand, an imagined utopia, free from the binding purposes of the existing order, would become powerless, a detached ornament, since it must take its elements and structure from that very order. On the other, any attempt to ban the utopian factor, like a prohibition of images, immediately falls victim to the spell of the prevailing order.[30]

The division between the useful and the useless, then, fails to resolve, even though it explains, the contradictions of the object in modern society.

What Adorno is suggesting, of course, is not that these contradictions can ever be overcome by some overarching and essential definition of usefulness and uselessness in art, the nonornamental and the ornamental, but precisely that such definitions will always be the response to specific historical conditions, that continually demand reflection and analysis. He is suggesting that the architect engage in what he calls 'constant aesthetic reflection' and self-criticism to avoid the all too easy lapse into self-justificatory hypotheses and the defence of fixed intellectual constructs.

> Such an aesthetics would not presume to herald principles which establish the key to beauty or ugliness itself . . . Beauty today can have no other measure except the depth to which the work resolves contradictions. A work must cut through the contradictions and overcome them, not by covering them up, but by pursuing them.[31]

Adorno's notion that the object of art would not be a given, that 'aesthetic thought must surpass art by thinking art', would, over 20 years later, suggest an excellent corrective for the over expressionist formulas of Post-Modern or deconstructivist 'constructs.' If we take, for example, those structures that have become the built signs, so to speak, of

their positions — Graves's Portland building and Eisenman's Wexner Center — both fall somewhat emptily into the trap of ornament/non-ornament: both in defining themselves as polemically on one side or the other of a debate framed in Kantian terms, emerge as the same. Adorno would have found both equally 'ornamental' in their formulaic application of artistic autonomy, their assertion of proscription, the one of functionalism, the other of ornamentalism.

Such an observation might lead us to a different interpretation of the contemporary 'ornamental monument' than that provided by Vattimo through Heidegger. In place of a 'weak' background, we might still see a strong foreground — one dedicated to the fullest expression of private property and display of acquisition. In place of a meditative state of 'post-history' we may find ourselves still immersed in the continuing struggle of historicity. Ornament would then, within the terms of the philosophy of money, become the greatest open secret of patronage and the paradoxical condition of patron's architecture. Architecture, passing through the 'primitive' stages of tattoo and dress, attains a status as pure ornament as the jewellery, the *schmuck* of capital investment.

This is not to deny the force of the notion advanced by Vattimo, and persuasively argued by, among others, Ignasi de Solà Morales.[32] But it would be to qualify what has every legitimacy as an *interpretative* position, suitable for consideration as an epistemological condition of the Modern period, in favour of a response to the uneven conditions of architectural production at any moment, so that, without denying the value of the 'oblique' perspective of weak architecture, we might also identify survivals of the post-Hegelian kind; survivals protected, so to speak, in the fortified enclaves of the developer.

Anthony Vidler is William R Kenan Jr Professor of Architecture at Princeton University. His publications include The Writing of the Walls — Architectural Theory in the Late Enlightenment *(Princeton Architectural Press, 1987);* Claude-Nicolas Ledoux: Architecture and Social Reform at the end of the Ancien Regime *(MIT Press, 1990) and* The Architectural Uncanny: Essays in the Modern Unhomely, *forthcoming, MIT Press. An abbreviated version of this essay was first published as 'From Tattoo to Trinket: Problems of Ornament in Contemporary Architecture', in* Ottagono 94, *Milan, 1990.*

NOTES

1 Gianni Vattimo, *The End of Modernity*, Baltimore, 1988, p87.

2 Ibid, pp87-8.

3 GWF Hegel, *Aesthetics. Lectures on Fine Art*, translated by TM Knox, Oxford, 1975, vol I, p423.

4 Gottfried Semper, 'Development of Architectural Style', translated by JW Root, *The Inland Architect and News Record*, vol XIV, no 7, December 1889, p77.

5 Semper, *Der Stil*, Munich, 1879, vol I, no 60, in Gottfried Semper, *The Four Elements of Architecture and Other Writings*, translated by HF Mallgrave and Wolfgang Herrmann, Cambridge, 1989, p254.

6 Ibid, p252.

7 Adolf Loos, 'Potemkin City', *Spoken Into the Void. Collected Essays 1897-1900*, translated by Jane 0 Newman and John H Smith, Cambridge, Massachusetts, MIT Press, 1982, pp95-6. This essay was first published in *Ver sacrum*, July 1898.

8 Loos, 'The Principle of Cladding', *Spoken Into the Void*, pp66-9. This article was first published in the *Neue Freie Presse*, September 4, 1898.

9 Loos, 'Ladies' Fashion', *Spoken Into the Void*, p102.

10 It was not by accident that the 1908 essay 'Ornament and Crime' appeared in its French translation in the same number of *L'Esprit Nouveau* as Le Corbusier's éloge to the Maisons Voisin, to the factory sheds and 'La Rhythmique' of the new dance.

11 Loos, 'Ornament and Crime',1908, in Ulrich Conrads, ed, *Programs and Manifestoes of 20th-century Architecture*, translated by Michael Bullock, Cambridge, MIT Press, 1975, p20.

12 Loos, 'Ornament and Crime', p21.

13 Ibid, p22.

14 Wagner, *Die Grosstadt*, cited in Schorske, op cit, p96.

15 Georg Simmel, 'Die Grosstadt und das Geistesleben', *Die Grosstadt. Jahrbuch der Gehe-Stiftung*, 9 (1903), translated by Edward A Shils, in *Georg Simmel in Individuality and Social Forms*, edited by Donald N Levine, Chicago University Press, 1971, p330.

16 Walter Benjamin, 'The Work of Art in the Age of Mechanical Reproduction', in Hannah Arendt, ed, *Illuminations*, New York, 1969, p239.

17 Simmel, 'Metropolis and Mental Life', p344.

18 Siegfried Kracauer, 'The Mass Ornament', translated with an introduction by Karsten Witte, *New German Critique*, 5, Spring, 1985, pp67-76.

19 Ibid, p69.

20 Siegfried Kracauer, cited in David Frisby, *Fragments of Modernity*, Cambridge, Massachusetts, 1986, p140.

21 Kracauer, 'The Mass Ornament', p70.

22 Ibid, p64.

23 Georg Simmel, *The Sociology of Georg Simmel*, translated, edited, and with an introduction by Kurt H Wolff, New York, 1950, p340. Originally published as 'Exkurs über den Schmuck', *Soziologie, Untersuchungen über die Formen der Vergesellschaftung*, Leipzig, 1908, p340.

24 Georg Simmel, *Excursus on Ornament*, p340.

25 Ibid.

26 Ibid, p344.

27 Theodor Adorno, 'Functionalism Today', translated by Jane O Newman and John H Smith, *Oppositions* 17, Summer 1979, p31.

28 Ibid, p35.

29 Ibid, p38.

30 Ibid, p39.

31 Ibid, p41.

32 Ignasi de Solà Morales, 'Architettura debole', *Ottagono 92*, September 1989, pp88-117.

PERPLICATIONS
JOHN RAJCHMAN

'Nothing is more disturbing than the incessant move-ments of what seems immobile.'
Gilles Deleuze.

As in the Baroque, It can happen that an architec-tural invention is enveloped in a larger event, implicated in a larger question that arises in our space, complicating it and our vision of it. A formal trait in architecture may then become part of the crystallisation of something unknown that is knocking at the door, something unforeseen we can only experiment or play with in our seeing, our thinking, our creations.

Peter Eisenman's development of Rebstockpark, a 40-hectare plot on the outskirts of Frankfurt, into a residential and commercial block, is about *the fold* — about the folding of architectural and urban space, and also the folding of that space into others. The fold is more than a technical device: it is the central Idea or Question of the project. But then what is a question — what is 'the Question' — in architecture?

In the first instance, 'folding' is the name Eisenman gives for the central formal technique employed in the generation of the design, and in this respect it plays a role analogous to that of the superpositioning of the L-grid in earlier works. The nature and the scale of project, however, allow Eisenman to think in urbanistic terms. In Rebstockpark he wants to depart from the urban contextualism that rejected the Modernist isolated point block or linear slab, and made the perimeter block the basic unit of Post-Modernism. In 'folding' the Rebstock plot, Eisenman would 'index' complexifications in urban space that have unfolded since the War, and that contextualism has been unable to treat.

The starting point for the folding transformation is an imagined *Siedlung* in the pre-war style of Ernst May — the once revolutionary style which supplanted the perimeter housing that the late 18th and early 19th centuries had carved out of the city, with what are now seen as its rather corrosive effects on the urban fabric. The formal transforma-tion then consists in successively putting this imagined design through the net of a 'folding' operation, derived from a modified version of a René Thom butterfly net. This 'folding' of the complex is what is meant to introduce another sense of space and time within the urban landscape, than that of the revolutionary *tabula rasa* of the Modern, or the kitsch, sentimental Context of the Post-Modern.

But this is not the only sense in which the Rebstock project is a project of 'the fold'. Rebstockpark is 'folded' in many senses and many times over — many things are implicated in it or implied by it. To explicate what it implies, or to unfold what is implicit in it, one must thus unravel the general questions of space, time, vision, technology and architec-ture, which its Idea involves. For, in architecture as else-where, an Idea is never exhaustively or integrally realised in a single work; in any given case, there are always 'complica-tions'. And that is why, as Leibniz once knew, in explicating something, it is always difficult to know where to begin and how to end.

Rebstockpark is then about 'folding' in architecture. But what is the fold, and what is it to fold? In his philosophy, and his reading of the history of philosophy, Gilles Deleuze has developed perhaps the most elaborate conception of folds and foldings, a conception that he sets forth in the book called *Le Pli*. The book is a study of Leibniz and the Baroque, and it ends with these words: '. . . what has changed is the organisation of the house and its nature . . . we discover new ways of folding . . . but we remain Leibnizian since it is always a question of folding, unfolding, refolding.'[1]

One may say that *Le Pli* is Deleuze's most architectural book, for it envisages Leibniz's philosophy as a great Baroque edifice, and supposes that his philosophy formu-lates the Idea of such edifices: the Idea of folds endlessly passing over into other folds, folding into folding to infinity. And yet, in the case of the new ways of 'folding, unfolding, refolding' which *we* continue today, while Deleuze discusses *l'informe* in music, painting, and sculpture, there is no reference to contemporary architecture. We may thus re-gard the 'folding' of Rebstockpark as Eisenman's attempt to take up the question about contemporary architecture and urbanism that these last sentences implicitly raise, discover-ing thereby something unnoticed, implicated all along in his own work and thought: as Deleuze invents a new philosophy of the *informe*, or an *informel* art of thinking, so with Rebstockpark Eisenman invents an architecture of the *informe*, or an *informel* way of building and designing.

Intensive Reading
The Rebstock project may then be taken as a reading — an 'intensive reading' — of *Le Pli*, and *Le Pli* of it. What Deleuze calls an intensive reading is not an internal formal reading or

an external contextual one, but rather an experimental encounter. An intensive reading is one that releases unnoticed 'complicities' between two spaces that remain divergent and singular, or common 'implications' between two things that remain differently 'folded' or constituted. One example is the use Deleuze himself makes of the passage from Malamud's *The Fixer*, which serves as an exergue for his book on the practical philosophy of Spinoza, and in which an old Russian Jew explains before an inquisitory authority that he read a few pages of Spinosa's *Ethics* and then 'kept on going as though there were a whirlwind at my back'.[2] This 'whirlwind' becomes important for Deleuze's conception of Spinoza as a 'practical philosopher', and for the concept of the intensive encounter in Spinoza's philosophy. And in discussing the fold, Deleuze uses it again to describe the sort of 'multilinear ensemble' through which, by intensive encounter, philosophy comes to connect with history and with something like architecture: such foldings of philosophy and architecture as the *Le Pli* and Rebstockpark into one another '. . . would be like the detours of a movement that occupies the space in the manner of a whirlwind, with the possibility of emerging at any given point'.[3]

Plica ex Plica

Deleuze explains that the arts of the *informe* are about two things: textures and folded forms. The Baroque invents one possibility of fold and texture: there are the textures through which matter becomes 'material', and the enfoldings of the soul through which form becomes 'force'. In the Baroque as in Leibniz, the metaphysics of formed matter is replaced by a metaphysics of materials 'expressing' forces. The Baroque thus opens, without prefiguring, possibilities of texture and fold, later taken up in other ways by Mallarmé or Heidegger. For example, Deleuze finds that the release of garment-folds from the contours of the body, shown in Baroque painting and sculpture, is unexpectedly continued in a different way in the mad theory of veils proposed by Clerambault, the French psychiatrist that Jacques Lacan (who himself kept a special affinity with the Baroque) took as his master.[4]

But there is also a linguistic point: the words belonging to the texture and the fold family have a philosophical use and lineage. For, the weaving — or *plex* — words (like 'complexity' or 'perplexity') and the folding — or *plic* — words (like 'complication' or 'implication') define, in modern European languages, a family whose members include terms like 'imply' and 'explain' with important places in the philosophical lexicon. And indeed the last words of Deleuze's book might be read as saying ' . . . we are still implicating, explicating, replicating'. But there is one member of this family — whose lineage goes back to a Latin 'enfolding' of the Greek, and thus to the Greek or dialectical fold — of

which Deleuze is fond above all others, and through whose eyes he sees all the others: the word 'multiple'. Thus on the first page of his book Deleuze declares: 'The multiple is not only what has many parts, but what is folded in many ways'.[5]

A defining principle of Deleuze's own philosophy is that the Multiple comes first, before the One. In this sense, states of affairs are never unities or totalities but rather 'multiplicities' in which there have arisen foci of unification or centres of totalisation. In such multiplicities what counts are not the terms or the elements, but what is in between them or their disparities; and to extract the ideas a multiplicity 'enfolds' is to 'unfold' it, tracing the lines of which it is made up. Multiplicity thus involves a peculiar type of com-plexity — a complexity in divergence — where it is not a matter of finding the unity of a manifold but, on the contrary, of seeing unity only as a holding together of a prior or virtual dispersion. Complexity thus does not consist in the One that is said in many ways, but rather in the fact that each thing may always diverge, or fold, onto others, as in the ever-forking paths in Borges' fabled garden. A 'multiple' fabric is such that one can never completely unfold, or definitively explicate it, since to unfold or explicate it is only to fold or 'complicate' it again. Thus, while it may be said that for Deleuze there are folds everywhere, the fold is not a universal design or model; and indeed no two things are folded in just the same way. The multiple is thus not fragments or ruins supposing a lost or absent Unity, any more than its incessant divergence is a dismemberment of some original organism.

In this image of complexity-in-divergence and the multiplex fabric, we may discern one complicity between the Deleuzian and Eisenmanian folds: the Idea of a folding-together, or complication, which does not reduce to relations among distinct elements in a space-time parameter, but which rather supposes a strange invisible groundless depth from which irrupts something that creates its own space and time. By reference to such 'intensive' complexity, the two attempt to depart at once from Cartesian space and Aristotelean place. As Deleuze puts it, 'I don't like points. *Faire le point* [to conclude] seems stupid to me. It is not the line that is between two points, but the point that is at the intersection of several lines.'[6]

Perplication

Deleuze, of course, is not the first to raise the question of complexity in architecture, or to connect it to Mannerism and the Baroque. On the contrary such discussion itself belongs to an entangled historical nexus, which includes, in the first generation of 'the Frankfurt School', Walter Benjamin's study of the Baroque *Trauerspiel*, to which Deleuze returns in *Le Pli*. But more important for Peter Eisenman's background, and for his generation, are two authors to whom Deleuze does not refer: Robert Venturi and Colin Rowe. Deleuze not only has a different view of 'manners' from these authors — not a mannered decoration attached to an essential shed or habitation, but rather manners detaching themselves from a habitation no longer seen as essential, something as the flowing folds of Baroque garb detach themselves from the body. He also starts from a different conception of 'complexity' itself. His conception is not Venturi's notion of a contradictory or 'difficult' whole; it is not Rowe's image of Cubist collage and Gestaltist perception. For the first reduces complexity to the totality and simplicity of compositional elements, and the second reduces depth to the simultaneity of figure and ground. Thus they eliminate what makes complexity multiple and divergent, and what makes depth intensive and ungrounded. They assume a bounded or framed space in which discrete elements may be associated with one another, more or less ambiguously; and so they subordinate diversity to unity, rather than seeing unity as a contingent operation holding together a potential divergence. That is why their thought leads to the sort of liberal-minded empiricist 'toleration of ambiguity' which they oppose to the Revolutionary-minded rationalist promise of a New Order. By contrast, Deleuze's conception of complexity-in-divergence leads to the Question; it leads to the practical ethic of not being unworthy of what is disturbing the spaces we inhabit — of this Other who is knocking at our door. It involves a notion of 'distance' or 'distantiation', which allows Deleuze to find something Baroque in Constructivism, as well as in Foucault's idea that the only sort of perplexity worth pursuing is the one that takes us from ourselves.

Deleuze thus speaks not only of implication, explication and replication but also of what, in *Différence et répétition*, he calls 'perplication' — a folding-through, or folding-across.[7] 'Perplications' are those 'cross-foldings' that introduce a creative distantiation into the midst of things. Such distance is the holding-apart — what Deleuze calls the 'disparation' — of a space that opens in it the chance of a 'complex' repetition (not restricted to the imitation of a pregiven model, origin or end), or a 'free' difference or divergence (not subordinated to fixed analogies or categorical identities). Perplications are thus what allows one to trace the 'diagonal lines' in a fabric that 'cut across' it so as to 'fold' it again. They are the times of 'the question'. For, it is just when a question comes into a space that the space discovers its free complexity; and conversely, when a space freely complicates itself it always opens itself to question. This 'perplexing' sort of complication is thus not a matter of resolving a contradiction, as with Venturi, but rather of what Deleuze calls 'vicediction', or the weaving together of a multiplicity. And it is concerned with a kind of depth that is not a ground, as with Rowe, but rather the 'groundless' depth of

an intensive space in the extensive one that includes or frames it. Perplications thus are the foldings that expose an intensive multiple complexity in the fabric of things rather than a contradictory framed one; they unearth 'within' a space the complications that take the space 'outside' itself, or its frame, and fold it again. For Deleuze this deep or groundless complexity is always *virtual* — 'disparation' is always a virtuality in a space, a sort of potential for free self-complication. But such 'virtuality' can not be a *dynamis* any more than such 'actuality' can be an *energeia*; for otherwise complexity would reduce to the unity of pregiven origins and ends. 'Intensity' is rather a nondynamic energy; and 'actuality' always occurs in the midst of things, just as 'virtuality' is always to be found in their intervals. Thus the sort of 'virtual space' that a 'line of actuality' exposes in a fabric is not at all a possibility or a design to be integrally realised within a fixed frame, but rather the movement of a question that opens onto new uncharted directions.[8] That is why the times of perplication that hold a space apart are times of a peculiar sort — not times of the instantiation of eternal Forms, not times of the continuation of traditional customs, but the 'untimely' moments that redistribute what has gone before while opening up what may yet come.

In such perplicational terms one may then read Peter Eisenman's motto, reported by Tadao Ando: 'In order to get . . . to a place, you have to . . . blow it apart . . . you have to look inside it and find the seeds of the new . . .'[9] One must 'disparate' a space or blow it apart to find the complexity of which it is capable; and conversely, the deep or intensive complexity of a space is shown in those moments that hold it apart, taking it out of itself, so that it can be folded anew. In Eisenman's words: one must make 'present' in a space its implicit 'weakness' or its 'potential for reframing'. The principles of his perplication are then that there is no space and no place that is not somewhat 'weak' in this sense; and that 'weakness' is always imperceptible, prior to the point of view one normally has on the space or the place. Thus where architectural or urban vision for Venturi and Rowe remains a matter of discovering an imperceptible unity in a perceptible diversity of elements, in the Rebstock project it becomes a matter of 'indexing' an imperceptible disparation in what presents itself as a perceptual totality.

The Rebstock Fold

What then is an 'architecture of the *informe*'? One of Eisenman's words for it is 'excess'. An architecture of the *informe* is one that exposes its containing grid as 'constraining' or 'framing' something that is always *exceeding* it, surpassing it or overflowing it. The grid has always been a central element in Eisenman's architecture and architectural discourse,[10] and in the Rebstock project, it does not disappear; it is not, and cannot be, abolished. The strategy is rather to introduce something into — or more precisely, to find something 'implicated in' — the gridded space, which it cannot contain, which leaks or spills out from it, linking it to the outside. In this way the grid becomes only a dimension of the 'folding' of the space in which it figures.

Eisenman uses the term 'frame' to discuss the grid, as that term has been elaborated by Jacques Derrida, notably, in his work on 'the truth in painting': much as Derrida says the dream of a completely unframed space is vain (and that 'deconstruction' is not that dream), so one might say there is no such thing as a gridless architecture. And yet, there exists a 'complexity', or a potential for folding, that is not contained within any frame or grid; on the contrary, a frame or grid only exists within a larger virtual complexity that exceeds it. And what is thus implicit in a space, which it cannot frame, may at any point or moment break out of it, and cause it to be reframed. 'Reframing', in other words, is a virtuality in all 'framed' complexities.

For Eisenman, in the case of architecture this means that there exists something exceeding Vitruvian commodity, firmness and delight — something that can't be simply read as the adequation of Form to structure, site or function, but that allows Form to detach itself from such determinants, and freely fold: namely the intensity that releases an 'excess' that takes a space outside its bounds, or through which it becomes 'beside itself'. The condition of the *informe* would then be that of this intensive space that seems to break out from the intervals of the articulating elements of the bounded space and the traditional place in which it occurs, with a free, smooth 'rhizomatic' energy that exceeds the framing of site, plan and programme.

This cluster of ideas is then what distinguishes 'the folding' of Rebstockpark from Eisenman's earlier attempts at 'superposition'. Superposition still preserves the simultaneity of figure and ground, and so does not yet find or invent a groundless smooth depth. In Rebstock, Eisenman starts to work instead with a type of com-plication which is no longer a matter of linear juxtaposition in an empty space or 'canvas', but which rather assumes the guise of a great 'transmorphogenic' irruption in three-dimensional space. Rebstock is a smooth, folded space rather than a striated, collage one, and so no longer appears rectilinear or 'Cartesian'. Thus the Idea of the project (as distinct from its programme or plan) passes from a punctual dislocation of a Place to a multilinear smoothing out of a Site, and from notions of trace and archeology to notions of envelopment and actuality — to the attempt to release new points of view or readings on the 'context', that are imperceptibly implicit in it.

In Rebstockpark, the housing and commercial units no longer figure as discrete extrusions out of a planar gridded space, but appear to have been deformed through an intensive *intrusion* that seems to have come from nowhere and to take one elsewhere. They appear as though they were the remains of an irruption that had broken out from the ground and returned to it, suggesting that such a 'catastrophic' occurrence might again arise anywhere in the calm solidity of things. The Rebstock Fold is thus not only a figural fold as in origami — not a matter simply of folded figures within a free container or frame. Rather the container itself has been folded together, or complicated, with the figures. Rebstock is folding in three dimensions. Hence one is not just dealing with an urban 'pattern'; rather it is the urban 'fabric' on which the pattern is imprinted that is folded along this line, becoming thereby more complex, more multiplex. The periphery of the plot thus ceases to be its defining edge, and becomes instead one dimension of an uncentred folding movement, which overtakes the site, pushing through and out of it like a sudden whirlwind.

Thus the units or their juxtaposition no longer define the spaces in between them as more or less filled voids. On the contrary, it is the space in between the units that has come alive, for the 'crease' of the fold intrudes from out of the midst of them. The crease line — an intrusive or fault line — now seems to differentiate or distribute the units in a non-contiguous continuity, where each unit becomes singular or disparate, even though it 'co-implies' the others along the line. The crease is thus not a co-ordinating, containing or directional line — it does not resolve an inner contradiction, establish a 'difficult whole', or juxtapose figures as in a collage. It is rather a free 'vicedictory' line that instead of going from one point to another, traces a multidimensional space, without fixed points of beginning and ending, or of which one can never be quite sure where it has come from or where it is going.

The Rebstock fold is thus an intensive line, energetic without being dynamic, dimensional without being directional. But it is also a 'perplicational' or 'perplectic' line. For it does not follow the 'strong' determinations of the programme, the structure or site alone, but tends at the same time to take one 'outside' them. For, while in functional terms, the crease of the fold is the connecting space between the various activities to be carried on in the modules, in architectural terms it offers the sense of the sudden emergence in the site and its activities of another 'free' space that escapes them. It has the look of the arrested moment of an irruption, whose cause is unknown or 'external' to the site and its uses, and the feel of an explosive energy that seems to come from somewhere else. Thus the fold 'distances' one from one's habitual perception or reading of the space, as if to transport one to this 'elsewhere' where things go off in unimagined directions, or are folded again.

Because Rebstock is in this way folding in three dimensions, its flowing movement can not be wholly captured in a figure-ground plan. The plan is only one point of view, one aperture or opening onto a movement which, since it is 'smooth', cannot be 'drawn' as in a coordinated projection. Indeed Eisenman thinks the whole relation to projective drawing changes. 'Folding' can't be projected from a combination of plan and section, but requires a topographical model, and involves another kind of sign: the index. In this case the proverbial index finger points to something unseen, to a virtual movement that would not destroy the site, but 'reframe' it, setting it off in other directions. For the deep complexity of a site is always 'implicit' — imperceptible in space, virtual in time. And that is why to discover it one must 'blow the place apart'. In Deleuze's idiom, one might say the index points to something that can't be 'mapped', but only 'diagrammed' — the intensive space within the extensive one, or the smooth space within the striated one.

What Eisenman calls 'weak urbanism' may then be defined as the attempt to provide for a moment of urban 'envelopment' in urban development, or to provide a place for urban 'diagrammatisation' within the space of urban 'planning'. The idea of the Rebstock Fold is to become this surface on which urban events would be inscribed with an intensive actuality. It thus involves a particular kind of point of view on the city.

Light Regimes

One can imagine different sorts of points of view or perspectives on the city: that of the cartographic photo from the plane above, which gives the impression of a god's-eye view; or that of someone who knows his own district or neighbourhood so well he can see the whole city refracted in it; or again that of the *flâneur*: the perspective of the Baudelairian walk or the Situationist *dérive*. Implicit in Deleuze there is another idea which is the point of view of the 'implications' and 'perplications' of the city. With his conception of 'complexity' goes an art of seeing.

Folding and seeing, complexity and clarity, perplexity and illumination — it has long been asked how these go together. In Neoplatonism, the One is a *Lumens Divinis*, faintly shining through the complications in everything, ever waiting to be read again. And, via Scholem, one can find something of this tradition in Walter Benjamin's account of Baroque allegory. But in the Deleuzian multiplex, complexity is such that things can never be folded back to a first seeing, to a single source or 'emanation' of Light. Rather than a god's-eye view on everything, there are only new points of view that are always arising everywhere, complicating things again. For light is not One but multiple: and one must always speak of *les lumières*. Illumination or clarification is thus

never a complete reduction of complexity to obtain an uncomplicated or unfolded planar surface or transparency. On the contrary, in the first instance, it is the multiple complications in things that illuminate or clarify, redistributing what may be visible and what obscure.

Thus, according to Deleuze, it is just when, in Leibniz and the Baroque, space becomes 'folded', or acquires the sort of 'texture' that can express force, that there is a dual departure at once from Cartesian logic and Cartesian optics — from the regime of the 'clear and distinct'. There arises another 'regime of light', in which things can be inseparable or continuous even though they are 'distinct', and in which what is 'clear' or 'clarified' is only a region within a larger darkness or obscurity, as when the figures emerge from a 'dark background' in the Baroque painting of Tintoretto or El Greco. Thus the windowless monads illuminate or clarify only singular districts in the dark complexities of the world that is expressed in them; and Leibniz becomes a 'perspectivist' philosopher for a world that has lost its centre, or can no longer be illuminated by the Sun of the Good.

But our own *informel* foldings involve no less a type of seeing or perspectivism. For one can never see the deep intensity or virtual complexity of a space without changing one's point of view on it. To inhabit the intervals or disparities of a city, tracing a diagonal line in its fabric, is to see the city as never before: to see something not given to be seen, not already 'there'. Divergences are what permit 'subjective' points of view or perspectives, and not 'subjective' views of an unchanging uncomplicated space that permit perspectival variation. That is why Deleuze says that the 'there is' of light is not given by the subject or in his field of vision; on the contrary, the subject and his visual field always depend on the light that there is. For illumination or enlightenment always comes from the midst or intervals of things; and the 'disparation' of a space is always a kind of illumination or enlightenment. It is as if, through the crevices of the city and the cracks of its edifices, light were always seeping in, illuminating the lines of its becoming-other. In its intervals and imperceptible holes, *la ville* is thus always virtually *radieuse*; and that is why the free folding of its fabric is always illuminating.

Disparate Vision

The Rebstock Fold implies a peculiar sort of architectural vision: an art of light and sight whose principle is not 'less is more', but 'more or less than what is there'. Folding is an art of seeing something not seen, something not already 'there'. For the jumbled lines and titled planes of the folding irruption, which deflect its surfaces onto its angular remnants, do not translate a 'freeflowing' or 'transparent' space. They do not possess even what Colin Rowe called 'phenomenal transparency': they do not fit in a 'pictorial' space where light is cast on a complex of 'clear and distinct' forms for an independent eye standing outside their frame. And yet if Rebstock has a different feel from a freeflowing Modern transparency, it is not achieved by enclosing the units and attaching to them a kitsch set of contextualising or historicising symbols. Rather the fold creates a different kind of 'flow' — the flow of an energy that the bounded space seems to be impeding, that is spilling over into its surroundings, interrupting the calm narrative of its context, and so opening new readings in it.

The heraldic and emblematic imagery of Baroque and Mannerist art presented visual enigmas that interconnected images and signs, seeing and reading. What Eisenman calls 'the index' is not exactly such 'allegory'. And yet it uncovers a 'complexity' in things, a complication that is prior to what is given to be seen or read, or that lies 'inbetween' the things that are seen or read: this free region where the visible and the readable are implicated in one another and the fabric folded anew. Thus, in Rebstock the eye is no longer directed, as in Modernism, to an 'uncomplicated' and unadorned space, where clarity is distinctness; it is no longer shown an 'illumination' of structure and use so 'pure' that all reading would be eliminated. But the eye is not shown either a cluster of allusions to tradition, and its reading is not an historicist one. Rather Rebstock 'complicates' the space in which forms might otherwise freely flow, and so 'intrudes' into its site, unfolding unnoticed implications. It works thus as an 'index' that points to a 'diagrammatic' rather than a 'programmatic' or a 'nostalgic' reading of the site — an illuminating 'disparation' in the midst of things.

The 'vision' of Modernism meant a *replacement* of what was already there; the 'vision' of contextualism meant an *emplacement* with respect to what was already there. What Rebstock would give to be seen is rather a *displacement* or 'un-placing', that would be free and complex, that would instigate without founding, that would open without prefiguring. And it is just when vision becomes multiple, complicating and 'perspectival' in this way, that Hermes becomes nomadic, inhabiting the intervals and the midst of things, rather than carrying messages from one place — or one master — to another. No longer content to simply re-establish the 'hermeneutic' places, sites, or contexts of messages, Hermes creates his own space, his own lines of flight, or creative divergences, rather as 'le pli' can refer to the envelope in which a message is sent — something which, of course, facsimile transmission would dispense with.

Urban Electronics

Rebstockpark is to be the first thing one sees heading from the airport for downtown Frankfurt, now announced by the new Helmut Jahn tower — a new gateway to the city. Once the home of a great critical-philosophical school, Frankfurt has become the finance, and, afterwards, a kind of 'museum capital' of the *Wirtschaftswunder*, museum and capital having discovered a new type of interconnection and, with it, of architecture.[11] Site of a former *Luftwaffe* airport, a *tabula* that was literally *rasa* by the War, (and that neither client nor architect find worth 'recalling' in the project), the Rebstock plot is now, in the postwar and post-postwar period, internationally noted for its proximity to the site of the annual Frankfurt book fair. One implication of the Rebstockpark fold is then the way it supplies a sort of contortionist vision of the whirl of this post-industrial capital of the *Wirtschaftswunder*.

Among the vectors that have transmogrified urban space, those of transport and transmission have performed a key role: in some sense it is the auto and the airplane that killed off or complexified the rational grids and the radial city of 19th-century industrialism. Such processes supply the starting point for the analyses of urbanist and philosopher Paul Virilio, who, like Peter Eisenman, thinks that to understand the complexities of the city, we must depart from a 'static urbanism' and view the city instead in terms of the movement, rhythm, speed, in a word the 'timespaces', that the various modes of transport and transmission make possible.

Along such lines Virilio proposes to analyse the intrusion into the urban environment of a 'timespace' rooted in electronics technology, spread out yet interconnected through the likes of facsimile transmission, and closely tied to the finance capital with which the Rebstock development is linked in so many ways. The result is what Virilio calls 'the overexposed city'. But if this 'overexposed' city is unlike the 'collage' city brought about through the transformations of 19th-century industrialism, it is because its complexity is not so much that of a Levi-Straussian *bricolage* of distinct elements as of a Deleuzian texture or interweaving of disparities. The 'overexposed city' is an intensive or explosive city, not a gridded one — a city in which incessant 'movement' is prior to the apparent immobility of traditional place or planned space.

Philosophers of science once debated what it means to 'see' electrons, and so whether such 'theoretical entities' are real or only inferred. Today everyone tacitly counts them as real, because without ever seeing them, one nevertheless cannot but 'inhabit' the space of what their ever miniaturised and transportable manipulation makes possible — a manipulation that is becoming ever more direct, interactive or 'live'. Towards this space, which 'exposes' the city and to which it is 'exposed', Virilio adopts the critical attitude of what he calls 'non-standard analysis'. In the Rebstock project, Eisenman seems to adopt what might be called an attitude of 'perplectic' analysis. For there is a sense, at once spatial and historical, in which the Rebstock site is 'framed' by the railway and the highway lines that lead into the city, where museums now cluster about the old river Main, which the Franks proverbially crossed. By contrast, the electronic space in which we move and make moves 'exposes' the city to something that can no longer be read as a structuring or framing network, or seen through the materials and locations that realise it. For it is in itself invisible and unlocalisable; it no longer requires the sort of physical displacements that provided the sense of mobility and congestion, captured in the progressivist and Futurist imagination.

The energy of Rebstock is thus not a directional 'dynamism' racing towards a sleek new future, but belongs rather to a sort of irruptive involution in space; and it is this multilinear nondirectional energy that serves to take one out of the traditional gridded city. Rebstock gives neither a 'futuristic' nor a 'nostalgic' sense of our electronic moment but an 'actualistic' one. Its attitude to the new electronic technologies is not rejection and nostalgia, yet not the manic embrace of a California cybercraze, It is rather an attitude of this perplexity of the multiple 'elsewhere' the technologies introduce into our ways of inhabiting spaces. Rebstock is not about the arrival of a new technological order any more than it illustrates the Post-Modernist sense that nothing can happen any more, that all that will be already is, as though history had come to an end in the self-satisfaction of the health club or the shopping mall. It is rather about this implicating, explicating, replicating energy that is always escaping or exceeding the space and the locale in which it is implanted, introducing a distance that allows one to look back upon the gridded or collage city with the mixture of nostalgia and horror with which one once looked back *from* it to the country.

Perhaps one might thus speak of a new relation between architecture and technology. The Bauhaus sought to display in architecture the pre-electronic industrial engineering that had made possible a whole new programme of 'rational' building and construction, artist and engineer joining in the new figure of the architectural *Gestalter*. But 'post-industrial' electronic technology shows itself architecturally in a different manner: in terms of a free excess in formal variation that still remains compatible with structure and use, and that is made possible by invisible means. It is shown in an exuberant detachment of form, in the sort of the contortions between the random and the regular which electronic modelling makes possible. Thus from the Bauhaus aesthetic of geometric abstraction one passes to the electronic aesthetic of 'free' abstraction, where an intensive line goes 'all over', released from its subordination to the grid — a passage from formal juxtaposition to *informel* smoothing-out, of the sort Deleuze associates with Klee rather than Kandinsky, in the points, lines and inflections of the Bauhaus painters.

Metroplex

We thus inhabit the metroplex. There is no completely rational space, no completely adequate place, and the alternative between topia and utopia no longer defines our possibilities. That is why the Rebstock style is neither 'international' nor 'regional', 'elitist' or 'populist', but rather moves in a space inbetween. While it always remains 'nowhere', it seems to come from 'nowhere'. For, in the words of Deleuze, while there are folds everywhere, the fold is not a universal design. Rather, singular or new foldings somewhere in the social fabric provide the chance for the emergence of this *peuple à venir*, this 'people-to-come', that is no longer identified by a rational space or an adequate place, of which Deleuze declares the architect always has need, even if he is not aware of it.

Deleuze presents the Baroque as marking a moment when the collapse of the old heliocentric *cosmos*, where man imagined he had his place and his task, gives rise to a decentred perspectival *mundus*, where each monad has a particular point of view on the world it includes or expresses — the moment when the traditional separation into two different realms is replaced by a single edifice with two stories, in which there is a 'new harmony' between an enclosed interior and an inflected exterior. But our own 'foldings' no longer transpire in such a Baroque *mundus* any more than in a ancient *cosmos*, for 'the organisation of the house, and its nature' have changed. Our manners of coexistence can no longer be held together through the principle of the Baroque house — the greatest or most complex variety in a single compossible world; for the world we inhabit is multiplex. We no longer have — we no longer need to have — the Good Cosmos or the Best World, the illumination of the Form of the Good, or the clarification of the Principles of the Best. Our foldings, our own 'mannerisms', have dispensed with the single Best World, turning rather to the complicities and complexities of the disparation through which things diverge into others; our invention of new 'manners' of being comes in response to events that disrupt our contextual frames, complicating things again, introducing new enfoldings, or free spaces of implication. From the Good City and the Best World, we have passed to an intensive cityspace or metroplex, where we are no longer supposed to find the identity of Context or of Reason, of Tradition or Eternity, but are free instead to practise an art of inhabiting the intervals, where new foldings arise to take our forms of inhabitation in new and uncharted directions. And so, in the place of the cosmopolitan or univeralist thinker, 'citizen of the world', there arises a strange new ubiquitous nomadic

121

community of *metroplexed* thinkers, perplectic inhabitants of our contemporary 'chaosmos'.

Games of Chance

What then is 'complexity', what is 'the Question' in architecture today? In the drama of philosophy, Deleuze finds the invention of various philosophical protagonists: there is Hume, the Inquirer, or Kant, the Judge at the Tribunal of Reason. In *Le Pli*, Leibniz figures as the Defence Attorney of God, a great inventor of 'principles' in philosophy, a whole Jesuitical jurisprudence to account for the incessant emergence of 'perplexing' cases. Leibniz was the genius of principles, and the principle of Leibnizian jurisprudence was inclusion in the Best World which God selects, and, which, in some sense, we ourselves are 'inclined without being necessitated' to select, even though that means that some of us must be damned. Deleuze calls Leibnizian Principles 'cries of Reason' in the Baroque world which theology seems to have deserted.

But as we today in our 'post-enlightenment' times find a multiple intensive complexity in things prior to simplicity and totality of compositional elements, the perplexing case — the Question — acquires a positive capacity to reframe or recreate our principles, our jurisprudence itself; and there emerges a new type of player in the game of the complexities of thought. Deleuze sees Nietzsche as announcing a new protagonist in philosophy, one who starts to play the game in the new way given by the two Whiteheadean principles that Deleuze makes his own: the abstract or the universal is not what explains but is what itself must be explained; and the aim of the game is not to rediscover the eternal or the universal, but to find the conditions under which something new may be created. In our folding, unfolding and refolding, we no longer inhabit the two-storied Baroque house, where, on the heights of the windowless walls of the interior, would be heard the elevating reverberations of the cries of Beelzebub below. For complexity no longer occurs within a house governed by the principles of such an 'elevating' illumination, but rather becomes a matter of a multiplex Play at once within and without the house — of this *pli*, this 'folding', which is a matter of an inexplicable Chance, prior to principles, prior to design, yet always virtual in them. The figure of our post-Baroque or *informel* complexity is thus a Player — the player of the new game of perplication.

It would seem that Peter Eisenman tries to introduce just this sort of game into architecture, and into architectural discourse. For, anterior to, yet inseparable from, the requirements of the programme and the site, and the space of the drawing plan, Eisenman discovers the Play of the Idea or the Question. His architecture plays a game where Chance becomes an inextricable part of Design, and not something

Design must master or eliminate — a game whose object is to maintain the play of Chance within the space of Design. Deleuze distinguishes two ways of playing the game of chance. Pascal, in his wager, exemplifies the bad way, where the game is played according to pre-existent categorical rules that define probabilities, and where one calculates gains and losses. The true player (like Nietzsche or Mallarmé) does not play the game in this way. Rather the table itself bursts open and becomes part of a larger more complex game that always includes the possibility of other new rules; and to play the game one must thus, in making each move, affirm all of chance at once. Thus a game of 'nomadic' or 'smooth' distributions replaces a game of categorical or striated ones; and chance itself ceases to be tamed or hypothetical, and becomes free and imperative. It is then this free multiplex game of chance that the Rebstock Fold tries to play in urban and architectural space.

The Baroque Fold, for Deleuze, is unlike the Oriental Fold which weaves together or com-plicates empty and full spaces, voids and presences. For in the Baroque, 'holes' are only the indication of more subtle foldings, and the principle is that there are no voids, that everything is included in a single expressive continuum, as in the principle of the Leibnizian Best that the greatest number of folds be fit within the same compossible world. Thus Jacques Derrida once wrote that Leibniz's God, in selecting the Best World, experiences nothing of the anxiety of the Jewish God, who must create out of Nothing, out of the Void; and that Baroque plenitude is thus symptomatic of an avoidance of the 'pure absence' which a Mallarméan sort of writing would suppose, and which would be incompatible with anything like a 'built visible *architecture* in its locality.'[12] And yet the free play of Chance that Eisenman's Rebstock Fold tries to introduce in Design is not a 'pure absence' — not a Lack or Void from which everything would have come. It is rather the virtuality in a space of what is 'more or less than what is there', of something that exceeds the space and that it cannot integrally frame. As Deleuze remarks, 'to speak of the absence of an origin, to make the absence of an origin the origin is a bad play on words. A line of becoming has only a midst . . .'[13] In the perplication game, untamed chance is not a place, not even a void or absent place, but rather the virtual space of the free line in the midst of things.

The supposition of the game in Eisenman's perplicational architecture is thus not 'absence' but 'weakness' — the complex chance of a space to be folded, unfolded and folded again. And it is in this sense that Rebstock remains a 'full' space — it is 'full' just because it is weak, or is 'filled by' its weakness. For the Fold, which fills up the space, is at the same time what takes the space out from itself, bursting it open and 'smoothing' it out, releasing an intensive energy that is neither theological nor mystical, neither Baroque nor Oriental, neither elevating nor quieting. Rebstock is rather 'full with' a 'distantiation', an unsettling question that clears out a space offering the chance of a complex repetition or a free divergence. And so, it fills its space in a manner different from the Baroque, and from the chequered pattern of voids and presences defined by the Modern slab or *Siedlung* —

through the intervals from which a new *lumière* peers through; from an intensive depth prior to figure and ground; and with a diverse complication that spills over into history and context with a perplexing tension. That is what Eisenman calls 'presentness'. Presentness is the splendour of the fold in the house we have come to inhabit, where the game of creation is played not *ex nihilo* but *ex plicatio*.

NOTES

1 Gilles Deleuze, *Le Pli: Leibniz et le baroque*, Minuit, Paris, 1988, p188.

2 Gilles Deleuze, *Spinoza: Practical Philosophy*, City Light, San Francisco, 1988.

3 Gilles Deleuze, *Pourparlers*, Minuit, Paris, 1990, p219.

4 On Lacan and Clerambault's veils, see Joan Copjec, 'The Sartorial Superego', *October #50*, Fall 1989; on Lacan and Baroque vision, see *Encore*, Seuil, 1974, pp95ff, and Christine Buci-Glucksmann, *La Folie du Voir*, Galilée, 1987.

5 Gilles Deleuze, *Le Pli*, op cit p5.

6 Gilles Deleuze, *Pourparlers*, op cit.

7 Gilles Deleuze, *Différence et répétition*, PUF, Paris, 1968, pp324-30; 359-60.

8 Deleuze proposes to use the terms 'virtual' and 'virtuality' in a special way. With these terms, he is not referring to what architectural criticism calls 'virtual space', or what Rowe also terms 'illusionism' in architecture. On the other hand, what Deleuze calls 'virtual' is not to be confused with what Silicon Valley has decided to call 'virtual reality', even though it is part of Deleuze's view that virtuality, unlike possibility, is always real. Perhaps the closest term in Peter Eisenman's own idiom would be 'immanence'. Deleuze introduces his sense of the virtual in his *Bergsonism*, Zone, New York, 1988, pp96-103, distinguishing it from the possible. 'Virtuality' is not the 'possibility' of something that might be 'realised'; it is already real, and it does not stand in a representational or mimetic relation to what 'actualises' it. Rather, what is virtual is always a 'multiplicity'; and it is actualised through a free or creative 'divergence'. This theme is further elaborated in *Différence et répétition* (pp269-76) in relation to Leibniz, before being taken up again in *Le Pli*. In that work it is also linked to 'perplication'; the 'perplication of the Idea' is defined as its 'problematic character and the reality of the virtual that it represents' (p324).

9 *Tadao Ando: The Yale Studio and Current Works*, Rizzoli International, New York, 1989, p19.

10 On the grid in Eisenman's early work see Rosalind Krauss, 'Death of a Hermeneutic Phantom: Materialisation of the Sign in the Work of Peter Eisenman', in Eisenman's *House of Cards* (Oxford, 1988); see also her 'Grids' in *The Originality of the Avant-Garde and Other Modernist Myths*, MIT, 1985; this book also includes two original essays on the index.

11 On the connection between contemporary museums and finance capital see Rosalind Krauss, 'The Cultural Logic of the Late Capitalist Museum' *October #54*, Fall 1990; the problem of banking and finance plays an important role in the analysis of capitalism Deleuze proposes in collaboration with Félix Guattari, as well as in a short text 'Postscriptum sur Les Sociétés de Contrôle' in *Pourparlers*, Minuit, Paris, 1990. It would seem timely to analyse along these lines the centrality of the museum as a type in contemporary architecture.

12 Jacques Derrida, 'Force et signification' in *L'écriture et la différence*, Seuil, Paris, 1967, p28. By 'pure absence', Derrida means 'not the absence of this or that — but the absence of everything, in which every presence is announced' (p17). This text first appeared in *Critique* in 1963, at a time when Derrida was still trying to work out a phenomenological contrast between geometric and literary 'ideality'. It is a review of a book by Jean Rousset, a central figure among those who, referring to Wölfflin and Wittkower, tried to establish the existence of a 'Baroque Age' in literature. And in *Le Pli*, Deleuze refers on several occasions to Rousset, remarking that those who have written best about the Baroque are those most sceptical of the category. Rousset's account of the attempts to discover a 'Baroque Age' includes reference to the rediscovery of the English Metaphysical Poets, and, in this sense, lends support to Geoffrey Bennington's impression that 'Mannerist and Baroque buildings are to Venturi [in *Complexity and Contradiction in Architecture*] what the English Metaphysical Poets were to Eliot'. For his part, in 1963, Derrida took Rousset's 'Baroquism' as only one instance of something called 'the structuralist passion', and he went on to advance the more general argument that the attempt to find 'spatial' or 'architectural' metaphors for literature is ultimately vain, since there is something inherent in 'literary ideality' that 'excludes' this sort of description 'in principle' (p29). After 1963 one of course finds in Derrida's continuing reflections a more complex (not to say Baroque discussion of the theme of absence; and, one may observe that the theme has an important part in his writings on the architecture of both Eisenman and Tschumi. And yet it might be argued that Derrida preserves from his early work the general problematic of the literary and the spatial, or the textual and the architectural. Deleuze, by contrast, was never motivated by a search for a phenomenological contrast between literary and geometrical ideality; instead, he invents a singular kind of spatial idiom in philosophy, using it in his readings of literature. Thus, he comes to the view that there is a sense in which architecture, regarded as a 'framing of territory', is the *art premier*.

13 Gilles Deleuze and Félix Guattari, *A Thousand Plateaus*, University of Minnesota, Minneapolis, 1987, p293.

AN INTERVIEW
PETER EISENMAN AND ROBERT E SOMOL

Robert E Somol: *Given the timing of this interview — four days after the massively televised 'deadline' — I would like to begin with one of the enabling bases for the shift in your recent thinking and design, namely the place, or non-place, of the media and the condition of mediation in the late 20th century.*

Peter Eisenman: The question of media concerns the issue of the aura of real physical space, and the question that Jacques Derrida asked me about the difference between the aura of a cathedral in history and what you would do for a cathedral today, would it have the same aura? Would that aura be the aura of a metaphysical condition of presence, of presencing? Architecture posits the question of aura whether we talk about an iconic or an indexical sign. The indexical sign tends to remove the traditional aura from the object and the iconic sign attempts to define the essence of the aura and maintain it. While the indexical sign generally removes the particular presencing aura that the iconic sign had, it cannot, in architecture, remove presence, or the aura of presence. Folding is interesting because it involves, in its being, an indexical condition of process, but in that condition it will have an aura. The real issue posed by the folded objects of this new Frankfurt project is whether they are displacing, dislocating, destabilising of the iconic condition of the sign. In another sense I believe that we are always going to have an auratic condition, meaning some kind of presence in architecture, because there is always going to be some *being-in* which is opposed to the condition of language which is *being-as*. The suggestion is that the being-in of architecture is being questioned by the condition of media. The nature of our real world experience has become so mediated that the condition of the actual event almost becomes a simulation. It is incredible when the military finds out from the television what is happening in Baghdad. Because of satellite distribution and monitoring of public TV we know that our news is 'all the news that's fit for enemy ears'. In fact there is a new condition of reality that is so suffused with media that reality is almost dictated by the media. It is so brought home when you begin to see the effect of watching, watching bombs actually explode and destroy things, something that in the past was only simulated by film. And then there is the fascination we have with these toys, the incredible anxiety-infatuation complex that they trigger.

RES: *That is part of the fascination with the media itself, a kind of futurist moment, an erotics of technology.*

PE: It has become so pervasive and available, but not any less eroticised, because it has become so much more real and that is what makes it more powerful. We are talking about real human sacrifices, testing our games now on real subjects, not simulated subjects, so when the Patriot missile first went up they were all excited because it was the first time they 'really' saw it work. And then you say what about architecture? In the face of all this what can one say about the aura of presence?

RES: *Is architecture only the vent that this technology goes down?*

PE: Yes, but perhaps architecture can become an e-vent. And then media begins to suggest the possibility for a change in the idea of real time, and real place. Traditionally, architecture defined reality — bricks and mortar, house and home, foundations, the architect of the plan — it was a defining instrument of reality. It no longer seems to occupy that territory. For me it is because it took its own discipline as its discursive structure. Architecture was the only medium that used its own discipline — that is, function and structure — as its *raison d'être*, its meaning. Perhaps its condition of text lies in other disciplines which begin to open up architecture as a discursive field. I believe that is where the movement in my work is. Certainly you and I in our teaching together have participated in moving from archaeological work and superposition to the cusp of this folding work. The Frankfurt project for Rebstockpark is something new. One does not have many breakthrough projects. Even though we were working with plate, as opposed to vertebrate structures at Nunotani and Cincinnati, they were still dealing with ideas of superposition and trace that were begun in Guardiola. Frankfurt is working with something entirely different. You can see it coming out of Cincinnati, but instead of taking the plates and superposing them, now they are being folded.

RES: *All of this discussion of mediation, including the issue of presentness and aura, has to do with your debate with one aspect of deconstruction, evident in your reply to Derrida. For you, the object possesses a certain residue, or excess, which you are calling aura or presentness. This seems both to replay Benjamin's fascination with the destructive qualities of media as well as his simultaneous nostalgia for a now lost aura. How do you situate your position in relationship to that Modern double bind, because it always seems to flip back and forth between being a revival of an historical avant-garde practice, and at the same time an extension of a high or classical Modernist position . . .*

PE: Do you think I see it as a *revival* of an avant-garde strategy?

RES: *No, but you have figures whose work or whose projects you proceed from.*

PE: In architecture?

RES: *Mostly in philosophy, literature, art and film. Within architecture, only Terragni seems to occupy this position, at least in the early work. But Terragni is an amazingly malleable figure.*

PE: Right. He is in some ways an invention.

RES: *Exactly, which makes one wonder, if that is the case, in what ways does Terragni's work display aura, if you can be such a powerful interpreter, or inventor?*

PE: Well that is an interesting issue which I am confronting now in the Terragni book. If you read the book I would argue that it is a total fiction.

RES: *And different from your previous fictions.*

PE: Completely different, yet there is still a trace, the fiction comes from *something*. That is the issue where I believe architecture is different; it is not a total tissue of traces. At some point there is a condition of presence. When you go to see the object — the Casa del Fascio — I think this is what the term *presentness* is about. Presentness is about the possibility of the maintenance in time and space of a certain condition of event. When you see the Casa del Fascio it has an auratic condition, and I believe this is so because its notational system is indexical. I think this is what most interpreters have not understood, that it is not iconic. Most of the interpretations of the Casa del Fascio have tried to take an indexical object and force it into an iconic strategy. And it does not go that way. However, when it is put through this other filter you begin to understand the limitation of the iconic sign and also how much the indexical sign is suffused with an aura. It is this aura of the index — of the process — that constitutes presentness. Terragni had no idea of this, but synchronic and mystical events happen.

RES: *And that is precisely how you describe your own work: 'I came across the fold, I did not plan to come across the fold.' I suppose the fold is exactly the thing one never expects to come across.*

PE: I think that luck is always part of design. It is about finding that moment, that click, when it is both clear and unclear at the same time. Because as you and I have talked about even out here in the studio, we can all be working theoretically on the same thing and yet at different desks there are different indications; I know where they are and that is where the aura is.

RES: *What is at stake in that ability to decide? Again, this raises the ambiguity between avant-garde and high Modernist attitudes. The project of the historical avant-garde would seem to be adverse to concepts like aura and presentness, because they recall, for example, Michael Fried's defence of postwar Modernism which concluded with the line 'Presentness is grace.'*

PE: I am not talking about presentness in the Michael Fried sense.

RES: *Which is why I invoke the term avant-garde. Obviously you are an aficionado and collector of avant-garde journals and materials, and began* Oppositions *with those models in mind, so it is not an unconscious alignment or interest. The position that the 'Modernist project' was never taken up in architecture largely forms the impetus for your work.*

PE: Perhaps it began there, but I do not think that is where I am right now. The Modernist project propelled me initially, and you can see that as it goes from house to house.

RES: *And even there, the early houses are not possible without the projection system employed to represent them, the axonometric. The houses begin an investigation of a particular representation system associated with the historical avant-garde which had been repressed in the immediate postwar period. The axonometric drawing — a supposedly neutral supplement — becomes activated. The houses are not possible apart from it and, by the end of the decade or so long series, that system is ultimately imploded. Is there a representational discourse associated with the current work that is analogous to that of the earlier work?*

PE: Have you seen the sections of Cincinnati recently? Cincinnati is being drawn, or better still has to be drawn, on a computer. Because of the tilting superpositions it would be impossible to calculate by hand.

RES: *And that is related to the idea of aura not as a present space or bounded figure, but as time or event. Is section, then, the technique that is about event, as opposed to plan?*

PE: I do not want to say that categorically. What I believe is that the vertical plane carries with it two sets of information. That is, you are literally experiencing it, at the same time you can read it. This is not the case for a plan. You apperceptively read a plan, but you do not apperceptively read a section or elevation. Apperception is the summation of single perceptions. You understand where you are in a plan because it is totalising; a section is there moment to moment, you are always moving through a datum of vertical projection, you are reading all the time. A section has a plan and elevation built into it, its own discourse is perceptual and conceptual at the same time.

RES: *Section is the index of a plan and an elevation.*

PE: Exactly. Whereas a plan is not an index of section. What no one has investigated is the real problem between vertical and horizontal. We always assume that one is figure and one is ground, but I think there is another condition, a non-dialectical third between figure and ground. The new work is the first time that the section is not mere extrusion from the plan. Extrusion is the ultimate classical formalist mechanism for architecture. The early Frankfurt studies are still plan-generated, or initiated, and that could be a limitation. I am not certain that if we were working with a computer that they would be. But what is interesting is that they are not extruded, you cannot just draw from plan what these things are in three dimensions.

RES: *Both scales of your work, that is 'weak form' and 'weak urbanism', can be seen as responses and critiques to the writing of Colin Rowe. In other words, weak form challenges the ideal of a transcendental typology —* The Mathematics of the Ideal Villa *you might say — while the weak urbanism pursued in the Frankfurt project operates as an alternative to the morphological, figure-ground gestalt of* Collage City.

PE: There is no question that there is some critique intended. There have been two strong theoretical conditions posited, one is the Venturi position and the other is the Rowe position. One still needs to articulate what the difference is between undecidability and complexity and contradiction. Fundamentally complexity and contradiction are still rooted in presence and ultimate decidability; the metaphysical presencing condition is not altered. Rowe's position was fully articulated by 1960, around the time of the La Tourette article, which is an incredible piece of writing. Having been with Rowe for two years in Cambridge, and being suffused with him throughout my early academic career at Princeton, he is certainly the father. And there is no stronger father. You can see it in the detritus of Colin Rowe's patronage which is in every academic institution in this country. Tafuri's work probably came closest to introducing another aspect of patronage through Rossi. If you read Rossi's idea of the city it is certainly an alternative to contextualism. But that discourse was never in my psyche. Rowe is still the dominating discourse as well as the problem for me.

RES: *In other words the dialectically opposed, but still 'strong', materialist alternative is not an option for you. You still operate within and against Rowe's formalism, the dominant American problematic. Hence, weak* form *and not weak programme or weak politics.*

PE: I would agree that my work has always been an attempt to extricate itself from the Colin Rowe discourse. Now another strong early influence on my work was Rosalind Krauss and therefore probably Clement Greenberg, Michael Fried, and *Artforum*, at that time. After all, we did start *October* at the Institute for Architecture and Urban Studies, which was a unique publication considering our overriding concern with architecture. You have to understand that these origins were repressed by *October* itself in their recent anthology. But Krauss's writing and thought were always very potent to me.

RES: *And that is the same lineage in the visual arts that yours was in the architectural realm. If you equate the postwar formalism of Rowe and Greenberg, then you and Krauss occupy similar positions. And so the discussion of the death or displacement of the author in both her work and yours always masks this latent formal discipline and training. And this leads back to the ability to walk around the office or the studio and being able to say when an indexical 'presentness' seems to be manifested and when it is not. This returns to the 'black box' of not being able to articulate it, but when we walk around we can identify it. Are your terms 'touch' (from production) and 'smell' (from reception) ways to register the ghost of the author in the design machine, or, more strongly, are they ways to smuggle back in the 'eye' and 'taste', have we just substituted the tactile and olfactory for the optical and oral?*

PE: You could argue that much of what we call literary or poetic writing is acculturated. That the repression of various groups has made it heretofore impossible to be sensitive to or understand certain kinds of poetry which have therefore remained outside a so-called literary canon. So you could say that art or architecture is a matter of acculturation or interpretation. But Jacques Derrida still chooses certain writers to critique over other writers. He does so, whether admitting it or not, because certain works have, for lack of a better word, an aura. The interest in my work is not merely theoretical but rather because it has an aura. Frankly if it was just theory and it was terrible work, it would be no good. If Godard was a great critic but his films did not have a certain aura we would not care about Godard. Godard is good because he *could* do it. The same with Renais or Robbe-Grillet. Without theory none of them would be as important, but it is also terribly important to have that other aspect.

RES: *But that is also the thing that one cannot teach. What we are coming up against at the University of Illinois is that — after design is divided into its constituent elements (typology, morphology, building science, theory, craft) — what is the design component of design supposed to do?*

PE: Design is a by-product. It is not a teachable subject; it is not part of a curriculum. We never taught design. It is interesting how close weak form is to Rowe in that sense. That is the interesting thing that Rowe taught me, that the eye is trainable, you can open somebody's eye to something. When I sat in front of a Palladian facade I saw nothing, and Rowe kept saying, 'Keep looking.' Now if you are forced to look for 90 days, for two or three hours a day, at more or less similar phenomena, you can begin to discern subtle things. It is all a question of training the eye.

RES: *So smell is not taste?*

PE: No, it is not taste. That is what I am trying to get the students to understand. Traditionally, however, design is connoisseurship.

RES: *How do you institutionalise connoisseurship?*

PE: You can institutionalise it because you can have master exemplars. Michael Graves can do that beautifully, he can get a student to see a plan, how it pulsates, and then go out and reproduce those conditions. You can almost catalogue the kinds of pulsations that will allow you to reproduce a good plan. Making a good plan is reproducible, if 'good' plans are what you want. And that is a big question. Colin Rowe would say to me that my stuff was bad because it did not have good plans. Good plans — that is taste, connoisseurship. And you can teach that. I could teach kids to make good plans. I think you could say there are two categories under design, taste and smell, one is connoisseurship and one is training an eye. Training the eye is not necessarily going to facilitate the ability to do anything.

RES: *So design is this residual other. What I find interesting about your comments on Michael Graves is that here is a case where design is embodied in a unique individual hand. But it is curious that the work itself is reproducible. Whereas with this other system you are not necessarily an originating agent, but the work itself is not reproducible, not predictable. Which makes sense since an original requires the iterative economy of the correct copy, whereas when there is not that original condition one may be able to produce events, or 'mappings', to invoke Deleuze, rather than tracings.*

PE: That is a good point. I think that is true. The issue — going back to the lectures and weak form — is that my work has always been situated, in the social and cultural milieu. It is always about the *Zeitgeist*. You cannot do classical architecture today and be relevant. But equally you cannot do Modernist architecture and be relevant. The notion of undecidability comes from the *Zeitgeist*.

RES: *The discussion of mediation in the recent discourse is quite compelling, but part of its seduction, its element of chance, is that it is incredibly ambiguous or undecidable. Is mediation a weakening event or a strengthening condition? On the one hand it deterritorialises, to use Deleuze's term, and on the other it is always engaged in reterritorialising. So when one begins to confront and internalise this thing called mediation, what is being swallowed and how will it manifest itself in the work?*

PE: I cannot answer that.

RES: *But your diagnosis speculates on how we got to where we are, it defines mediation as the distinguishing characteristic of this moment, this Zeitgeist. Weak form is a relevant alternative or possibility because of this condition of mediation, and this is not something that traditional, classical, strong form has addressed. This ambiguity is especially evident in your discussion of 'weak food' — the blurred food of nouvelle cuisine — but what about the mediated instance of fast food, which, whatever else it does, may engage in an initial deterritorialising, a displacement of regional identity?*

PE: First I think fast food is strong food, because strong is also reductive. Media is definitely in reduction and thus strong. Now we have not addressed the issue of excess in all of this. The question of aura must be considered outside of necessity, that is not as an immanent condition of form and function. Function is a requirement of the condition of architecture. But if presentness, as a presence, is in the excess, the not necessary, then it is a very different condition. And it is this question of being in the excess — this non-metaphysical excess, not the excess related to the metaphysics of presence — which is interesting about the process of folding. Because folding is a condition of excess in terms of the metaphysics of presence.

RES: *And related to this question of excess, then, is the issue of beauty and aura. If it is another aura is it an other beauty?*

PE: Well if you study the Vitruvian triad, commodity and firmness are conditions of necessity and delight is a condition of excess. Commodity and firmness are not conditions of propriety, they are conditions of necessity, that is, they also have an excess about them, when something is seen to be functional it is not merely that it is functional — it has to *look* functional. Now beauty does not have that *is* and *look*: that is why the question of beauty is interesting. You can make the distinction, that what Vitruvius is talking about is function, not as the literal function, but the *propriety* of function. The language of function. It has to function, but it also has to deploy the iconicity of function. *What about beauty?* What is actual beauty as opposed to the iconicity of beauty? Or the sign of beauty? I think beauty is a different condition than that of function. The Vitruvian triad has always put beauty in a condition which is similar, that is, in a condition of necessity, but it is not. It is something displaced. And nobody has really done anything on beauty. If you were to ask me where the really hot subject is, the hot subject for me is beauty. Beauty really summarises aura and excess.

RES: *So your current project is to investigate the condition of beauty in some non-classical, non-Modernist manner?*

PE: A critical practice today would be to investigate the notion of beauty. I would say that beauty is a central issue, not technology, not function, not space, not place, not site, not context, but beauty. That is the issue.

AN INTERVIEW
PETER EISENMAN AND ANDREW BENJAMIN

Andrew Benjamin: *One of the distinguishing aspects of your work has been your involvement with philosophy. Perhaps we could start by exploring that involvement. It must be added that it is to my mind a restless involvement. You have moved from an interest in structural linguistics to deconstruction and more recently, to the writings of Charles Saunders Pierce. Before coming to the use or place of specific philosophies, you might like to respond to the more general question of philosophy and architecture or architecture and philosophy.*

Peter Eisenman: First of all I do not believe it is possible to do architecture without some sort of idea structure. What I would argue is that the structure of ideas — that is any theoretical matrix, a discourse — has been as far as architecture is concerned, traditionally at a very pragmatic level. That is, we have had a history of theory in architecture, but that theory has been related to how to build buildings, how to site buildings, how buildings look. Of the categorical treatises, very few of them deal with the discourse itself. In other words, have any kind of attitude towards such things as the object, the subject and the relationship between the two. Questions of form are often raised outside of architecture, particularly in philosophy.

If one says to oneself, as an architect, 'what does one do?' or 'why does one do it?', most architects would answer that we accommodate function and symbolic meaning. In the case of libraries, churches and public buildings, we accommodate society in some way. This accommodation assumes that at any one time society is known and also in some way predictable and may be translated into some discourse. My attitude has always been that this is not the case. That, in fact, one can never know at the same time what is the condition of society, its so-called *Zeitgeist*, and how architecture should respond to it. So that one has always had to go outside of architecture. I have had to do so in order to address the question of 'what should I do?' And I would argue that philosophy is one of the most readily available.

Although one could argue that recently, in 20th-century fiction or film, one can also find philosophic attitudes have already been digested in a way in which they have not been in architecture. My argument would be that architecture in fact, insofar as it has digested any philosophical thought, stopped doing so with Kant or Hegel; for example, Modern architecture was, in many ways, Hegelian. Anything post-Hegel that is dealing with Nietzsche, Heidegger, Derrida has never been formulated discursively for architecture.   One can say that the current problematics in philosophy, in post-structural thought, rarely entered into architectural discourse. For me, the problematic of architecture is a discursive field lying virtually untilled, untended, and unopened. And that is the possibility of the post-Hegelian architectural problematic.

If one were to read my Cambridge thesis one would find that it seems like a formalist doctrine, but at that point I was exposed to traditional architecture formalisms, coming from Colin Rowe, Rudolf Wittkower, Frank Wölfflin. That is what I knew. My PhD thesis, *The Formal Basis of Modern Architecture*, attempted to shift from a reading of an essential formalism to a kind of textuality, a kind of more open textuality which talked about the possibility of an interpretive field outside function and meaning entering into the discussion of the architectural object, as a deep structure. I began to become restless with the problem of valued origins and began to realise that I was dealing with issues that had very problematic philosophic implications. Therefore, this restlessness that you spoke of charts the movements away from my thesis (which was essentially an escape from formalism) into another kind of discourse, let us say, structuralism. From there it was a short step to post-structuralist thought. I moved from Chomsky to Foucault to Derrida, trying to find a way of forming in architecture.

The issue of philosophy and architecture is complicated because the making of architecture is not merely the reading of philosophy as architecture. Derrida calls it 'deconstruction *as* architecture'. The problem with that is that deconstruction as architecture is not the same as deconstruction in writing or deconstruction as text. It leaves out the problematic which is proposed when you look at the difference between the work of Valerio Adami and the work of Jasper Johns. Adami for me is a painter who is philosophising through the canvas. He might as well be writing on the canvas. There is no question of its textuality. Just as there are many symbolic painters who are psychologising in painting, but they are not painting.

Jasper Johns, on the other hand, addresses the problematic not of writing so much, but of painting as textuality. Not as textuality in the form of painting, but painting as a textual condition. Johns has, for me, proposed an open condition of the work; Adami does not. The distinction that I make in architecture is the question of the aura of the work. This is not aura in the traditional metaphysical sense, but rather something to do with what I call 'presentness', seen within a different institutional frame. This is neither a condition of the object, nor an interpretation of the object, but something that is between being and language. It falls between the two. What I would argue is that it is possible to introduce this auratic condition not as in Walter Benjamin's, but rather like Pierce's idea of the index or an indexical operation.

AB: *I wonder if we could pursue this relationship between the aura and the indexical. Is the aura a formal component of all works, or is the aura simply something that can be said of all works, although the way in which it is present will be different in each work? The auratic element of Jasper Johns is specific to a specific painting while the auratic element in a building or a piece of architecture will be specific to the architecture.*

PE: It could be argued that all painting is textual whether it is colour field painting, figurative painting, or symbolist painting. One could then argue that all architecture is textual. It has a text of function, of structure, of its aesthetic, of meaning, and so forth. So that the mere presence of a textuality is not necessarily any guarantee of the presence of aura. Aura is not necessarily a condition of textuality. It could be argued conversely that aura is something that resists textuality. It is that almost mute condition that is outside of the indexical or the iconic. The aura proposed here is, however, a product of writing, but a writing, again within a different institutional frame,that may not be textual. This is no longer the aura of the original in mechanical reproduction. Therefore, the condition of aura has changed. In other words, it is no longer necessarily value-laden in the same way. For example, if we were to build a Gothic cathedral today its aura would no longer be value-laden in the sense of 'a Gothic cathedral' in the sense of its received historical value. The aura proposed here is the aura of an indexical or weakened relationship between meaning and form.

AB: *It seems to me that you are touching on what I think is a very interesting problem. That while the aura is clearly not the sublime, there is an interesting parallel in the way that Kant sets up the sublime. Of the many problems involved, one of them, I think one of the more central, is the problem of exemplarity. By definition, you can't give an example of the sublime because the sublime actually involves experience and the play of the understanding and therefore you can't simply imposite the sublime because it's a relation between a subject and an object. In that sense it is relational. This gives us a way of addressing what it is that the aura would be.*

PE: For you the aura may be in the experience?

AB: *Well, the experience would be auratic.*

PE: Could be, but not all experiences are auratic.

AB: *No. Of course. This would distinguish between everyday experiences that were almost marked by the forgetting of experience, such that one is unaware that one is experiencing, and some fundamentally different conception of experience such that that which was experienced could never be sited outside of the experience because its force is located in its being experiential. That's one way of beginning to come to terms with the ontological nature of the auratic.*

PE: How does this definition then help me as an architect to make an auratic condition; does it only work for you as a philosopher?

AB: *The way in which it would work is simply that if one takes this linkage, tenuous though it may be, between the auratic and elements of the Kantian sublime, what would emerge is that conditions of possibility for the auratic could not be predictable. In other words you could not inscribe, as it were, the auratic moment in a particular part of the building as though one would have to respond in a particular way.*

PE: But you would have to set up the conditions where such a non-predictability was possible. We are then talking about the conditions for chance. In other words, the auratic has something to do with the possibility for chance and the arbitrary. And also, what we have called that new necessity that may lie within the arbitrary. But nevertheless, one which can be known. Not necessarily predicted, but known.

AB: *But therefore the problem emerges of what is it that you are knowing. What is the object of knowledge. And this goes back to the other approach I'd like to take — to the question of the aura — and also touches on the question of weakness. The reference is to a paper by Roland Barthes called 'The Third Meaning'. In his analysis of Eisenstein's films he links the iconic and the indexical on the one hand and the symbolic on the other. And he says that the iconic and the indexical can be approached through theories of science, the symbolic can be approached through psychoanalysis and theories of signification. Then he asks the question, 'Is there not something that remains?' To which his answer is, yes. Then he gives what one may view at times as an unsatisfactory response to his own question, but what he is alerting us to is that there is something which looks back. There is something that looks back beyond any reducibility to either the iconic and indexical or the symbolic. There is this third element.*

PE: I think Barthes was talking before the paradigm shift from the mechanical to the electronic had become a fact. My argument would be that the aura that Benjamin would talk about — the nostalgia for the aura prior to mechanical reproduction and the new aura of mechanical reproduction has been displaced by another aura. That is the aura of the mediated, unvalued reproduction. The aura of that unmediated condition which now takes on its own aura. Architecture, in order to have an aura which can stand in face of this electronic necessity, has got to look not to the traditional modes of aura as described by Barthes, but perhaps in the indexical itself. In other words, not in the strong iconic symbolic relationships or relation between icon and index but in the indexical itself, which is by Pierce's definition a secondary condition.

AB: *Why isn't then the aura an ornament?*

PE: Because that assumes that the institutional frame of architecture is always described by the relationship between form and function, and is also the appropriate metaphoric presentation of that relationship. My argument is that the relationship of form and function can exist without it being necessary or appropriate to represent it in architecture. That is, we can have form and function, but the architecture may not be symbolic of that relationship. It is only assumed that this relationship is natural to architecture. And that aura comes from the assumed naturalness.

This assumption represses the possibility that there may be manifestations of presence which are not essential to architecture. The form-function relationship has always seemed to be the essence of architecture. And therefore, the symbolic role of architecture came from this essential relationship. But one may say that in fact there are also other possibilities for the indexical that may lie in what one calls the excess. The excess that is not necessarily more than the object, but the excess that lies within the object itself which is always present. And the index that I am speaking of may be the manifestation of that already present, inscribed within excess and therefore, not ornamental.

AB: *Is it necessary therefore to distinguish between at least two sorts of excess, one that lurks within and that comes to be released through the process of reading, and another sort of excess, one whose presence is affirmed in its very being? In other words, if excess is simply a necessary part of the event itself, then either it is released or it is repressed within it, and if it is repressed within it then it needs a second reading to release it. If it has always already been released then the question is not simply how that comes to be experienced, or understood, but how that comes to be differentiated from an excess that is repressed. And the real question is, to my mind, whether or not this distinction is the basis for a possible aesthetics. One that was no longer formalistic or concerned with form.*

PE: Are we looking for the basis of an aesthetic? This is back in a kind of metaphysical ontology. I think it is language that is tripping us up. It seems to me that we are trying to displace the transcendence of the form-structure-meaning relationship. That form is in some way a secondarity with respect to function.

The opposite response to that is some kind of formalism. Where form is a priority and function follows from it. What I am suggesting is that neither of these is adequate. There can be no architecture without form. How does one do this without the aura of an aestheticised formalism? We're talking about a third condition, that is, a presentness which lies in the excess which has always been there, but because of this dialectical structure, the narrative structure of language, has in itself been repressed. In other words, it is not just a new idea. That it has always been available but unavailable because of language. The description of architecture — its categoric descriptions as strong form categories have repressed it in itself.

AB: *Excess therefore is constitutive of the mode of being of the event.*

PE: Yes. It is an aspect of an architectural aesthetic. But only an aspect. That is why architecture is always going to be what I call a second language; no one speaks architecture first. Also, architecture as a second language means that in architecture itself there is a condition of secondarity which will always be secondary because we can never displace, we can only reframe. We cannot erase function, we can displace it and reframe it. But in the displacing and the reframing it is never going to become dominant. We can only bring it to a condition that is no longer supplemental in the traditional iconic sense.

AB: *Does this mean that displacing becomes a form of repetition?*

PE: Displacement concerns iteration. Repetition is self-sameness, while iteration is a non-self-same repetition. In displacement, there is the superposition of the original and the displaced condition which in itself is never a repetition. Because a repetition would be a self-same condition where there was no displacement. In other words, the displacement would fall over itself like a square on a square. The distinction is important because there is a form of repetition in transformation that exists in architecture, and this is not displacement. If one were to draw a square repeatedly it is repetition. However, when you draw a square on a rectangle, the displacement is a third figure as it is inscribed on the original square, the superpositions become a constantly shifting and reframed construction.

GRONINGEN VIDEO PAVILION

The project 'What a Wonderful World' was a collaboration between the Museum and the Department of City Planning in Groningen, near Amsterdam. It was an attempt to work at the image of the city and the quality of public places in an experimental fashion, free from the restrictions of immediate usefulness. It was decided that the music video would be the central issue of the manifestation, in a presentation that would be radically different from ordinary circumstances at home. Peter Eisenman, chosen as one of the architects, said of it:

'Our project is based on the idea that the new video technology nurtured by the growing home video industry is revolutionising the notion of the moving image. The traditional notions of time and space have become suspended. Our pavilion marks the attempt to redefine the traditional relationship between three-dimensional artificial, man-made, space and architectural time through an immediate contrast with the experience of time and space in video movies.

'The structure is based on an analysis of the way a video image is produced on a picture screen. An electron beam sweeps across a screen, moving from left to right, filling in an image point by point . . . The visitor in this pavilion follows a path which is analogous to that of the scanning beam — he or she moves along the chevron path, and is constantly repositioned within space. Thus, the visitor becomes part of the medium itself, passing in front of viewing screens and continually crossing through images, shifting his or her position to form images in different ways. Though the pavilion provides neither a traditional auditorium nor a static point of orientation for the spectator, it does allude to the traditional auditorium in its sloping floors.'

Pages 140/141: Site Plan
Pages 144/145: Sectional Plan

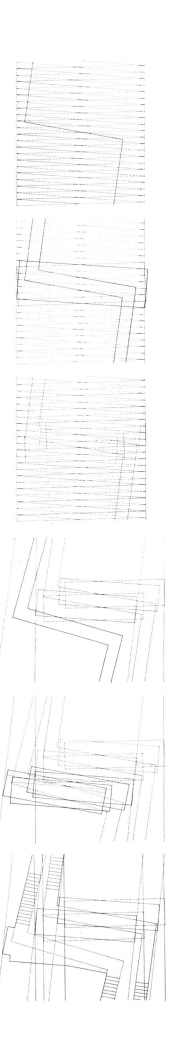

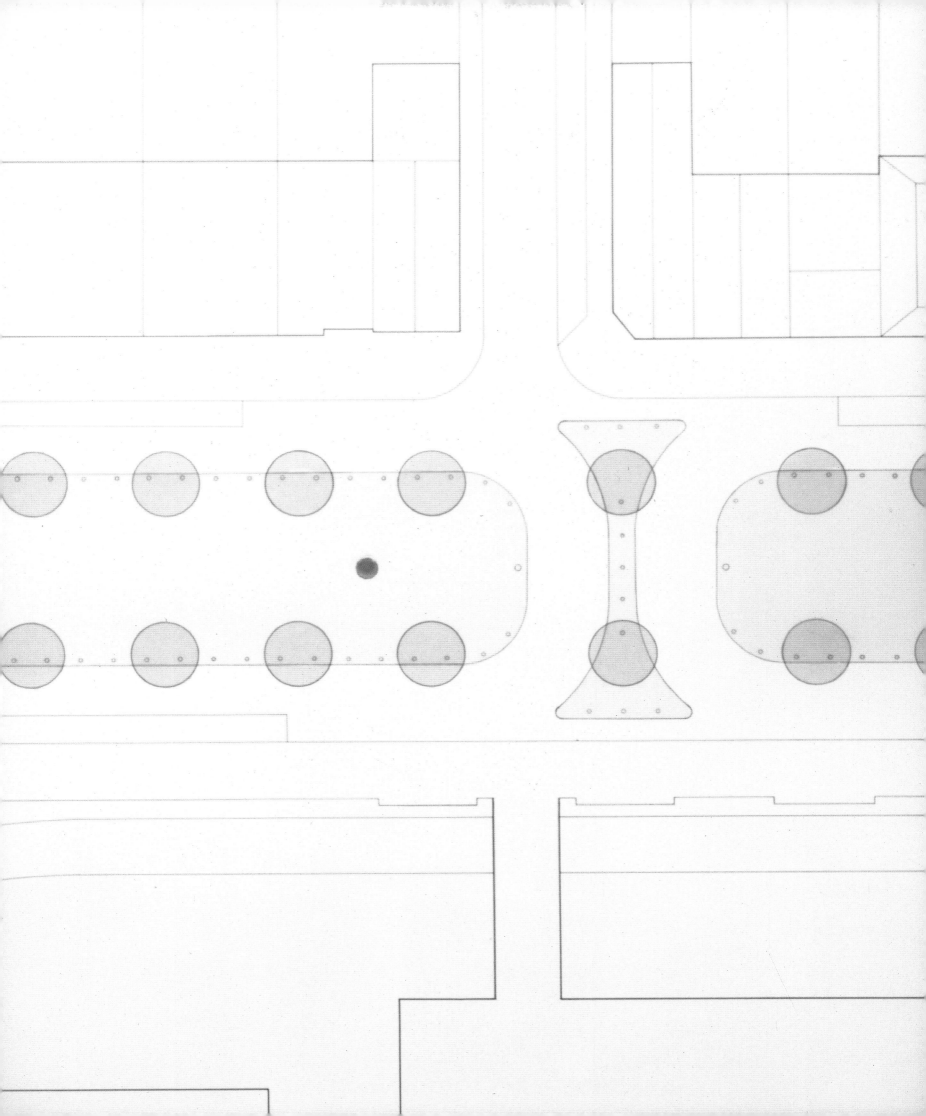

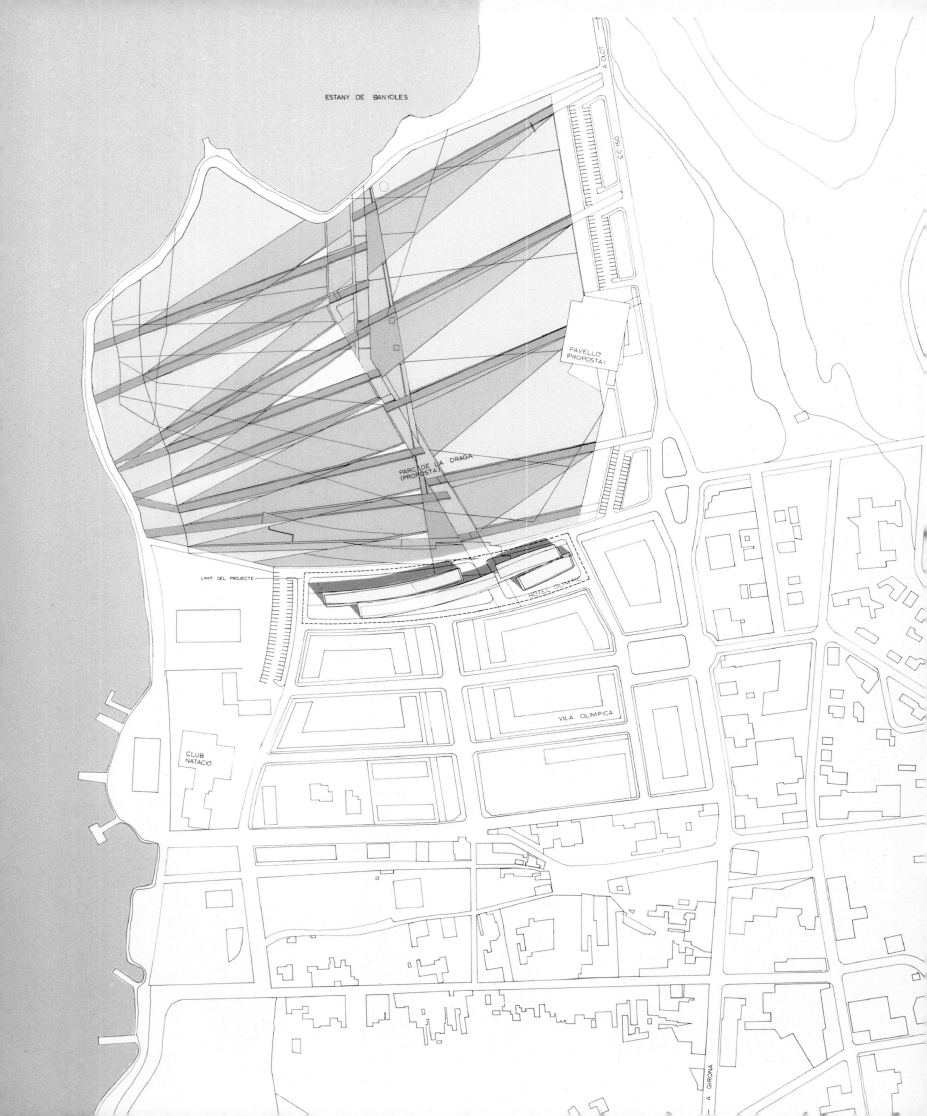

ESTANY DE BANYOLES

PAVELLO
(PROPOSTA)

PARC DE LA DRAGA
(PROPOSTA)

LIMIT DEL PROJECTE

HOTEL OLIMPIC

VILA OLIMPICA

CLUB
NATACIÓ

A OLOT

CC-150

A GIRONA

BANYOLES
OLYMPIC HOTEL
BARCELONA

In this project, the building is no longer a primary form. The line of its geometry (necessitated by the repetition of seemingly like units) is no longer Cartesian. This produces a building of incredible richness and complexity, while at the same time preserving the simple autonomy and replication of bedroom units. It is a building which is not a building in the traditional sense but is also part-landscape. Equally the landscape becomes part of the displacement of the building. It exists as three different trace conditions of time; the trace of time past as represented in the form of the agricultural divisions that existed around the turn of the century; the trace of time present in the extension of the building form into the landscape and the trace of two notions; one in which the agricultural divisions and the building divisions become the arcs of the sweeps of an eight-oared shell; the other, the sliding of the divisions backwards as the sliding of the seats of the shell backwards as the shell skims forwards. Because of these displacements from 'primary' building and 'secondary' landscape, a new secondarity becomes evident. The resulting form and space no longer can mean in the conventional sense of architectural meaning. Another level of potential significance, previously repressed by conventional meaning, is now liberated. The 'interior' space of the building is no longer the static lobby-corridor-room stacking of the traditional hotel. Instead there is a sliding and a sloping found in the possibility of the form of the line creating another condition of interior/exterior space.

Pages 146/147: Site Plan
Pages 150/151: Longitudinal Sections
Pages 152/153: Third Floor Plan
Pages 154/155: North Elevation, South Elevation
Page 156 from above left to right: Elevations: East Facade, West Facade, Main Entrance, Meeting Room Entrance
Page 157: Cross Sections

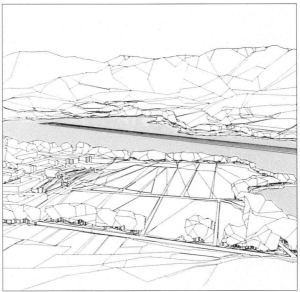

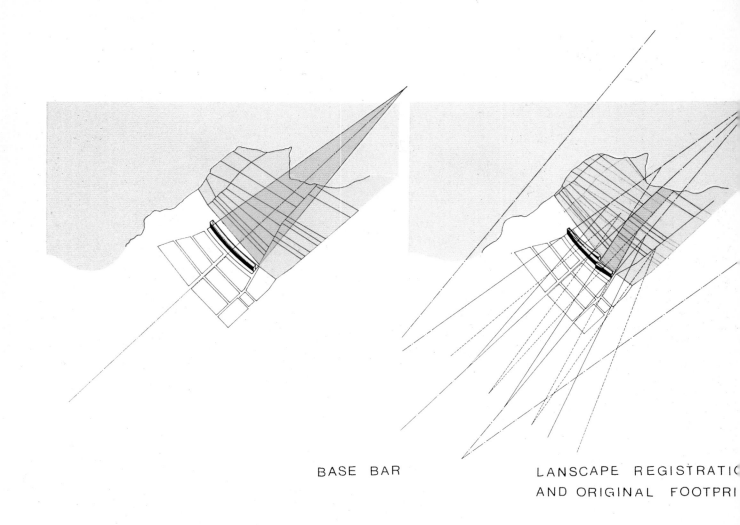

BASE BAR

LANSCAPE REGISTRATIO
AND ORIGINAL FOOTPRI

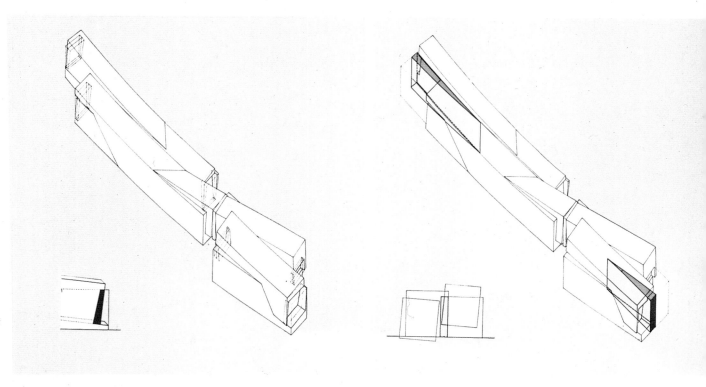

IMPRINT OF OVERLAP IN
THE SAME PAIR

VOIDING OF OVERLAP C
OPPOSITE PAIR

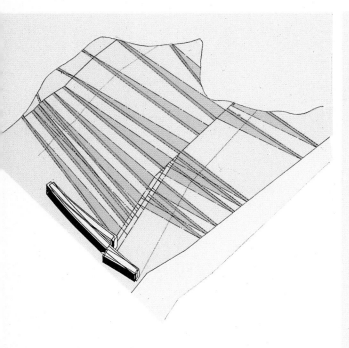

ROWING DISPLACEMENT
OF PARK AND BUILDING

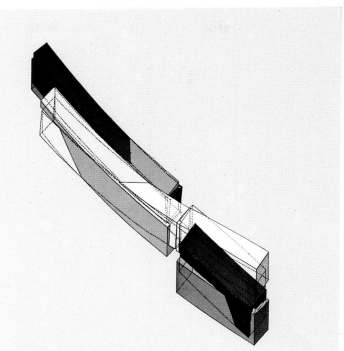

TILT OF SHADOW BARS

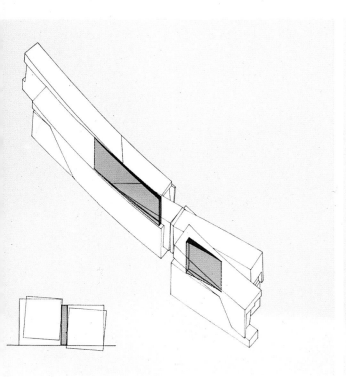

TRACE OF THE VOID
BETWEEN STABLE BARS

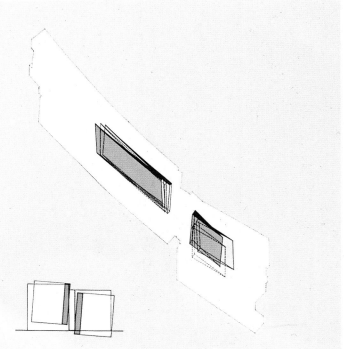

IMPRINT OF THE VOID
INTO UNSTABLE BARS

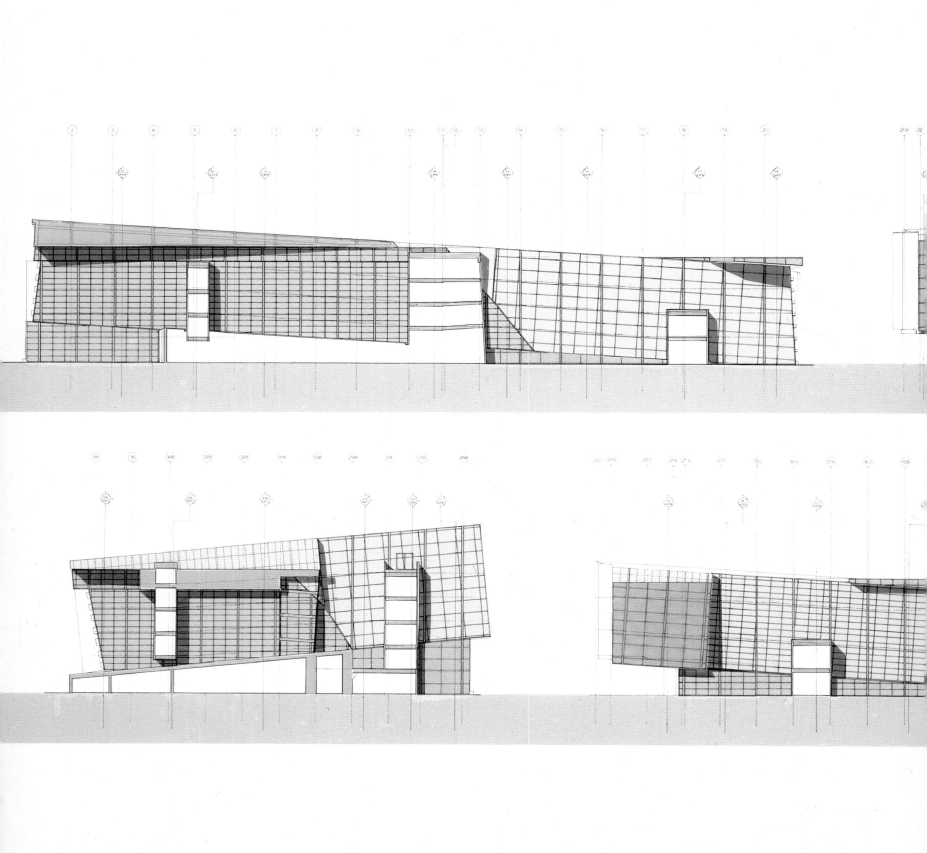

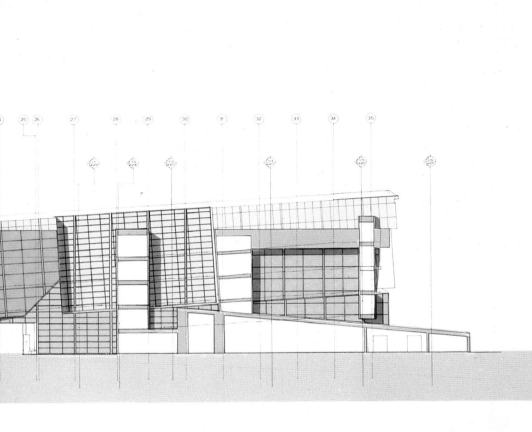

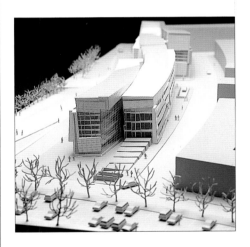

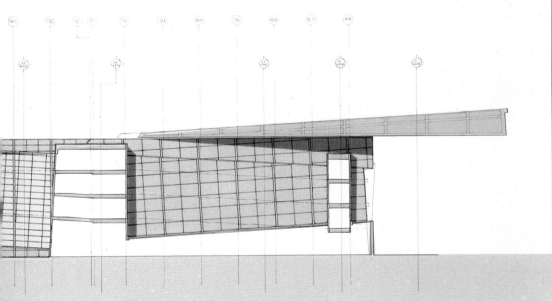

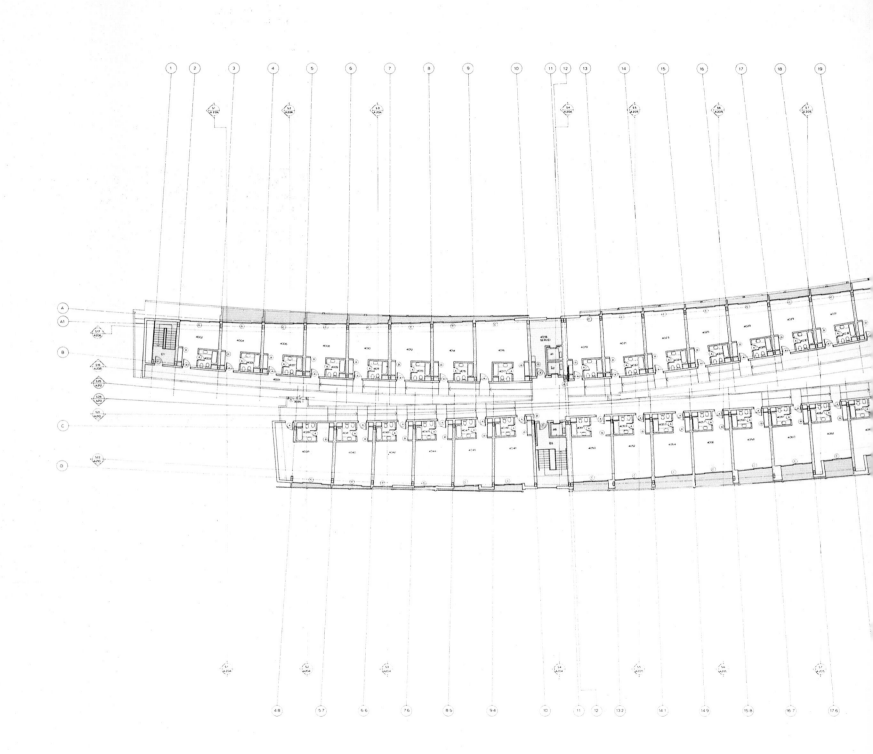

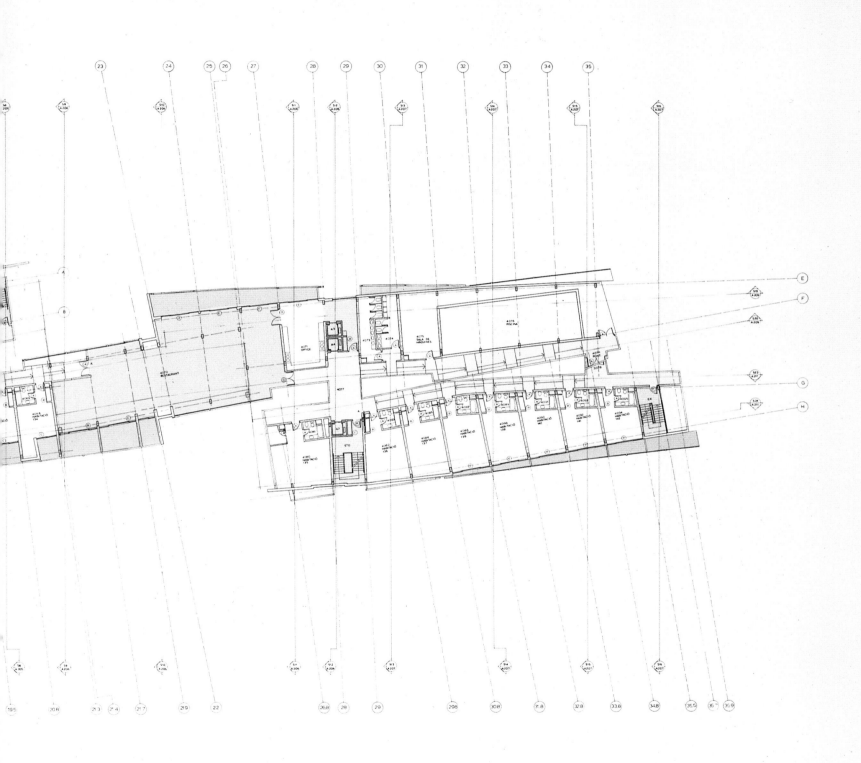

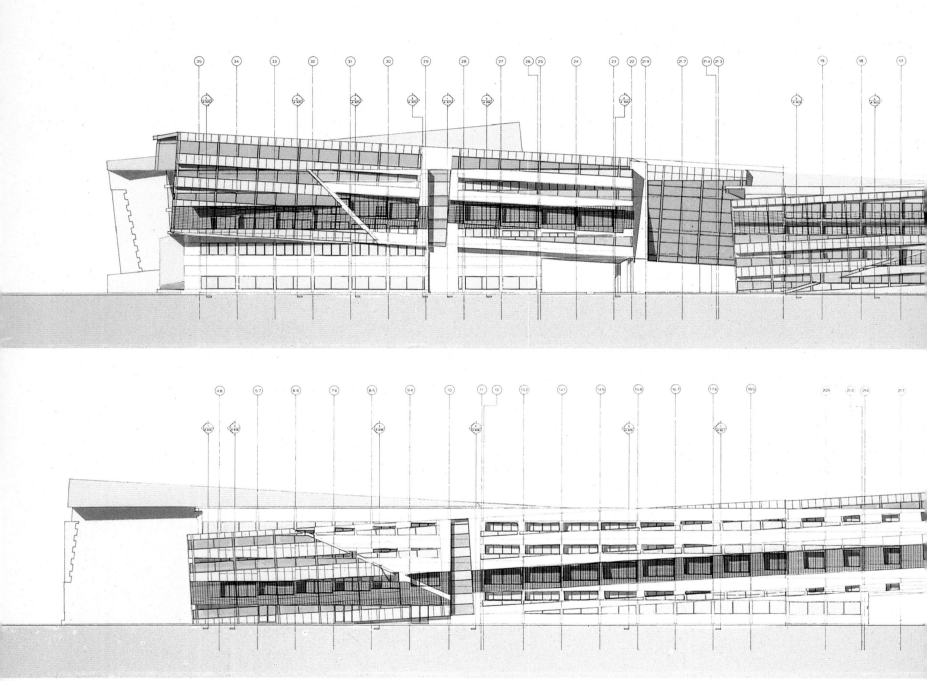

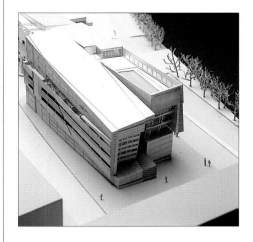

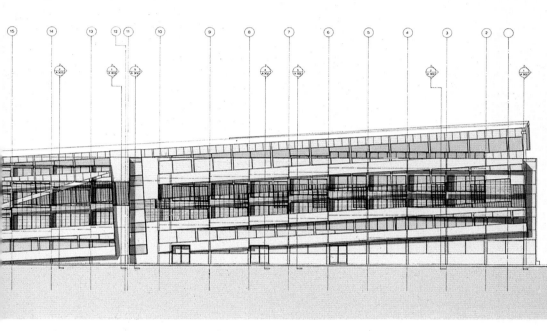

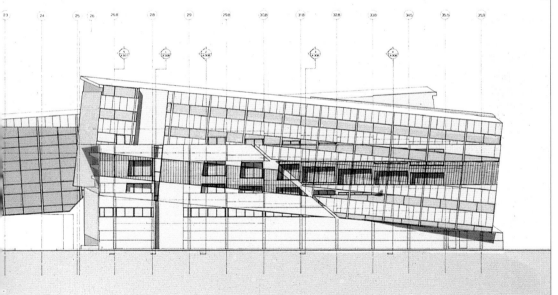

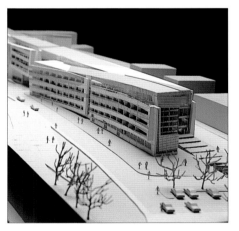

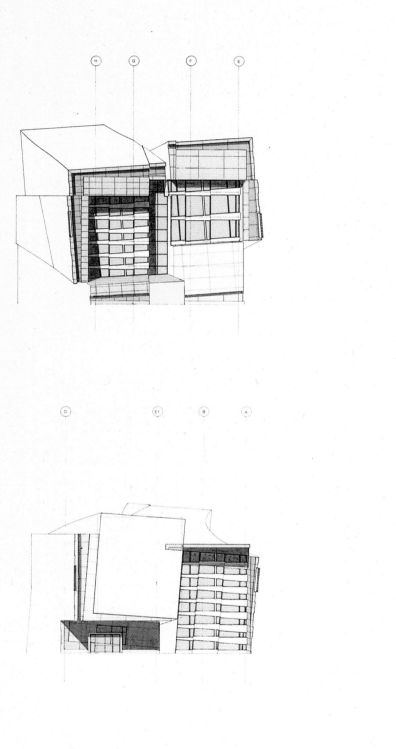
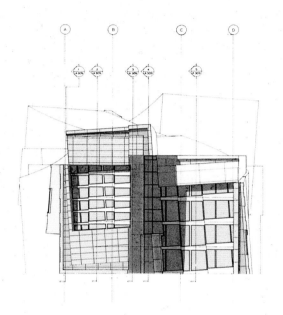
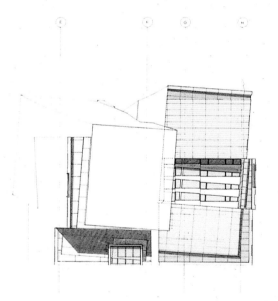

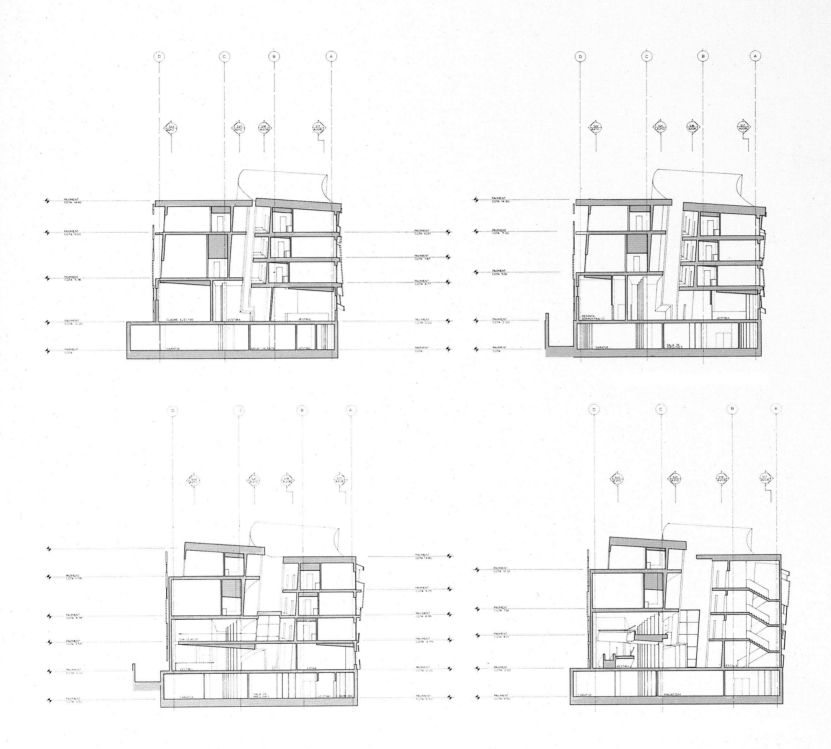

REBSTOCK REFINeD

Framed by a segment of the Mercator Grid, Rebstockpark floats within its rectilinear container to obscure the residual position it occupies within Frankfurt's third green belt. By compressing the large grid segment onto the site perimeter and similarly compressing the small-scale grid onto the close site, contingent readings emerge as the two site figures fold and unfold, each relative to its expanded (or compressed) position. As the new figure of the site boundary opens to interpretation the nature of its perimeter, so does the interior edge of the close site to Rebstockpark through the webbed morphology of the ambiguous container edge. Similarly, the striated site divisions, now webbed continuously, begin to articulate warped planes of various dimension and proportion as they fold over and underneath themselves into and again back out of a neutral orientation.

By overlaying a typological index of urban development in Frankfurt, perimeter housing and perimeter commercial blocks now merge with the German seidlung type to form a combined sub/urban category. Subdivided by the grain of the large site folds as they pass through the close site, the typologos figures separate and align themselves with both the control surfaces and adjacent cusps of the web. Typologies, now severed and refigured by the grain of the large site, occupy in a weakened version their traditional urban syntax.

Page 159: Volumetric concept
Pages 160/161: Site Plan
Pages 162/163: Sectional Plan
Pages 164/165: Roof Plan

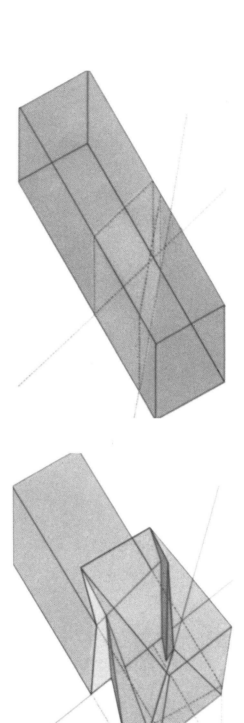

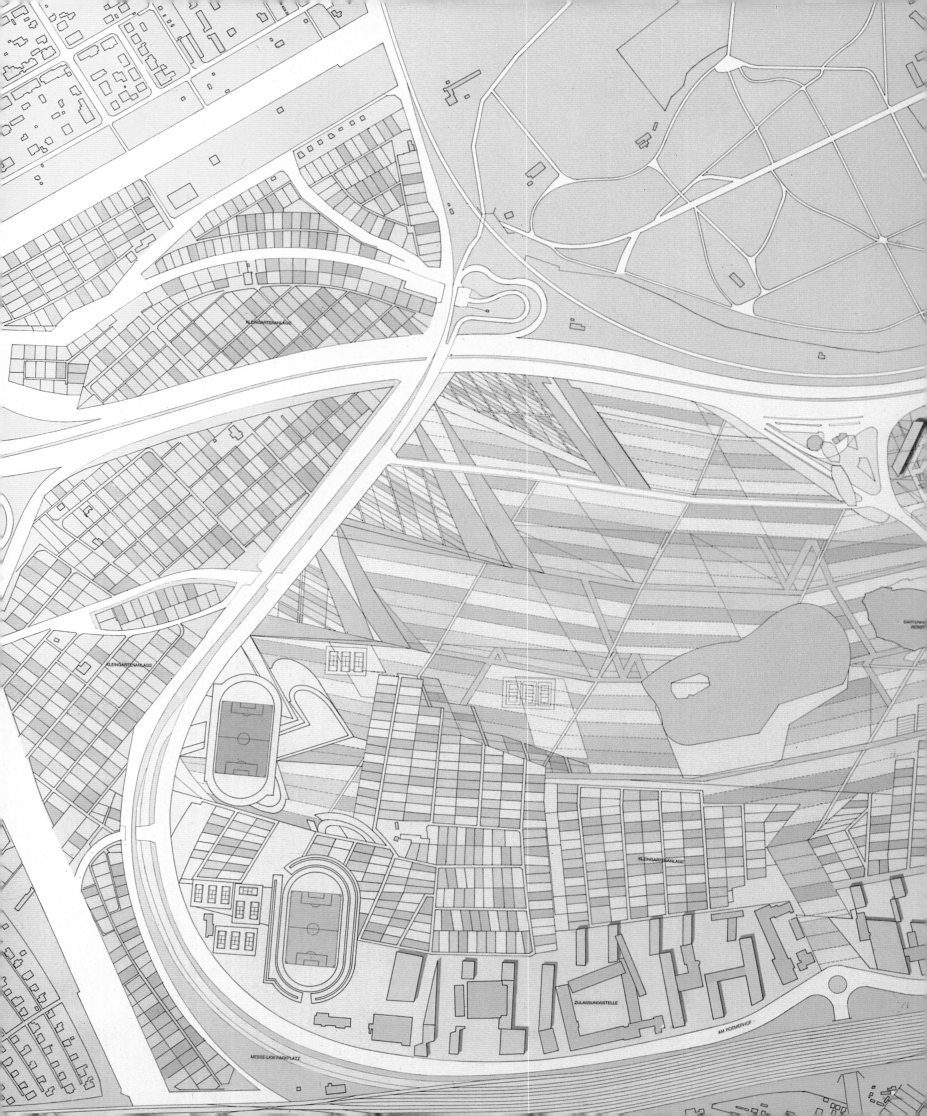

MESSEBUS - HALTESTELLE

GARTENHALLENBAD
REBSTOCK

TENNISPLATZ

ZUM REBSTOCKPARK

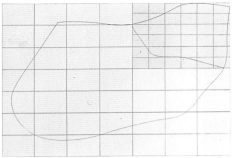

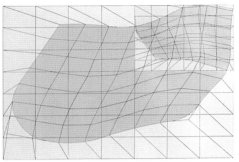

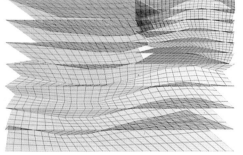

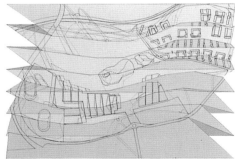

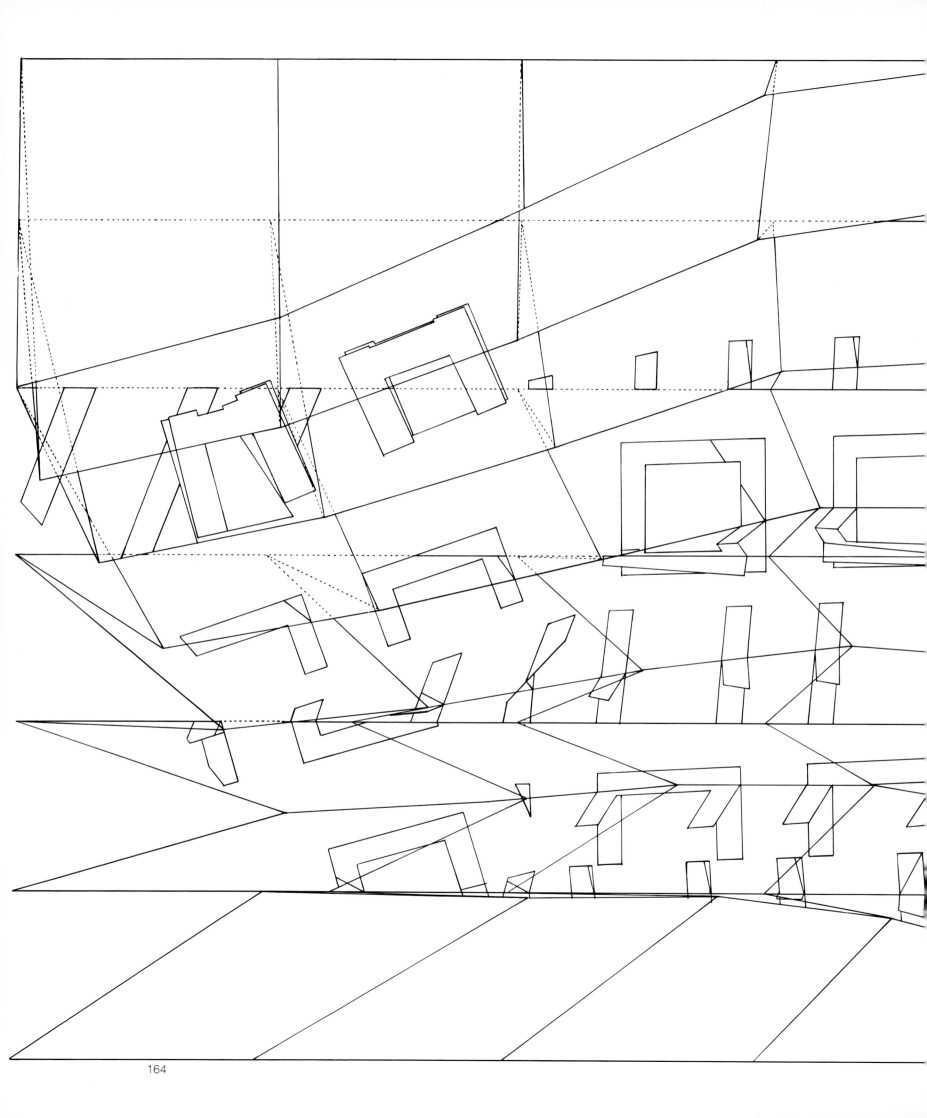

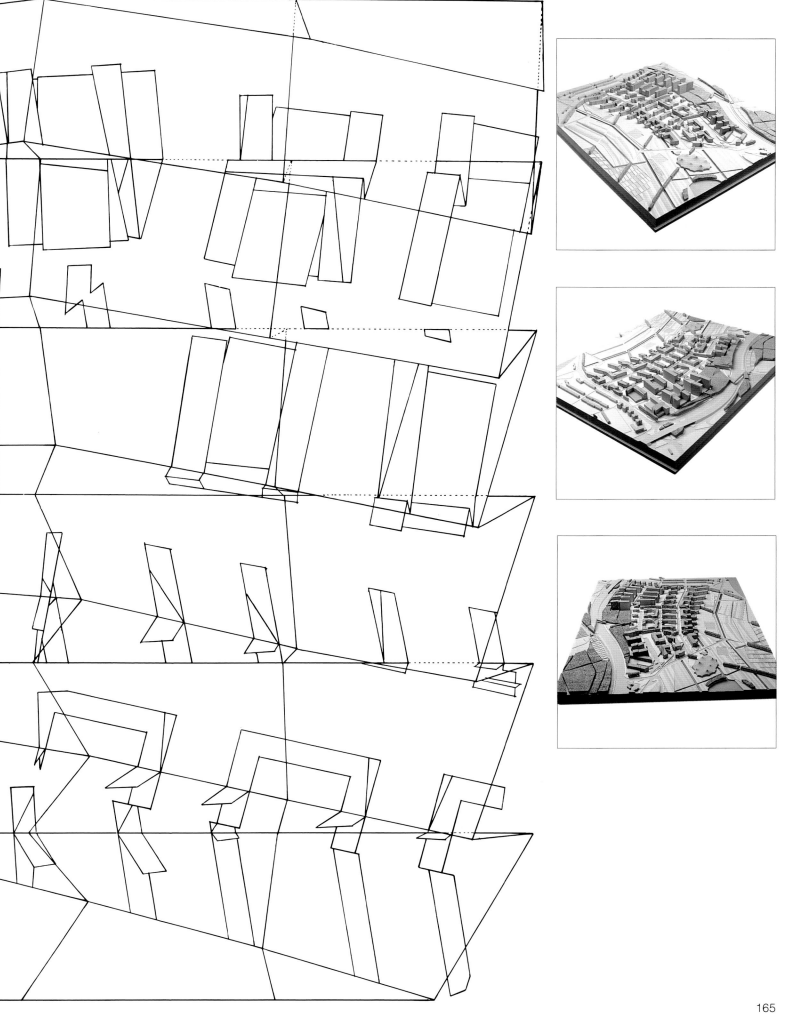

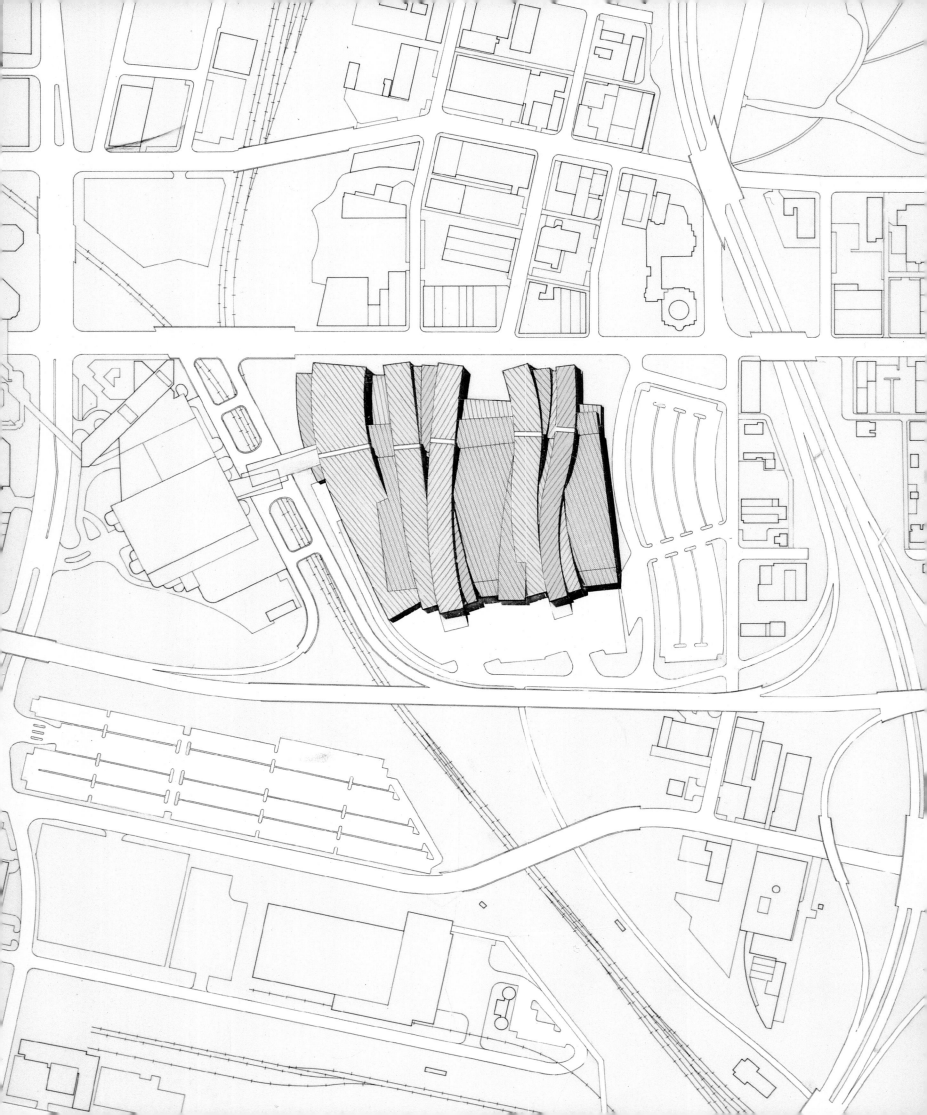

COLUMBUS CONVENTION CENTER OHIO

In order to realise the vision for the Center and the City of Columbus, we proposed that a convention centre was a place for convening, not a place to redeploy old conventions of architectural thinking in a new skin. The convention centre should not be a conventional centre, but must go beyond being merely an amenity for a visitor, turning on and off according to the convention scheduling: rather it should enter into the daily life of the city as an ongoing participant and contributor.

I think the convention centre will be the monument of today. Every city is going to have one. It's the way people are going to meet, the way business is going to be done and we had better find a way to solve the problem of monuments and the need for them today. I think it's very different from the need in the 19th century or the 15th century for a monument.

Peter Eisenman

Page 166: Site Plan
Page 168 Above: Ground Floor Plan; Below: Meeting Rooms Section, looking east
Page 169 Above: Mezzanine Plan; Below: Concourse Section, looking east
Page 170 Above: North Elevation; Below; East Elevation
Page 171 Above: South Elevation; Below: West Elevation

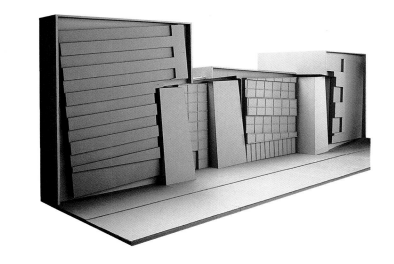

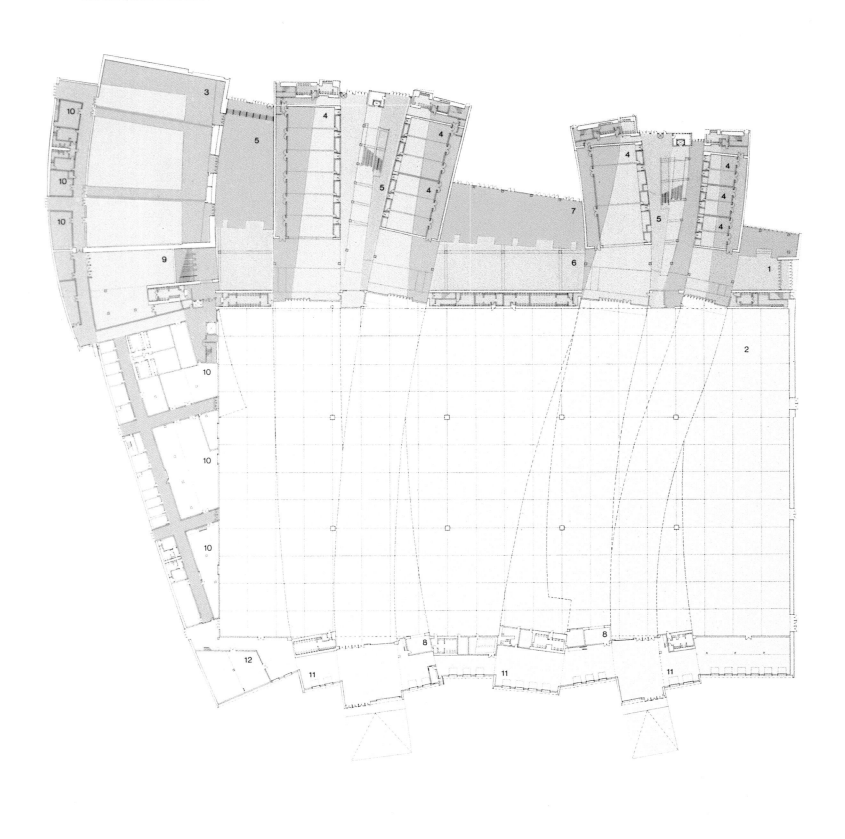

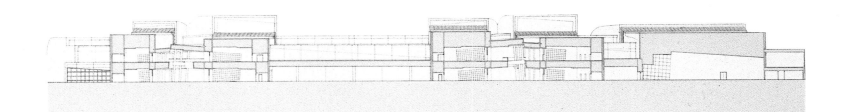

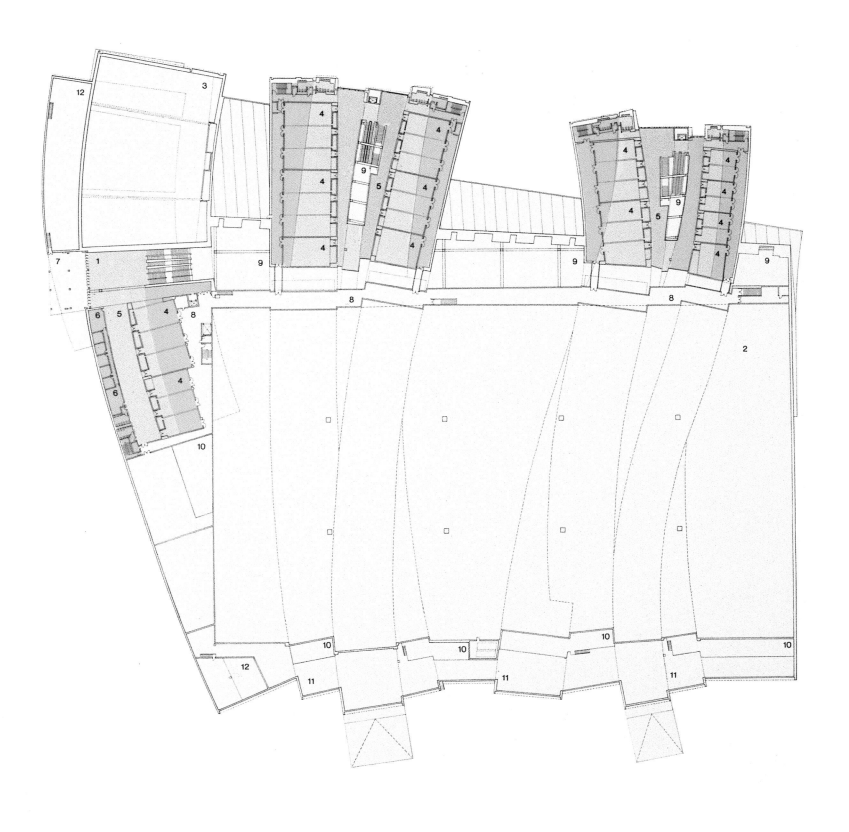

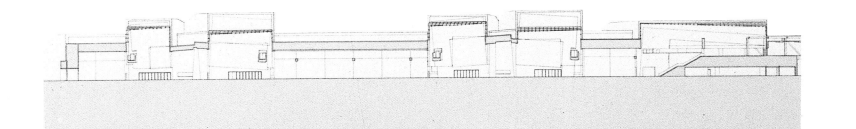

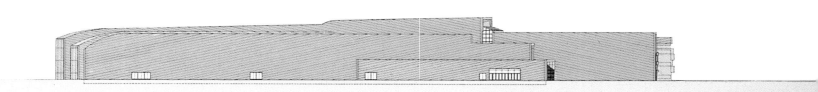

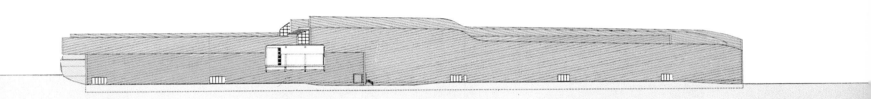

NUNOTANI HEADQUARTERS EDOGAWA DISTRICT TOKYO

The client for this building in Edogawa, on the present outskirts of Tokyo, desired an 'aggressive contemporary image' for the building.

Japan is located on top of the point of collision between the western Pacific continental plate and the Pacific oceanic plate. The Nunotani building is seen as a metaphoric record of waves of movement as the plates overlap. Simultaneously, the project represents an attempt to rethink the symbolism of the vertical office building. Traditionally this had two metaphoric connotations, the one as a metaphor of anthropocentrism, the other, a symbol of power and dominance, in particular phallogo-centrism. Our building symbolically attempts to undermine these two centrisms, first by producing a building that is not metaphorically skeletal or striated, but made up of a shell of vertically compressed and translated plates, and second, by producing an image hovering somewhere in between an erect and a 'limp' condition. As such the building provokes a discussion which is already commonly understood in related discourse.

Page 175: Site Plan
Page 176 Above: Third Floor Plan; Below: Ground Level Plan
Page 177: South Elevation
Page 178: Sections
Page 179: North Elevation

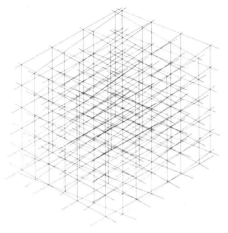

STRIATED CONTEXT

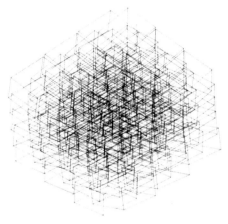

INTEGER TRANSLATION

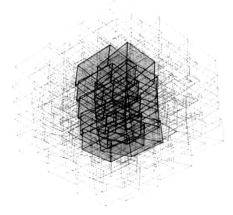

INTEGERS

INTEGER OVERLAP

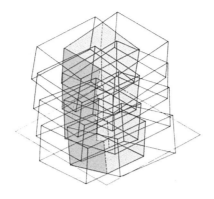

ISOMETRIC

PLAN

INTEGER IMPRINT

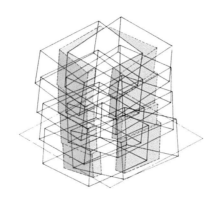

ISOMETRIC

PLAN

IMPRINT OVERLAP

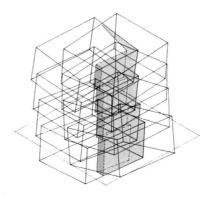

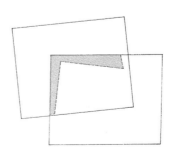

ISOMETRIC

PLAN

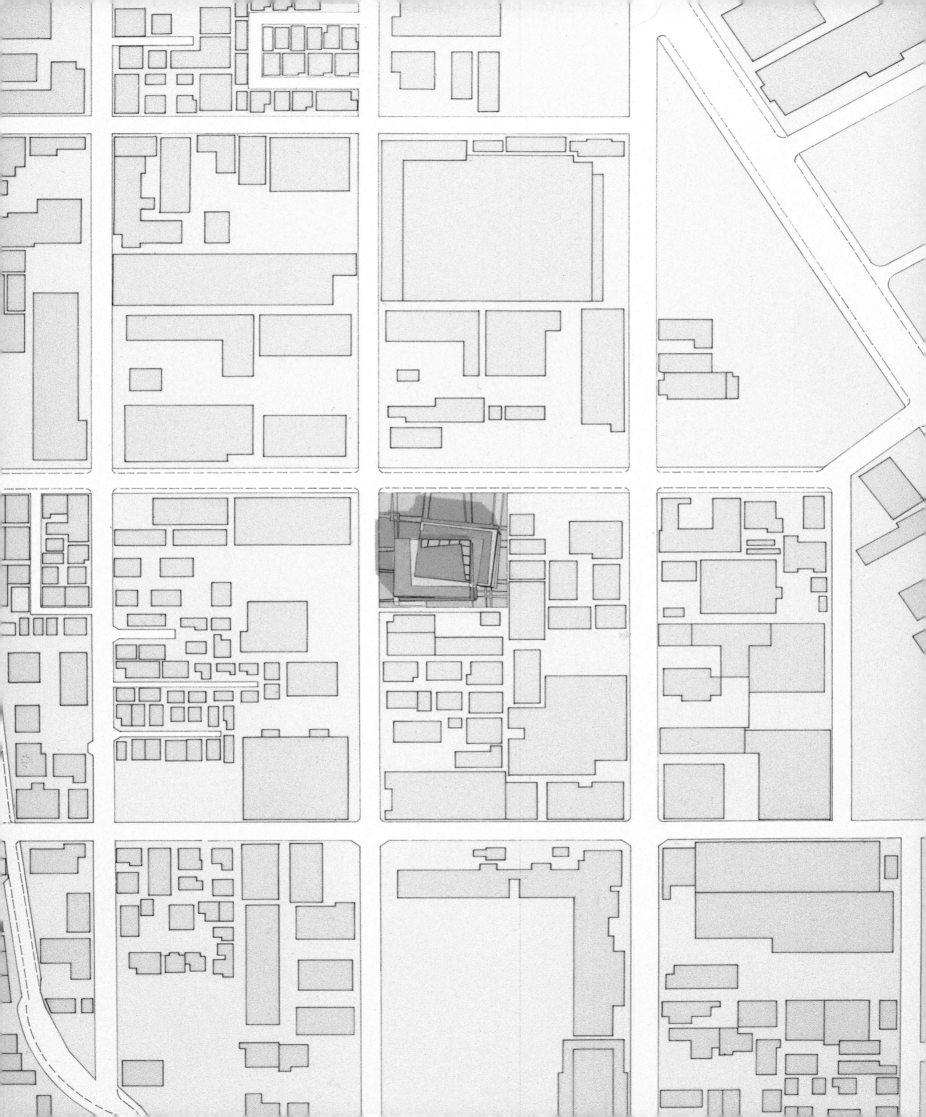

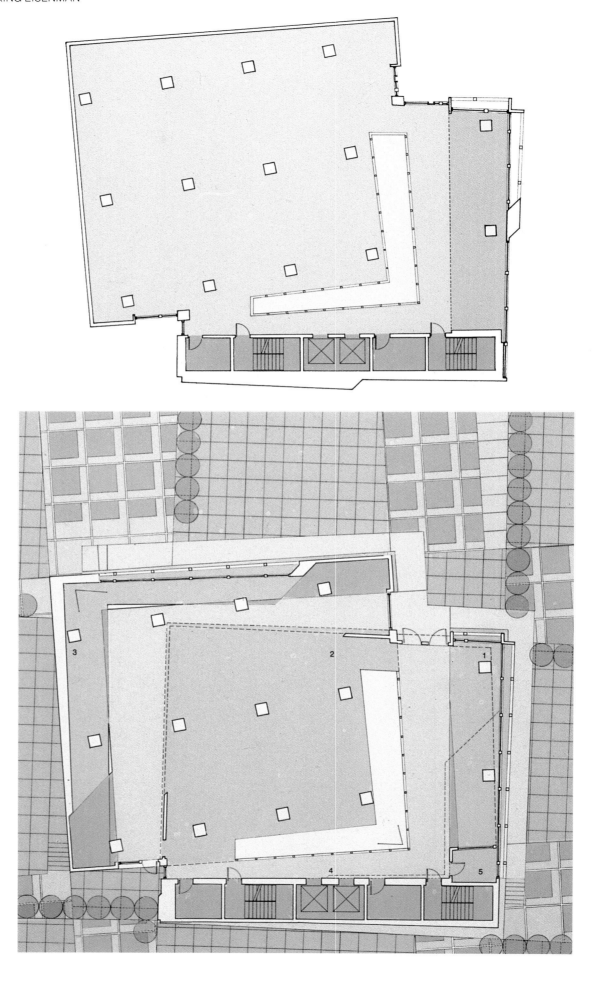

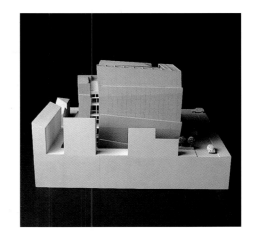

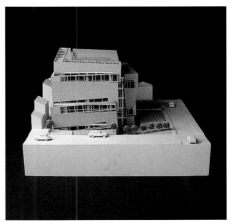

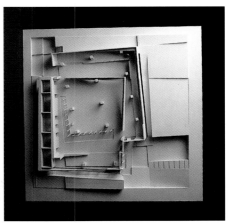

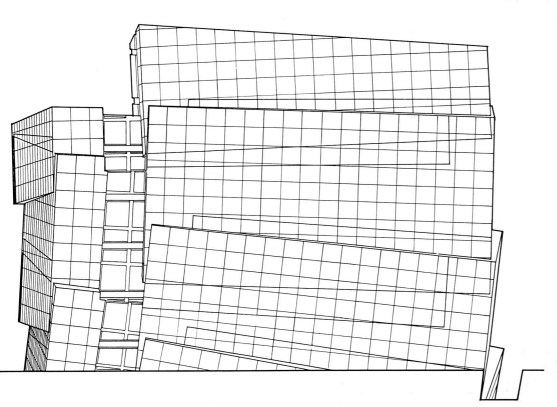

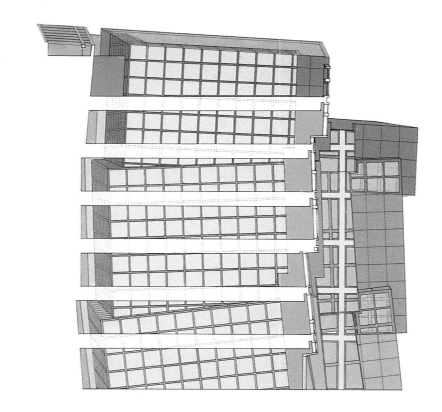

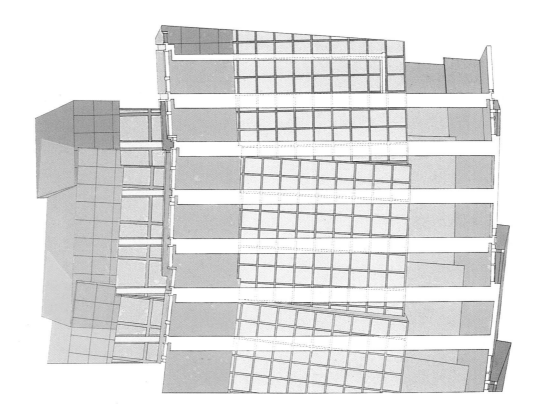

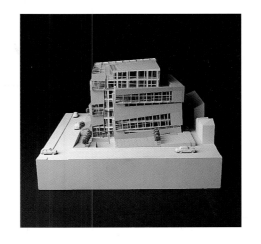

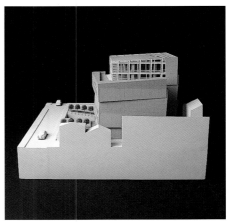

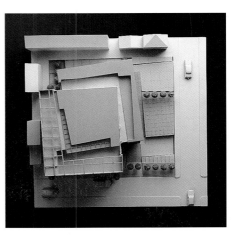

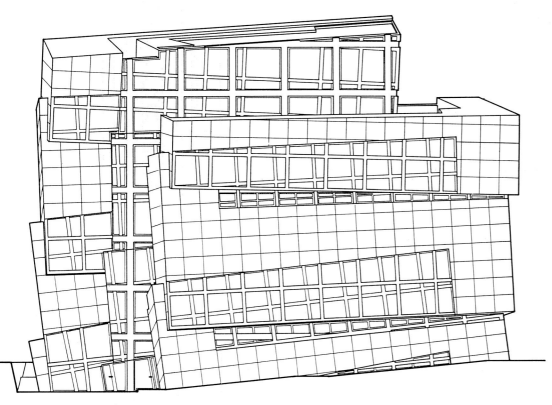

UNIVERSITY OF CINCINNATI DAAP

Peter Eisenman's addition to the University of Cincinnati's Department of Art, Architecture and Planning consolidates four existing schools with new shared college facilities into a combined complex with the 144,000 sq ft new structure and the 145,000 sq ft existing building. The additional programme area allows for the movement of off-campus facilities to the site, along with the addition of new shared programme spaces. The new structure contains a 350-seat auditorium, library, lecture and seminar rooms, administrative offices, café, photo lab and gallery as well as adding to the existing studios, labs and offices. Between the addition and the existing building a large multi-purpose College Hall is created as a symbolic shared space for juries and exhibitions. The project is scheduled for completion in 1993.

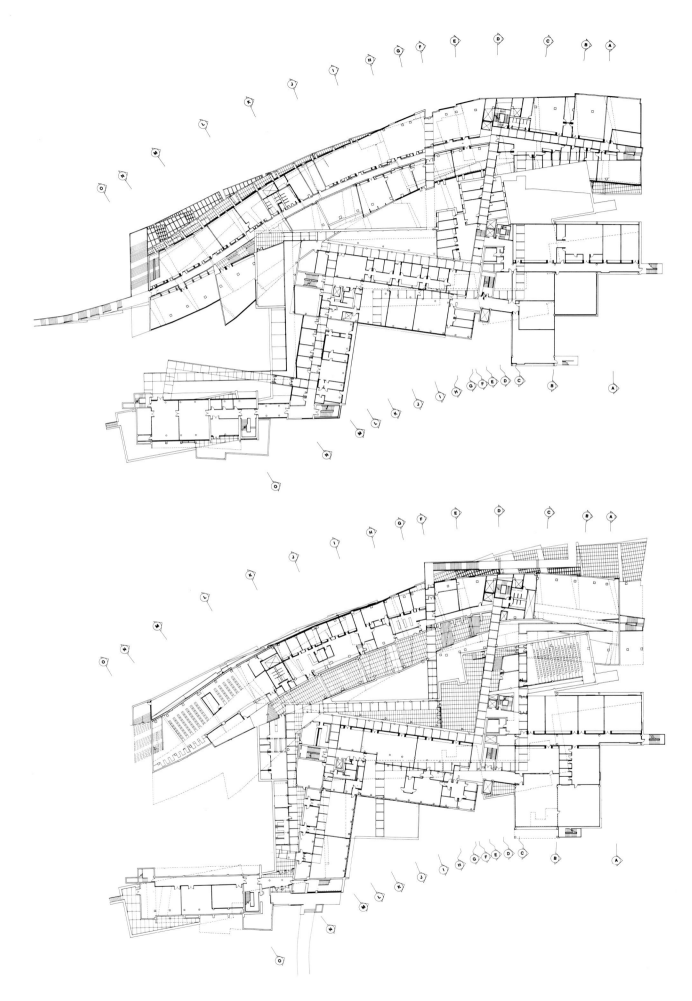

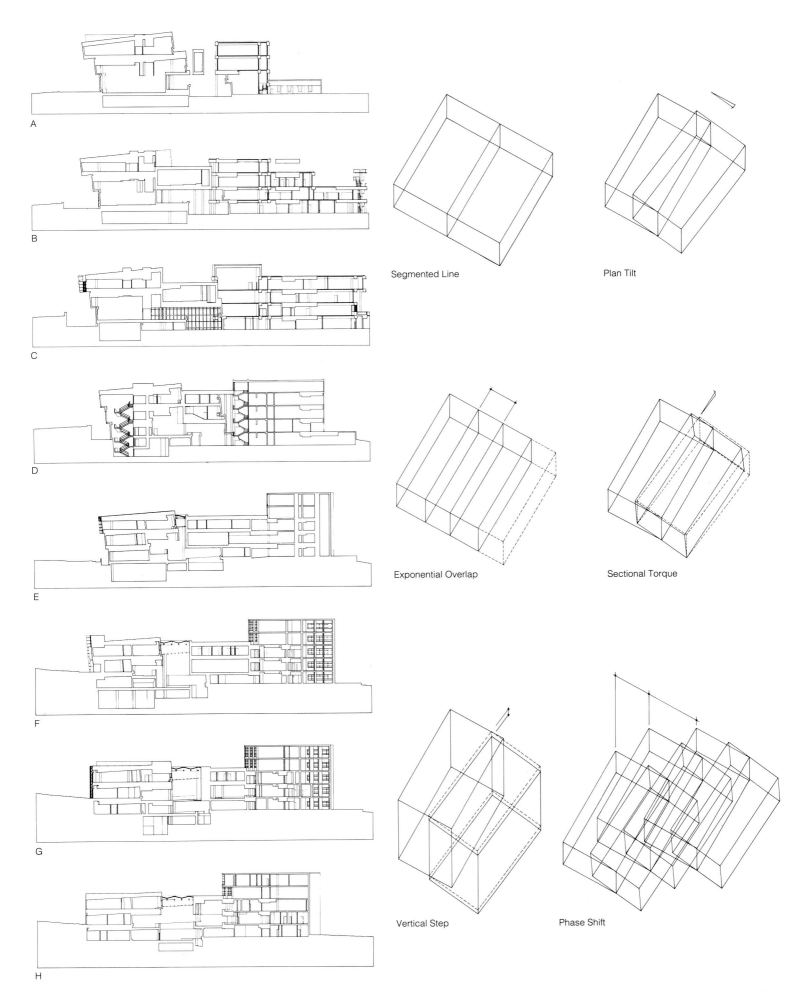

A

B

C

D

E

F

G

H

Segmented Line

Plan Tilt

Exponential Overlap

Sectional Torque

Vertical Step

Phase Shift

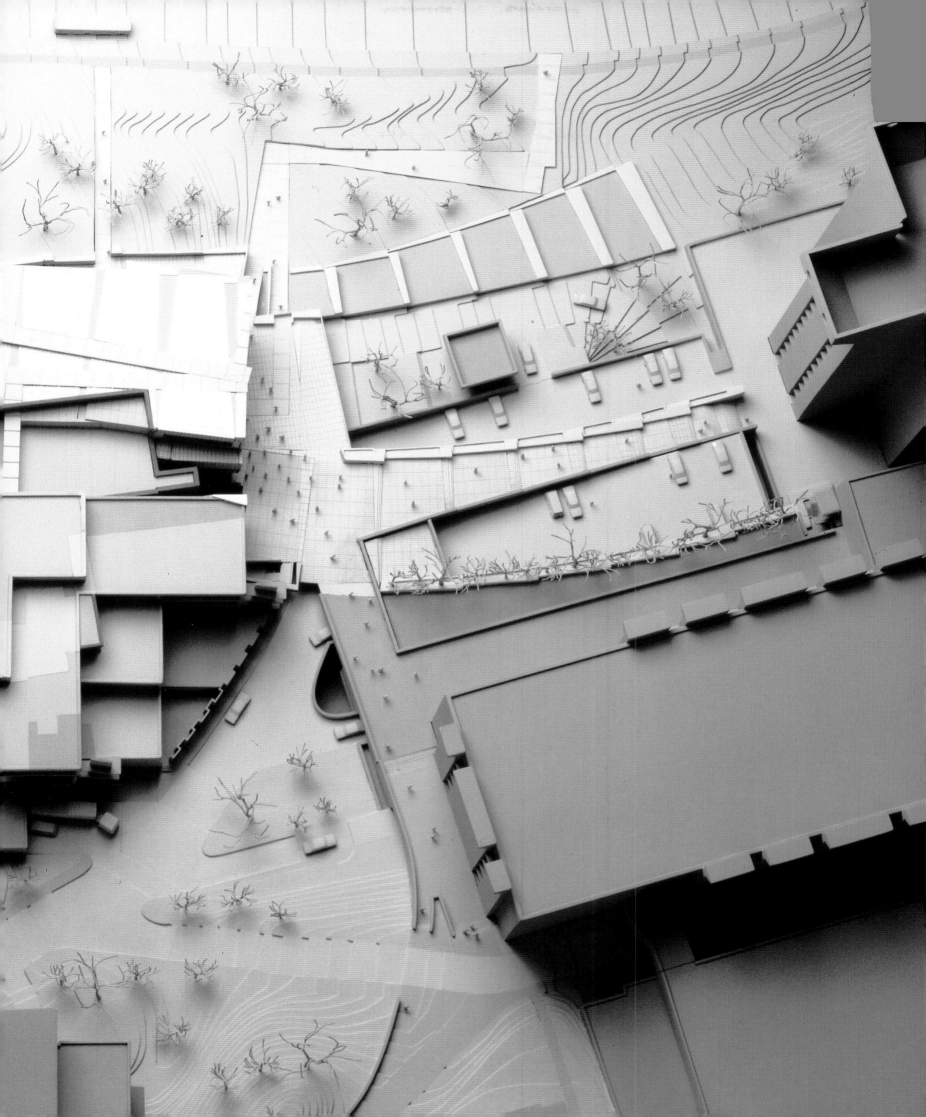

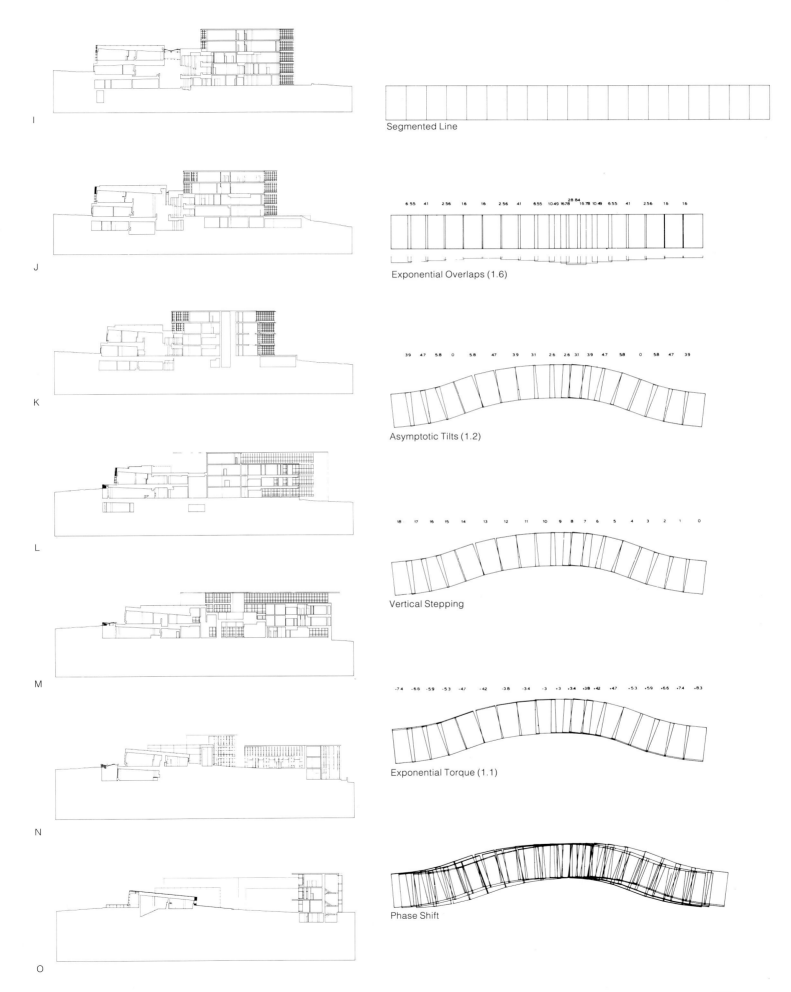

I

Segmented Line

J

Exponential Overlaps (1.6)

K

Asymptotic Tilts (1.2)

L

Vertical Stepping

M

Exponential Torque (1.1)

N

Phase Shift

O

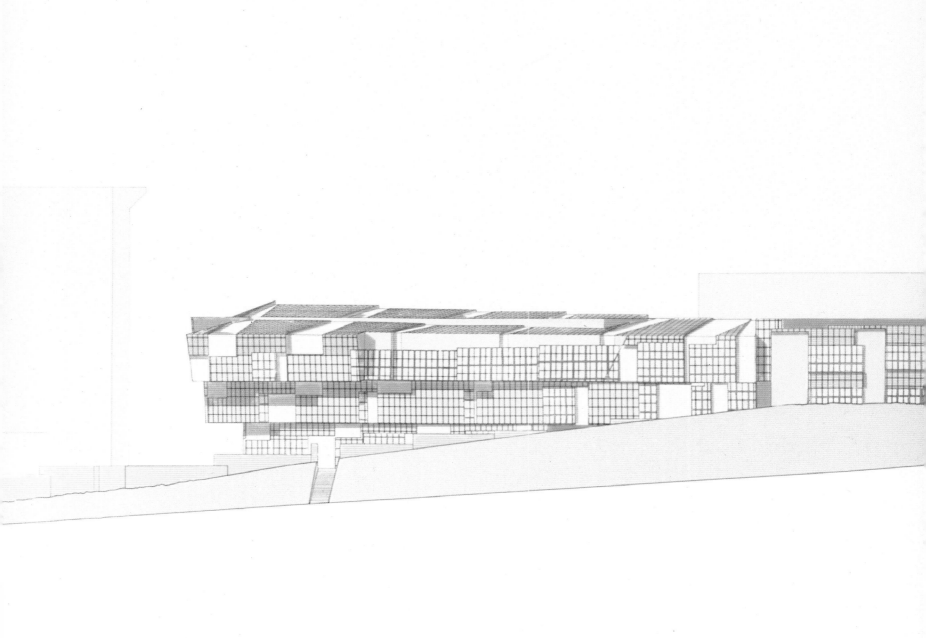

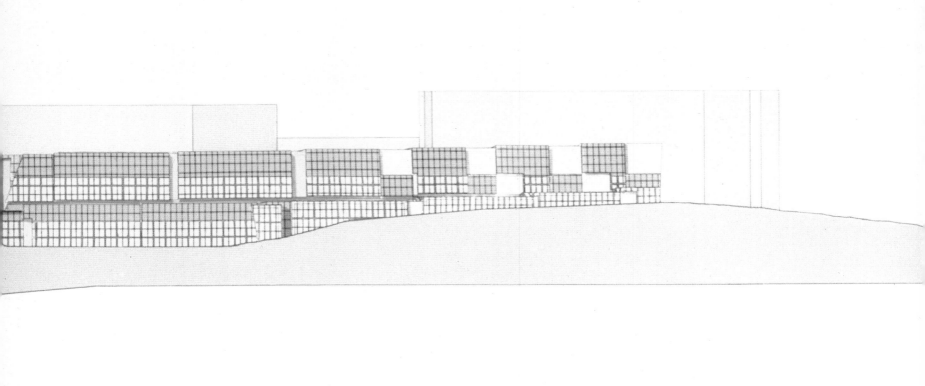

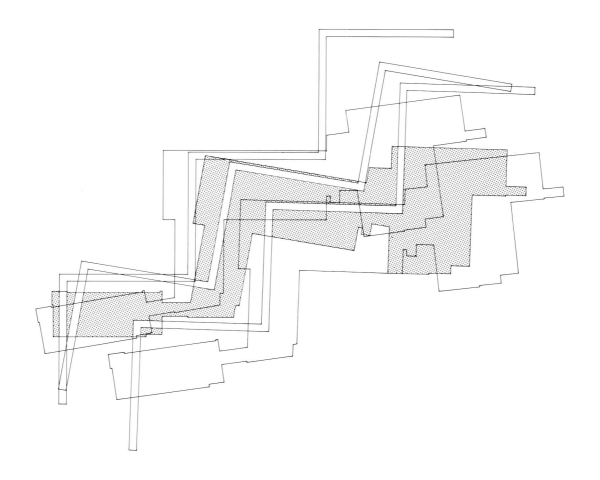

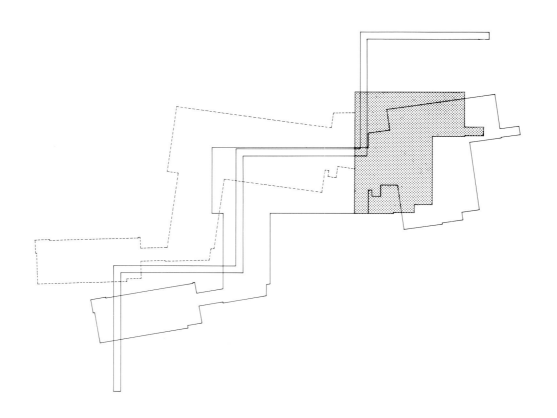

192

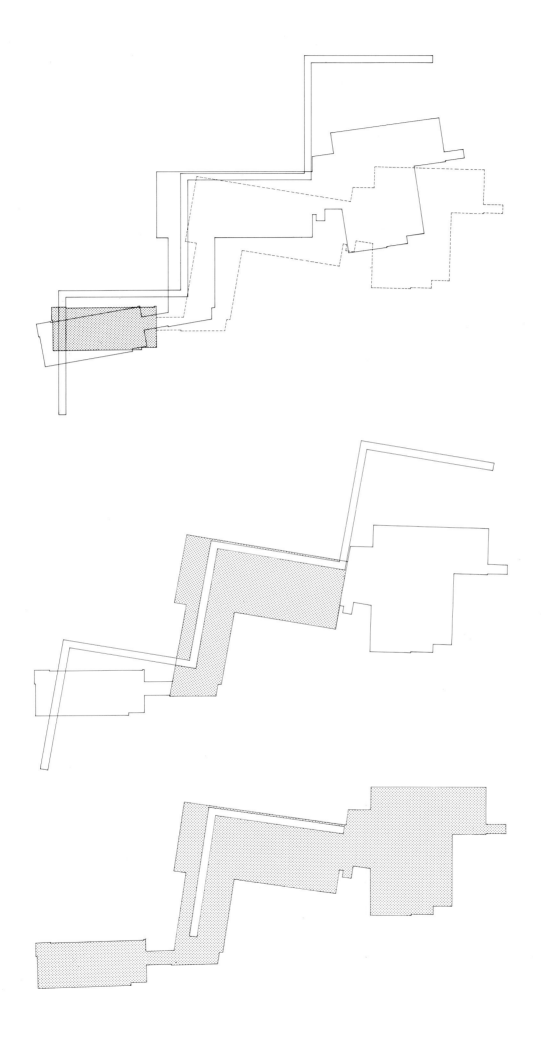

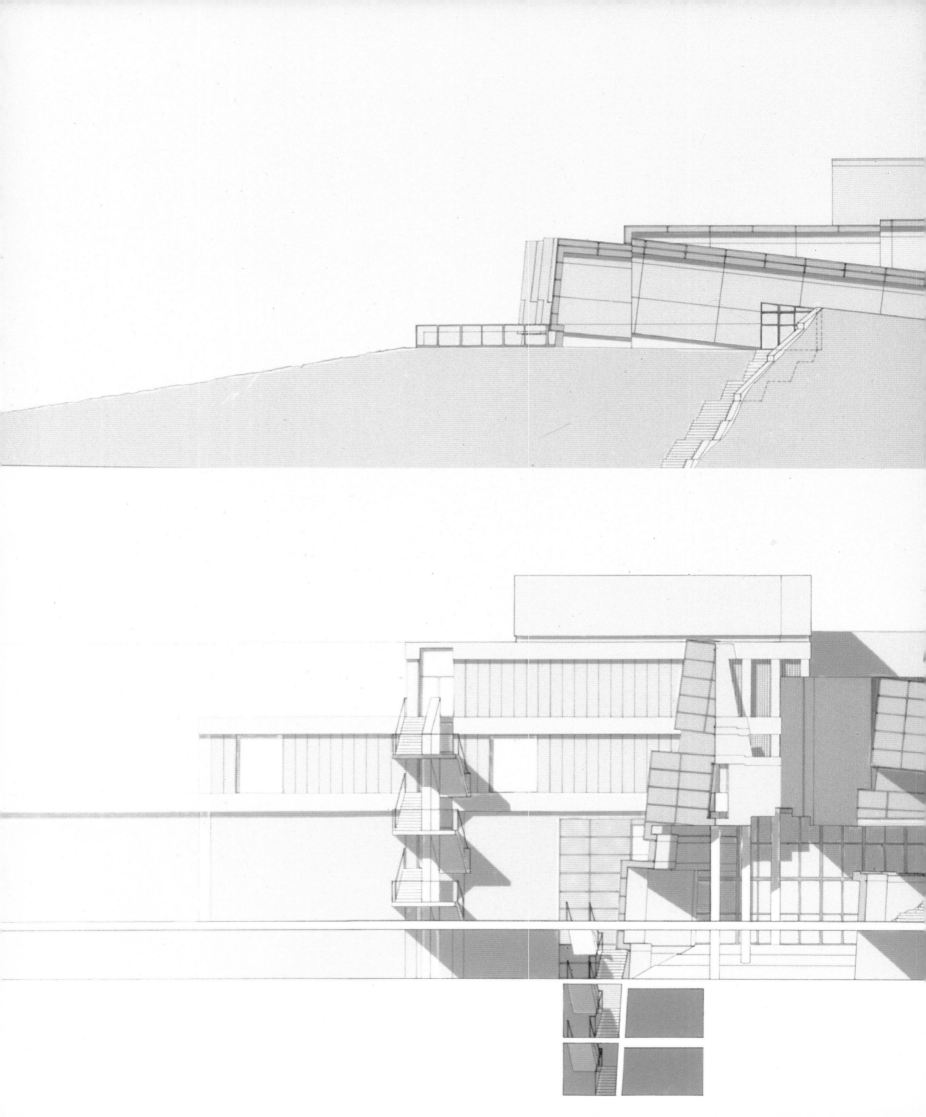

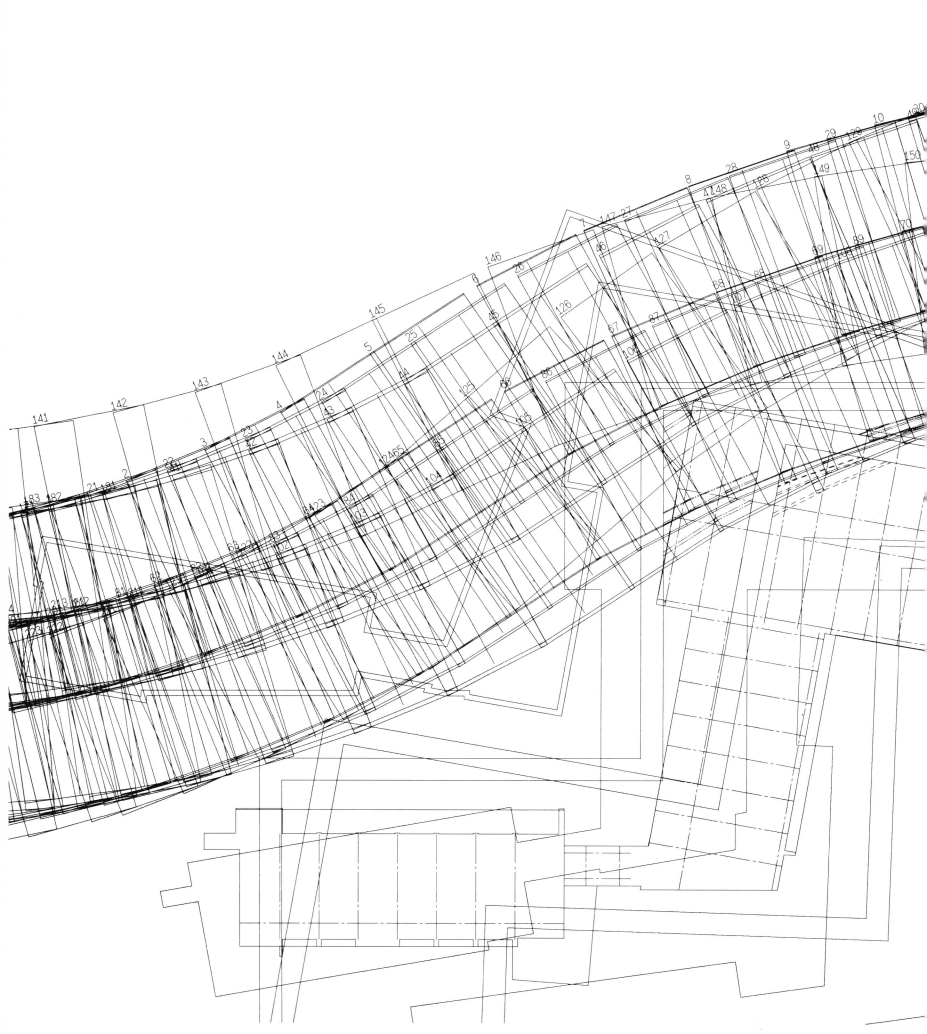

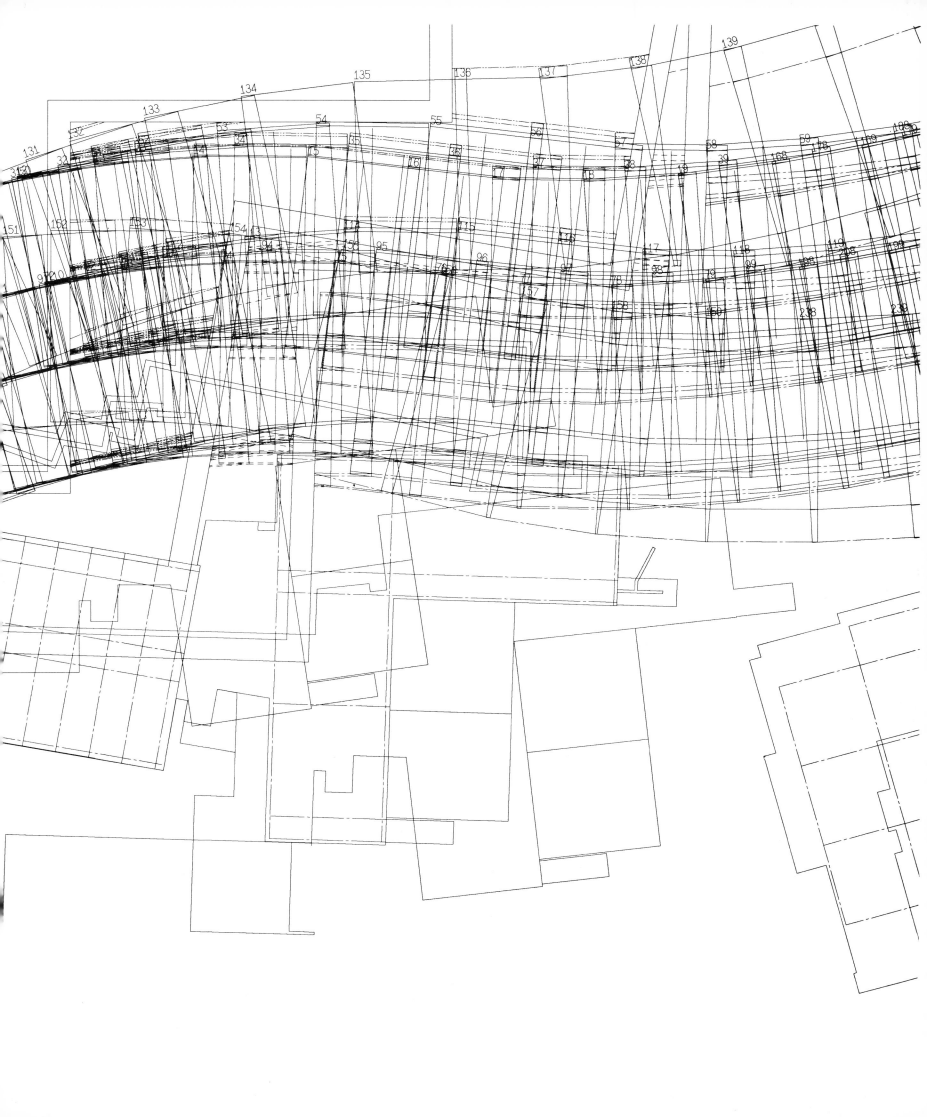

SELECTED BIBLIOGRAPHY

Books

1982 * Indicates major critical writings
* Eisenman, Peter, *House X*, New York: Rizzoli International Publications, Inc., 1982.

1985

* Eisenman, Peter, *Fin D'ou T Hou S*, Folio IV, London: The Architectural Association, 1985 (with Jeff Kipnis and Nina Hofer).

1986

* Eisenman, Peter, *Moving Arrows, Eros, and Other Errors: An Architecture of Absence*, Box 3, London: The Architectural Association, 1986.

1987

* Eisenman, Peter, *La Fine del Classico*, Venezia: Cluva, 1987 (Italian translation of 'Postfunctionalism', 'The Representation of Doubt', 'The Representation of Limits', 'The City of Artificial Excavation', 'The Futility of Objects', 'The End of the Classical', 'The Beginning, the End, and the Beginning Again'. Introduction by Franco Rella, Post-Script by Renato Rizzi, Venezia, CLUVA editrice, texts translated by Renato Rizzi and Daniela Toldo).
* Eisenman, Peter, *Houses of Cards*, New York: Oxford University Press, 1987.

1989

* Eisenman, Peter, *Recente Projecten/ Recent Projects* (Nijmegen: SUN Publishing Co, 1989) (in Dutch and English).
Eisenman, Peter with Anthony Vidler and Raphael Moneo, *The Wexner Center for the Visual Arts: Ohio State University* (New York: Rizzoli, 1989).

1991

Unfolding Frankfurt (a catalogue for the exhibition of Rebstockpark project at Aedes Gallery), Berlin: Ernst & Sohn, 1991, 80 pages (in German and English).
Peter Eisenman & Frank Gehry (a catalogue for the Fifth International Exhibition of Architecture at the 1991 Venice Biennale) (New York: Rizzoli, 1991).

1992

FRANKFURT REBSTOCKPARK: Folding in Time (a catalogue for the exhibition of the Rebstockpark Master Plan project at the Deutsches Architekturmuseum in Frankfurt) (Munich: Prestel-Verlag; and Frankfurt: Deutsches Architekturmuseum, 1992), 128 pp. (in German).

1993

Ciorra, Pippo, *Peter Eisenman: opere e progretti*, serie Documenti di Architettura, no 71 (Milan: Electa, 1993).
Griddings, Scalings, Tracings and Foldings in the Work of Peter Eisenman (a catalogue for the exhibition of the same title at the Museu de Arte de Sao Paolo in Sao Paolo, Brazil) (Sao Paolo: Editora Pini, Ltda., 1993) (in Portuguese and English).

Forthcoming Books

Eisenman, Peter with Jacques Derrida and Jeff Kipnis, *CHORAL WORKS* (New York: Rizzoli).
* Eisenman, Peter, *Giuseppe Terragni: Transformations, Decompositions, Critiques* (New York: Rizzoli).

Writings on Eisenman in English

1966 * Indicates major critical writings
Stern, Robert AM, 'Jersey Corridor Project: Peter Eisenman, Michael Graves and Michael Eardley' in *40 Under 40: An Exhibition of Young Talent in Architecture*, New York: The Architectural League of New York and The American Federation of the Arts, 1966, p. 7 (Catalogue).

1967

Hatch, CR, 'The MOMA Discovers Harlem', *Architectural Forum*, No 126, New York: March, 1967, pp 38-47.
* 'Manhattan Waterfront Design Project: Peter Eisenman and Michael Graves' in *The New City: Architecture and Urban Renewal*, New York: Museum of Modern Art, 1967, pp 36-41 (Catalogue including Manhattan Waterfront design project with Michael Graves).

'The Other Architect', *Architectural and Engineering News*, V. 9, New York: February 1967, pp 33-51.
Roberts, Steven, 'MOMA & Cornell Help to Found IAUS', *New York Times*, New York: October 15, 1967, p 52 (including comments with the director, Peter Eisenman).

1968

Clark, Robert Judson, 'Modern Architecture 1919-1939: Polemics', *Princeton University Library Chronicle*, Vol XXIX No 3, Princeton: Spring 1968, pp 216-218.
Glaeser, Ludwig, 'Pavilion for Antique Toys, Princeton', *Architecture of Museums*, New York: Museum of Modern Art, 1968, p 9 (Catalogue).

1971

Rykwert, Joseph, 'The Institute for Architecture and Urban Studies', *Casabella*, Vol 35, Milan: 1971, pp 100-102 (in Italian and English).

1972

Frampton, Kenneth, 'Frontality vs. Rotation', *Five Architects*, New York: George Wittenborn & Company, 1972, pp 9-15.
* Gandelsonas, Mario, 'On Reading Architecture', *Progressive Architecture*, Vol 53, Stamford: March 1972, pp 68-88.
Rowe, Colin, 'Introduction', *Five Architects*, New York: George Wittenborn & Company, 1972, pp 3-9.

1973

Bonicalzi, Rosaldo, and Uberto Siola, 'Architettura e Ragione: XV Triennale di Milano: House I', *Controspazio*, Rome: December, 1973, pp 16-27 (in Italian).
Frampton, Kenneth, 'Criticism: Eisenman's House I', *A+U*, no 11, Tokyo: November 1973, pp 190-192.
* Gandelsonas, Mario, 'Linguistics in Architecture', *Casabella*, No 374, Milan: 1973, pp 17-30 (in Italian and English).
* Giurgola, Romaldo, 'Five on Five: the Discreet Charm of the Bourgeoisie', *Architectural Forum*, Vol 138, No 4, New York: May 1973, pp 46-57.

* Goldberger, Paul, 'Architecture's "Big Five" Elevate Form', *New York Times*, New York: 26 November, 1973, p 33.

Greenberg, Allan, 'Five on Five: the Lurking American Legacy', *Architectural Forum*, Vol 138, No 4, New York: May 1973, pp 46-57.

Moore, Charles, 'Five on Five: in Similar States of Undress', *Architectural Forum*, Vol 138, No 4, New York: May 1973, pp 46-57.

Papadementiou, PC, 'Five Architects', Book Review in *Architectural Design*, Vol 43, No11, London: 1973, pp 690-1.

* Robertson, Jaquelin, 'Five on Five: Machines in the Garden', *Architectural Forum*, Vol 138, No 4, New York: May 1973, pp 46-57.

Stern, Robert AM, 'Five on Five: Stompin' at the Savoye', *Architectural Forum*, Vol 138, No 4, New York: May 1973, pp 46-57.

1974

Gandelsonas, Mario, 'On Reading Architecture II', *A+U*, no3, Tokyo: March 1974, pp 93-100.

Miller, Robert, 'I guess you win, Peter (House III)', *Progressive Architecture*, Stamford: May, 1974, pp 94-98.

Morton, David, 'One Man's Fit. . .(House III)', *Progressive Architecture*, Stamford: May, 1974, pp 92-94.

Nakamura, Toshio, 'The New York School', *A+U*, no3, Tokyo: March 1974, pp 81-82.

Rykwert, Joseph, 'XV Triennale', *Domus* 530, Milan: January, 1974, pp 1-22 (in Italian and English).

Scully, Vincent, *The Shingle Style Today or the Historian's Revenge,* New York: George Braziller, 1974, pp 39, 70, 129, 130.

Tafuri, Manfredo, 'L'Architecture dans le Boudoir', *Oppositions 3*, New York: May 1974, pp 37-62 (in English).

1975

Frampton, Kenneth, 'Five Architects', *Lotus*, Vol 9, Milan: 1975, pp 146-161, 231-234 (in Italian and English).

'Idealist Cycles', *Architectural Design*, London: November 1975, pp 703-4 (Exhibition diagrams from Art Net, London).

O'Raleigh, Flann, 'Idealist Cycles', *Architectural Design*, no 45, London: November 1975, pp703-4.

Pelli, Cesar, 'White and Gray', *A+U*, No 52, Tokyo: April 1975, pp 25-180 (in Japanese and English).

1976

Gandelsonas, Mario, 'Neo-Functionalismo: After Modern Architecture', *Oppositions 5*, Cambridge: Summer, 1976, pp i-ii (Editorial).

Jencks, Charles, 'Fetishism and Architecture (with Apologies to Adolf Loos and Gore Vidal)', *Architectural Design*, London: August, 1976, pp 492-5.

* Pommer, Richard, 'The New Architectural Supremacists', *Artforum*, Vol XV No 2, New York: October 1976, pp 38-43.

Sky, Allison and Michelle Stone, *Unbuilt America*, New York: McGraw Hill, 1976, pp 113-115 (Jersey Corridor Project).

Tafuri, Manfredo, 'European Graffiti: Five X Five = Twenty-five', *Oppositions 5*, Cambridge: Summer 1976, pp 35-74.

1977

'American Architectural Drawings', *Progressive Architecture*, Vol 58, Stamford: August, 1977, pp 56-57.

* Gass, William, 'House VI', *Progressive Architecture*, Stamford: June 1977, pp 60, 62, 64.

Gebhard, David and Deborah Nivens, *200 Years of American Architectural Drawing*, New York: Whitney Library of Design, 1977, pp 246-247 (House VI).

Goldberger, Paul, 'The House as a Sculptural Object', *New York Times Magazine*, New York: March 20, 1977, pp 74-84.

* Gutman, Robert, 'House VI', *Progressive Architecture*, Stamford, June 1977, pp 57-67.

Smith, C Ray, 'Design: Peter Eisenman', *Avenue Magazine*, Vol 2, No 2, New York: October 1977, pp 48-54.

Staats, Margaret and Sarah Staats, 'Dream Houses', *Quest '77*, Vol 1, No 4, September/October 1977, pp 60-61.

Stephens, S, 'Role-models; Polemicist-theorist', *Progressive Architecture*, Stamford: May, 1977, p 68.

Stern, Robert AM, *New Directions in American Architecture* (Revised Edition), New York: George Braziller, 1977, pp 117-125.

Stern, Robert AM, 'America Now: Drawing Towards a More Modern Architecture', *Architectural Design*, Vol 47, No 6, London: June, 1977 House X (entire issue).

1978

Jencks, Charles, 'Late Modernism and Post-Modernism', *Architectural Design*, Vol 48, No 11-12, London: November-December, 1978,

pp 593-609 (Drawings of House VI, pp 27-9).

* Jencks, Charles, *Post Modern Architecture* (Revised, Enlarged Edition), London: Academy Editions, 1978, pp 8, 64, 66, 100, 101, 118, 121, 122, 126, 127.

Sharp, Dennis, ed *The Rationalists: Theory and Design in the Modern Movement*, New York: Architectural Book Publishing Company, 1978, pp 121, 218-219.

1979

* Bletter, Rosemary Haag, 'Five Architects — Eisenman, Graves, Gwathmey, Hejduk, Meier', *Journal of the Society of Architectural Historians*, New York: May 1979, pp 205-207.

'Citation: Architectural Design (House 11a)', *Progressive Architecture*, Stamford: January, 1979, pp 84-85.

* Gandelsonas, Mario, 'From Structure to Subject', *Oppositions 17*, Cambridge: Summer 1979, pp 6-29.

1980

Archer, BJ, ed 'House El Even Odd', *Houses for Sale*, New York: Rizzoli International Publications, Inc, pp 17-30 (Catalogue of the exhibition at the Leo Castelli Gallery, 18 October–15 November 1980).

* Dal Co, Francesco, 'Ten Architects in Venice', *A+U*, No 121, Tokyo: October 1980, pp 26-33 (in English and Japanese).

* Filler, Martin, 'Peter Eisenman: Polemical Houses', *Art in America*, Vol 68, No 9, New York: November 1980, pp 126-133.

* Fuji, Hirome, 'From Conception to Decomposition', *A+U*, No 112, Tokyo: January 1980, pp 249-252 (in Japanese and English).

Fuji, Hirome, 'Architectural Metamorphology: in Quest of the Mechanism of Meaning', *Oppositions 22*, Cambridge: Fall, 1980, pp 15-16.

Gandelsonas, Mario, 'From Structure to Subject: The Formation of an Architectural Language' *A+U*, Tokyo: January 1980, Special Issue, pp 153-188 (in Japanese and English).

Goldberger, Paul, 'Beyond the Modern Movement', *Harvard Architectural Review*, Vol 1, Cambridge: Spring 1980, pp 19, 191 (on a conference sponsored by the *Review* 1977).

Hubbard, William, *Complicity and Conviction: Steps Toward an Architecture of Convention*, Cambridge: MIT Press, 1980, pp 7, 9, 209-10, 212.

* Huxtable, Ada Louise, 'The Troubled State of Modern Architecture', *New York Review of Books*, New York: 1 May 1980, pp 22-29.

* Krauss, Rosalind, 'Death of a Hermaneutic Phantom: Materialization of the Sign in the Work of Peter Eisenman', *A+U*, No 112, Tokyo: January 1980, pp 189-219.

Kutnicki, Lawrence, 'On Eisenman: Houses I to VI', *Archetype*, Melbourne: Vol I, No IV, Winter 1980, pp 33-36.

Lym, Glenn Robert, *A Psychology of Buildings: How We Shape and Experience our Structured Spaces*, New Jersey: Prentice Hall, Inc, 1980, pp 65-66, 81-82.

* Mendini, Alessandro, Editorial; 'Dear Peter Eisenman', *Domus*, No 611, Milan: November 1980, p 1 (in Italian and English).

Sorkin, Michael, 'Drawings for Sale', *Village Voice*, New York: News Group Publications, Inc, Vol XXV, No 46, November 12-18, 1980, pp 85-86.

Stern, Robert and Deborah Nivens, *The Architect's Eye*, New York: Pantheon Books, 1980, pp 158-160.

* Taki, Koji, 'Dialogue on Peter Eisenman', *A+U*, No 112, Tokyo: January 1980, pp 245-248 (in Japanese and English).

1981

Bernhard, Schneider, 'Perspective refers to the Viewer, Axonometry refers to the Object', *Daidalos*, Berlin Architectural Journal, Berlin: 15 September 1981, pp 81-95 (in German and English).

Doordan, D, 'New York-Como Connection', *Architectural Design* 51, no1/2, London: January/February, 1981, pp 76-79.

* Forster, Kurt, 'Eisenman/Robertson's City of Artificial Excavation', *Archetype*, Volume II, No II, Melbourne: Spring 1981, pp 84-85.

Foster, Hal, 'Pastiche/Prototype/Purity', *Artforum*, New York: March 1981, Volume XIX, No 7, pp 77-79 (Review of 'Houses for Sale', Leo Castelli Gallery, New York).

Huxtable, Ada Louis, 'Troubled State of Modern Architecture', *Architectural Design*, 51, no 1/2, London: January/February, 1981, pp 2-14.

Lipstadt, Helene, 'Self-reflection: Eisenman in Berlin', *Progressive Architecture*, Stamford: September, 1981, p 38.

Reichlin, Bruno, 'Reflections Interrelations between Concept, Representation and Built

Architecture', *Daidalos*, Berlin Architectural Journal, Berlin: 15 September 1981, pp 60-73 (in German and English).

1982

Frampton, Kenneth, 'Five plus Ten; a Symposium', *Colonnade: The News Journal of the School of Architecture*, University of Virginia, Charlottesville: Spring 1982.

Frampton, Kenneth, 'Neo-Plasticism and Architecture: Formation and Transformation', *De Stijl: 1917-1931, Visions of Utopia*, Minneapolis: Walker Art Center, 1982, pp 120-123.

* Gandelsonas, Mario, 'From Structure to Subject: The Formation of an Architectural Language' in *House X* by Peter Eisenman, New York: Rizzoli, pp 7-31 (op cit7).

1983

Dunster, David, 'Declining in the East', *Building Design*, London: March 25, 1983.

Dunster, David, 'Eisenman: Art of the Post-Modern Lecturing', *Building Design*, London: June 17, 1983, p 7.

* Hofer, Nina, 'Fin d'Ou T Hou S', text, *Architectural Follies*, Leo Castelli Gallery, New York: October 22 - November 19, 1983.

Huxtable, Ada Louise, 'After Modern Architecture', Review of House X, *New York Review of Books*, New York: 8 December, 1983.

* Jencks, Charles, 'The Perennial Architectural Debate, The Eisenman Paradox: Elitism, Populism and Centrality', *Architectural Design Profile*, London: 1983, pp 4-23.

* Lemos, Peter, 'The Triumph of the Quill', *Village Voice*, New York: May 3, 1983, pp 96, 99.

* Lerup, Lars, 'House X by Peter Eisenman', *Design Book Review*, San Francisco: Summer 1983, pp 44-8.

Merkel, Jayne, 'Architects Compete to Design OSU Center for the Visual Arts', *Dialogue/The Ohio Arts Journal*, Columbus: July, August 1983, pp 7-8.

* Merkel, Jayne, 'Looking for the Future: The Center for the Visual Arts Competition at Ohio State University', *Inland Architect*, Chicago: December 1983, pp 110-16.

Noone, Peter, 'The Hero Within', *Threshold*, University of Illinois, Volume Two, Autumn, Chicago: 1983, pp 105-109.

Paplow, Michael, 'The Competition for the

Center for Visual Arts at Ohio State University', *Columbus Art*, Vol 4, No 4, Columbus: Summer 1983, pp 10-13.

Stephenson, William, 'Toward a New Cosmology: An Interview with Peter Eisenman', *Art Papers*, New York: May-June, 1983, pp 3-5.

1984

* Colquhoun, Alan, 'The Competition for the Center for the Visual Arts at Ohio State University', *The Ohio State Center for the Visual Arts Competition* New York: Rizzoli International, 1984, pp 132-135.

* Davis, Douglas, 'Modernism Revisited', *The Ohio State Center for the Visual Arts Competition*. New York: Rizzoli International, 1984.

* Davis, Douglas, 'The Death of Semiotics (in Late Modern Architecture), the Corruption of Metaphor (in Post-Modernism), the Birth of Punctum (in Neomania)', *Art Forum*, New York: May, 1984, pp 56-63.

* Davey, P, 'Urban Eisenman [Visual Arts Center Ohio State University, Columbus]', *Architectural Review*, London: December 1984, pp 48-52.Forster, Kurt, 'Monuments to the City', *Harvard Architectural Review*, Cambridge: Spring, 1984, pp 107-121.

* Davey, P, 'Traces and Treason of a Tradition', *The Ohio State Center for the Visual Arts Competition*, New York: Rizzoli International, 1984, pp 135-140.

* Kipnis, Jeffrey, 'The Ohio State University Center for the Visual Arts and the Architecture of Modification', *Casabella*, 488/9, Milan: January/February, 1984, pp 96-99 (in English).

* Libeskind, Daniel, 'Peter Eisenman and the Myth of Futility', *Harvard Architectural Review*, MIT Press, Cambridge, Massachussetts, Volume 3, Winter 1984, pp 61-64,1985.

* Abrams, Janet, 'Misreading Between the Lines', *Blueprint*, No 14, London: February, 1985, pp 16-17.

Cofer, Doug, 'Eisenman and Graves: Modeling in Architecture', in *Crit XV The Design Process*, edited by Laura Todd, Washington, DC: American Institute of Architecture Students Inc, 1985, pp 44-47.

* Evans, Robin, 'Not to Be Used for Wrapping Purposes — Peter Eisenman: Fin d'Ou T Hou S', *AA Files*, London: Autumn, 1985, pp 68-78.

Finken, Kathleen Enz, 'House VI', *The Critical Edge: Controversy in Recent American Architecture*, Exhibition catalogue/Rutgers University, Cambridge: 1985, pp 125-136.

Latham, Ian, 'Shrink Rap', *Building Design*, London: March 8, 1985, pp 24-25.

* Macrae-Gibson, Gavin, 'The Anxiety of the Second Fall: House El Even Odd, Peter Eisenman', in *The Secret Life of Buildings: An American Mythology for Modern Architecture*, Cambridge: MIT Press, 1985, pp 30-51.

Morton, David, 'Stone Lions in Venice', *Progressive Architecture*, Stamford: September, 1985, p 23.

'The OSU Center for the Visual Arts', *Progressive Architecture: 32nd Annual P/A Awards*, Stamford: January, 1985, pp 98-100 (Award).

'Syntactic Architecture (House II and Other Works)', *The Toshi Jutaku*, Tokyo: November, 1985 (in Japanese and English).

1986

Brown, Andrea, 'In Caesura', *Investigations in Architecture/Eisenman Studios at the GSD: 1983-85*, Cambridge: Harvard Graduate School of Design, 1986, pp 14-26.

Cobb, Henry, 'Forward', *Investigations in Architecture/Eisenman Studios at the GSD: 1983-85*, Cambridge: Harvard Graduate School of Design, 1986, pp 5-6.

* Hacker, Marc, 'With a Certain Laughter and Dance', *Investigation in Architecture/ Eisenman Studios at the GSD: 1983-85*, Cambridge: Harvard Graduate School of Design, 1986, pp 26-42.

* Kipnis, Jeffrey, 'Star Wars III: The Battle at the Center of the Universe', *Investigation in Architecture/Eisenman Studios at the GSD: 1983-85*, Cambridge: Harvard Graduate School of Design, 1986, pp 42-47.

* Kipnis, Jeffrey, 'Architecture Unbound: Consequences of the Recent Work of Peter Eisenman', in *SD*, Special Issue on Peter Eisenman, Tokyo: March, 1986, pp 26-33 (in Japanese and English).

* Maruyama, Hiroshi, 'Of a mis-Leading, for a mis-Leading', in *SD* Special Issue on Peter Eisenman, Tokyo: March, 1986, pp 7-8 (in Japanese and English).

Turner, Judith, 'Five Architects', *Annotations on Ambiguity: Photographs of Architecture*, Tokyo: Axis Publications, pp 27-39 (Exhibition catalogue; in English).

* Whiteman, John, 'Site Unseen — Notes on Architecture and the Concept of Fiction: Peter Eisenman: Moving Arrows, Eros and Other Errors', *AA Files*, no 12, London: Summer 1986, pp 76-84.

* Yatsuka, Hajime, 'The Adventure in the Labyrinth of the Knight for Purity', in *SD*, Special Feature on Peter Eisenman, Tokyo: March, 1986, pp 70-71 (in Japanese and English).

1987

The Chicago Tapes: Transcript of the Conference at University of Illinois, November 7 & 8, 1986, New York: Rizzoli, 1987.

Clelland, Douglas and Davey, Peter, ed,' Neubau: Housing, Kochstrasse (Southern Friedrichstadt): Eisenman/Robertson', *The Architectural Review*, London: April, 1987, pp 60-63.

* Doubilet, Susan, 'The Divided Self', *Progressive Architecture*, Stamford: March, 1987, pp 81-92 (Cover; Berlin, Travelers, Artifacts).

* Frampton, Kenneth, 'Apropos Eisenman', *Domus*, No 688, Milan: September, 1987 (in Italian and English).

* Krauss, Rosalind, 'Death of a Hermeneutic Phantom: Materialization of the Sign in the Work of Peter Eisenman', in *Houses of Cards*, by Peter Eisenman, New York: Oxford University Press, 1987, pp 166-184.

* Tafuri, Manfredo, 'Peter Eisenman: The Meditations of Icarus', in *Houses of Cards* by Peter Eisenman, New York: Oxford University Press, 1987, pp 167-187 (originally written in 1980).

1988

'Deconstruction at the Tate Gallery', *Architectural Design: Deconstruction in Architecture*, London: Vol 58, 3/4 1988, p 6.

* Derrida, Jacques, 'Why Peter Eisenman Writes Such Good Books', *A+U: EISENMANAMNESIE* Tokyo: August 1988 Extra Edition, pp 113-124 (in Japanese and English). (Translation of the French original in Jacques Derrida, *Psyche: L'invention de l'autre*, Paris: Galilee, 1987, pp 495-508) (cover)

Dietsch, Deborah, 'Prime Dislocation', *Architectural Record*, New York: mid September 1988, pp 78-87 'EISENMANAMNESIE', *A+U: EISENMANAMNESIE*, Tokyo: August 1988, Extra Edition, pp 12-55, 70-111, 126-145 (cover).

* Frampton, Kenneth, 'Eisenman Revisited: Running Interference', *A+U: EISENMANAMNESIE*, Tokyo: August 1988 Extra Edition, pp 57-69 (in Japanese and English) (reprint from *Domus*, No 688, September 1987) (cover).

Jencks, Charles, 'Deconstruction: The Pleasures of Absence', *Architectural Design: Deconstruction in Architecture*, London: Vol 58, 3/4 1988, pp 17-31.

Johnson, Philip, 'Biocenter for the University of Frankfurt', an interview, *A+U*, No 209, Tokyo: February 1988, pp 30-36.

* Johnson, Philip, 'Philip Johnson on Peter Eisenman', *A+U: EISENMANAMNESIE*, Tokyo: August 1988 Extra Edition, pp 9-11 (in Japanese and English) (cover).

Johnson, Philip and Mark Wigley, *Deconstructivist Architecture*, The Museum of Modern Art, Boston: Little Brown & Co., 1988, pp 56-67.

Kimball, Roger, 'The Death and Resurrection of Postmodern Architecture', *The New Criterion*, New York: June 1988, pp 21-31.

'Peter Eisenman: Wexner Center for the Visual Arts', *Architectural Design: Deconstruction in Architecture*, London: Vol 58, 3/4 1988, pp 62-63.

'Tom's Loft, New York', *Architectural Design: Contemporary Architecture*, Vol 58, London: 1988, pp 39-43.

* Vidler, Anthony, 'After the End of the Line', *A+U: EISENMANAMNESIE*, Tokyo: August 1988 Extra Edition pp 147-161 (in Japanese and English) (cover).

Wigley, Mark, 'The Displacement of Structure and Ornament in the Frankfurt Project: An Interview', *Assemblage*, No 5, Cambridge: February 1988, pp 51-57.

1989

Benjamin, Andrew, 'Derrida, Architecture, and Philosophy', *Deconstruction: Omnibus Volume*, New York: Rizzoli, 1989, pp 80-83. (Reprint from *Architectural Design: Deconstruction in Architecture*, London: Vol 58, 3/4 1988, pp 8-11)

'Carnegie Mellon Research Institute', *A+U*, Tokyo: January 1989, pp 33-52.

'Correspondence: Peter Eisenman X Tadao Ando', *SD*, Tokyo: September 1989, pp 33-40 (in Japanese and English).

Davis, Douglas, 'Slaying the Neo-Modern Dragon', *Art in America*, New York: January 1989, pp 43-49.

Deconstruction: Omnibus Volume, Academy Editions, London, 1989, pp 79, 128-130, 140-143, 146, 151, 154-173.

Derrida, Jacques, 'In Discussion with Christopher Norris', *Architectural Design: Deconstruction II*, London: No 1/2 1989, pp 6-11.

Derrida, Jacques, 'In Discussion with Christopher Norris', *Deconstruction: Omnibus Volume*, New York: Rizzoli, 1989, pp 71-78. (Reprint from *Architectural Design: Deconstruction II*, op cit)

* Derrida, Jacques, 'Why Peter Eisenman Writes Such Good Books', *Threshold: Restructuring Architectural Theory*, ed Marco Diani and Catherine Ingraham, Evanston: Northwestern Univ Press, 1989, pp 99-105. (Reprint from *A+U: EISENMANAMNESIE*, August 1988, pp 113-124) (French original in Jacques Derrida, *Psyche: L'invention de l'autre*, Paris: Galilee, 1987, pp 495-508.)

Diani, Marco and Catherine Ingraham, 'Introduction: Edifying Projects: Restructuring Architectural Theory', *Restructuring Architectural Theory*, Evanston, IL: Northwestern University Press, 1989, pp 1-6.

Doubilet, Susan, 'The Pied Piper Syndrome', *Progressive Architecture*: Special Issue-Eisenman, Stamford: October 1989, pp 90-99 (cover).

Fisher, Thomas, 'Introduction: Wexner Center', *Progressive Architecture*: Special Issue — Eisenman, Stamford: October 1989, p 68 (cover).

Fisher, Thomas and John Morris Dixon, 'Wexner Center for the Visual Arts', *Progressive Architecture*: Special Issue-Eisenman, Stamford: October 1989, pp 68-85 (cover).

Frampton, Kenneth, 'Eisenman Revisited: Running Interference', *Peter Eisenman: Recent Projects*, ed Arie Graafland, Nijmegen: SUN, 1989, pp 47-62 (in Dutch and English) (Reprint from *Domus*, No 688, Milan: September 1987).

* Graafland, Arie, 'Peter Eisenman: Architecture in absentia', *Peter Eisenman: Recent Projects*, ed Arie Graafland, Nijmegen: SUN, 1989, pp 95-126 (in Dutch and English).

* Green, Jonathan, 'Algorithms for Discovery', *The Wexner Center for the Visual Arts, The Ohio State University*, New York: Rizzoli,

1989, p 28-31.

'Guardiola House', *A+U*, Tokyo: January 1989, pp 9-33.

Jencks, Charles, 'Deconstruction: The Pleasures of Absence', *Deconstruction: Omnibus Volume*, New York: Rizzoli 1989, pp 119-131. (Reprint from *Architectural Design: Deconstruction in Architecture*, London: Vol 58, 3/4 1988, pp 17-31.)

* Kipnis, Jeffrey, 'The Law of ana-. On Choral Works', by Jeffrey Kipnis, *Peter Eisenman: Recent Projects*, ed Arie Graafland, Nijmegen: SUN, 1989, pp 145-160 (in Dutch and English).

'Making/History: Eisenman/Trott's Wexner Center', *Newsline* (Columbia University School of Architecture), New York: December 1989-January 1990, p 2.

McLeod, Mary, 'Architecture and Politics in the Reagan Era: From Postmodernism to Deconstructivism', *Assemblage 8*, Cambridge: February 1989, pp 23-59.

* Moneo, Rafael, 'Unexpected Coincidences', *The Wexner Center for the Visual Arts, The Ohio State University* (New York: Rizzoli, 1989) pp 40-45.

'Peter Eisenman', *El Croquis* 41, Madrid: December 1989, pp 24-51, 62-119 (cover).

Progressive Architecture, 'Special Issue-Eisenman' Stamford: October 1989. Whole issue devoted to Peter Eisenman and the Wexner Arts Center (cover).

Scully, Vincent, 'Theory and Delight', *Progressive Architecture*: Special Issue-Eisenman, Stamford: October 1989, pp 86-87 (cover).

* Sola-Morales, Ignasi de, 'Cuatro Notas Sobre la Arquitectura Reciente de Peter Eisenman', *El Croquis* 41, Madrid: December 1989, pp 16-23. (in Spanish and English) (cover).

* Somol, RE, 'O-O' (Wexner Center), *Progressive Architecture*: Special Issue-Eisenman, Stamford: October 1989, p 88 (cover).

* Sorkin, Michael, 'Architecture: Solid Geometry: Coming off a Theoretical Tangent, Architect Peter Eisenman Puts a New Spin on Design', *House and Garden*, 'Notes', New York: October, 1989, pp 62-66.

Stearns, Robert, 'Building as Catalyst', *The Wexner Center for the Visual Arts, The Ohio State University*, New York: Rizzoli, 1989, pp 24-27.

Taylor, Mark, 'Deadlines Approaching

Anarchetecture', *Restructuring Architectural Theory*, eds. Marco Diani and Catherine Ingraham, Evanston, IL: Northwestern University Press, 1989, pp 18-25. (Reprint from *Threshold*, Journal of the School of Architecture at the University of Illinois at Chicago, Vol IV, Spring 1988, pp 71-75.)

* Stearns, Robert, 'Eisenman's Coup', *Progressive Architecture*: Special Issue-Eisenman, Stamford: October 1989, p 89 (cover).

Stearns, Robert, 'Messages from/to the Post Age: A Letter to Peter Eisenman', *Tears*, State University of New York Press, New York: 1989, pp 51-53.

'Tom's Loft in New York', *Detail*, New York: March/April, 1989.

Townsend, David, 'The Man who Puts Windows in the Floors', *Blueprint*, no 58, London: June, 1989, pp 34-35.

* Vidler, Anthony, 'Counter-Monuments in Practice: The Wexner Center for the Visual Arts', *The Wexner Center for the Visual Arts, The Ohio State University* (New York: Rizzoli, 1989) pp 32-38.

1990

A + U, No 232, Special Feature: Recent Works by Peter Eisenman, Tokyo: January 1990 (Wexner Center on cover).

* Barris, Roann, 'Eisenman and the Erosion of Truth', *20/1 Art & Culture*, School of Architecture & Design, University of Illinois at Chicago, Vol 1, no 1, Chicago: Spring 1990, pp 20-37.

* Benson, Robert, 'Eisenman's Architectural Challenge', *New Art Examiner*, Summer 1990, pp 27-30.

* Benson, Robert, 'Wexing Eloquent in Columbus', *Inland Architect*, Chicago: May/June 1990, pp 34-43 (cover).

Bess, Philip, 'Peter Eisenman and the Architecture of the Therapeutic', *Inland Architect*, Chicago: May/June 1990, pp 52-55 (cover).

Connors, Thomas, 'Museum Wexner Center', *Contemporanea*, January 1990, pp 78-81.

Davidson, Cynthia Chapin, 'Cubic Disturbance', *Architecture*, Washington DC: September 1990, pp 80-85.

Davidson, Cynthia, 'Taking Risks: Eisenman in Ohio', *Inland Architect*, Chicago: May/June 1990, pp 44-51 (cover).

* Derrida, Jacques, 'A Letter to Peter

Eisenman', *Assemblage*, Cambridge: No 12, August 1990, pp 7-13.

Moore, Rowan, 'All That's Solid Melts into Air', *Blueprint*, London: April 1990, pp 27-31.

* Somol, R E, 'Peter Eisenman: Wexner Center for the Visual Arts, Columbus/Ohio', *Domus*, Milan: January 1990, pp 38-47.

Stephens, Suzanne, 'Beyond Criticism? The Opening of the Wexner Center for the Visual Arts by Eisenman/Trott', *Oculus*, New York: Vol 52, no 5, Jan 1990, pp 10-11.

1991

Benjamin, Andrew, 'Pavilion Display: The American Pavilion', Venice Biennale, 1991: *Newsline*, Nov/Dec 1991.

Benjamin, Andrew, 'Eisenman and the Housing of Tradition', *Art, Mimesis and the Avant-Garde*, Routledge, London, 1991, pp107-131.

Breakthroughs: Avant-Garde Artists in Europe and America, 1950-1990, Wexner Center for the Arts, The Ohio State University(New York: Rizzoli, 1991).

'Cartolina 91 / Postcard 91', *Casabella*, 584, Milan: November 1991 (in Italian and English, image diagram of House III).

* Davidson, Cynthia, 'A Game of Eisenman Seeks', *A+U*, Tokyo: September 1991, pp 12-13 (in Japanese and English) (cover).

Forster, Kurt, 'Shrine? Emporium? Theater? Reflections on Two Decades of American Museum Building', *Zodiac*, Milan: No 6, 1991, pp 30-76.

Frampton, Kenneth, 'Reflections on the Autonomy of Architecture: A Critique of Contemporary Production', *Out of Site: A Social Criticism of Architecture*, Seattle: Bay Press, 1991, pp 17-26.

Ghirardo, Diane, 'Introduction', and 'Two Institutions for the Arts', *Out of Site: A Social Criticism of Architecture*, Seattle: Bay Press, 1991, pp 114-128.

* Johnson, Philip, 'Introduction', *Peter Eisenman and Frank Gehry* (a catalogue for the Fifth International Exhibition of Architecture at the 1991 Venice Biennale), New York: Rizzoli, 1991, pp 2-3.

Kipnis, Jeffrey, '/Twisting the Separatrix/', *Assemblage* No 14, Cambridge: April 1991, pp 31-61.

* Kwinter, Sanford, 'The Genius of Matter: Eisenman's Cincinnati Project', *Peter Eisenman and Frank Gehry* (a catalogue for the Fifth International Exhibition of Architecture at the 1991 Venice Biennale), New York: Rizzoli, 1991, pp 8-9.

Lynn, Greg, 'The Deference of Anyone', *Arquitectura*, Madrid: October 1991, pp 74-80 (in Spanish and English).

Moneo, Raphael, 'On the American Pavilion of the Venice Biennale: Peter Eisenman and Frank Gehry', *Arquitectura* Issue 290, Madrid: January 1992 pp 47-52 (in Spanish and English).

Pecora, Vincent, 'Towers of Babel', *Out of Site: A Social Criticism of Architecture*, Seattle: Bay Press, 1991, pp 46-76.

'Peter Eisenman: University of Cincinnati, College of Design, Architecture, Art and Planning', *GA Document* 29, Tokyo: April 1991, pp 22-25 (in Japanese and English).

Pidgeon, Monica, 'Global Diversity at Venice Biennale', *Progressive Architecture*, Stamford: November 1991, pp 25-26.

* Rajchman, John, 'Perplications: On the Space and Time of Rebstockpark', *Unfolding Frankfurt* (a catalogue for the exhibition of the Rebstockpark project at Aedes Gallery), Berlin: Ernst & Sohn, 1991, pp 20-77 (in German and English).

'Recent Projects of Peter Eisenman', *A+U*, Tokyo: September 1991, pp 16-138 (in Japanese and English) (cover).

Sheeley, Glenn, 'Architecture of the '90s: softer and womblike', *Atlanta Journal and Constitution*, Atlanta: July 25, 1991, p C2.

* Somol, Robert, 'Accidents Will Happen', *A+U*, Tokyo: September 1991, pp 4-7 (in Japanese and English) (cover).

Somol, Robert, 'Peter Eisenman: Shell Games, Incorporate Forms, Impaired Liabilities', *Forum International*, Belgium: No 9, Vol II, Sept-Oct 91, pp 41-46 (English and Dutch).

1992

Johnson, Philip, 'Philip Johnson on Eisenman and Gehry', *Architectural Design: Modern Pluralism: Just Exactly What is Going On?*, London: Jan/Feb 1992, pp 28-31.

1993

'Max Reinhardt Monument Challenges "Business as Usual"', *Architectural Record* 3/1993 (March 1993).

'Nunotani Building', *The Japan Architect 9*, 1992 Annual (Spring 1993) pp 150-53

(in Japanese and English).

Articles by Eisenman

1963   * Indicates major critical writings

* Eisenman, Peter, *The Formal Basis of Modern Architecture*. Dissertation for the Degree of Doctor of Philosophy, University of Cambridge, Cambridge: August 1963 (unpublished).

Eisenman, Peter, 'Towards an Understanding of Form in Architecture', *Architectural Design*, London: October 1963, pp 457-58.

1969

Eisenman, Peter, 'The Big Little Magazine: *Perspecta 12* and "The Future of the Architectural Past"', *Architectural Forum*, Volume 131, No 3, New York: October 1969, pp 74-75, 104.

1970

* Eisenman, Peter, 'Notes on Conceptual Architecture: Towards a Definition', Special Double Issue of *Design Quarterly*, Nos 78-79, Minneapolis: 1970, pp 1-5 (cover).

1971

Eisenman, Peter, 'Meier's Smith House: Letter to the Editor', *Architectural Design*, London: August 1971, p 520.

Eisenman, Peter, 'A Review of Alison and Peter Smithson's *Ordinariness and Light*', *Architectural Forum*, Vol 133, New York: May 1971, pp 76-80.

Eisenman, Peter, Guest Co-Editor, 'The City as Artefact', Special Issue of *Casabella*, Nos 359-360, Milan: November/December 1971 (in Italian and English) (cover).

* Eisenman, Peter, 'Notes on Conceptual Architecture: Towards a Definition', *Casabella*, Nos. 359-360, Milan: November/December 1971, pp 48-58 (in Italian and English).

* Eisenman, Peter, 'From Object to Relationship II: Giuseppe Terragni', *Perspecta 13-14 The Yale Architectural Journal*, Cambridge: 1971, pp 36-75.

1972

* Eisenman, Peter, 'From Golden Lane to Robin Hood Gardens; or If You Follow the Yellow Brick Road, It May Not Lead to Golder's Green', *Architectural Design*, Vol 42, No 9, London: September 1972, pp 557-

573, 588-592, and *Oppositions* 1, Cambridge: September 1973, pp 27-56.

1973

Eisenman, Peter, 'Notes on Conceptual Architecture II A', *Environmental Design Research Association*, Volume II, Stroudsburg, Pennsylvania: 1973, pp 319-22.

Eisenman, Peter, 'Notes on Conceptual Architecture II A', *On Site*, No 4, New York: 1973, pp 41-44.

Eisenman, Peter, 'Cardboard Architecture', *Architecture and Urbanism,* no 11, Tokyo: November 1973, pp 185-189.

1974

*   Eisenman, Peter, 'Real and English: Destruction of the Box I', *Oppositions* 4, Cambridge: May 1974, pp 5-34.

*   Eisenman, Peter, 'House III: To Adolf Loos and Bertolt Brecht', *Progressive Architecture*, Stamford, Connecticut: May 1974, p 92.

1975

Eisenman, Peter, Guest Editor with Robert AM Stern, 'White and Gray: Eleven Modern American Architects', *Architecture + Urbanism*, No 52, Tokyo: April 1975, pp 25-180 (in Japanese; English summary pp 2-4).

*   Eisenman, Peter, 'Post-Functionalism', *Oppositions* 6, Cambridge: Fall, 1976, pp i-iii (Editorial).

1977

*   Eisenman, Peter, 'Behind the Mirror: On the Writings of Philip Johnson', *Oppositions* 10, Cambridge: Fall 1977, pp 1-13.

Eisenman, Peter, 'House VI', *Progressive Architecture*, Stamford, Connecticut: June 1977, pp 57-59.

Eisenman, Peter, 'Residence, Critique of Weekend House by Philosopher, Sociologist, and Architect Himself', *Progressive Architecture*, Stamford: June, 1977, pp 57-67.

Eisenman, Peter, 'Semiotica e Architettura (la Casa del Fascio), *Casabella*, Milan: October, 1977, p 25 (in Italian and English).

1978

*   Eisenman, Peter, 'The Graves of Modernism', *Oppositions* 12, Cambridge: Spring 1978, pp 36-41.

1979

*   Eisenman, Peter, 'The House of the Dead as the City of Survival', Introduction, *IAUS Catalogue 2: Aldo Rossi in America: 1976-1979*, New York: The Institute for Architecture and Urban Studies, 1979, pp 4-15.

1980

Eisenman, Peter, 'House El Even Odd', *Architecture and Urbanism*, No 123, Tokyo: December 1980, pp 96-98 (in Japanese and English).

*   Eisenman, Peter, 'Aspects of Modernism: Maison Dom-ino and the Self-Referential Sign', *Oppositions* 15/16, Cambridge: Winter/Spring 1980, pp 119-128.

*   Eisenman, Peter, 'Sandboxes: House 11a', Special Issue of *Architecture and Urbanism*, No 112, Tokyo: January 1980, pp 221-224 (in Japanese and English).

*Eisenman, Peter, 'Transformations, Decompositions and Critiques: House X', Special Issue of *Architecture and Urbanism*, No 112, Tokyo: January 1980, pp 14-151 (in Japanese and English).

Eisenman, Peter, 'Three Texts for Venice', *Domus*, No 611, Milan: November 1980, pp 9-11 (in Italian and English).

*   Eisenman, Peter, 'House VI: The Frank Residence', *GA Document Special Issue: 1970-1980*, Tokyo: 1980, pp 172-3 (in Japanese and English).

Eisenman, Peter, 'Stadium Ghosts', *The New York Times*, New York: April 2, 1980, Op Ed Page.

Eisenman, Peter, 'House VI: Frank Residence', Text for Catalogue and Exhibition, *Houses for Sale* at the Leo Castelli Gallery, New York: Rizzoli International, 1980, pp 172-6.

Eisenman, Peter, 'In My Father's House are Many Mansions', *IAUS Catalogue 12 John Hejduk: Seven Houses*, New York: Rizzoli International, 1980, pp 8-20.

1982

*   Eisenman, Peter, 'The Houses of Memory: The Texts of Analogy', Introduction to Aldo Rossi, *The Architecture of the City*, Cambridge: MIT Press, 1982, pp 3-12.

*   Eisenman, Peter, 'Le Rappresentazioni del Dubbio: Nel Segno del Segno', *Rassegna* 9, Milan: March 1982, pp 69-74 (in Italian); also 'The Representations of Doubt: At the Sign of the Sign', *Rassenga* 9, op cit (English original,unpaginated).

Eisenman, Peter, 'Peter Eisenman', *Yale Seminars in Architecture*, Volume 2, New Haven: Yale University Press, 1982, pp 49-87.

1983

Eisenman, Peter, 'House X', *At Home with Architecture: Contemporary Views of the House*, San Diego: Mandeville Art Gallery, 1983, pp 18-21 (Catalogue).

*   Eisenman, Peter, 'Representations of the Limit: Writing a "Not Architecture"', *Chamberworks: Architectural Meditations on Themes from Heraclitus* by Daniel Libeskind, London: Architectural Association Folio, 1983, pp 6-8.

*   Eisenman, Peter, 'The City of Artificial Excavation', *Architectural Design*, London: Nos 1-2, January, 1983, pp 91-93.

Eisenman, Peter, 'Fin d'Ou T Hou S', *Follies: Architecture for the Late Twentieth Century Landscape*, New York: Rizzoli International Publications, 1983 (Catalogue from exhibition at Leo Castelli Gallery), pp 54-56.

1984

Eisenman, Peter, 'Banff Transcripts', *Section* A, Volume 2, Nos. 3/4, Montreal: September, 1984, pp 20-26.

Eisenman, Peter, 'The Futility of Objects', *Harvard Architecture Review*, Vol 3, Cambridge: Winter 1984, pp 65-82.

Eisenman, Peter, 'Giuseppe Terragni: Casa Giuliani-Frigerio, Como', *Lotus* 42, Milan: 1984, pp 69-71 (in Italian and English).

*   Eisenman, Peter, 'The End of the Classical', *Perspecta 21, The Yale Architectural Journal*, Cambridge: Summer 1984, pp 154-172, op. cit.

Eisenman, Peter, 'Firehouse for Engine Company 233, Ladder Company 176, Brooklyn, New York', *Architectural Design 54*, London: November-December, 1984, pp 14-15.

1985

Eisenman, Peter, 'The City as Memory and Immanence', *Zone*, Volume 1, New York: Fall 1985, pp 440-1.

Eisenman, Peter, 'The OSU Center for the Visual Arts' and 'Fin D'ou T Hou S', *Architectural Design*, Vol 55, No 1/2, London: January, 1985, pp 44-55.

1986

* Eisenman, Peter, 'miMISes READING: does not mean A THING', in *Mies Reconsidered: His Career, Legacy, and Disciples*, Art Institute of Chicago, New York: Rizzoli Publications, 1986, pp 86-98 (Catalogue).

* Eisenman, Peter, 'Metaphysics, Mystique, and Power', in *AA Files*, n.12, London: Summer, 1986, p. 107 (A Review of John Hejduk's *Mask of Medusa*).

Eisenman, Peter, 'The Beginning, the End, and the Beginning Again', *Nerot Mitzvah: Contemporary Ideas for Light in Jewish Ritual*, Catalogue for the Israel Museum, Jerusalem: 1986, p 62.

1987

Eisenman, Peter, 'University Campus, Long Beach, California: The Museum Rediscovered', *Lotus* 50, Milano: 1986, p. 128-135 (in Italian and English).

Eisenman, Peter, 'University Art Museum, California State University, Long Beach, California', *GA Document 18: GA International '87*, Tokyo: April, 1987, pp 13-15.

* Eisenman, Peter, 'TEXt AS Zero Or: the Destruction of Narrative', a postscript to Lars Lerup's book, *Planned Assaults*, Centre Canadienne d'Architecture /MIT Press: Cambridge, 1987, pp 93-98.

Eisenman, Peter, 'Architecture and the Problem of the Rhetorical Figure', *Architecture and Urbanism*, Special Feature: Eisenman/Robertson Architects, No 202, Tokyo: July, 1987.

* Eisenman, Peter, 'Moving Arrows, Eros and Other Errors', *The Culture of Fragments, Precis 6*, New York: Columbia Graduate School of Architecture, Planning and Preservation, Spring 1987, pp 139-143.

* Eisenman, Peter, 'Misreading Peter Eisenman', *Houses of Cards*, New York: Oxford University Press, 1987, pp 167-186.

1988

* Eisenman, Peter, 'En Terror Firma: In Trails of Grotextes', *Form, Being, Absence/ Architecture and Philosophy - Pratt Journal of Architecture*, New York: Rizzoli 1988, pp 111-121.

* Eisenman, Peter, 'Architecture as a Second Language: The Texts of Between', *Threshold, Journal of the School of Architecture, University of Illinois at Chicago*, Vol IV, Illinois: Spring 1988, pp 71-75.

* Eisenman, Peter, 'The Authenticity of Difference: Architecture and the Crisis of Reality', *Center, A Journal for Architecture in America, University of Texas at Austin*, Vol 4, Rizzoli, New York, 1988, pp 50-57.

Eisenman, Peter, 'Biology Center for the J. W. Goethe University of Frankfurt, Frankfurt am Main, 1987', *Assemblage* No 5, Cambridge: Feb 1988, pp 29-50.

1989

Eisenman, Peter, 'Architecture as a Second Language: The Texts of Between', *Threshold: Restructuring Architectural Theory*, ed. Marco Diani and Catherine Ingraham, Evanston: Northwestern University Press, 1989, pp 69-73. (Reprint from *Threshold*, Journal of The School of Architecture, University of Illinois at Chicago, Vol IV, Spring 1988, pp 71-75.)

Eisenman, Peter, 'The Blue Line Text', *Architectural Design: Contemporary Architecture*, London: Jan./Feb.1989, pp 6-9.

Eisenman, Peter, 'Blue Line Text', *Deconstruction: Omnibus Volume* (New York: Rizzoli, 1989), pp 150-151. (Reprint from *Architectural Design: Contemporary Architecture*, op. cit.)

Eisenman, Peter, 'The Carnegie Mellon Research Institute', *GA Documents 23*, Apr, Tokyo: 1989, pp 82-84.

Eisenman, Peter, 'The Story of AND O', *Tadao Ando: The Yale Studio & Current Works*, New York: Rizzoli Books, 1989, pp 137-39.

Eisenman, Peter, 'Recent Works', *Architectural Design: Deconstruction II*, London: No 1/2, 1989, pp 40-61.

1990

* Eisenman, Peter, 'Post/El Cards: A Reply to Jacques Derrida', *Assemblage*, No 12, Cambridge: August 1990, pp 14-17.

1991

Eisenman, Peter, 'The Author's Affect: Passion and the Moment of Architecture', *Anyone* (New York: Rizzoli, 1991), pp 200-211.

Eisenman, Peter, 'Indicencies: In the Drawing Lines of Tadao Ando', *Tadao Ando: Details*, Ed. Yukio Futagawa, *GA* (Tokyo: A. D. A. Edita, 1991) pp 6-9 (in Japanese and English).

Eisenman, Peter, 'Strong Form, Weak Form', *Architecture in Transition: Between Deconstruction and New Modernism* (Munich: Prestel, 1991), pp 33-45(in German and English).

Eisenman, Peter, 'Unfolding Events: Frankfurt Rebstockpark and the Possibility of a New Urbanism', *Unfolding Frankfurt* (Berlin: Ernst & Sohn, 1991) pp 8-17 (in German and English).

1992

Eisenman, Peter, 'Aratacism: On the Theoretical Ruins of Arata Isozaki', *Arata Isozaki: Works 30: Architectural Models, Prints, Drawings* (Rikuyo-sha Publishing, Inc., Tokyo: 1992), pp 186-197 (in Japanese and English).

Eisenman, Peter, 'Oltre Lo Sguardo: L'Architettura nell'Epoca dei Media Elettronici' ('Visions Unfolding: Architecture in the Age of Electronic Media'), *Domus*, Milan: January 1992, pp 17-24 (in Italian and English).

Eisenman, Peter, 'Hollein's Cave(at): The Haas Haus', *A+U*, Tokyo: January 1992, pp 122-123 (in English and Japanese).

Interviews

1981

Eisenman, Peter, 'Interview: Wolfe and Eisenman', *Skyline*, New York: Rizzoli International Publications, October 1981, pp 12-14.

Eisenman, Peter, 'Interview: Wolfe and Eisenman, Part II', *Skyline*, New York: Rizzoli International, November 1981, pp 3-4.

Eisenman, Peter, 'Interview: Robert Hughes and Peter Eisenman', *Skyline*, New York: Rizzoli International, December 1981, pp 10-11.

Eisenman, Peter, 'A Poetics of the Model: Eisenman's Doubt', taken from an interview with Peter Eisenman by David Shapiro and Lindsay Stamm, March 8, 1981, in *IAUS Catalogue 3: Model as Idea*, New York: Rizzoli International, 1981, pp 121-125.

1982

Eisenman, Peter, 'Interview: Cesar Pelli and Peter Eisenman', *Skyline*, New York: Rizzoli

International, May 1982, pp 22-25.

Eisenman, Peter, 'Interview: Gerald D Hines and Peter Eisenman', *Skyline*, New York: Rizzoli International, October 1982, pp 18-21.

Eisenman, Peter, 'Interview: Goldberger and Eisenman', *Skyline*, New York: Rizzoli International, January 1982, pp 6-9.

Eisenman, Peter, 'Interview: Henry Cobb and Eisenman', *Skyline*, New York: Rizzoli International, June 1982, pp 12-14.

Eisenman, Peter, 'Interview: Johnson and Eisenman', *Skyline*, New York: Rizzoli International, February 1982, pp 14-17.

Eisenman, Peter, 'Interview: Robert Venturi and Peter Eisenman', *Skyline*, New York: Rizzoli International, July 1982, pp 12-15.

Eisenman, Peter, 'Interview: Peter Eisenman', *Archetype*, Vol 1, No 4, Winter, 1980, pp 30-32, 36.

1983

Eisenman, Peter, 'Interview: Tigerman and Eisenman', *Harvard GSD News*, Cambridge: Vol II, No 2, 1983, p 10.

'Discord over Harmony in Architecture: the Eisenman/Alexander Debate', *Harvard GSD News*, Cambridge: Spring, 1983, pp 12-17.

Eisenman, Peter, 'Contrasting Concepts of Harmony in Architecture: Debate Between Christopher Alexander and Peter Eisenman', *Lotus* 40, Milan: 1983, pp 60-68.

Eisenman, Peter, 'Interview: John Portman and Peter Eisenman', *Skyline*, New York: Rizzoli International, January 1983, pp 12-15.

Eisenman, Peter, 'Interview: Leon Krier and Peter Eisenman', *Skyline*, New York: Rizzoli International, February 1983, pp 12-16.

Eisenman, Peter, 'Interview: Robert Maxwell and Peter Eisenman', *Skyline*, New York:

Rizzoli International, March 1983, pp 12-16.

Eisenman, Peter, 'Interview: Richard Serra and Peter Eisenman', *Skyline*, New York: Rizzoli International, April 1983, pp 14-18.

1984

Eisenman, Peter, 'Interview: Peter Eisenman', *Transition*, Volume 3, Nos. 3/4, Melbourne: April/July, 1984, pp 37-42.

1986

Eisenman, Peter, 'Interview with Peter Eisenman', *Journal*, Notre Dame, Indiana: School of Architecture, Notre Dame University, 1986, pp 19-25.

1988

Breslin, Lynn, 'An Interview with Peter Eisenman', *Form, Being, Absence: Architecture and Philosophy: Pratt Journal of Architecture*, New York: 1988, pp 106-110.

Jencks, Charles, 'An Architectural Design Interview by Charles Jencks', *Architectural Design: Deconstruction in Architecture*, London: Vol 58, No 3/4, 1988, pp 48-61.

Nieto, Fuensanta and Enrique Sobejano, 'Entrevista a Peter Eisenman', *Arquitectura*, n 270, Madrid: Jan/Feb 1988, pp 124-130 (in Spanish and English).

1989

Cohn, David, 'Interview', *El Croquis* 41, Madrid: December 1989, pp 7-15 (in Spanish and English – cover)

Jencks, Charles, '*An Architectural Design Interview by Charles Jencks*', *De-construction: Omnibus Volume*, New York: Rizzoli, 1989, pp 141-149. (Reprint from *Architectural Design*, Vol 58, No 3/4, 1988, pp 48-61.)

1990

'A Conversation with Peter Eisenman and Michael Graves', *Dimensions*, Journal of the University of Illinois, Chicago: Spring 1990, pp 10-13.

1991

'A Conversation Between Peter Eisenman and Frank Gehry: June 1991', *Peter Eisenman & Frank Gehry* (a catalogue for the Fifth International Exhibition of Architecture at the 1991 Venice Biennale) (New York: Rizzoli, 1991) pp 4-5.

Mann, Lian Hurst, 'Why ANYone Writes Such Good Books', *L. A. Architect*, Los Angeles: July/August 1991, pp 6-7.

Muschamp, Herbert, 'Moral Fiber', *Interview*, New York: April 1991.

'Interview with Robert Somol', *Newsline*, Columbia University School of Architecture, New York: March 1991, p 2.

1992

'Du Processus à la Presence: Entretien avec Peter Eisenman', *L'Architecture d'Aujourd'hui*, No 279, Paris: February 1992, pp 100-108 (in French and English) (cover).

'Interview: Peter Eisenman', *CSPA Practices*, Issue 1, Cincinnati: Spring 1992, pp 5-11. (Cover: Department of Art, Architecture and Planning).

'Vices Versus Verses (or Vice Versa): Peter Eisenman/Stanley Tigerman debate', *Dimensions* vol 6 (Journal of University of Michigan College of Architecture), Michigan: Spring 1992, pp 92-101.